BAFFY

The Diaries of Blanche Dugdale
1936–1947

BAFFY

THE DIARIES OF BLANCHE DUGDALE
1936-1947

Edited by
N. A. ROSE

Foreword by
MEYER WEISGAL

VALLENTINE, MITCHELL—LONDON

First published in Great Britain in 1973 by
VALLENTINE, MITCHELL & CO. LTD.
67 Great Russell Street, London, W.C.1B 3BT

ISBN 0 85303 145 2

ACKNOWLEDGEMENTS

For permission to reproduce photographs acknowledgement is
gratefully made to the Radio Times Hulton Picture Library for
the pictures of Wauchope, Peel, MacDonald and Sinclair, de la
Warr, MacDonald, Amery, Masaryk and Eden; to the Jewish
National Fund for Ben-Gurion, Shertok (Sharett), and Berl
Locker; to United Press International for the Weizmanns; to
the Jewish Chronicle for Balfour and Weizmann, Namier and
group outside number '77', and Brodetsky.

Printed in Great Britain
at the St. Ann's Press, Park Road, Altrincham, Cheshire WA14 5QQ

CONTENTS

LIST OF ILLUSTRATIONS

Many of the characters are referred to throughout the diaries by their first names or nicknames. The following list has been compiled for the reader's convenience.

ANTHONY Eden
ARCHIE Sinclair
BERL Locker
BERL Katznelson
BILLY Ormsby-Gore
BOB Boothby
BOB Cecil
BOBBITY Cranborne
BUCK De la Warr
CHAIM Weizmann
COLIN Coote
DAVID Ben-Gurion
DIANA De La Warr
EDGAR Dugdale
EVA Reading
FRANCES Fergusson
HANNAH Hudson
HENRY Melchett
JAN Masaryk
JIMMIE Fergusson
LEO Amery
LEWIS Namier
MALCOLM MacDonald
MICHAEL Dugdale
MOSHE Shertok
NEVILLE Chamberlain
OLIVER Stanley
PETER Rutenberg
ROB Bernays
VERA Weizmann
VICTOR Cazalet
WALTER Elliot
WINSTON Churchill

FOREWORD

My own recollections of 'Baffy' Dugdale date from long before the period covered by these diaries. She was known to me as the niece of Arthur James Balfour, and I first met her in connection with her activities on behalf of Zionism. I well remember the occasion when Dr. Weizmann introduced Baffy Dugdale to some friends of his, who asked, *sotto voce:* 'Who is this distinguished lady?' His answer, in his usual sardonic tones: 'She is what is left of the Balfour Declaration.' She was of course a close and intimate friend of Chaim Weizmann and acted as the Chief's loyal aide and adviser during many moments of crisis in the Zionist movement's relations with the British Government. But this was not all. She was an integral part of what we would now define as the British establishment. This was a world in many ways foreign to us—esoteric, unassailable, often incomprehensible. Baffy brought it to life. She breathed into our lives, through her inexhaustible range of family and social and political contacts, the atmosphere of a world which was vital for our survival but which obstinately remained remote from our grasp.

It is for this reason that I find the impressions and thoughts she privately recorded so fascinating in their scope and penetration. For here revealed are both her worlds; and one can only now fully understand how one was dependent upon the other. This volume enhances our understanding of the political motivations and developments preceding the establishment of the state of Israel. But it also provides an intimate record of the protagonists and events of that crucial decade of over a generation ago. Baffy's brilliant and original mind penetrated into the heart of problems no less than into the hearts of men. She will long be remembered with gratitude and reverence by all those to whom she gave her inimitable friendship.

Autumn 1972   Meyer W. Weisgal

ACKNOWLEDGEMENTS

Editing these diaries has proved to be a far more exacting task than I had previously anticipated. And it most certainly could not have been done without the active assistance and encouragement of many individuals and institutions. In particular, I am deeply grateful to the late Mr. Michael Dugdale, whose sad and untimely death in November 1970 occurred while this volume was still in an early stage of preparation. He set me upon this task and his unfailing courtesy did much to ease my assignment. I hope that the result would have met with his approval. Upon his death, his brother-in-law and sister, Sir James and Lady Fergusson, and his literary executor, Mr. Adam Fergusson, continued to give every support to the project. Sir James and Lady Fergusson and Mr. Adam Fergusson have read the manuscript in full and I owe much to their critical eye and informed comments.

A special debt is owed to Mr. Meyer Weisgal, now President of the Weizmann Institute of Science. His understanding, spontaneity and generosity made the publication of this volume possible.

I am indebted, too, to Lady Elliot of Harwood, wife of the late the Rt. Hon. Walter Elliot, C.H., M.C., F.R.S., M.P., for her interest in this work, her encouragement, and her readiness to help. I also wish to thank Lord Boothby, Sir Colin Coote, Earl De la Warr, Mr. Joseph Linton, Mr. Berl Locker, Mr. Arthur Lourie, and Miss Elizabeth Monroe, for at times taxing their patience and exploiting their time. I am also grateful to the Institute of Contemporary Jewish History at the Hebrew University for providing me with a grant to cover secretarial expenses. Above all, I owe special thanks to my wife and daughter who, with remarkable patience and understanding, lived with this project from its outset.

N.A.R.

INTRODUCTION

Blanche Elizabeth Campbell Balfour was born in London on 23 May 1880. Her family roots were predominantly Scottish. Her maternal grandfather, George Campbell, eighth Duke of Argyll, was the acknowledged chief of the Clan Campbell. The family home was at the castle of MacCaillean Mor, near the town of Inveraray, Argyll. It was here that the Duke retired after his excursions into English politics. For he was no mere Highland landlord. Actively interested in politics, the Duke served in Gladstone's first and second administrations, holding the posts of Secretary of State for India and Lord Privy Seal. He was, as Baffy[1] recalls, a short, stout, commanding figure, with high forehead, blue eyes, and a small imperious mouth. Politicians of all persuasions were frequent visitors to the castle. And although the household was not dedicated entirely to politics, the very nature of the Duke's activities—he was also an authority on the social and natural history of the Highlands—forced the remaining members of the household into an awareness of the political controversies of the hour, a fact which Baffy soon took note of.

Lady Frances Campbell, Baffy's mother, was the tenth child in a family of twelve. She was a woman of remarkable qualities. Fierce, single-minded, loyal to her Scottish ancestry, possessed of a dominating personality with a touch of aristocratic eccentricity, Baffy once had occasion to note that her mother behaved 'even more than usual like the Red Queen in Alice in Wonderland'.[2] Lady Frances's influence upon her daughter is beyond dispute. The stories about her are legion. One will suffice. During the periodical journeys made by the Balfours to and from Scotland, Lady Frances imposed upon her brood a curious national ritual.

> At last the train slowed down on the curve before Berwick Bridge, and weariness was temporarily forgotten as the great moment approached. Rigid I sat, with eyes fixed upon Mamma, waiting for her signal that we were exactly half-way across Tweed. Then we all cheered. On the south-bound journey we hissed like serpents at this point.[3]

---

1. Baffy was the name by which Mrs. Dugdale was universally known. It was, apparently, her earliest attempt at pronouncing the name, Balfour.
2. Blanche E. C. Dugdale, *Family Homespun* (John Murray, London, 1940), p. 64.
3. *Ibid.*, p. 65.

Lady Frances was no blind martinet, unconscious of change in a changing world. She was prominent in the suffragette movement and developed into one of the most effective public speakers on behalf of that controversial cause. Nor was life under her care dull or tedious or devoid of interest. With such an unpredictable character there was little of the routine and monotonous discipline that plague the children of most families. She possessed a vivid sense of humour and unerringly perceived the ludicrous in otherwise ostensibly sane situations. She would often collapse with laughter at some private joke of her own, regardless of place or company, much to the consternation of her guests or of her host. And although there was much tension in her presence, there was also perpetual variety and much fun in her company. Baffy regarded her mother with awe and from afar, but with affection and respect.

Eustace Balfour, Baffy's father, does not figure very prominently in her book of family reminiscences. He was an architect by profession and re-designed, among other buildings, Crown Court Church in 1907, the oldest congregation of the Church of Scotland in London, which still stands near the Drury Lane theatre; Baffy attended Crown Court throughout her life. He alone among the Balfour brothers (there were five brothers and two sisters in all) did not reveal an aptitude for politics. Rather, his extra-professional activities took a military turn. He was a member of the Volunteers, that typically Victorian institution which one authority has described as 'the English businessman in arms'.[4] Eustace Balfour served as Colonel of the London Scottish. Baffy remembered well visiting the volunteers at camp on Wimbledon Common every summer, eagerly searching for the Lion Rampant flying over the lines of the London Scottish, and finally the great moment when her 'father would come out of his tent, very tall and good-looking in his grey kilt and doublet'.[5] Nevertheless, he leaves the overall impression of moving quietly and unobtrusively through the intellectually demanding life of the Balfours. This, however, did not make him immune from the true-bred Whig prejudices of the Campbells, and the Duke and Duchess hesitated for some time before allowing a daughter of theirs to marry a nephew of Lord Salisbury.

The Balfours lived at 32 Addison Road, Kensington. Here Baffy lived the life that befitted a young lady of her position. She 'came out' in the accepted manner and met Queen Victoria on at least three occasions, the second occasion in the Jubilee year of 1887 at Kensington Palace, the home of her aunt, Princess Louise, daughter of the Queen and husband of her uncle Ian, ninth Duke of Argyll. The district at the time was a quiet backwater of London, disturbed only occasionally by passing hansom cabs, or even more rarely by an omnibus. Baffy recalls how, with private access into Holland Park, she could visit her Campbell relatives at Argyll Lodge on

4, M. Howard, *Studies in Peace and War*, (London, 1970) p. 87.
5. *Family Homespun*, p. 116.

Campden Hill without hardly ever having to set foot upon a pavement. It was here that Lady Frances lived until her death in 1930, defying innovation, resisting until the end the introduction even of electric light.

Baffy, in later life, remained a resident of the same area, and strayed only slightly south to 1 Roland Gardens, South Kensington, where she lived for most of her married life. She married, in her early twenties, Edgar Trevelyan Stratford Dugdale, second son of a Warwickshire landowner and coal-mines proprietor, whose family could be traced back to Sir William Dugdale, author of *Monasticum Anglicanum* and Garter King of Arms to Charles 1.

The Balfour family home was at Whittingehame, near the Firth of Forth. It had been built by Baffy's great-grandfather, James, who had sought and made his fortune in India. Whittingehame was then in the possession of her famous uncle, Arthur James Balfour, and presided over by her aunt Alice, Balfour's sister.

The atmosphere at Whittingehame contrasted strongly with that at Inveraray. With the Campbells children generally 'fidgeted' or 'fussed' or behaved in other unsuitable ways. At Whittingehame the axiom that children should be seen and not heard did not prevail. Those who held an opinion, no matter what age, were expected to voice and defend it, a trait that once provoked Lady Frances into commenting: 'The Balfours spent their time pulling red and white balls out of a bag and losing their tempers because this proved nothing.'[6] It was among the Balfours that Baffy was brought up.

Her paternal grandmother was the sister of Robert Cecil, third Marquess of Salisbury, Leader of the Conservative party and Prime Minister of three administrations. Salisbury was then at the height of his fame and influence. Baffy was a frequent visitor to Hatfield, the Cecil country home, and she relates what must have been a very gratifying experience for a young and impressionable girl.

> As we enter the town of Hatfield, people are gathered on the pavements, and a crowd fills the market-place. They cheer, and my great-uncle and aunt acknowledge their salutations. I do my best to copy their dignified inclinations to right and to left. Mamma whispers that the plaudits of the people are meant for Uncle Robert, not for me. I ignore the remark which seems to strike a discordant note on an occasion which otherwise exactly fulfils one's ideals of how life should be.[7]

The occasion of this family triumph was to hear the poll declared for the elections of 1886; the result of which saw the formation of Salisbury's second government.

Of all her Balfour-Cecil relatives it was to A.J.B. that she became most

6. *Ibid.*, p. 96.
7. *Ibid.*, pp. 101–102.

greatly attached. She quickly formed a deep and lasting admiration for him, and, as she tells us, came to prefer his society over that of any other uncle, aunt or cousin, without exception. Baffy eventually came to write an official two-volume biography of Balfour, and it was unquestionably through his example that she came to take an interest in Zionism, an interest that rapidly became the dominating passion of her political life.

Baffy's parents were as well off as most younger children of great families in Great Britain in which the eldest son—or sometimes the only daughter—inherits the bulk of the property, thereby keeping the family estates intact from generation to generation. She remembers that 'our house was smaller than almost any other house I knew'.[8] But it must be remembered that her childhood was spent largely in the great homes of London—Argyll Lodge (the home of her grandfather, the Duke of Argyll), 4 Carlton Gardens (then Balfour's private home), Kensington Palace (the home of her aunt, Princess Louise, and her uncle Ian), Stafford House (the home of her great-grandmother, the Duchess of Sutherland), and Sion House (the home of her aunt and uncle, the Duke and Duchess of Northumberland)—virtual palaces by any standard. 32 Addison Road comfortably housed Col. Eustace and Lady Frances Balfour, their two sons, three daughters, and five servants. After it was sold in 1931 it was converted into seven well-appointed flats. Money, or the lack of it, was never the subject for family discussion. It was considered 'bad manners' to talk about incomes, either one's own or other people's. And, so we are led to believe, what is not talked about is often not thought about. This was a habit which Baffy adopted with comparative ease, for these considerations appear only rarely in the diaries, and then to be dismissed in one or two curt phrases.

There was never any question of Baffy going to school. Her formal education was acquired through private governesses, and she soon picked up 'an odd patchwork of knowledge and ignorance'. The physical sciences utterly eluded her, though she quickly took to pen and ink and did not remember a time when she could not read. Inevitably, Lady Frances attempted to impose her own austere standards upon her daughter. Even Grimm's *Fairy Tales* did not escape her censorship, and she would resort to the simple if inefficient device of marking 'No' above so-called stories of horror, those which told of ogres and witches. These methods did not materially alter Baffy's reading habits. It was a rather haphazard method of education; but not without its advantages. It never occurred to Baffy to wonder whether she was backward or forward, clever or stupid. For apart from Lady Frances's periodic exhortations to 'show a little intelligence', these somewhat arbitrary classifications were never applied to Baffy. There might have been some loss in this, but there was certainly much gain.

Religion constituted an integral part in her upbringing and education. Both at Whittingehame and at Inverary regular churchgoing and prayers

8. *Ibid.*, p. 118.

were considered an essential aspect of family life. Both the Campbells and the Balfours were Church of Scotland. And although the Balfours were more liberal and could envisage the existence of other denominations, Baffy retained for ever a good-humoured distaste for the Anglican service and a deep, lasting suspicion of Catholic ritual and Papistry. Her religious education was of the utmost importance, not only because it provided her with an inner strength and conviction [she remained a regular church-goer until the end of her life], but also because it afforded her a profound understanding of the roots of Zionism. After her first visit to a synagogue she wrote:

> I had never been to a Synagogue before, except for a wedding. I found it less impressive in some ways than I expected (the prayer-shawls are so very like bathing towels!), in some ways far more so. I was unprepared for the ritual when the Ark is opened and the Torah unwrapped, very reminiscent of Papistry. But these are indeed The People of the Book and two thousand years seemed but as yesterday. Once or twice the sound of their sighing was like wind in the trees.[9]

Nurtured on the scriptures and fortified by a deeply-felt bond with the Old Testament, it was the prophecies of the Book she knew so well that were being redeemed by the twentieth-century descendants of the Children of Israel. 'Do not drop "Zionist philosophy" from your propaganda,' she once adjured the Zionist leadership, 'It was "Eretz Israel" ["The land of Israel"] which converted A.J.B. and "Eretz Israel" is really [your] only message to the British public.'[10] The spiritual-historical aspect of Zionism is one to which she continually returns to seek comfort when the Zionist movement found itself drowning in the whirlpools of *realpolitik* in the late 1930's and 1940's.

Baffy's fascination with politics also evolved from her earliest experiences. As she herself remarked, 'The multiplication table might remain a sealed book, but if you had asked me the difference between a Conservative and a Liberal-Unionist, I could have told you by the time I was ten.'[11]

Her first practical introduction to politics was accomplished in a manner wholly symbolic of her future political activity. She was taken behind-the-scenes of the House of Commons by the Speaker, Mr. Peel [son of the late prime minister], and shown, in an informal and chatty manner, how the House functions. It was a tradition which Baffy perpetuated within her own family. Her grand-daughter Alice was shown the cabinet room at Number 10, sat in the prime minister's chair, and acquired one of his pencils. 'This,' Baffy concluded, 'is how interest in politics is born.'[12] The

9. Entry for 13 December 1942.
10. Entry for 18 March 1936.
11. *Family Homespun*, p. 143.
12. Entry for 13 November 1944.

B

same was no doubt true for Baffy herself.

It was from the Speaker's chair that she first surveyed the government and opposition benches. Baffy, however, never attained the impartiality that is reputed to go with that high dignitary's office. She rarely saw two sides of a question, or if she did she never allowed it to interfere with her opinions. Her political convictions were held with an iron determination. Objectivity, so comforting to those in authority, was no favourite of hers. This was no doubt a Campbell quality, for one finds no trace of it in the detached, philosophical treatment of events so evident among the Balfours.

Baffy was in the fortunate position of being able to pursue her own interests without undue concern for the more mundane considerations of life. She exploited the First World War to break out of the traditional pattern of female occupations—or non-occupations—and was employed from 1915–19 in the Department of Naval Intelligence at the Admiralty, no doubt on the recommendation of Balfour who joined Asquith's Coalition Government as First Lord in May 1915. At the end of the war Baffy flung herself whole-heartedly behind the principle of international cooperation and was a fervent adherent of the League of Nations. She, together with her cousin, Lord Robert Cecil, was a founding member of the League of Nations Union, and headed its Intelligence Department until 1928. For the whole period of its existence she served as a member of the Executive Committee of the Union, and the diaries provide some interesting sidelights on the discussions that went on in that increasingly academic institution.

> A day of Committees with the L.N.U. ghosts. Often I think it is time I left them, lest I become a ghost myself, but then something diverting always happens. Today it was discussion of an idea to set up a Standing Conference of representatives of foreign governments here, to 'keep in touch' with their ideas of a Peace Settlement, and, even more, to influence them to accept ours! This had drawn forth a letter from Dr. Benes [then leader of the Czech government-in-exile], which shocked all the ghosts very much, for it said that he thought there would be plenty of time before we could get down to the real Peace Settlement. A number of local wars would have to be fought out first, and a little blood-letting would do us no harm! With such ideas about we settled that we must lose no time in starting our Conference![13]

By temperament and upbringing Baffy was a Conservative. But as the Conservative-dominated National Government of the 1930's moved along its chosen path of seeking out agreements with Germany and Italy, Baffy found herself in instant sympathy with those voices critical of government policy. During the summer of 1937 she joined National Labour. In November of the same year she took the initiative in forming a foreign-policy-making-

13. Entry for 15 May 1941.

body, with the avowed aim of injecting new vigour and ideas into her new political connection. At about the same time she was offered and accepted the parliamentary constituency of Central Southwark. She descended to the grass-roots of party work. She nursed her constituency; attended meetings; pushed and prodded the local organization. All this collapsed under the strain of the Munich crisis. On 20 September, even before the agreement had been signed, she resigned from the party and went into opposition.

Harold Nicolson recalled:

> The morning begins by Baffy Dugdale ringing me up. She said she had been sick twice in the night over England's shame, and that at breakfast she read *The Times* leader. She came upon the words 'The general character of the terms submitted to the Czechoslovak Government could not, in the nature of things, be expected to make a strong *prima facie* appeal to them.' Having read these words she dashed to the lavatory and was sick for a third time. She then returned and wrote a letter to Buck [Earl De la Warr, a leader of National Labour] saying that she must resign from the National Labour Party.[14]

The entries for September 1938 are among the most dramatic in this volume. She followed the crisis in detail and with a view from the inside. She was not swept away by the almost universal feeling of relief which encompassed the country after Munich. After the settlement she recalled: 'About 10 p.m. Jan Masaryk [Czech minister in London] came in. We all rose, and Vera [Weizmann] and I kissed him. He sat down, and talked for nearly an hour—discursively—a little excitedly, of course. But the story he told—the black shame of the story he told!'[15]

September was a critical month for Baffy apart from Munich. For it then became apparent that the Government was preparing to sell the Zionists just as it had sold the Czechs. Indeed it is abundantly clear that both questions were closely connected. The point at issue here was the partition of Palestine. The previous year, in July 1937, the Palestine Royal Commission—the Peel commission—had recommended a tripartite partition of Palestine as a solution for the Arab-Zionist conflict. The Government immediately accepted and endorsed this proposal. Partition was also enthusiastically taken up by Chaim Weizmann, the Zionist leader. Baffy was an accepted member of Weizmann's *entourage* and she quickly moved into battle both to swing the Zionist movement into line behind its leader's policy and to champion that policy in government and parliamentary circles. The crucial debate was at the twentieth Zionist congress in Zurich

---

14. N. Nicolson, ed., *Harold Nicolson: Diaries and Letters,* 1930–39, (Collins, Fontana Books, 1969), p. 355.
15. Entry for 1 October 1938.

in August 1937. Here, once again, Baffy was an eye-witness to the drama that unfolded. She recorded the political infighting and manoeuvring for position, the doubts, the hesitations, and finally, Weizmann's great triumph: 'The birthday of the Jewish State, as it will prove.'[16]

The government failed to keep faith with its own convictions for long. Wilting under pressure from various quarters it soon began an inexorable retreat from its pledge of partition. The new policy took a long time to mature. But by September 1938, Malcolm MacDonald, then Colonial Secretary, felt confident enough to make it perfectly clear that partition was no longer practical politics. This signified a return to the 1922 mandate under conditions far worse for the Zionists than those which had existed prior to the publication of the Peel report. Here was the first, definite hint of the May White Paper of 1939,[17] a document eternally damned in the eyes of all Zionists.

Baffy had an extensive range of relatives and friends at all levels of social and political life, and she could number among her close acquaintances several cabinet ministers. They were not, it is true, of the front rank. But their friendship gave her a clear insight into government policy and the differences of opinion, such as they were, that existed at cabinet level. Her most prolific source of information was Walter Elliot [Minister of Agriculture, 1932–36; Secretary of State for Scotland, 1936–38; Minister of Health, 1938–40]. Almost daily Elliot and Baffy would discuss the issues of the hour. When he was excluded from Churchill's government in May 1940, Baffy lost her most important single contact. This is reflected in the diaries. Until 1940 she is able to comment with a great deal of authority on government policy; after 1940 she has neither more nor less information than the average, well-informed person of her standing. In any case, it was perhaps inevitable that the exigencies of war would tend to diminish her sources of information.

Baffy's first introduction to the Jewish problem took place at a very early age. The occasion was a sermon on the subject 'Mission to the Jews' at Inveraray church. Baffy had intended to put a threepenny-bit into the plate at the church door. One of her Campbell aunts objected. Threepence was not enough; the subject was worthy enough to warrant all of Baffy's savings, one whole shilling. Baffy railed violently at this decision but to no avail. Campbell will prevailed over Balfour logic.

It was my first introduction to the Jewish question. Further experience

16. Entry for 4 August 1937.
17. The May White Paper appeared on 17 May. It provided for the establishment of a Palestinian state in treaty relations with Great Britain after a transitionary period of ten years. The possibility of a federal solution was hinted at, and there were to be constitutional safeguards for the National Home and British interests. Eventual independence would depend upon the degree of cooperation attained between the two communities. Immigration was to be restricted to 75,000 over the next five years at an annual rate of 10,000; and in addition 25,000 refugees were to be allowed to enter Palestine. There were also to be severe restrictions on land sales.

has never made me doubt that my instincts of resistance were right on this occasion, and that any developments which the future may hold in store for the Jewish faith will come from within, not from without. My shilling was ill-spent, and I have never ceased to regret it.[18]

Baffy once noted that it was part of Orde Wingate's strength to identify himself completely and unequivocally with whichever minority group he happened to be championing at the time.[19] The same was true for Baffy. In no sphere of her activity is this more apparent than in her Zionist work. Zionism is, indeed, the dominant theme of the diaries. For although there is much comment on other political events, her obsession with Zionism increased in intensity over the years. She was often accused of being more Zionist than the Zionists. She bore this accusation lightly. Questions of dual loyalty held no fear for her. Upholding the Zionist cause, defending it from attack, rescuing it from defeat, was for her a British interest. Great Britain, she would doubtless have claimed, had a mission to fulfil: to help create a Jewish National Home in Palestine. Any deviation from this path she considered as a betrayal of a sacred trust. She had nothing but contempt for those who disregarded pledges given in good faith; or for those who attempted to rationalize Great Britain's steady retreat from her mandatory obligations in terms of political expediency. Such arguments were not only morally wrong, they were also politically bankrupt. And this combination of political conviction and moral indignation was usually sufficient to sweep away all opposition.

Family considerations also counted for much. She was conscious of the responsibility she held as Balfour's niece in safeguarding the legacy of the Balfour Declaration.[20] What Balfour started, Baffy would continue. And after her the family would inevitably take the same path. When her cousin, the third Earl of Balfour, made his debut at a Zionist function in London, Baffy noted as if full of fulfilment:

I felt so proud to see him (Ral) standing up there at the very table in the very same room where I remember A.J.B. speaking at that very dinner —I have waited and hoped for so many years that the great tradition might be carried on, and now in the time of greatest need it happens.[21]

Baffy was in every sense of the word the heiress to the Balfourian tradition in Zionism.

Her connection with Zionism centred on her friendship with Chaim

18. *Family Homespun*, p. 29.
19. Entry for 20 November 1944.
20. On 2 November 1917 Balfour, then Foreign Secretary, sent a note to Lord Rothschild in which he expressed the British Government's readiness to facilitate the establishment in Palestine of a National Home for the Jewish people.
21. Letter to M. Shertok (Sharett), 5 June 1939, S25/969, Central Zionist Archives, Jerusalem.

Weizmann. It is not absolutely clear when they first met but it appears to have been in 1923 and almost certainly through Lewis Namier, Professor of Modern History at Manchester University, a great friend of Baffy's and a dedicated Zionist. Weizmann was the greatest figure in Zionism from 1917, the year of the Balfour Declaration, until the years 1946–48, when age, ill-health, and the harsher realities of the post-war world pushed his leadership into the background. Weizmann was the only Zionist leader whom the British took seriously; the only one who spoke to them in a language adapted to their terms of reference. At times a powerful and moving orator, particularly in Yiddish, his main strength lay in his powers of exposition before small, intimate gatherings.

Weizmann was a genuine Anglophile, a not altogether uncommon phenomenon among East European Jews of his generation, particularly as they tended to endow the British way of life with a certain mysticism when comparing it with the Tsarist autocracy. He appreciated the necessity of gaining great-power support for Zionism. And of all the powers Great Britain appeared to him the most suitable. The Balfour Declaration and the drawing up of the mandatory terms for the administration of Palestine marked the culmination of Weizmann's policy. From then on his policy, in effect, turned on persuading successive British governments to keep faith with those fast receding obligations. This was no easy task at the best of times. But from the mid-nineteen-thirties onwards, international factors widened the already existing divisions of opinion between the Zionist leadership and the Government.

In many ways, the years the diaries cover were the most momentous in the history of Zionism. They saw the first, fateful armed Arab uprising in Palestine against Zionist aims and British policy; they witnessed the first suggestion, however faint and ambiguous it then appeared, to establish a Jewish state; they noted the effects of appeasement upon the fortunes of the Jewish people. Above all else, these were the years of the Second World War and the holocaust. The traumatic impact of this tragedy gave an added bite to the movement's struggle against the Labour Government during the post-war years, and determined both psychologically and politically the necessity for a Jewish state and its unceasing, even obsessive preoccupation with security problems in after years.

This was a period of mounting tension and the Zionists stumbled from one crisis to another in their relations with the Government. Weizmann's policy of Anglo-Zionist cooperation was in danger of breaking down. It was in this kind of situation that Baffy was of most help. Her immense range of contacts proved to be of tremendous value to Weizmann. She helped to unlock hitherto barred doors; or at least ensured an easier entrance.

Her commitment to Weizmann was absolute. When Weizmann failed to be re-elected to office in December 1946, Baffy quickly realized that her day-to-day work for Zionism had come to an end. Her disappointment was great and she fully shared the old leader's bitterness at the 'intrigues' which had jockeyed him, and her, from office.

There were of course many Gentiles sympathetic to Zionism. Some of the best known names in British politics were associated with the movement. Many of them worked together with the Zionists consistently and with great devotion. But their Zionism was only one facet of their overall political activity: it could hardly have been otherwise. With Baffy it was everything. Her identification with Zionism was complete and irrevocable. It must sometimes have even alarmed her friends. While on a visit to Palestine she wrote, 'The past two weeks have made me love it [Palestine] and its Jewish people more passionately than ever.'[22] And in Palestine again: 'What an utterly different world the British officials inhabit—and how much more at home I feel with the Jews.'[23] And again during the Twenty-First Zionist Congress at Zurich: 'So here I am again, with my *other* people, and in the atmosphere which is also home.'[24] And yet again, after participating in a Passover celebration: 'The true spirit of Eretz Israel, wonderful and moving. What a tremendous thing it is to be welcomed by them to their innermost festivals, to be made part of so great a movement.'[25] She spoke on behalf of Zionism up and down the country, and, significantly, found great difficulty in adapting herself to Gentile audiences: 'In the evening went down to Sevenoaks to talk about Palestine to a Drawing-Room Meeting of Goyim . . Did not speak very well—it is difficult to change the key to suit non-Jewish audiences.'[26]

Of all the Gentile Zionists, Baffy alone was admitted into the inner circle of Zionist policy-making bodies. Always a member of Weizmann's team, she became later a member of the London Political Committee, a body chiefly responsible for Zionist political work in England, and, for a period, even acted as its chairman. This must have raised acute questions of conscience for both the Zionists and her other friends. But it is a remarkable fact that none of Baffy's friends, Jew or Gentile, ever questioned her fidelity.

The Zionists regarded her as a full and equal member of their councils. Most decisions were not voted upon but were thrashed out in open discussion until a unanimous decision was reached; and Baffy's opinion was valued more than most. It was, after all, in the Zionists' interests to have someone well placed in political life who could and would push their views outside of the formal world of official memoranda and meetings. Although there was no question of subterfuge and Baffy was a willing and convinced participant, it would be a little more than naïve to suppose that this factor escaped the notice of her Zionist colleagues. Baffy's relationship with her government friends posed even more delicate problems. She unquestionably

22. Entry for 3 May 1936.
23. Entry for 23 April 1939.
24. Entry for 19 August 1939.
25. Entry for 24 April 1940.
26. Entry for 10 November 1937.

knew what was going on inside the cabinet. At times she saw government documents which were not intended for her eyes, the most pertinent example being her access to the Peel report more than two weeks before it was published and while its main recommendations were still being discussed in cabinet.[27] How did she use this information? Of course, when in debate with the Zionists she based her argumentation upon her prior knowledge. But there is no evidence to assume that she passed on *verbatim* the knowledge that she had acquired. Quite the contrary, she was extremely conscious of the exacting nature of her position, and desperately anxious not to abuse old friendships. Thus:

> Walter [Elliot] said that once the Cabinet had agreed to a [Royal] Commission it was probably the opening of War between the Jews and them, and that he and I must revise technique of what he tells me. It would be impossible for him to give me information which I should be bound to use against his colleagues. I fear this is true. I must simply trust him, tell him everything, but never consult him. This we settled.[28]

Baffy constituted in fact an essential ingredient in all diplomacy. Well-informed, trusted by both sides, she acted as an unofficial channel of communication, freely passing information back and forth, while keeping both sides talking and in contact with each other. Of course, one should not overestimate her importance. She was not indispensable and would never have made such a claim. But she was at times a vital element in Zionist diplomacy; and, while not indispensable, her abscence would have been sorely felt.

Baffy's day-to-day work at 77 Great Russell Street, the Jewish Agency and Zionist Federation[29] headquarters in London, consisted mainly of helping to draft documents needed to promote the Zionist viewpoint. If a letter was required for *The Times,* a memorandum for the Colonial Office, or a Weizmann speech in need of polishing, Baffy was usually on call to lend a hand. Her chief collaborator in these endeavours was Lewis Namier, and a formidable combination they made. Baffy's fire tempered by Namier's original and pedantic mind produced, more often than not, the correct formulae.

The diaries appear not to have been written with an eye for literary style, although Baffy was undoubtedly a skilful and attractive writer. They are blunt and matter-of-fact, direct and to the point. Only rarely does she indulge in embellishment and descriptive passages. This seems to be wholly in

27. Entry for 22 June 1937.
28. Entry for 14 May 1936.
29. The original terms of the Mandate stated that a Jewish agency should act in cooperation with the Palestine administration in National Home affairs, and that initially the Zionist Organization should be that agency. However, it was not until 1928–29 that the Jewish Agency was established in its final form with the incorporation of representatives of non-Zionist world Jewry, particularly from the U.S. It was by then a most complex organization which has been defined, with some justification, as 'a state within a state'.

keeping with her personality. It was not Baffy's intention to evoke the social atmosphere of the period. She recorded what people said and did; not in what setting they appeared. Like all diaries these too have to be treated with some caution. The reader may often disagree with her opinions, or the historian question her judgement. None of this seriously affects their importance. They are valuable precisely because they portray a highly personalized interpretation of events. And it is Baffy's single-minded, unyielding devotion to a particular viewpoint that gives the diaries a unique flavour of their own.[30] She sometimes had unkind things to say about her political opponents, or those who chanced to stray from her chosen path. She was not one to pull her punches. Her comments are at times perceptive, often biting, and invariably reflect the passions aroused by the controversies of those years.

The original diaries consist of some thirteen typewritten volumes—about seven hundred thousand words. Much of the material, being mainly of a family and personal nature and of little interest to the general reader, excluded itself. Nevertheless, the task of selection posed extremely thorny problems; and inevitably an element of arbitrary decision-making intruded. On the one hand, there were the unavoidable remarks about her contemporaries which, if published, might cause offence or embarrassment. Those of a purely personal character have been omitted; those which have some bearing on the political events recorded have been retained. For the rest, there are included in the main only those comments which have a recognizable historical relevance. This course was dictated by the functional style of the diaries.

It must be admitted that such a manner of approach may lead to misrepresentation, for it does portray a somewhat unbalanced portrait of Baffy. It would be totally wrong to regard her merely as a political *savant,* interested in little else, whiling away her life flitting from one political *salon* to another. Few would deny that Baffy needed politics; but there were other interests. The diaries record her continuous interest in painting, travel, the theatre, films, architecture; and she was, of course, an avid reader on most topics. Above all else there was Scotland and her family. If Baffy lived in London, she returned home to Scotland as many times during the year as duty allowed. Caponflat, East Lothian, was the home of her daughter and son-in-law, Frances and James [Jimmie] Fergusson[31] and her three grandchildren. It was here that Baffy relaxed. She tended the garden, went for long walks, renewed old acquaintances, immersed herself in local and family gossip. It was here that she found shelter and relief from the buffetings of political life, and here that she unwound in preparation for renewing the political merry-go-round in London.

30. Nevertheless, on the numerous occasions that I have had need to check the facts recorded in the diaries, I have found them remarkably accurate; only the interpretation is Baffy's.
31. Sir James Fergusson succeeded to his baronetcy in 1951.

Baffy's health began to deteriorate in 1946. Until then she appeared as a most robust person. But obviously the strain and tension of her life took its toll. She began to suffer from the effects of high blood pressure and bronchial asthma, and her doctor prescribed a less active timetable as part of a cure. Baffy voiced protest after protest at this maddening limitation upon her activities; but she was eventually forced to bow before the inevitable. The entries for 1947 are sparse and they cease altogether from August of that year.

She died suddenly on 15 May 1948, at the age of sixty-seven, in her native Scotland at Kilkerran, by then the home of her daughter and son-in-law. On the previous day, David Ben-Gurion had announced the establishment of the State of Israel, the first president being her old comrade-in-arms, Chaim Weizmann. Her life-long dream had come true. On hearing of this momentous news from her son-in-law, Baffy clapped her hands and said, 'It will all come right now. You'll see.'[32] This sentiment was, of course, little more than a reflection of her unwavering belief in the destiny of Zionism, for it was not at all certain at the time that everything would come right. But it was a wholly characteristic reaction, and as such deserves to be set on record as a worthy epitaph for her life's work.

I have intervened in the narrative of the diaries as little as possible. On the rare occasions where it has been necessary, I have done so in square brackets. Biographical details have been included for the reader's convenience. For the rest, explanatory footnotes and other comments have been kept to the barest minimum.

The Hebrew University,   N. A. ROSE.
Jerusalem, 1972.

---

32. Berl Locker relates [*BeChavlei Kium VeTeKuma* ('Jewish Survival and Revival'), (Jerusalem, 1963), p. 285], that Baffy said: 'This is the happiest day of my life.' This may well have been an afterthought. Her immediate reaction, as related to me by Sir James Fergusson, was as above.

1936 *January 1st—The Cottage, Oldbury Wells, Bridgnorth, Alison's House*[1] I begin a Diary again for the first time since 1918 . . .

January 14th—1 Roland Gardens, London[2] This afternoon went to a Refugee Committee at League of Nations Union. Bob[3] in chair . . . Afterwards asked Bob whether he thought Neill Malcolm[4] would make a good High Commissioner for German Refugees. He said, failing Victor Lytton,[5] he thought so. This was the idea of Lewis Namier,[6] who dined here, and I went with him after dinner to discuss the matter at Zionist Office . . . It was agreed that Lewis and I should go to Foreign Office tomorrow and press the name of Neill Malcolm on Bobbitty Cranborne[7] (who is now Under-Secretary and goes to Geneva in a few days for Council Meeting where this matter will be decided). It was nice to be working again with Lewis in 77 Great Russell Street.[8]

January 20th—London, 10.50 p.m. The King is dying, perhaps will die tonight . . .
  Jack Wheeler-Bennett[9] and Peter Rutenberg[10] came to tea. Peter told me

1. Mrs A. D. Milne, Mrs Dugdale's younger sister.
2. Mrs Dugdale's home.
3. Lord Robert Cecil: Held cabinet office under Asquith, Bonar Law and Baldwin; a devoted advocate of the League of Nations and President of the League of Nations Union, 1923–45; Nobel Prize for Peace, 1937. Cr. first Viscount of Chelwood, 1923.
4. Major-General Sir Neill Malcolm: High Commissioner for German Refugees, 1936–38.
5. Victor Lytton, 2nd Earl: Served in Indian Civil Service; Chairman of the League of Nations mission to Manchuria, 1932; and of Palestine Potash Ltd.
6. Lewis Namier: Political Secretary of the Jewish Agency, 1929–31; Professor of Modern History at Manchester University, 1931–53. Knighted, 1952.
7. R. A. J. Gascoyne-Cecil: Under-Secretary of State for Foreign Affairs, 1935-38; Paymaster-General, 1940; Secretary of State for Dominions, 1940–42, 1943–45; for Colonies, 1942; Lord Privy Seal, 1942–43, 1951–52. Cr. Viscount Cranborne, 1903; fifth Marquess of Salisbury, 1947.
8. The Zionist headquarters in central London.
9. John Wheeler-Bennett: Author and Historian. Knighted, 1959.
10. Peter Rutenberg: Ex-Russian revolutionary and Zionist civil engineer; founder of the Palestine Electric Corporation—the Rutenberg Works.

I

about his conversations with J. Thomas[11] in which he thinks he impressed Thomas with the critical state of affairs in Middle East, which would make the giving of a Legislative Council in Palestine very unwise.[12] Peter returns to Palestine in a day or two and promised to keep me informed of any further talk with Thomas before he goes. But the King's death will prevent that, I fear.

Soon after midnight Stew's[13] friend, Mrs Manson, rang up to tell us that the King died a few minutes before twelve o'clock.

January 21st—London . . . Lewis Namier dined with us and we went round to Michael's[14] in Elizabeth Street, to listen on his wireless to Mr Baldwin[15] speaking to the nation about the King. Half-an-hour *quite* perfect, as only Stanley Baldwin could be on that theme. The mixture of homeliness, dignity and feeling. He will probably regain through that talk much of the ground he lost before Xmas at time of Sam Hoare's[16] resignation.[17]

Much speculation rife today about Edward VIII. Brendan Bracken[18] told Hannah[19] that the question is being asked—Who is the next Prince of Wales?—Answer, Mrs. Simpson!

. . . Lewis stayed, and we talked Palestine. It is evident that Jimmy Thomas will be a very bad Colonial Secretary from our point of view. Weak, ignorant, blustering, insolent and indiscreet. All these qualities have shown themselves in the last week or two over Legislative Council controversy, and another regarding the proposal to exclude immigrants in the Capitalist class with £1,000.[20] The minimum is to be raised to £2,000. We

11. J. H. Thomas: Labour [from 1931, National Labour] M.P. for Derby, 1910–36; General Secretary of National Union of Railwaymen, 1917–31; Secretary of State for Colonies, 1924, 1935–36; for Dominions, 1930–35.

12. The question of a Legislative Council for Palestine had reappeared in an acute form in the winter of 1935–36. The Zionist were opposed to the establishment of such a body on the grounds that the fate of the National Home would then be turned over to those who totally rejected both the Balfour Declaration and the Mandate. The British argued that the setting up of a representative body was implicit in the terms of the Mandate and other Government statements issued since. The Zionists, hard pressed, stumbled upon a compromise formula: parity. But this found no positive echo in Government circles.

13. Mrs Elizabeth Stewart: Mrs Dugdale's cook and housekeeper for 46 years.

14. Mrs Dugdale's son.

15. Stanley Baldwin: Prime Minister, 1923, 1924–29, 1935–37; Lord President of the Council, 1931–35; Lord Privy Seal, 1932–34. Cr. Earl, 1937.

16. Sir Samuel Hoare: Secretary of State for Air, 1922–24; for India, 1931–35; for Foreign Affairs, 1935; First Lord of the Admiralty, 1936–37; Home Secretary, 1937–40; Ambassador to Spain, 1940–44. Cr. Viscount Templewood, 1944.

17. As a result of the public outcry following the publication of the Hoare-Laval proposals to settle the Italo-Abyssinian war.

18. Brendan Bracken: Conservative M.P. for North Paddington; Parliamentary Private Secretary to Churchill, 1940–41; Minister of Information, 1941–45; First Lord of the Admiralty, 1945. Cr. Viscount, 1952.

19. Hannah Hudson, wife of Rob Hudson: Conservative M.P. for Southport; Minister of Pensions, 1935–36; Secretary for Department of Overseas Trade, 1939–40; Minister of Agriculture, 1940–45.

20. According to the Immigration Ordinances, immigrants were admitted into Palestine under the following categories: A. Persons of independent means with a guaranteed capital of

decided to fight this, on grounds of psychological and actual cruelty it would inflict on German Jews to make this change at this moment. Method of fighting, to form a block, inside and outside Cabinet, to coerce J. Thomas. No good trying for his friendship, it is worthless. Laid some plans.

January 22nd . . . Dined with Walter[21] at Caledonian Club . . .

Talked with him about J. Thomas, who has been acting most annoyingly on affairs of Palestine. I made up my mind he ought to leave Colonial Office.

January 23rd   L.N.U. Executive—Then to Hannah for lunch. Mrs Gunston,[22] Rob Bernays,[23] little Robin [Hudson] and Walter also there. Some discussion of Stanley Baldwin's broadcast on King's death. None of them admired it as I did. Walter had given us seats in Members' Gallery and we went there after lunch to hear the tributes to King's memory from the Party leaders, Baldwin was adequate but not 'inspired'. Attlee[24] read commonplace speech. Archie Sinclair[25] good, in Victorian manner which suits him. Then with Hannah to the Minister of Pensions' room in House of Commons. The only Minister's room that looks out on Palace Yard. . . . We stood on a table by window and had an excellent straight view of pavement in front of entrance to Westminster Hall. Harold Nicolson[26] told us afterwards the scene inside was too splendid for words, light concentrated on the coffin in the centre of the Hall. The heralds walked round. Harold Nicolson said the Commons talked too much as they walked by. We had hoped to be allowed in accompanied by M.P.'s after the service was over, but the Hall was closed till 8 p.m. Nicolson said that part of the Crown, somewhere on the gun carriage or coffin, had partly fallen off on road from St Pancras. I hope not a bad omen! Much speculation about the habits of the new King. Walter says he has a dual personality. Which will be uppermost?

£1,000; members of the liberal professions with a capital sum of £500, provided that a need existed for their employment; and skilled craftsmen with £250, under the same conditions. B. Orphans; religious functionaries; and students. C. Persons who have a definite prospect of employment in Palestine. D. Dependents of permanent residents, and of categories A, B, and C. The labour schedule, the scale of which was always the subject for long and acrimonious argument, referred to category C. The proposal noted here concerned the capitalist class and was later dropped.

21. Walter Elliot: Conservative M.P. for Kelvingrove from 1924; Minister of Agriculture, 1932–36; Secretary of State for Scotland, 1936–38; Minister of Health, 1938–40.
22. Gardenia Gunston, wife of Derrick Gunston: Conservative M.P. for Thornbury; Parliamentary Secretary to Neville Chamberlain, 1931–36.
23. R. H. Bernays: Liberal M.P. for Bristol North from 1931; Parliamentary Secretary to Ministry of Health, 1937–39; to Ministry of Transport, 1939–40.
24. C. R. Attlee: Leader of the Labour Party, 1935–55; Lord Privy Seal, 1940–42; Deputy Prime Minister, 1942–45; Prime Minister, 1945–51. Cr. Earl, 1955.
25. Sir Archibald Sinclair: Leader of the parliamentary Liberal Party, 1935–45; Secretary of State for Scotland, 1931–32; for Air, 1940–45. Cr. Viscount Thurso, 1952.
26. Harold Nicolson: National Labour M.P. for West Leicester, 1935–45; author and critic. Knighted, 1953.

January 27th . . . Lewis lunched with me. A telegram from Chaim[27] in Palestine (cyphered) begging us to stop the proclamation of Five Feddan Law[28] announced for 29th January . . . Chaim has told Arthur Wauchope[29] it is against promises in 'P.M.'s letter'.[30] I got on to Buck[31] on telephone at lunch and begged him to ask Ramsay MacDonald[32] to use influence for delay.

About 6 p.m. Buck rang up to say he had talked to Ramsay MacDonald, but got no change out of him. He said Cabinet had considered the point and were satisfied there had been no going back on promises. I begged Buck now to get hold of Malcolm[33] to delay Proclamation in Palestine.

February 2nd—Sunday . . . Walked with Lewis Namier, more Zionist politics. He feels strongly that Chaim is too much at Rehovoth,[34] not enough in Jerusalem at present.

February 10th—London . . . Lewis came to discuss the campaign about Palestine. It is settled that I am to speak to the Palestine Committee of the House of Commons next Monday . . .

February 15th—London Opened *Times* on account of Austen's[35] unexpected onslaught on Stanley Baldwin in Defence Debate yesterday. What a sign of the approaching fall! Talked to Colin[36] about it on the telephone and also whether he could not further idea of Winston Churchill as Defence

---

27. Chaim Weizmann: President of the World Zionist Organization, 1921–31, 1935–45, from 1929 he combined this office with that of President of Jewish Agency; first President of Israel, 1948–52.
28. This legislation forbade the sale of land except on condition that the landowner retained a minimum area sufficient for subsistence for himself and his family. This area was to be inalienable and revert to the Palestine Government should the owner-occupier cease to cultivate it. One feddan is equivalent to 1·038 acres.
29. General Sir Arthur Wauchope: High Commissioner for Palestine and Transjordan, 1931–38.
30. On 13 February 1931, Ramsay MacDonald, then Prime Minister, addressed a letter to Weizmann in which he reinterpreted, in a more positive manner, the Passfield White Paper of October 1930, a document generally held to have been damaging to Zionist interests.
31. H. E. D. B. Sackville, ninth Earl De la Warr; Parliamentary Under-Secretary of State for Colonies, 1936–37; Lord Privy Seal, 1937–38; President of the Board of Education, 1938–40.
32. J. R. MacDonald: Leader of the Labour Party, 1911–14, 1922–31; Prime Minister and Foreign Secretary, 1924; Prime Minister of Labour Government. 1929–31; of National Government, 1931–35; Lord President of the Council, 1935–37.
33. Malcolm MacDonald, son of Ramsay: Secretary of State for Dominions, 1935–39; for Colonies, 1935, 1938–40; Minister of Health, 1940–41.
34. Where Weizmann lived in Palestine. His home was situated just by the Sieff [later Weizmann] Institute.
35. Sir Austen Chamberlain: Conservative M.P. for Birmingham West from 1914; Secretary of State for India, 1915–17; member of War Cabinet, 1918; Chancellor of Exchequer, 1919–21; Lord Privy Seal and Leader of the House of Commons, 1921–22; Foreign Secretary, 1924–29.
36. Colin Coote: Journalist and author; deputy editor of *Daily Telegraph,* 1945–50; editor, 1950–64; at the time he was leader writer for *The Times.* Knighted, 1962.

Minister. He said he had mentioned it in *Times* office and found Geoffrey Dawson[37] not disposed. Colin agreed that if Winston would only do what I suggested[38] . . . it would be easier to push. Colin said he would do anything to oppose appointment of either Sam Hoare or Eustace Percy,[39] both which disastrous ideas seem to be under discussion. Colin again said how dismally out of touch with reality this cabinet is. I feel it, even with Walter.

Lewis Namier to lunch and spent afternoon here going over points for my speech to Palestine Parliamentary Committee on Monday.

February 16th—Sunday Stayed in all day working at speech. Lewis lunched with us and was here for tea when Harry Sacher[40] also came. He says the more this Palestine Land Legislation is looked into the more obvious that H.M.G. had no idea what they were doing. There will be intense discontent among Arab peasants over it. We made plans for getting it modified before Chaim leaves Palestine, which he does on February 29th. Harry will go tomorrow to talk to that fool J. H. Thomas.

February 17th—London In till 4 p.m. polishing up my speech. . . .

At 4.30 p.m. joined Henry Melchett,[41] Lewis and Brodetsky[42] for tea in House of Lords, we talked over names of peers to take part in debate on Palestine.

At 5.30 we went up to Committee Room 11, where Wedgwood[43] took Chair. A good many people came and did not go away. There were almost forty I suppose and among them people I was very pleased to see, such as Bob Cecil and Leo Amery[44] and James de Rothschild.[45] Rob and Hannah were there. I spoke for about forty-five minutes on Land and Legislative Council and afterwards there was long and fruitful discussion, for they settled to have Sub-Committee to watch developments and to ask some questions. A lot of people now certainly know what is on the tapis.

Rob said my speech was too feminine and not statesmanlike enough and did not enough catch right tone for House of Commons.

37. Geoffrey Dawson: Editor of *The Times*, 1912–19, 1922–41.
38. Mrs Dugdale had suggested that Churchill make a public speech allaying the alarm people felt about him.
39. Lord Eustace Percy: Minister without Portfolio, 1935–36.
40. Harry Sacher: Journalist and lawyer; director of Marks and Spencer; Zionist functionary and friend of Weizmann.
41. Henry Mond, second Baron Melchett: Industrialist; Director of Imperial Chemical Industries; of Barclay's Bank.
42. Professor Selig Brodetsky: Member of the Executive of World Zionist Organization and Jewish Agency for Palestine; Professor of Applied Mathematics at Leeds University.
43. J. C. Wedgwood: Labour M.P. for Newcastle under Lyme; Chancellor of the Duchy of Lancaster, 1924; fervent Gentile Zionist. Cr. Baron, 1942.
44. L. S. Amery: Conservative M.P. for Sparkbrook from 1911; First Lord of Admiralty, 1922–23; Secretary of State for Colonies, 1924–29; of Dominions, 1925–29; for India, 1940–45.
45. James de Rothschild, eldest son of Baron Edmond: Liberal M.P. for Isle of Ely from 1929.

February 26th—London Went to House of Lords to hear Debate on Palestine Legislative Council on Lord Snell's[46] Motion. Marvellous result: some ten Peers from all sides spoke against Government and not one in favour. We now hope for a further Debate in both Houses. Spent evening writing an article about it for Palestine papers.

March 2nd Dined with Walter . . . He told me that about a week ago he had conveyed to Stanley Baldwin a message (he did not tell me through whom) that if Sam Hoare is made the Chairman of the C[ommittee] I[mperial] D[efence] then he [Walter] would resign. Baldwin was furious! Walter thinks he has dished Sam Hoare but of course also himself for the job. I said, nevertheless, I was overjoyed. *That* is the way to act, *before* not *after* the event, and do what you feel right and then hope for the best. I do think Walter is recovering form!

March 8th—Sunday, Caponflat[47] The papers had the news that Hitler had marched troops into the demilitarized zone without warning. Thus breaking Locarno Treaty.[48]
. . . After dinner we heard Sarraut the French P.M. on wireless—saying French Government would not examine German proposals, put forward after such a brutal violation of Treaty. We sat discussing new European situation created today. Abyssinian War fades into background. About 11 p.m. Walter rang me up from London. Cabinet meets tomorrow morning. He seemed to think we should tell the French we would support them along their own frontier line, but not in an invasion of Germany.

March 9th—Caponflat . . . we listened to the News and heard that Anthony Eden[49] had said in the House that we should go to the help of France and Belgium if attacked. He also said we should examine German proposals of return to League and so forth.[50] I fear this is the right and only line under the circumstances. . . .

---

46. Henry Snell: Pro-Zionist Labour peer; member of the Shaw Commission in 1930 and author of its minority report. His motion asked the Government to defer the proposal until greater experience in Local Government had been acquired.
47. Caponflat, East Lothian, the home of Mrs Dugdale's daughter, Frances, and her son-in-law, James Fergusson.
48. The Locarno treaties of 1925 had guaranteed the Franco-German, Belgium-German frontiers and had provided for the continued demilitarization of the Rhineland. The treaties had been underwritten by Great Britain and Italy.
49. Anthony Eden: Lord Privy Seal, 1934–35; Minister for League of Nations affairs, 1935; Foreign Secretary, 1935–38, 1940–45, 1951–55; Prime Minister, 1955–57. Cr. Earl, 1961.
50. In place of Locarno, Hitler had proposed a non-aggression pact with France and Belgium for 25 years, supplemented by a similar air agreement, and to be guaranteed by Great Britain and Italy; a new demilitarized zone on both sides of Germany's western frontier; non-aggresion pacts with Germany's eastern neighbours; and the possibility of Germany returning to the League of Nations.

March 10th—London . . . After lunch shopped, saw Mr. Watt,[51] then went up to Zionist Office and had tea with Chaim, just back from Palestine, and arranging interviews with politicians of all sorts. He said time is come when H.M.G. must make up its mind whether it intends actively to assist the National Home, or just go on holding the balance. The Jews must know where they are—and on the answer will depend much of their loyalty to us, and perhaps the peace and defence of Palestine.

I dined with Walter at Club. Told him I thought that while we ought not to fight Germany unless she crosses the frontier, likewise we ought not to negotiate with her on basis of broken Treaty. He would not quite agree, though he said it was a sustainable point of view. He would prolong talking period under any conditions. I walked with him to House of Commons—we were joined on the way by Rob Bernays. Then I went on to Savoy Grill (it was by now about 10.30) where I met Buck. Diana [De la Warr] came later and finally Walter from House after the end of the Debate on Defence. Winston had made a very good speech—his chances of Vice-Chairmanship of C.I.D. are increasing, Walter thought. But nothing is settled. Sam Hoare considered to have ruined his own chances by maladroit speech night before. It was T. Dugdale[52] who persuaded him to speak, hoping that would happen, for he himself is a strong advocate of Walter! Walter told us that Neville[53] announced League Council to be held *here* on Saturday!

March 11th—London   There came to lunch Chaim, Neill Malcolm, and Lewis. This was first meeting between Chaim and Neill, and Chaim talked of Palestine conditions and difficulties with Government. Neill asked him how many immigrants he thought Palestine could hold. Chaim said he personally would run a ten-year plan, on basis of some 30,000 agricultural settlers a year, who would provide work for twice that number in the towns, thus about 100,000 new settlers a year for ten years, and then we would see! He begged Neill to remember that Palestine is the only place in the world where the Jew does not *fill* room—he *makes* room. I think Neill was much struck with Chaim.

. . . After getting home Walter came to see me about 11.30 p.m. There was a Cabinet this evening. The French want to march into the Rhineland. Anthony went tonight to see Hoesch,[54] to try to persuade Hitler to evacuate If not, our legal advisers have no doubt of our obligations under Locarno.

51. Mrs Dugdale's literary agent.
52. T. L. Dugdale: Conservative M.P. for Richmond, Yorkshire; Parliamentary Private Secretary to Sir P. Cunliffe-Lister (Lord Swinton), 1931–35; to Stanley Baldwin, 1935–40; Minister of Agriculture, 1951–54. Cr. Baron Crathorne, 1959.
53. Neville Chamberlain: Chancellor of Exchequer, 1931–37; Prime Minister, 1937–40; Lord President of the Council, 1940.
54. Leopold von Hoesch: German Ambassador to Great Britain, 1932–36; his sudden death in April, ostensibly as a result of his exertions during the crisis, became the subject of much rumour.

C

The Cabinet will be much divided. I hope and believe Walter will be where he should be, but he says he will not make up his mind till the moment comes. It may be—in fact it *is* so—that this is a greater crisis than 1914. As Walter said, it was just a War that hung in the balance then. But if Anthony succeeds in his mission tonight perhaps few will ever know. The country is quite unawakened.

March 12th—London Spent morning and afternoon at L.N.U. committees. A full Exec. in morning. Austen Chamberlain started off with impressive statement of his views. He said he had felt something missing from Anthony Eden's speech on Monday, nothing said about the entry of Zone being a violation of frontier according to Locarno. There could be no clearer case of the breach of a voluntary engagement. Nothing could strike so fatal a blow at Collective Security than to let Germany get away with this. *We can break our Locarno obligations—as Germany has broken them—but we cannot evade them.* We ought not to negotiate with Germany until she had withdrawn. We should note the despatches of *Times* Berlin correspondent, regarding the internal struggle in Germany. Our public is totally unaware of the solemnity of our engagements under Locarno. France now asks us— will we *stand* by her? If we don't the League is gone. *We* forced France into Sanctions against Italy. Unless you can teach Germany that she must not do these things we move towards World War. Austen would bring the Fleet back from the Mediterranean. The peril is now in Europe.

I agreed with every word Austen said.

The Dean of Chichester[55] said the ordinary man almost breathed a sigh of relief when we heard that Hitler had entered the Zone!! Austen gasped. But I fear it is true. *At present* ninety out of every hundred people feel no anger against the Germans. . . . I found it terribly true at a crowded (and amusing) Sherry Party at the Rayleighs.[56] No other topic was discussed, but nearly everybody abused the French, said we must restrain them, but if they insist on Germany evacuating before we talk to her, then we must abandon them. At least that is what most people seemed to want to do. The Franco-Prusian Pact[57] is blamed for much. Harldy anywhere does one meet a person who thinks clear. The horror of war is upon them. I don't wonder, but we shall have it all the more certainly if we don't do right now—and then we shall be without a friend in the world.

March 14th Tom Inskip[58] is Defence Vice-Chairman. The one person nobody had thought of! But, if we are not to have someone of the type of

55. The Rt. Rev. George Kennedy Allen Bell.
56. Robert John Strutt, Lord Rayleigh: Physicist; Mrs Dugdale's cousin.
57. Signed in May 1935; ratified, February 1936. Hitler argued that tne ratification of the pact destroyed the basis of the Locarno treaties.
58. T. W. H. Inskip: Attorney General, 1932–36; Minister for Coordination of Defence, 1936–39; Dominions Secretary, 1939; Lord Chancellor, 1939–40; Lord Chief Justice, 1940–46. Cr. Viscount Caldecote, 1939.

Winston or Walter, I think he may prove quite a good appointment. A very astute move on Baldwin's part.

March 15—Sunday, London   Dined at Nancy Astor's.[59] Forty-six people, including the German Ambassador von Hoesch, the Russian Ambassador Maisky, Titulesco the Roumanian Foreign Minister, Sam Hoare, Bobbitty Cranborne, the Salisburys, Walter and Katherine Elliot, M. Avenol, the Secretary-General of the League, and many more!! An extraordinary party. I thought it might be like the ball before Waterloo?

At dinner I sat between Sir Roderick Jones[60] and Sir Sam Hoare. Talked to the latter first about the novels of Tolstoy and Balzac, and then about British Foreign Ministers who had been a danger to their country. He started this topic—not I! He referred to Lord Aberdeen and to Dizzy.

After dinner Nancy started off with Musical Chairs. A number of people played . . . But neither Hoesch nor Maisky so my hopes of seeing those two scrabbling for the last chair were not fulfilled.

Afterwards people moved about and talked in groups. The news came that the Germans have accepted invitation to attend Council, on condition of equality and consideration of their proposals. Avenol and Titulesco sat down one on each side of me, and Titulesco tried to pump Avenol without success as to exact meaning of these conditions. He seemed highly suspicious.

March 18th   A Conference of Zionists at Mulberry House—the Melchetts.

About twenty were present. Chaim exposed the present position in Palestine and foresaw the time when there would be no more land. The question was debated whether this is the moment to begin to urge openly the development of Transjordan. No decision on that, but it was decided to start systematized 'break-through' of ignorance and apathy of British public, by organizing a campaign in Parliament, Press, etc. This to be done gradually and wisely, by means of Sub-Committees to deal with each subject. I shall probably be in on this. My own chief contributions to discussion tonight were to beg them to believe that much is due to faults in British Colonial System —nothing is due to ill-will on part of His Majesty's Government—and secondly to remind them that they must not drop Zionist philosophy from their propaganda, nor try to meet the British mind too much. It was *Eretz Israel (the Land of Israel)* which converted A.J.B., and *Eretz Israel* is really their only message to the British public. Gwen Melchett gave us a caviare supper after, and I came home in Simon Marks'[61] car with Eva Reading,[62] Lewis and Chaim.

Lewis told me a good saying of Schmaryahu Levin,[63] 'If you take away the

---

59. Viscountess Astor: Conservative M.P. for Sutton, Plymouth, from 1919.
60. Chairman of Reuters News Agency.
61. Simon Marks: Chairman and Joint Managing Director of Marks and Spencer.
62. Eva Reading: Henry Melchett's sister, married to the Marquess of Reading.
63. Schmaryahu Levin: A Zionist functionary and publicist.

money of a Russian Jew, there is a Jew left. If you take away the money of an American Jew, there is nothing left.'

March 19th—London . . . Dined with Walter at Club. He told me what had been decided and told already privately to the Germans. I should think they will go home. All turns on the conversations between the French and British Staffs. We are back at Agadir and 1911. Hitler has done for the French what for 20 years they have failed to do for themselves, driven us into a military alliance, however it may be disguised.[64] I never thought this Government would have the guts! But the country won't like it. It is *shocking* how much pro-German feeling exists even among one's own friends. I met it tonight . . . at an amusing musical party at Tom Inskip's. He came in late after the second Cabinet Meeting of his life.

The first was this morning! He has certainly begun at a moment when Cabinets are 'peu banal'! Talked to Harry Crookshank[65] and Tony Muirhead.[66] Tony, speaking of Winston taking his exclusion so much to heart, said, 'It's a pity Winston's swimming bath has no shallow end.' Tony also said, 'When I was a child I used to hear sermons which said, "If you do right you can't go wrong". I always wondered what that meant. I suppose the Government thinks it understands.'

March 20th   After lunch I went to Zionist Office for small conference about sudden resolve of Labour Party to have a Palestine Debate next Thursday. Rather annoying, but if it is to be then we must organize some speakers.

March 24th—London . . . House of Commons for Palestine Debate. Got there just as Jimmy Thomas began. He made a poor defence of policy re Legislative Council, and the Government had a bad time on all sides till Debate ended about 8.15. No one in favour of Leg. Co. except one, Crossley.[67] Winston made a very fine speech. On way to dinner with Jos. Wedgwood I met Brendan Bracken and Winston in the corridor. They both thought Leg. Co. dead if the two oppositions choose to pursue their advantage. I am not so sure—and indeed if it were to lead to Wauchope's resignation I am not so sure it is to be wished—but certainly the Debate in both Houses has been a triumph for us. . . .

March 25th—London . . . Bob Boothby,[68] to talk of Palestine Debate. He too thought Leg. Co. proposals dead and foresaw Wauchope's resignation. He

---

64. On 19 March the Government had promised that it would come immediately to the assistance of the French in accordance with the Locarno treaties and would take all practical measures to ensure France against unprovoked aggression. This guarantee was followed by joint staff talks; but they petered out towards the end of the year.
65. H. Crookshank: Conservative M.P. for Gainsborough from 1924; Secretary for Mines, 1935–40; Postmaster-General, 1942–45; Minister of Health, 1951–52; Lord Privy Seal, 1952–53. Cr. Viscount, 1956.
66. Lt.Col. A. Muirhead: Conservative M.P. for Wells, Somerset, from 1929.
67. A. Crossley: Conservative M.P. for Stretford from 1935.
68. Robert Boothby: Conservative M.P. for East Aberdeenshire from 1924. Cr. Baron, 1958.

said Duff Cooper[69] had a successor in mind—a General Burnett Stewart 'the only intelligent soldier' Bob had ever met. I repeated this later to Chaim, for there might be a certain advantage in having the nominee of the War Minister, if we want to develop point of Jews being an asset in defence of Middle East.

Edgar and I lunched with the Salisburys. . . . I sat next Lord Lloyd.[70] We discussed Palestine Debate. He has just been in Palestine and had much confidential talk with Wauchope. I asked him whether withdrawal of Leg. Co. proposals under Parliamentary pressure would necessitate Wauchope's resignation? He said no, but he thought Wauchope *would* resign, having pinned his personal honour to the point and fearing to 'lose face' with the Arabs.

At 4 p.m. I went with Lewis to Chaim's house for a final consultation (Chaim leaves for Palestine tonight). He has lunched alone with J. H. Thomas and Simon Marks. J. H. T. *literally* lachrymose over position in which last night's Debate had placed him, said that he was left to 'carry the baby' that Malcolm MacDonald and Philip Lister[71] had landed him with, that he might have to resign, etc., etc. Simon said 'Never mind, Jimmie, we'll look after you.' Humiliating! Then he told Chaim that he had wired that morning to Wauchope, instructing him to drop all idea of raising qualifications for immigrants with capital—*and to open negotiations re Transjordan!* I subsequently discovered that he had *not* informed his colleagues at today's Cabinet before taking this step, and had in fact refused to circulate the telegram in question, saying it was only a private wire!!! Chaim, Lewis and I decided that we should make no effort at present to influence course of events. Lewis quoted to me Lord Shelburne's saying 'Inactivity may be a political curb, when it proceeds neither from indolence nor from vice.' It is indeed hard to say whether the resignation of Thomas and Wauchope is immediately desirable and whether one would prefer to see Leg. Co. break down—or never be set up. Break down, I think it would now.

March 26th—London . . . Lewis . . . told me Lord Lothian[72] proposes to suggest in House of Lords a *purely advisory* Council with *parity*—and a cable has gone to Ben-Gurion[73] suggesting that might be acceptable to

69. A. Duff Cooper: Secretary of State for War, 1935–37; First Lord of the Admiralty, 1937–38; Minister of Information, 1940–41; Chancellor of the Duchy of Lancaster, 1941–43; Ambassador to France, 1944–48. Cr. Viscount Norwich, 1952.
70. G. A. Lloyd: High Commissioner for Egypt and Sudan, 1925–29; Secretary of State for Colonies, 1940–41. Cr. Baron, 1925.
71. Philip Cunliffe-Lister: Secretary of State for Colonies, 1931–35; for Air, 1935–38. Cr. Viscount Swinton, 1935.
72. Philip Kerr, 11th Marquess of Lothian: Secretary to Lloyd George, 1916–21; Chancellor of the Duchy of Lancaster, 1931; Ambassador to the U.S., 1939–40.
73. David Ben-Gurion: General Secretary of the *Histadruth*, 1921–35; Chairman of the Zionist Executive and Jewish Agency, 1935–48; Prime Minister and Defence Minister of Israel, 1948–53, 1955–63.

Jews. Probably the Arabs would *not* accept and the position would thus be very advantageous.

March 27th . . . I gave a very successful Sherry Party to say good-bye to myself before going to Palestine. About thirty people—no bores—indeed none had been asked! Best bit at the end, when only about a dozen left, . . . Walter said 'Let's beat Megan[74] up'. So we formed a circle with her in the middle, and argued the case whether the Lloyd George Family were Public Enemy Number One on this German business. Megan of course defended her sire with spirit, but Walter was really magnificent when he declared that if Lloyd George yesterday, instead of backing up the whines about the Treaty of Versailles, had declared that we must stand shoulder to shoulder with the French, *then* he might have done something to avert the shadow of war, which otherwise will hang over all our lives, even the life of Megan, the youngest in our circle.

April 1st—London   Went to see Watt, to discuss American contracts, etc. All London is placarded with *Daily Telegraph* advertisement of my book[75] in letters many feet high!

Later went to Zionist Office for a policy Conference. Henry Melchett, Eva Reading, Lewis, Brodetsky, Perlzweig,[76] etc. Propaganda campaign discussed and sub-committees formed, all with a view to raising the whole Jewish problem in the autumn and meanwhile educating every section of public opinion—English and Jewish—in this country, from H.M., the Treasury, Parliament, general public, etc., etc. Henry's idea. They will have to use tact! Then we discussed immediate position. I urged that objective should be to get rid of J. H. Thomas from Colonial Office, even if wrecking his proposals involves resignation of Wauchope also.

Only Janner[77] agreed with me fully. The others were afraid that they might get a *less* malleable Colonial Secretary and were in favour of building a bridge for his retreat from Leg. Council proposals. I think they are wrong. Thomas is not of the calibre to understand the problem of Palestine.

[Mrs Dugdale's arrival in Palestine coincided with the outbreak of the Arab disturbances of 1936–39. On 19 April serious rioting flared up in Jaffa. This was the culmination of many months of mounting tension between the two communities. The immediate cause of the riots was the murder of two Jews on the Nablus-Tulkarem highway on the night of 15

74. Megan Lloyd George: Independent Liberal M.P. for Anglesey from 1931; daughter of David Lloyd George.
75. Her biography of Balfour.
76. Rev. M. Perlzweig: Head of the Political Department of World Jewish Congress, 1936–47; deputy member of the Executive of Jewish Agency, 1935–46.
77. Barnett Janner: Liberal M.P. for Whitechapel and St. George's, 1931–35; Labour M.P. for N.W. Leicester from 1945; President of Board of Deputies of British Jews, 1955–64; and of Zionist Federation of Great Britain and Ireland. Cr. Kt., 1961, Life Peer, 1971.

April. The following night two Arabs were found murdered in a hut outside Petach Tikva; it was taken for granted that this was an act of Jewish retaliation. The funeral of one of the Tulkarem victims became an excuse for anti-Arab demonstrations, and some Arabs in the Tel Aviv area were assaulted. As a result the riots of the 19th followed and Arabs, incited by false rumours that the Jews were killing their brethren, ran riot in Jaffa, killing and wounding several Jews. A curfew was imposed on the area and emergency regulations brought into force. The following day an Arab national committee was set up and a general strike declared throughout Arab Palestine. On 25 April a Supreme Arab Committee was established, subsequently known as the Arab Higher Committee. In this manner the Palestine disturbances, which were to continue intermittently until the outbreak of the Second World War, began.]

April 20th—Chez Rutenbergs, Haifa, Palestine   We left Nicosia yesterday morning, drove to Larnaca, lunched in the inn there, and went on board *Jerusalemme Lloyd—Triestino,* a fine boat of some 9,000 tons, packed to bursting in every class with German Jews, some on their way to settle in Palestine, others to visit friends. We sailed from Larnaca at 5 p.m., bound (as we thought) for Jaffa. There was a little movement, I went early to bed. Was awakened about 5 a.m. by Edgar who said we were in harbour and mooring at a quay. This seemed odd for Jaffa, and presently he returned to say that we were at *Haifa* not Jaffa, on account of riotings that broke out there yesterday, and the ship had been directed by wireless to change her port of call. It suited us much better at the moment, as we had meant to come here by road. . . . motored up here to stay with his brother [Peter Rutenberg] and wife in their new and charming house on Carmel. Breakfast etc. and then we later started out by car and saw first of all the magnificent Power Station which Peter has built since I was here two years ago, 45,000 h.p. engines etc. and the whole not being big enough. They will soon double its size. Then with Mrs Rutenberg we drove out to Kiryat Ovdim —the new Histadruth [The General Confederation of Jewish Labour] settlement of Haifa town workers. Nearly 1,000 little houses already, situated just on the sand. Marvels are being done with houses and gardens.

Peter is convinced the whole thing was pre-arranged as an introduction to the visit of Arab leaders to London,[78] in hopes of frightening H.M.G. into granting Leg. Co. demands, and he thinks it should be made an opportunity for the exact reverse, and thus letting Wauchope out of his rash promises without loss of face. I wrote these views tonight to Walter . . .

78. The lack of confidence expressed by Parliament in the Legislative Council policy had led the Government to invite an Arab delegation to London to continue discussions on the subject. However, when the disturbances broke out the Arabs claimed that the political situation was not conducive to such talks and therefore delayed their departure. In mid-May the Government retaliated by stipulating that the restoration of law and order was a necessary prerequisite before the talks could commence.

April 21st—King David Hotel, Jerusalem   At breakfast in Haifa this morning, we reluctantly decided to move here. . . . There was a lot of telephoning to Weizmanns, etc. about our change of plan, otherwise the morning passes in re-packing, and taking a drive around Carmel with Mrs Rutenberg. The whole hill is covered with villas now. What would Elijah think?

About seven we arrived at Jerusalem. Met at station by Dr Leo Kohn,[79] who waited in King David lounge for a talk with me before dinner after we had seen our rooms, etc. He told me (1) that Chaim has lunched with Arthur Wauchope, the High Commissioner, who was deeply depressed, and became quite emotional when Chaim said it was not his fault. He (the H.C.) highly praised restraint of Jews and admitted bad behaviour of Arab police.

Edgar and I then sat down to dinner, when George Antonius[80] walked in with Miss Graves (daughter of the author[81] of *The Land of Three Faiths*). They joined us in the lounge after dinner. . . .

George Antonius professed entire ignorance of what is going on. It may be a fact that he is not in the confidence of the Arab leaders now. I am quite at sea there, though it seems to be known that there is great division in their Councils about whether the Delegation should go to London and who should compose it.

Last of all Agronsky[82] came to see me about 10.30. He says the thing has not spread beyond the neighbourhood of Jaffa, though there was more 'tension' in Haifa this afternoon. He is very apprehensive lest the H.C. should not be firm enough and complained bitterly of wording of Empire broadcast last night, talking of 'clash' between Jews and Arabs etc., says this wording was also used in first draft of first official communiqué for the press, but Shertok[83] went and complained and the H.C. himself altered it. They (the Jews) suspect Hall, the Chief Secretary, of being responsible for attempt to infer that both sides were equally to blame. There seems no doubt whatever that the attack was quite unprovoked and (contrary to what Peter thought yesterday) probably quite undesired by Arab leaders.

April 22nd—Jerusalem . . . went sight-seeing . . . Gethsemane, University, War Cemetery, all looking *so* lovely. Jerusalem, Jerusalem!

April 23rd—Jerusalem . . . went to Jewish Agency, Ben-Gurion was speaking on telephone to Lourie[84] at Zionist Office in London, bidding him contradict false rumours that Jews had made reprisals. Ben-Gurion and Shertok then

79. Dr Leo Kohn: Secretary to the Political Department of the Jewish Agency in Jerusalem.
80. George Antonius: Christian Arab publicist; author of *The Arab Awakening*.
81. Philip Graves: Foreign Editor of *The Times*; exposed *The Protocols of the Elders of Zion* as a forgery.
82. Gershon Agronsky (Agron): Editor of the English language daily, *Palestine Post*.
83. Moshe Shertok (Sharett): Head of the Political Department of Jewish Agency and a member of its Executive; Foreign Minister of Israel, 1949–53; Prime Minister, 1953–55.
84. Arthur Lourie: Political Secretary to the Jewish Agency in London; since 1948 has held high office in Israel diplomatic service.

told me of bad reports from Jerusalem District of intended trouble tomorrow. They (the Jews) would have liked the H.C. to send for more troops from Egypt and had even sent a code telegram to Melchett asking that C. Office should order that from London on its own hook. Shertok said the Mufti[85] could stop all disorder beginning tomorrow in this District if he chose. I said this later on to George A., who replied, 'What! How could he stop the Moslems coming into the Mosque on a Friday? All he could do would be to direct his preachers to bid them keep quiet.'

Before leaving J.A. Office I saw over it, the Golden Books, Herzl Room etc.

. . . Chaim thinks we are at the beginning of much trouble which should be made to end in a final re-settlement of many outstanding things. He thinks Jews should be given more definite voice in Government. He cites many unpleasant small indications which make him uneasy, e.g. the H.C. had tea yesterday with the *Arab* Mayor of Ramleh, after visiting wounded in Jaffa and Tel Aviv. His own lunch at Government House on Tuesday was not reported for the press, but this other visit was.

April 24th—Jerusalem   At six went to a cocktail party in Antonius's garden, inexpressibly lovely in the gathering dusk and cool of evening. Chiefly English officials there, a pretty poor crowd, very depressingly mediocre. Dined with Weizmanns and Sacher. Back early to hotel, found Edgar much brighter and temperature sub-normal.

Shertok and Ben-Gurion told how 120 young citrus trees just come into fruiting were uprooted last night near Ain Harod.[86] How true Chaim's saying—it is a struggle between civilization and the desert. This strange Eretz Israel, the land of contrasts. How one loves it all! And how sad to see so many English—officials and tourists—walk unseeingly amidst so many miracles!

April 25th—Jerusalem   Edgar better, he decided to leave for England. Went with him to Cooks etc. Telephone from High Commissioner's Private Secretary, asking us to lunch today and to talk over my letter.[87] We went of course. Lunch passed pleasantly, but without any talk of present situation.

. . . At 6.15 George Antonius came to appointment to hotel for tête-à-tête talk. He said (among other things) he was strongly opposed to Legislative Council in form proposed and had told the High Commissioner so some months ago and had been coldly received ever since! He opined Legislative

---

85. Haj Amin al-Husaini: Mufti of Jerusalem; Chairman of the Supreme Moslem Council; of the Arab Higher Committee; generally admitted to have been the guiding hand behind the disturbances of 1936–39.

86. A communal settlement in Lower Galilee.

87. Wauchope had taken offence at an article which Mrs Dugdale had written in the *Manchester Guardian* claiming that he had sprung the Legislative Council proposals on the Zionists. Mrs Dugdale wrote him a letter elaborating upon her version of the incident.

Council now dead and also thought this implied that Wauchope's position was fatally impaired. He spoke of Syrian strike and of how after 40 days, it had caused French Government to give way.[88] I said I could not suppose Palestinians so misguided as to imagine the same effect could be produced with us? George appeared eagerly to agree.

April 26th—Club at Sieff Institute, Rehovoth At 3.30 we left Jerusalem by road in two cars— . . . Chaim's usual Hagana[89] guard in the car. Very, very little traffic on roads but no incidents of any kind. Met two armed police lorries.

Got here at tea-time. I have charming quarters here and eat at Chaim and Vera's, at present inhabiting a bungalow about a quarter of an hour's walk away.

Chaim heard through Smilansky[90] that an Arab leader had come, offering a deal, £20,000 to call off strike, £20,000 more to bring Arabs to Round Table Conference in London. Can he deliver these goods? Much consideration and negotiation will be required.

Vera walked back with me—by moonlight—from her garden scented heavy with oleanders, down the road, the car following us, with its lights on us and an armed guard beside the driver. The Hagana (fifteen of them) are on guard in the Institute grounds all night. The jackals are howling among the orange-groves. Eerie. The Desert *v.* the Sown.

The Hagana keep watch and ward beside the police all over the country. They keep iron discipline. Chaim has two, one for night, one for day, whose orders are never to leave him for a moment.

April 27th After dinner Chaim talked bitterly on the old subject of the hostility of the English official world here. It is a misfortune that these seem to have touched the nadir of such a world. When above all things first-rate officials are needed in this most difficult country. I never loved it so much as this time! The oleanders and the jackals of Rehovoth! Both are in great form on this moon-lit night. I hear the footsteps of the Hagana guards below my window. Reassuring.

April 30th—Rehovoth Quiet morning reading and writing. Found Chaim and Vera both very edgy and tired at lunch. Vera on the warpath against Mendelssohn[91] about her new house. Everything wrong! Drove with them, with usual police escort to Tel Aviv for opening of Levant Fair by the High Commissioner. All went well. Four or five thousand people listened

---

88. The French administration in Syria had succumbed to the pressures of nationalist agitation and a general strike in February 1936, and had allowed the formation of a nationalist government.
89. Hagana: the secret Jewish defence organization.
90. Moshe Smilansky: President of the Palestine Farmers Union; a veteran settler and noted Hebrew author.
91. Eric Mendelssohn: Architect of the Weizmanns' new home in Rehovoth.

to H.C.'s speech and though they gave him a chilly reception, there was no hostile demonstration as was feared. J. H. Thomas broadcast from London, and the Mayor (Dizengoff) spoke in Hebrew. All these languages were translated into the other two official languages, interminable! The High Commissioner's speech was criticized for its reference to 'victims' of recent disturbances, instead of boldly saying *Jewish* victims. A good moment when the Exhibition flag (blue, with design of a flying camel in white) was broken on the tower, to the loud blast of a siren. Then there *was* cheering and in fact the opening of the Fair on appointed day is the most impressive demonstration that Jews could have made. But owing to the strike in Jaffa port only the Palestine pavilions were opened. The H.C. refused to order the unloading of goods from the other countries for fear it might lead to bloodshed. But we heard tonight that they are all landed. The brother of Dov Hos[92] took £100 and therewith bribed sufficient Arab stevedores. They got military protection and did what was needed, perfectly calmly. It is now believed that the Arabs are longing to find a way to end the strike. They may ask for suspension of immigration if only for a week or a day. It will be fatal if this granted them.

May 1st—Rehovoth This morning I had bathed and breakfasted in my room at the Club, when a knock at the door at 9 a.m. announced that Shertok was below and I was urgently wanted by Weizmann at the bungalow. I dressed hastily, and as we drove there Shertok related that he and Kaplan[93] had come that morning from Jerusalem, with disquieting news re Government policy[94] which made them want me to fly today to London. This plan, rather to my relief, was frustrated by news that there is no seat in a plane for next few days. We had a long confabulation, and they went back to Jerusalem to arrange for Chaim to see Wauchope tomorrow, and for a telephone call from Lewis in London tonight. This duly came through at 8.15 and Chaim, speaking Russian, told him all he could. But the espionage on telephones etc. is one of the great difficulties here. Spent the whole day in bungalow with Chaim and Vera, discussing tactics in light of Shertok's information and speaking on telephone to people, also helping Chaim to draft a letter to the High Commissioner which he will probably send as an Aide Memoire after his interview tomorrow. Vera was exceedingly clear-headed and constructive. Chaim himself feeling deeply affronted by treatment of himself, and if Shertok's news is true (as I feel sure it is) Chaim has indeed been ill-treated. We think the whole affair goes to explain the amazing fuss to justify himself shown in the H.C.'s letters to me. 'Qui s'excuse' etc.

92. Dov Hos: A founder of Hagana; Palestine labour leader.
93. Eliezer Kaplan: Head of the Financial and Administrative Departments of the Jewish Agency; later, first Finance Minister of Israel.
94. This was the first hint of the Government's decision to send a Royal Commission to Palestine to investigate the underlying causes of the disturbances.

May 2nd—Chez A. Rutenbergs, Carmel, Haifa Walked with them on Carmel and sat some time at dusk on balcony of Peter's house, gazing at Mount Hermon, Bay of Acre and Emek spread below in glorious panorama. Gradually the lights came out in Haifa town till the whole firmament of stars seemed spread below me. My last evening in Palestine—this time.

After dinner Chaim on telephone told Peter something of his interview with the High Commissioner, who admitted that the points we knew of are being discussed in London. This frees our hands somewhat, but Chaim had not been warned. Today's interview is of his seeking. He told the High Commissioner that if a Royal Commission is appointed to enquire into the Mandate, the Jews will fight it. I know he contemplates a possible boycott of it.

May 3rd—S.S. Spinz between Haifa & Alexandria As I came aboard I was handed a *third* long letter from Wauchope—very friendly this time. This I shall answer before we arrive at Alexandria tomorrow morning. Before ship left Haifa, but after my friends had gone ashore, a very fierce fire was to be seen raging in the very centre of Haifa—it spread and was a large one. What this means I do not know, but it was a very sad last sight of this dear country. The past two weeks have made me love it and its Jewish people, more passionately than ever.

May 11th—1 Roland Gardens, London Morning—telephones—vain effort to cope with letters . . . Then to Marks & Spencer's for a confabulation. Present, Lourie, Lewis, Henry Melchett, Harry Sacher, Simon Marks, Dov Hos who left Palestine by air later than I. A fresh cable in from Chaim, warning that Commission may be sprung. Decided that Harry and Simon should try to see J. H. Thomas at once. I went off to tea with Leo Amery at House and asked him to try to see Stanley Baldwin before Cabinet which was summoned for 6 p.m. This he did and wrote me he had tried to impress that firmness is required. I then, at twenty to six, went to see Maurice Hankey[95] and begged him to prevent the Cabinet doing anything until Chaim shall arrive. Maurice listened attentively, took the point, but of course did not commit himself in any way. I felt all was done that I could do for the moment.

May 12th

> 'The Fathers of the City, they sat all night and day
> For every hour some horseman came, with tidings of dismay'

For 'Fathers' read 'Jewish Agency'! We had two meetings today, one at Marks & Spencer office, one in the House of Lords tea-room! Telephoning

---

95. Maurice Hankey: Secretary to the Committee of Imperial Defence, 1912–38; to War Cabinet, 1916–18; to Cabinet, 1919–38; Minister without Portfolio and member of War Cabinet, 1939–40; Chancellor of Duchy of Lancaster, 1940–41; Paymaster-General, 1941–42. Cr. Baron, 1938.

to Jerusalem etc. Increasing evidence of how Wauchope and J. H. Thomas have been going behind the backs of Chaim and others. But I *hope* our united exertions will prevent Cabinet here granting any concessions to Arab demands at least till Chaim comes home.

May 14th—London   Home hot and exhausted to lunch, to find urgent telephones from Henry Melchett and others, to say a wire had come from Jerusalem that British Cabinet gave way yesterday on question of Royal Commission. This without waiting for Chaim and in spite of many pledges (given in talk or alleged to have been). Henry wanted immediate advice whether Attlee should move a Private Notice Question, adjourn the House and try to defeat Government that very night. I advised against until we knew more, and am glad I did, for when Walter and I dined together, though he admitted our information true, he said J. H. Thomas would have been able to evade answering, as Wauchope's reply had not yet come.

I said to Walter I had trusted to being told. He then said he *alone* had fought against it, all the friends, so lavish in assurances, had given way, including Billy Ormsby-Gore.[96]

Walter said that once the Cabinet had agreed to a Commission it was probably the opening of War between Jews and them, and that he and I must revise technique of what he tells me. It would be impossible for him to give me information which I should be bound to use against his colleagues, I fear this is true. I must simply trust him, tell him everything, but never consult him. This we settled . . .

May 15th   In all day, writing, telephoning etc. Cable came from Palestine that the Arabs had refused Royal Commission, insisted on their complete demands. This is good, I think.

May 16th—Menham-le-Hatch[97]   . . . While at dinner I got a telephone from Lewis to say Wauchope has asked to be allowed to suspend immigration. This was of course news to Walter, but after recent telegrams he is not surprised. Chaim is home tomorrow. Will seek an interview with Baldwin before Monday's Cabinet. But if Government does this we shall make war upon them by every possible means.

May 17th—London   Went to the Weizmanns. They flew over today. Lewis and Henry there. Heard the High Commissioner had been told from London he must grant Schedule and that he will announce it tomorrow! We suspect this haste. It will probably cause a great row with the Arabs. Could it be in hopes of being able to put more pressure on London to compromise? Dreadful to be driven into suspecting such a thing! But there has been so

96. W. Ormsby-Gore: Conservative M.P. for Stafford, 1918–38; Secretary of State for Colonies, 1936–38; succeeded his father as Lord Harlech, 1938.
97. The Hudsons' country home at Ashford, Kent.

much deception! Long, long talk about tactics and strategy. Thank goodness Chaim is home. _____

May 18th   Before lunch went to Zionist Office to see Chaim, who was just off to lunch at Claridges alone with J. H. Thomas. He was in good firm spirits. Later saw in paper that Cabinet this morning decided to despatch a Royal Commission of Enquiry to Palestine. Also today, they announced granting of schedule of 4,500 immigrants. This may neutralize for the moment the bad effects of Commission, but nevertheless the latter is a grave mistake at present juncture. What we should do should depend on terms of reference, but it seems to me impossible that these should not touch terms of Mandate itself.

May 19th   ... Lunched Carlton Grill with Chaim, Lewis, Lourie, Dov Hos. Yesterday, Government announced Royal Commission. J. H. Thomas had previously asked Chaim to give him lunch at Claridges and informed him. (Tommy Dugdale told Chaim this was by desire of Cabinet. I thought this very indiscreet of T.D.) We concerted plans. Chaim had seen Baldwin this morning and found him rattled and quite ignorant of Palestinian questions! Chaim told him Jews 'quite interested' in Royal Commission. We must in fact wait to see terms of reference before deciding on a policy. I think it will be found impossible to frame them *without* touching the Mandate. Invented one or two Questions for Attlee and Sinclair to put tomorrow.

May 25th—London   ... Lunched with Buck at Carlton Grill. Mostly discussed chances of his being put in Cabinet en suite of changes consequent on J. H. Thomas's resignation.[98] Speaking later to Colin on telephone, he seemed to think it probable that Billy Gore may go to Colonial Office and Buck to Board of Works. I hope the latter. As to the former, if (as seems the fact) nearly the whole world is divided into Rabbits and Gangsters, is it best to have a friendly Rabbit? For I think that is what B.O.G. will prove to be from the Jewish point of view.

   To Zionist Office, Chaim, Henry, Lewis, Lourie, Dov Hos, later Perlzweig. Chaim went off by request to see Geoffrey Dawson. We gave him to take, an extract from *Corriere dela Sera* which helps towards establishing fact of Italian complicity in Palestine disturbances. The High Commissioner has taken a much firmer line in past ten days. We date this from Cabinet after the return of Anthony Eden from Geneva[99] and think Government are probably aware of Italian manoeuvres. It is all to the good from Jewish point of view, but makes the whole affair much more serious. . . . Heard of Billy Gore's appointment to Colonial Office. Am glad on the whole. . . .

98. Thomas had recently been involved in a budget leakages scandal and, as a result, had been forced to resign.
99. Eden had been in Geneva in April for League discussions on the Abyssinian war.

June 10th   Went to Zionist Office for a Conference. Chaim, Lewis, Lourie, Ben-Gurion, later Henry Melchett and Perlzweig. Topic a despatch, suggesting alternatives to put an end to present situation. (1) Stoppage immigration; (2) Martial Law; (3) going on as at present. (1) not recommended; (3) considered ineffective without (1). Writer evidently very worried. Chaim put forward a proposal that Jewish Agency should offer *itself* to suspend immigration for a period in order to help Government. The idea was so passionately turned down by all except myself that it is obviously impracticable. Ben-Gurion's opposition was the most important, for as Chaim himself said, the unity of Jewry is our chief asset and he would never do anything to split it. *I* see many objections to the proposal, but I like the idea of getting initiative into our hands. But Ben-Gurion's attitude makes it obvious that Palestinian Jewry would never understand it. B.G. says it would not only rend the Zionist movement in twain, *but* would instantly start Civil War in Palestine, for nothing has kept the Jews from retaliating all these seven weeks except the determination to do nothing to stop immigration. Ben-Gurion spoke with passion. The discussion showed the strain on the leaders. But Chaim is in good spirits and full of confidence that we shall win through. It was decided to wire to Shertok to fly as soon as may be to Cairo and there to telephone. Chaim wants approval of his writing to Billy Gore to announce that the Jews will facilitate work of Royal Commission, subject to terms of reference. This as a gesture of response to Billy's firm statement in the House last night.

I lunched at Club with Walter and told him *all* this. He was (of course) struck with Chaim's idea. I gather that J. H. Thomas left his office in an awful state. It will take Billy days to get straight and there are crisis brewing in Kenya and Hong Kong as well as Palestine. I believe any constructive suggestion re Middle East would be welcome and I told Chaim this. Nuri Pasha[10] has been in touch with Chaim the last day or two re plans for a Confederation of Arab States. Big things are brewing, but the way is dark and it is so easy to make false steps! I tried to make Walter understand the sabotage going on on part of the officials in Palestine.

. . . Returned to office after lunch and raised Chaim's idea again. No good. But in the car, alone with me, he said he thought it would have to come. But he will not speak of it again at present.

June 11th   Drove to House of Commons with the Cazalets.[101] Walter had got me a ticket in Members' Gallery for the Debate on Budget Leakages. I heard J. H. Thomas and Sir Alfred Butt[102] make their statements and leave the House for ever. House crowded to the utmost. I never witnessed so

---

100. Nuri al-Sa'id: Iraqui politician; at the time, Foreign Minister; assassinated in the anti-Hashemite coup of 1958.
101. Victor Cazalet: Conservative M.P. for Chippenham from 1924. Thelma Cazalet-Keir: Conservative M.P. for East Islington, 1931–45.
102. Sir Alfred Butt: Conservative M.P. for Balham and Tooting, 1922–36.

appalling a scene. It was as if one had gone to witness an execution. The House behaved very well. Thomas was utterly changed in appearance. White and shrunken. His speech was perfect. Butt's was received in icy silence. Yet I think his wild complaint that the refusal to prosecute left him no appeal had justice behind it. Baldwin spoke under great stress of emotion, very well I think. But the whole scene was terrible.

Dined alone with Hannah Hudson. Buck and Rob came in after. We talked of Neville Chamberlain's speech last night at a dinner which spilled the beans about the forthcoming Sanctions policy.[103] I think there will be a row. Rob thinks not. Anthony Eden's name ought to be mud. But who knows? All decency is gone from this Government. The ups and downs of politics! I saw Sam Hoare on the Front Bench again. What a day . . .

June 16th   Home for breakfast, loaded with Caponflat flowers. Went to a Mandates Committee at L.N.U. Then to lunch at Carlton Grill with Chaim, Lewis, Israel Sieff.[104] Chaim reported on a very satisfactory interview with Billy Gore. Lord Plymouth[105] had also been present. Billy had declared his intention of dealing with the point of Jewish *right* to be in Palestine in next Friday's debate. He had also spoken of disloyalty of certain Palestine officials. He had also said that in his view the proposed Land Legislation was 'bunkum'. He also told Chaim that the Cabinet had decided to raise Sanctions!!! Chaim very pleased, I rather less confident in view of other things I had heard from Walter. Chaim foolishly left with him the translation of a cypher telegram from Shertok. In consequence they had to wire to Palestine to change the cypher.

June 17th   Buck, Colin, Walter dined here with me. A most interesting, rather distressing conversation, about the present situation.

We all agreed that the Government is a scorn and a derision, but we could not see the elements of another one. It is humiliating. Colin said we must make up our minds for the next two or three years to being and behaving like a third-class Power. He said that when the Staff Talks began recently the French and Belgians opened by saying 'What can *we* do for *you*?' Horrible!

June 25th   to Zionist Office for Conference. Felix Frankfurter[106] and Stephen Wise[107] over from New York. Discussion of probabilities of Govern-

---

103. His 'midsummer of madness' speech which presaged the adandonment of League sanctions against Italy.
104. Israel Sieff: Vice-chairman and Joint Managing Director of Marks & Spencer. Cr. Baron, 1966.
105. Lord Plymouth: Parliamentary Under-Secretary of State for Foreign Affairs, 1936–39.
106. Felix Frankfurter: American jurist; Justice of the Supreme Court, 1939–62; a veteran Zionist supporter.
107. Rabbi Stephen Wise: Founder and First Secretary of Federation of American Zionists; at various times President of World Jewish Congress, American Jewish Congress, and Zionist Organization of America.

ment remaining firm. Chaim said public opinion with us *now,* but we should be prepared for change any minute if troubles go on in Palestine. All seemed of opinion that military measures there are even now half-hearted. Decided that F.F. should see Anthony Eden as soon as possible and also that Lord Willingdon[108] should be asked to tell Billy Gore (what he has said privately to Henry Melchett) that he thinks any sign of weakening in Palestine would be fatal in India. But he also said to Henry that of course the India Office is not asking the opinion of an ex-Viceroy on any subject!

June 27th—Haseley Court, Oxon. Came here after lunch to stay with Tony Muirhead. Walter and Kay Elliot arrived later and the Donald Fergussons (he a Treasury official about to become Permanent Secretary to Board of Agriculture—Walter's choice—but it raised a storm in Whitehall). A perfectly charming man, charmingly indiscreet for a Civil Servant! For instance he told us all after dinner that the speech made in Paris two days ago by Duff Cooper (Minister for War) practically advocating an Anglo-French Alliance was all written out and talked over with the Foreign Office! This is interesting for the Cabinet did *not* know, and the policy is not that of a triple Franco-German-British understanding which they are supposed to be pursuing! Less than a fortnight since Neville let off his Sanctions bomb-shell. Not too good for Anthony's reputation, every Minister in turn making an unexpected pronouncement on Foreign Affairs!

June 29th Went to Zionist Office in p.m. found Chaim very depressed, partly because of an indiscretion committed by himself when talking to Nuri Pasha.[109] He toyed with the idea of flying to Palestine for a week and I encouraged this, for I think it would be good both for him and for the Yishuv [the Jewish Community of Palestine]. But when I went to his house after dinner for a cup of tea with him and Vera, he said no more on the subject.

July 1st Summoned early to Zionist Office, where Chaim told us of interview yesterday between Billy Gore and Ben-Gurion and himself. Gore had told them that not only did he intend to suspend immigration while the Royal Commission sits, but that he thought it would hereafter have to be limited by political and not merely economic considerations. Even after Walter's warnings this took me aback, after Billy's speech a fortnight ago! The others were shattered. It reminded me of 1929[110]—may the issue be as

108. Lord Willingdon: Viceroy and Governor-General of India, 1933–36.
109. Nuri had reported to Ormsby-Gore that Weizmann had agreed, in a private conversation, to suspend immigration for a year as a gesture of good-will. Weizmann later insisted that Nuri had misunderstood him, and in a letter to Ormsby-Gore [28 June 1936] vehemently denied the story. However, the story appears to fit in well with Weizmann's own feelings on the subject [see entry for 10 June].
110. The riots of August 1929 led to a series of government investigations and documents, all of which were considered as damaging to the Zionist cause; they culminated in the Passfield White Paper of October 1930. This document raised a cry of anguish from world

D

successful. Spent nearly all day at Zionist Office helping draft a letter which it was decided Chaim must send to Billy at once, warning him of the gravity of his decision. The letter was of course not perfect, being composite drafts by Lewis, self, Ben-Gurion, Henry Melchett. We discussed next steps. It is unlikely that the Jews will keep quiet when this is once known. Ben-Gurion flies back on Friday for a few days, to consult with Shertok. Here, all friends of all parties in House and elsewhere to be sounded about their attitude. Chaim and Henry may have to go to Palestine later, but would first warn Billy of possible consequences, but are anxious not to do this until Ben-Gurion returns. Billy's attitude was shrugging his shoulders and implying he could not help himself. But it appears that only three days ago he gave Henry quite another impression! How disgusting!

July 6th   Morning at Zionist Office—Conference on policy in absence of any answer from Billy to Chaim's letter of July 1st. In the late afternoon I went to cocktail party at the Salisburys, before wedding of Billy's daughter. There saw Billy himself who told me he had just posted a letter to Chaim saying there had been a complete misunderstanding, and he had never suggested any change in basis of immigration, nor could he do so before Royal Commission had reported. I said 'I wish you had let me know this sooner.'

Billy (who looked tired and rather distracted) said he had only got the letter on Saturday 4th. He went on to say I had no idea of the pressure from all sides to which he was subjected. Walter almost his only support in Cabinet. Often he felt inclined to tell everybody to leave him alone, and he would settle Palestine himself, but when he took office he found himself too deeply committed to the Royal Commission for this to be possible.

I went home at once and telephoned to all concerned that there has been a 'misunderstanding'. No use now to probe mystery of how it arose. . . .

July 8th   Dined with Melchetts (certainly there is *too* much contrast for comfort of mind in this world), Lewis there. We decided four things as objective: (1) Jewish Defence Force, (2) Tel Aviv Harbour, (3) Parity, (4) Cantonization.

July 9th . . . Tea also with the Felix Frankfurters, to talk to him about the sale of my book in U.S.A. Lewis and Dr Wise came in. Wise seemed only just to have realised the implications of what was said to him by Billy twenty-four hours ago[111] and wanted to stimulate a violent demonstration

Jewry and let to the resignation of Weizmann and other Jewish leaders. The Government, under mounting pressure from public opinion, Gentile as well as Jewish, eventually agreed to reconsider its declared policy. On 13 February 1931 the Prime Minister, Ramsay MacDonald, sent an official letter to Weizmann in which he re-interpreted, in a manner more favourable to the Zionists, Lord Passfield's paper.

111. Ormsby-Gore had told him that immigration would be suspended during the sittings of the Royal Commission.

of Jewish feeling in U.S.A.—remonstrances by Roosevelt, etc. etc. With Felix's aid we threw cold water on this project. I like the Frankfurters, but how awful the ordinary Yankee is, so childish and so verbose!

July 13th—London Found Chaim very depressed. Anti-semitism growing in Paris. All the world disturbed and Jews the scapegoats everywhere. 'I felt' he said (when alone with me) 'as if an iron band were round my throat.' All the tragedy of Jewry is in Chaim's eyes at such moments.

Lewis irritates him frightfully. But it's no good saying anything. It would only hurt Lewis and he can't change.

Lewis talked to me today about future of this new German-Austrian Agreement.[112] He thinks Hitler may have been 'too clever by half' and that the first result must be that the Little Entente[113] will consolidate itself against Germany, and that the Franco-Russian Alliance will be strengthened. But all the news from Paris makes one fear that France is not a force at the moment. Chaims has heard that the Germans and the Italians covet a bit of Syria. He told Viénot[114] this today, but did not mention it to Blum.[115]

July 15th . . . After lunch went to Zionist Office. There was Ben-Gurion, just back by air from Palestine. Conference in Chaim's room to hear his news . . . He reports High Commissioner more cheerful, seeing that worst is over and becoming firmer in attitude. B.G.'s foreign news very serious. Wilensky, the Jewish representative in Cairo, was approached by Donato Italian (Consul?) with offer of land for Jewish settlement in Abyssinia immediately, with *promise* later of Jewish State in Palestine when Italy has got control of Syria and Palestine!! Wilensky reported this at once to Miles Lampson.[116] Chaim is also writing to Billy Gore on the subject for he has long taken a very serious view of Italian policy in Middle East.

July 17th To Zionist Office—and saw Chaim alone, telling him some rather depressing impressions I got of Palestine affairs after my morning talk on telephone with Walter. The military pressure upon the Cabinet to finish the 'War' is very great. There are eight battalions in Palestine now and the question of winter barracks becomes urgent. The Cabinet seem to think more of these secondary immediate questions than of a long-term policy. Suspension of immigration seems more and more likely. It is hard to see what cards we still have to play *now* with a view to preventing such a disaster.

112. The so-called 'Gentlemen's Agreement' of 11 July 1936. By this agreement Germany promised to respect Austrian sovereignty. In return, Austria acknowledged herself as a 'German State'; promised an amnesty for political prisoners; and held out the prospect of including some 'nationally-minded' Austrians in the government.
113. The Little Entente: Czechoslovakia, Rumania, and Yugoslavia. They were bound together by a loose series of agreements signed in 1920–21.
114. Pierre Viénot: Under-Secretary at Quai d'Orsay.
115. Léon Blum: Prime Minister of the Popular Front Government in France, 1936–37.
116. Sir Miles Lampson: High Commissioner for Egypt and Sudan, 1934–36; Ambassador to Egypt, 1936–46. Cr. Baron Killearn, 1943.

July 20th—London . . . Went to Zionist Office and then out to lunch at Carlton Grill with Chaim and Ben-Gurion . . . Chaim had received a letter from Billy, which plainly shows that no argument drawn from British former promises has much chance of being listened to. Others must be found! Chaim and Ben-Gurion talked for first time of possible necessity of placing their own resignation before Congress as their policy has (apparently) failed. They will never agree to suspension of immigration, but I still feel some compromise might be possible if Billy were an abler man and stronger!

July 21st   Rang up Leo Amery and asked for a cup of tea in House. Then went to Zionist Office and went over points, also got Chaim and Ben-Gurion's approval. A letter in from Billy to Chaim, very stuffy and not improving matters! Home to lunch . . . Went to House at 5 p.m. and had an hour's talk with Leo, who is sympathetic,[117] but promised no more than to consider the idea. He thought the great difficulty would be Lord Winterton,[118] but thought Winston *might* deal with him. He told me that he had suggested to Billy that before the Royal Commission goes out it might take evidence from people such as himself, Lloyd George, etc. as to background of Mandate and Administration. Billy not unfavourable, but had not committed himself. I urged Leo to get busy on all these notions.

July 28th—London   To Zionist Office, Lewis, Lourie, Ben-Gurion. Discussed what I might say to Billy (if he gives me a chance). (1) Parity, (2) Defence Force, estimated at a possible 50,000, (3) Purchase of land in Transjordan *for Arabs,* (4) Results of suspending immigration.

July 29th   Lewis to dinner and *finished* my proof at 3 a.m. *The Book is done.*

August 26th—Balbirnie[119] . . . Lewis very depressed about situation, and the consultation by H.M.G. of Nuri Pasha and the Arab Kings.[20] He says Ben-Gurion begins to favour cutting loose from H.M.G. But that decision could only be taken by the Yishuv and will not be mooted at the Actions Committee[121] now assembling in Zürich.

117. An idea had been mooted to send a letter to *The Times* under the signatures of Amery, Churchill, Lord Winterton, and Lord Lloyd, arguing that 'political parity under the British crown in perpetuity' was the only solution for the Palestine problem.
118. Earl Winterton: Under-Secretary of State for India, 1922–24, 1924–29; Chancellor of the Duchy of Lancaster, 1937–39.
119. Balbirnie, Fife: Home of Col. Edward William [Bill] Balfour, officer commanding Scots Guards Regiment; married Lady Ruth, daughter of Gerald Balfour, 2nd Earl.
120. These negotiations had been in progress throughout the summer. The Zionists were naturally apprenhensive of a deal being made behind their backs and to their detriment.
121. The Greater Actions Committee. This was the authority to which the working executive of the Zionist Congress, the Smaller Actions Committee, was directly responsible. In 1921 the executive was divided into two sections, one based in Jerusalem the other in

August 31st   We[122] all lunched with Chaim at Carlton Grill and after he
and B.G. went off to interview with Billy Ormsby-Gore and the rest of us
went back and waited for their report. They returned about 4.45. Interview
had lasted over an hour. Sir J. Shuckburgh[123] and Billy's Private Secretary
Boyd[124] had also been there. Billy said to have shown his discomfort and embarrassment very visibly all through. Notes of conversation were made by
Lourie from Chaim and B.G.'s report, so will only say that Chaim told
Billy that the Jews could no longer continue political co-operation with
H.M.G., if a settlement was arrived at with Arab leaders outside Palestine
behind the backs of Jewish Agency. He was, however, as ready as he had
always been to meet any Arabs in open conference under aegis of H.M.G.
Billy jumped at this, and at once cabled it to Wauchope, as we know,
because Chaim, on returning to Zionist Office telephoned Shuckburgh to
ask to see exact wording of that part of Billy's cable, and it was at once
read out over telephone. Chaim seems to have behaved with utmost coldness
and calm, simply declining all responsibility for giving Billy advice how to
get out of position into which H.M.G. has put itself. We decided that this
must be his last word before Cabinet makes up its mind on Wednesday,
and that he should see no other Ministers or officials before that. He rather
spoiled the effect of this by asking Shuckburgh to lunch over telephone! We
persuaded him to get out of it. But what a curious genius his is—rising to
greatest heights then by some foolish, unpremeditated act undoing his own
work and making one wonder whether it is instinct—or intellect—which
is uppermost with him. I have seen it again and again!

September 1st   To Zionist Office before lunch (which I had at Chaim's
with him and Lewis). At three went to Foreign Office by appointment to
see Bobbitty. Put to him grave consequences to F.O. of admitting settlement of Palestine by Nuri Pasha. Bobbitty listened sympathetically, asked
some questions, showing his mind running on using greater force, but did
not betray his agreement with my point of view re Nuri. On my return to
the Zionist Office however I found one of the telegrams in which told
that the Foreign Office are very much aware of this and very uneasy.

Walter appalled by 'light-hearted amateurishness' with which Billy has
embroiled the existing difficulties by approving intervention of Nuri. Some
decision *must* be taken by Cabinet tomorrow on that point (recognition, or
not, of Nuri as negotiator) but probably on no other, owing to absence of
Stanley Baldwin and other important Ministers, including Anthony him-

London. The executive was required to furnish members of the Actions Committee with
periodic reports and to consult them on all matters of importance. Both bodies were
elected at the bi-annual Zionist Congress.
122.   Namier, Ben-Gurion and Lourie.
123.   Sir John Shuckburgh: Assistant Under-Secretary of State at the Colonial Office, 1921–31;
Deputy Under-Secretary, 1931–42.
124.   E. B. Boyd: had been principal private secretary to successive Colonial Secretaries—
Passfield, Swinton, Malcolm MacDonald, Thomas.

self (probably) who is ill. . . . Also *enormous* length of Cabinet Agenda, on which Palestine is only fifth item, first being Reform of the League, the last threatened march on London of *blind pensioners*! !

Walter inclines to work for (A) repudiation of Nuri, (B) Cabinet Committee to eliminate dangers of leaving things to Billy, (C) Martial Law in Palestine. This last my idea, mainly because I think suspension of immigration under that would be less mildly inacceptable to Jews. Walter favours it because it might hasten possibility of sending out the Royal Commission. But he points out that Martial Law applied gently soon loses its terrors. Air Marshal's[125] Report says that he could soon reduce Palestine to order by ruthless bombing of Samaria, but in no other way. Martial Law would probably *not* rid us of Wauchope. God, what a mess lack of firmness at the beginning has got us into!

September 3rd—Caponflat Yesterday in London Cabinet considered Palestine. I went in morning to the Zionist Office. At 1.15 Walter rang me up to say that subject had only just been reached on Agenda, and they would go on after lunch. So Lewis and I lunched with Chaim at Carlton Grill, rather cheered because Walter said discussion beginning well. Returned to Roland Gardens to pack, then again to Zionist Office to wait. About 4.30 Walter rang up to say *all was well*. No departure from Billy's statement in House last July that violence must cease before negotiations. I went into Chaim's room where were he, Lewis, Ben-Gurion and Arthur Lourie, and told them on condition news should go no further, not even to Shertok. A moment of great emotion and thankfulness and then we began discussing the next steps, for after all this is (to some extent though not entirely) only the story of the Rabbi and the goat,[126] and when it reaches Palestine this may increase violence and fresh difficulties. About 5 o'clock Henry Melchett came in longing for news, but was given none—nor Brodetsky.

. . . About 7 I said goodbye to all at Zionist Office and joined Walter for dinner at Hyde Park Hotel, and he told me more of what had passed and of what is now to be done. A fresh Division is to go out!! . . .

September 16th—London . . . Lewis came, in great agitation, Sir Herbert Samuel[127] and Lord Winterton have opened negotiation on their own with Nuri Pasha, who is travelling from Istanbul to Paris for the purpose. Chaim knew, but concealed the knowledge from his Exec. and it was 'gathered'

125. Air Vice-Marshall R. E. C. Pierse: air officer commanding Palestine, 1933–36.
126. The story runs as follows. An old Jew living in hard circumstances, burdened down by a nagging wife, obstreperous children, and little material comforts, sought consolence from his Rabbi. The Rabbi listened attentively to his tale of woe and advised him to take in a goat to live with his family.
    The Jew returned some time later and complained that things were now far worse than ever before. Then remove the goat, the Rabbi retorted, and you will have little to complain of.
127. Sir Herbert Samuel: Home Secretary, 1916, 1931–32; High Commissioner for Palestine, 1920–25; leader of the Liberal Party, 1931–35. Cr. Viscount, 1937.

in Jerusalem. . . . B.G. telegraphed in great agitation. There was a Conference at No. 77 today—Peter Rutenberg present—and Lewis spoke very strongly to Sir Herbert about the vast responsibility he takes upon himself in opening these unofficial negotiations and bringing Nuri into it again. Billy Gore seems to have spoken to Chaim about the doubtful wisdom of this.

There seems much confusion and considerable mistrust. On the other hand I think Sir Herbert is an experienced and honest negotiator.

The terms, as at present sketched, seem to include a Jewish immigration aiming at 40% of total population within ten years, the opening of Transjordan to Arab and Jewish immigration, a Legislative Council with parity of numbers for Arabs, Jews and officials. Restriction of land sales to Jews within certain areas, and a Zoll-Verein of all Arab states in which *Jewish* Palestine forms a definite unit.

September 28th   Spent whole day at Zionist Office helping reconcile Lewis and Brodetsky to accept each other's amalgamated drafts of a Declaration on Parity, soon to be put forth. Most exhausting . . .

September 30th . . . Lunched with Rob Bernays. Went to Zionist Office, saw Chaim and Lewis, just off to interview with Billy Ormsby-Gore. Chaim showed him the draft policy on Parity and told him that he (Chaim) intends to go shortly to Cairo and take initiative in negotiating with Arabs. He told him that Wauchope would be no match for the Arab Kings in 'bazaar politics'. Billy moaned as usual, blamed Anthony Eden (by implication) because Foreign Office did not want Palestine discussed at Geneva; so Billy had to give the Kings some sort of sop. He said H.M.G. would not start negotiating with them till all four were united. I fancy this will never be! Abdullah[128] would do anything he was told for 6d. The Colonial Office has weakened its position vis-à-vis the Jews by all the jiggery-pokery with the Arab Kings. No respect and no fear is now felt for Billy. Dined at Athenaeum Club Annex (newly opened) with Walter. He came back here for late tea and saw my reviews and letters regarding Book.[129] We agreed that sudden rise to power of Sam Hoare since he became First Lord is the political phenomenon of the moment. But what an extraordinary career Sam's has been in the last year. It's a year, almost to the day, since he made his famous Geneva speech,[130] so acclaimed, which was the beginning of all our troubles. Since then he has been hurled from power and now is almost the most important Minister—has swept Tom Inskip right off the board.

128. Abdullah: Amir, later King, of Transjordan.
129. The reviews of Mrs Dugdale's first volume of her biography of Balfour had just appeared; and they were generally favourable.
130. In which he proclaimed Great Britain's wholehearted support 'for the collective maintenance of the Covenant . . . and for collective resistance against all acts of unprovoked aggression'. This was generally interpreted as a rallying call to League members.

Winston said to Walter last night 'We are just *drifting* but fortunately drifting in the right direction!'

October 14th Lunched with Walter at Club, after his Cabinet. He told me things seemed moving our way re suspension, and strongly advised 'no pin-pricks'. I am sure he is right, but Jerusalem shows signs of being a little rattled in various ways.

October 18th—London . . . Dined at Chaim and Vera's, Lewis and Henry Melchett also there. Later came Lourie, Stein,[131] Brodetsky. Long confabulation, during which Jerusalem rang up for advice on whether to press for disarmament. We advised NO.

Parity Declaration not yet out, Jerusalem has not agreed as to date. It is getting rather late, for Commission goes out about November 15.[132] Word comes that W. Peel is not unfavourably inclined.

Word comes that Poland and Little Entente are excercising *violent* pressure on H.M.G. against suspension of immigration. On the whole it seems best to let the tides run just now without too much interference.

November 3rd—London Lunched with Rob and Hannah Hudson. Rob said Shakes Morrison's[133] sudden advancement had caused a great deal of feeling.

We discussed rumours, now current everywhere that the King means to marry Mrs Simpson. Hannah said she had heard that Mrs S. does not intend to do it.

November 5th—Vol. II of my book out. *The Evening Standard* started it off with a very nice review . . . Also at L.N.U. Exec. Vyvyan Adams[134] passed me a note saying he thought Vol. II 'even better' than Vol. I.

After lunch went to House of Commons. Heard Billy's statement that Schedule of 1800 to be given to the Jews in the next six months. On balance it is a victory, but it is far too small. I hope Chaim will apply for an emergency Schedule as soon as he reaches Palestine.

Heard Anthony on Foreign Affairs. As usual, he sounded all right!

After dinner two young Jews came to drive me to the Synagogue Hall in Bow. A wonderful meeting there! I suppose about 600, wildly enthusiastic. I never enjoyed making a speech more! But what a closed community it

131. Leonard Stein: Barrister; political secretary to World Zionist Organization, 1920–29; advised the Jewish Agency on the presentation of its case before the Palestine Royal Commission (1936) and the Woodhead Commission (1938); President of the Anglo-Jewish Association, 1939–49.
132. The Royal Commissioners were: The Earl Peel, chairman; Sir H. Rumbold, vice-chairman; Sir W. Carter; Sir H. Morris; and Professor R. Coupland. Mr J. M. Martin served as secretary.
133. William Shepherd Morrison: Minister of Agriculture, 1936–39; Postmaster-General, 1940–43; Speaker of the House of Commons, 1951–54. Cr. Viscount Dunrossil, 1959.
134. Maj. S. Vyvyan Adams: Conservative M.P. for West Leeds, 1931–45.

still is. The little, fat, Polish-born Rabbi who has been years in London is still unable to make a speech in English.

Altogether rather an exciting day!

November 7th   Went in morning to bid final farewell to Chaim and Vera. Simon and Miriam Marks also there. News just in that Arabs had decided to boycott the Royal Commission. Chaim doubted if that determination would persist. Best would be if Nashashibi and Co.[135] *did* give evidence and the Mufti Party not.

November 11th   Spent most of the day packing Nunk's[136] papers. Dorothy Macmillan[137] came in after tea. She said Bob Boothby, who is just back from U.S.A., says American papers are full of *every detail* of Mrs Simpson's life! She says British Press are now conferring what line to take about it. It is amazing how little the press has said, and yet, how everybody knows.

November 18th   After lunch Arthur Lourie and Mr Shane Leslie[138] later. He was amusing, about books, reviewers, etc. Also said he was with Winston last Sunday and Bob Cecil came over. Reason for this explained later on telephone by Mark Patrick,[139] who said Bob had given in about L.N.U. and I.P.C.,[140] owing to Winston's persuasions. A great victory, a great relief. I predict that Winston will take on L.N.U. and use it! Also that he will shortly form a Government, drawing the Right by his Armament programme, the Left by his support of the League.

Shane says Winston's admiration of Blum, knows no bounds. All these are strange portents of coming changes.

November 24th   Dined at House of Commons with Colin, Thelma and Victor, some Americans called Bonner, and Walter who was in tremendous form. We argued about the date of the next war, and Mrs Simpson was only mentioned when Bonner pointed out to me that the marriage would do more than anything to bind America to us. Every American woman sees the Cinderella story come true as it were in her own person.

November 27th . . . First report of Chaim's evidence before the Royal Commission came through. Clearly quite first-rate.

135. The Nashashibis constituted the chief political rivals to the Husainis in Palestine Arab politics.
136. i.e. Balfour, so known to his nephews and nieces.
137. Lady Dorothy Macmillan, wife of Harold Macmillan: Conservative M.P.; Under-Secretary of State for Colonies, 1942; Minister resident at Allied headquarters in North West Africa, 1942–45; Prime Minister and Leader of the Conservative Party, 1957–63.
138. The author and journalist.
139. Mark Patrick: Conservative M.P. for Tavistock from 1931.
140. For some time now there had been talk of cooperation between the League of Nations Union and an International Peace Congress. Some members of the Union considered that the origins of the Congress were dubious and hesitated before committing themselves. Now, apparently, all had been settled.

December 2nd—London Oswald[141] came after tea. He had an early edition of *The Evening Standard,* which had in it the Bishop of Bradford's sermon[142] and comments quoted from *Manchester Guardian, Yorkshire Post* and other provincials. So the fat is in the fire! But this page is omitted from the later editions! They say Max[143] has not made up his mind. Esmond Harmsworth[144] tells Him he cannot get away with it, and must go. Buck told me that later tonight.

Lunched with Rob Bernays. We agreed that it is already obvious from today's Press that there is little danger of a national cleavage on this matter. I do not think He could form a party even if He wished. The Empire will probably be solid also.

December 3rd I feel tonight, however, as if abdication might be the least of many evils, and also the most likely thing to happen. But *nobody* knows. Joan C[145] says that Mrs Simpson's house in Chester Gate was surrounded last night by a booing, stone-throwing mob! There have been quiet and orderly crowds all day outside Buckingham House and No. 10, where mounted police had to be. Baldwin was warmly cheered by all parties in House today. Everybody relieved by attitude of *Daily Herald.*

December 4th Mrs Simpson has fled the country! Lilli-bullero! She has made a mistake. Cabinet sat in the morning and Stanley Baldwin made a statement in House at 4 p.m. explaining facts of the situation. Walter told me that the Cabinet had no hand in drafting this though they liked it when they heard it. The situation really cannot be discussed by twenty-two people; and Baldwin with Simon,[146] Malcolm MacDonald and (I suppose) Neville, really run it, and tell the others. There is no difference of opinion among them, Duff Cooper, contrary to rumour, being quite sound.

December 5th Dominion Governments will apparently be solid. De Valera[147] is restrained by reflection that if he stands out his Catholic country may be the only one over which Mrs Simpson will be Queen! But there are nasty signs of split, fomented by Beaverbrook and Rothermere in this country.

141. Lt.Col. Oswald Balfour; Mrs Dugdale's brother.
142. The Bishop of Bradford, aptly named the Rt. Rev. Blunt, had publicly criticized the King's behaviour, thereby breaking an unofficial silence. Rumour had it that the Bishop was referring to the King's absence from Church and knew nothing of Mrs Simpson. However, it was the signal which opened the floodgates.
143. Max Aitken: Newspaper proprietor; Minister of Aircraft Production, 1940–41; of Supply, 1941–41; member of War Cabinet, 1940–42; Lord Privy Seal, 1943–45. Cr. Lord Beaverbrook, 1917.
144. Esmond Cecil Harmsworth: Newspaper proprietor and President of their Association; succeeded his father as 2nd Viscount Rothermere, 1940.
145. Joan Campbell, Mrs Dugdale's cousin.
146. Sir John Simon: Home Secretary, 1915–16, 1935–37; Foreign Secretary, 1931–35; Chancellor of Exchequer, 1937–40; Leader of National Liberal Party, 1931–40; Lord Chancellor, 1940–45. Cr. Viscount, 1940.
147. Eamonn de Valera: Prime Minister of Ireland, 1932–48, 1951–54, 1957–59.

Lunched with Walter at Club. Went there feeling that every hour's delay in a settlement increased our danger. He pointed out to me the other side. Ministers must not put a pistol to the King's head, as already they are falsely accused of doing. Nor should they drive matters to a point where they might have to resign. If they have to go, *he* must dismiss them. He will probably play for time, because (as things seem now) time will help him to form a Party. I fear Winston may be mixed up with Beaverbrook in this. All the distrust of Baldwin may bear fruit now. I asked what the King's attitude was. He is perfectly civil to Baldwin but seems undecided, and is inclined to listen to anybody, but nobody with a good influence comes to Fort Belvedere.[148] Walter did not leave me with the impression that abdication is a certainty, but I would still say it is the most probable and the least evil way out of a position which may—*must*—leave permanent traces behind.

Letters from Chaim and Vera from Jerusalem, which might be the Heavenly one, so far away do their voices and preoccupations seem! Chaim was very depressed after his 'in camera' evidence. He warns me that the Commission are for us in their hearts, but will attempt to 'crystallize' the National Home for fancied Imperial interests. If so be, the Jews will never give in. Vera thinks Chaim pessimistic. Lewis has been telegraphed for to go out. There seem indications that I may be asked to follow soon.

December 7th   No! Not yet. Lunched at Club with Walter who explains the King's *one* idea is Mrs Simpson. Nothing that stands between him and her will meet his approval. The Crown is only valuable if it would interest *her*. He must have marriage because then she can be with him always. Therefore he has no wish to form a 'Party' who would keep him on the Throne and let her be his mistress. Therefore he has no animosity against Ministers who are not opposing his abdication. On the contrary, he is very matey with Baldwin and *asked his permission* to see Winston, which was readily given and Winston dined with him on December 4th, though the Press has not got this. What really got him was Baldwin's parting remark yesterday. 'Well, Sir, I hope, whatever happens, that you will be happy.' He is very upset by the newspapers, never having seen anything but fulsome adulation in all his forty years! Baldwin will be very careful not to press him. So the situation may remain as it is for some days, though this is bad, for unrest must grow. Nevertheless, I do not think, in light of this knowledge, that there is much danger of a King's Party. It is impossible to be 'plus royaliste que le roi'.

December 8th   Rob Bernays drove me home. He says Winston was absolutely howled down yesterday,[149] and is in a very chastened mood today, and

148. The King's private home in Windsor Great Park.
149. Churchill had attempted to ask a supplementary question to Baldwin's statement. He was twice called to order by the Speaker and subjected throughout to hostile cries of 'sit down'; he eventually did so in a state of parliamentary collapse.

told him (Rob) that when he put his question he really had not read Baldwin's Statement!! I think he is done for. In three minutes his hopes of return to power and influence are shattered. But God is once more behind his servant Stanley Baldwin.

December 10th   Went with Melchetts to House of Lords tea-room, also crowded. Speculations about where he will live and about money. Henry says Duchy of Cornwall revenues mortgaged for many years for her jewels. But above all, the difficulties about the divorce decree. He *must* be allowed to marry her!

As Henry said, we all make muddles of our lives, but none can make so great a muddle as that poor miserable creature!

December 11th   King George VI came to the Throne.

Lunched at Ritz with Jack Wheeler-Bennett . . . [He] talked about Germany. He is convinced that Ribbentrop *used* Mrs Simpson,[150] but proofs are hard to come by. But I think Government and *Times* have them. There must in that case be wailing and gnashing of teeth! Oswald told me on telephone, Beaverbrook had predicted two days of rioting all over the country. But the calm is unbroken.

Jack had heard what Mrs George Keppell[151] said, 'The King has shown neither decency, nor wisdom, nor regard for tradition.'! !

. . . At ten o'clock H.R.H. Prince Edward spoke on the wireless to the world. Fine and moving, ending on a firm harsh cry of 'God Save the King.' Nothing became him in his kingship like the leaving of it.

December 13th   Stanley Baldwin is quite unmoved by his personal prestige. He says he was on a pinnacle before (at the time of the General Strike) and within six weeks all were abusing him. The House of Lords were such mugs that they went on with business after the King abdicated and a Special Act may have to be passed to indemnify them from treason!

December 15th . . . Victor Cazalet drove me back to the House, where I had tea with Rob Hudson. Saw Winston for a second. He looked distraught. I hear he is very miserable. Hear also Sibyl Colefax[152] wept at hearing Archbishop's[153] broadcast strictures on The Hostesses. Lady Cunard[154] said 'Ridiculous—I hardly know Mrs Simpson.' Rat Week![155]

150. Edward VIII was known to favour an Anglo-German rapprochement and it was widely believed that he had intervened to that effect during the Rhineland crisis.
151. A mistress of King Edward VII who had skilfully managed to preserve her relationship with the King for many years.
152. Lady Colefax: Famous hostess and a leading figure in London society.
153. Archbishop of Canterbury, the Most Rev. Cosmo Gordon Lang.
154. Lady Cunard: Often considered as Lady Colefax's most serious rival.
155. 'Rat Week'. An unpublished privately-circulated, satirical poem by Osbert Sitwell, on the behaviour of the King's former friends. The first three lines run: Where are the friends of yesterday/That fawned on him,/That flattered her?

Oswald told me Low had done a cartoon which was thought a bit too much, so it never appeared. Three portraits of men, hanging on a wall—Mr Spencer, Mr Simpson and H.M. Edward VIII. Labelled 'The Wallace Collection'! !

December 28th . . . Had a most interesting letter from Lewis in Palestine. More hopeful, saying disorders are expected when the Royal Commission reports, and the Jews are warned to stand by with 3,000 more volunteers. The soldiers are disgusted by Sir Arthur Wauchope and the Administration and say no more politics next time, but Martial Law at once. If only all this be true!

$I937$ *January 18th—London* . . . Went to Zionist Office where were Arthur Lourie and Lewis, he just home from Palestine. He talked for half an hour about Royal Commission, but has no conception of what the Reports will be. Willy Peel is pretty rude to *all* the witnesses—officials, Jews and Government. Coupland is strongly pro-Jewish—Morris indecently pro-Arab. Lewis thinks a unanimous Report is not likely if anything is said either way. The soldiers and the Jews are very friendly—not so the soldiers and the Administration, or Wauchope and the Commission. Stein's evidence was magnificent. The Commission will take more evidence here before issuing their Report, which is hardly to be expected before May. There will probably be more violence in Palestine before that time.

Lunched with Walter at Club, and told him all this. He argued that it was no easier to define an economic basis for immigration[1] than any other. It all came down, in the long run, to what H.M.G. decided. I told him *nothing* will keep the Jews out now—but if they think the basis of immigration unjust they will come in illegally somehow or other—and Britain will lose the asset of their loyalty.

January 25th To Zionist Office at tea-time for confabulation: Lewis—Brodetsky—Arthur Lourie—Perlzweig—Henry Melchett. Discussed whether Henry should offer evidence before R.C. when they return here about need for a special Palestine Civil Service. Settled *yes, if* Warren Fisher[2] would keep his promise of backing it up.

February 1st Chaim returned yesterday from Palestine, and will be here for a month at least, having decided not to go to USA at present—(1) because he wants a rest, (2) because he has a hunch he ought to be here while the Royal Commission is cogitating its Report, and (3) because he may have to go to America later and rouse opinion if the Report is unfavourable. He is probably right.

1. 'Economic absorptive capacity' was the formula which had governed immigration policy ever since the Churchill White Paper of 1922. See Cmd. 1700.
2. Sir Warren Fisher: Permanent Under-Secretary to the Treasury and head of the Civil Service, 1919–39.

It appears from something Coupland said to him on very last day of Commission's stay, that there is a possibility of recommending—*not* Cantonization, but an actual division into two halves, making the Jewish portion a real Jewish State, and possibly arranging an exchange of population! ! I do not believe the Arabs would accept this; it would have to be imposed. The Jews would be fools not to accept it, even if it were the size of a table-cloth. This Chaim strongly feels. He says Leon Blum is also strongly in favour. (He saw him in Paris.) But what difficulties! *Jews* must make the schedule—*Jews* must control immigration—*Jews* must deal with illegal immigrants! But—on the other hand—what a beginning at last! A real Home where no-one can interfere. They may not be ready for it yet—and indeed, the very unedifying spectacle of the internal quarrels . . . makes one doubt whether they *are*. But Time and Tide wait for no man.

Jos. Wedgwood told me Billy Gore has told Wauchope to come home on leave, and wants to get him out of Palestine for good.

February 2nd When Walter talked on telephone this morning he said that Heathcote-Amory (Willy Peel's secretary in Palestine) had told him a Jewish State was under discussion. It would involve the end of the Mandate. As now envisaged it would involve putting the Jordan Works into the Arab part, which would be joined up with Transjordan. It would involve complete stoppage of immigration during the process of arrangement. The Arabs would be coerced into accepting it.

Had tea at Chaim's and long further talk. He had seen Billy this morning, who professed not to have heard of the idea. Chaim told him the Jews would accept it in principle. To me Chaim said that he would agree to stoppage of immigration for a year at longest. He would not agree to sacrificing Peter's works. Vera said the non-Zionist Jews would not accept such a Jewish State. Chaim thought this would not matter much. We *must* have the whole Emek. Internal defence would have to be in Jewish hands.

February 3rd Lunched at Boulestin's with Bob Boothby. . . .
On Christmas Day he met Mrs Simpson at lunch at Somerset Maugham's on the Riviera! He sat between her and her Aunt Bessy from Baltimore—who said to him: 'Poor Wallis has had a dreadful time!' to which he replied: 'Yes, I think I saw something about it in the paper'!

February 17 Lunched at Horse Shoe with Moshe and Arthur. Discussed (1) a tiresome split[3] between Chaim and Ben-Gurion and (2) the general situation. Moshe was interesting on attitude of British Foreign Office to Iraq Government. This is *not* pan-Arab—the paradox therefore arises that H.M.G. is more suspicious of it because it might lean on some other European State. Therefore the F.O. has refused to bless a loan it wants to float

3. This turned on whether to accept partition or whether to continue with the Mandate.

in London. We decided this loan ought to be floated and subscribed by Jews—and we must try if the F.O. attitude can be changed.

February 19th   Went to Zionist Office for long talk alone with Chaim about Lewis. Whether he ought to join the Agency Executive if asked.[4] Chaim clear he should do so only if he can combine it with Manchester. On whole Chaim would obviously be relieved if he did *not*. Lewis's faults are much on his nerves. We went into the row with Ben-Gurion, which I fear L. did *not* soothe in Palestine.

February 27th—Swifts, Cranbrook, Kent   This house . . . has been bought by Victor Cazalet, who is about to pull it down and rebuild. Already it is utterly altered in atmosphere. Orchids, central heating etc.!
      Found Mrs Cazalet—Mrs Neville Chamberlain—the McKennas.[5] Neville Chamberlain and Victor came in when we were half through lunch; they had been inspecting orchids at Tonbridge. At lunch, talk about Winston and Stanley Baldwin—it seems clear that Winston will *not* be invited to join Chamberlain's Cabinet. He quoted with approval a description of him made (I think) by Haldane when they were in Asquith's Cabinet: 'It is like arguing with a brass band.' He also said to me later how deficient in judgment Churchill is. He told, very amusingly, how Baldwin had scored an enormous success when speaking at the Oxford Union by saying: 'I have always been a great admirer of Randolph Churchill'—then a pause— 'I mean *Lord* Randolph Churchill.'

March 2nd   Went to Zionist Office where there was a presentation of an album of photographs prepared for me by the Board of Keren Hayesod[6]— Chaim, Perlzweig and Brodetsky spoke—I answered—all the Z.O. staff present—rather embarrassing—but the photographs are really an historic souvenir.
      Chaim had a conversation this morning with Wauchope (home on leave), from which it appears certain that the Royal Commission will put forward a Jewish State as one recommendation. Chaim told Wauchope that all would depend on size of territory. It would be no good to 'hand him the key of Tel Aviv.' There must be room for immigration. Wauchope asked: How much? Chaim answered 50,000 or 60,000 a year. Wauchope answered 'You might get more', and offered to help all he could. He returns to Palestine soon, rather contrary to what I expected. He told Chaim he thought the attitude of the Arab Kings had changed. They were less interested in Palestine than before. (The truth is that unless Wauchope had encouraged them,

---

4. This was a particularly delicate problem. Namier was in many ways invaluable to Weizmann, but his relations with other leading Zionists were in a state of permanent crisis.
5. R. McKenna: First Lord of the Admiralty, 1908–11; Home Secretary, 1911–15; Chancellor of Exchequer, 1915–16.
6. Foundation Fund.

E

they would never have been very interested.) Things are evidently coming to
a head soon—and the Jews must walk like Agag. It will never do if this
idea is prematurely bruited abroad, and it must not seem inspired by the
Jews. I do not much like the idea of a group of M.P.'s forwarding a Memo
to the Commission, advocating a Jewish State—said Memo to be drafted
by Lewis. This is Cazalet's intention. What makes me most nervous is the
growing rift between Chaim and Ben-Gurion—who is making most foolish
and intransigent speeches in Palestine. Shertok is here, and it is hard to
know what best to do. We all try to soothe Chaim, who is very angry.

March 3rd   Went to Zionist Office. Relieved to find that Chaim has said
the Memo. for Cazalet had better wait until after he (Chaim) sees Peel on
March 15th. A code wire came from Palestine saying Agency is demanding
martial law in certain areas, especially Haifa, owing to the growth of outrages there. The Chief Secretary has promised to consult General Dill.[7]
Shertok is to see Billy Gore on Friday, and will mention the subject. I told
Chaim . . . that Willy Peel had said that Chaim's evidence was the only
evidence which had impressed the Commission. Chaim delighted at this. . . .

March 9th   Chaim much on edge. Brodetsky talked to me about need for
a conference of a few clear minds about this Jewish State proposal—what is
the common measure of agreement as to what could be accepted, etc. He
puts (1) Area, (2) Autonomy, (3) Haifa, (4) Jerusalem. I would transpose
(1) and (2). Leo Amery in a letter to me today raised question of *name*—
could we call it Judea? All this seems to me premature!

March 15th   Conference at Zionist Office on the scheme. Chaim—Brodetsky
—Shertok—Lewis—Perlzweig—Stein—Arthur Lourie—self—all agreed
that Scheme must be accepted, subject to conditions of area and *real*
autonomy. All, that is, except Stein, who was purely *défaitiste*. Much interesting discussion of frontiers etc., and whether the Scheme would prove workable. Much trouble ahead, but all will be well—it is a step to fulfilment,
and believe that in 20 years we shall see all Palestine as a Jewish State.
Membership of League and Empire said today to be essential.

April 7th—London   Lunched at Palace Hotel with Brodetsky, Arthur
Lourie, Perlzweig and Eva Reading. She is just back from two months in
Palestine—very full of stories all showing disgraceful weakness and mal-
administration. It is imposible not to believe in definite malevolence against
Jewish work. Eva is convinced (rightly or wrongly) that 'six months of
resolute Government' would make it unnecessary to have partition. She is
much against this, but I think I shook her a little. But there is evidently
going to be a great division of opinion in Jewry, and the task of statesman-

---

7. General Sir John Dill: C.I.C., British forces in Palestine, 1936–37; Chief of the Imperial
    General Staff, 1940.

ship will be to prevent this rending the Movement (*vide* 1903[8]) and making a public division. At the present stage, there is no harm in the world seeing that the Partition Scheme is not of Jewish origin. Chaim's position gets increasingly difficult—it is known in Jewry that he is very keen about the Scheme. How strange it would be if the result of all this were to be to bring Jews and Arabs together in common opposition! Speaking of the Scheme, Eva said: 'But the child is born too soon.' Maybe—but we do not strangle seven-month children at birth.

April 9th   Jos. Wedgwood to lunch. We discussed Palestine—he is not very favourable to The Scheme, but not as violent as I had been led to think. He takes the same line as Eva Reading—namely that 'six months of resolute Government' would make all other plans unnecessary.

April 10th . . . Lewis dined with Edgar and me. He told me of a conversation he had with Coupland just before I went to France.[9] The Scheme is really pretty drastic evidently, and Coupland was evidently afraid that the Jews would welcome it too openly. He seems to be writing the Report.

Lewis was interesting about the Ministers' Salaries Bill.[10] He approves of the £2,000 for the Leader of the Opposition, as fixing him as a necessary part of our machinery of Government.

April 14th   Spent most of the day at Zionist Office. A conference in the morning. Present: Chaim, Shertok, Katznelson,[11] Stein, Lourie, Namier and self.

Discussion sterile and futile. Only Chaim and Lewis see that The Scheme *must* be accepted. The others dare not say Yes or No to it. It will fall to Chaim in the end, but he is weary and ill, and in the meantime there has been talk enough. Till the Report is issued it is only beating the air.

April 17th   Had tea with Lewis, kept indoors by a bad throat. He thinks the best would be if the Mandates Commission accepts the Scheme, and the Jews then acquiesce in it under protest. He is startled by the amount of opposition developing in the Jewish world.

April 27th   Chaim called unexpectedly abroad . . . Went to see him before he started—Vera and Osinka[12] there too. He told me of a long talk with Coupland the night before. Points—Report will be unanimous and

---

8. In 1903 the Zionists received an offer from the British Government to settle a territory in East Africa: the famous 'Uganda' proposal. The repercussions of this offer almost split the movement.
9. Mrs Dugdale had been on a motoring-tour of northern France in late March.
10. The Ministers of the Crown Act was introduced to the House on April 12th.
11. Berl Katznelson: A prominent Palestine labour leader and ideologue.
12. Dr Joseph Blumenfeld: Chemist and specialist in rare metals; married to Vera's sister, Rachel.

presented to H.M.G. early in June. Frontiers fairly satisfactory to Chaim—all the north—the most important after Emek [the Vale of Esdraelon]. Complete independence. Chaim told him he would go as far as he could—but would not break the Jewish Agency. But I think he may have to. He may have to be Michael Collins.[13] Great events lie ahead. The Jews in the plains—so it must be before Armageddon.

May 7th Went to Buck's after tea, and had sherry. He mentioned Central Southwark.[14] I did not say no. Michael dined. We played bezique.

May 8th . . . Thought a good bit about *all* aspects of Central Southwark.

May 11th Lunched at Club with Walter. Told him idea of Central Southwark and *all* the reasons. I think he was pleased.

May 18th Looked in to see Buck, virtually promised him to try at Central Southwark.

May 20th League of Nations Union Executive. Discussion about Spain and break-down on 'non-intervention'[15]. Began *Palestine Post* article. Dined with Peter Rutenberg in Whitehall Court. He told me about his negotiations with Abdullah for land. Also how Abdullah was paid to keep Transjordan quiet last year—but double-crossed by sending an anti-Zionist Memo to the Royal Commission. So when he asked Peter for £2,000 more before Coronation, he only got £1,000 and was told he must mend his ways before he got the rest. He excused himself, and promised. Then a Jewish jeweller in Jerusalem showed Peter a golden dagger ordered by Abdullah as a present to King George (with Peter's money!) and told Peter how the inscription was first to have been 'From the Emir of Transjordan', but later had it changed to 'the Ruler of the Transjordan lands'. Clearly the Royal Commission had consulted *him* about Partition! . . .

May 21st . . . Lewis rang up—very worried about rumour that frontier is not to be contiguous with Syria. He wants Chaim (now at Meran[16]) to get Blum to expostulate about this.

13. Michael Collins: Irish nationalist leader; negotiated the Anglo-Irish settlement of 1921; assassinated in August 1922 by a group of Republican extremists.
14. He had suggested that Mrs Dugdale stand as National Labour candidate for that constituency.
15. The Spanish Civil War erupted in July 1936. In an attempt to localize the conflict, the Powers met in London on 9 September for the first meeting of the International Committee for the Application of the Agreement regarding non-intervention in Spain. It was an agreement in name only, it being flouted quite openly by Italy and Germany and, later, by the Soviet Union, hence its 'break-down'.
16. A health resort in the Italian Alps.

May 25th   Heat wave! 79°. Stayed in, struggling with an article on Stanley Baldwin. After 5, Edgar and I went to a perfectly delightful garden party given by Chatham House in St James's Square. Saw many people. Long talk with Sir Alfred Zimmern[17] about foreign policy of National Labour group, which I have now openly decided to join. Told several people. Harold Nicolson, Vivyan Adams, etc. Vivyan Adams said it was a shock to him, as National Labour is so High Tory. Talked with Harold about changing name to 'Radical'. He is much in favour.

Very disquieting telegram from Jerusalem that the Royal Commission does not intend to recommend a contiguous frontier with Syria—in fact means to withhold all Upper Galilee. If this is so, it is fatal, and Jews cannot acquiesce. It is also plain, from answers given by Gore in the House, that H.M.G. does not intend to give the House the opportunity of discussing the Report before announcing policy. There are two things to be done: (a) get Blum to give his views—only Chaim can approach Blum. Chaim is still at Meran and loth to come away; (b) get protests in House against ignoring Parliament. Spoke to Vera, and she promised to ring up Chaim.

May 26th   Had tea in House of Lords with Buck and talked about my eventual candidature for Central Southwark. He did not tell me his news *then,* but rang up after dinner and told me he is to be Lord Privy Seal! I am very, very glad.

May 28th—London   Slept well in Paris in spite of very hot night. Chaim telephoned early to say he had arrived at Plaza, from Meran. Went round there, found him in good mood and looking well . . . all went to Inauguration of Palestine Pavilion. Many speeches, and very, very hot. Then back alone with Chaim to lunch at the Plaza and to talk business. He will see Blum tomorrow. He says the Jews *could* not accept a State unless they control the head-waters of the Jordan and the Huleh Concession. If these are not given, they will passively resist the Scheme—and I think thus wreck it. He will, in the last resort, formally communicate this to Peel before the Report is published.

May 29th   Walter said on telephone that Hore-Belisha's[18] appointment is very unpopular, especially with the soldiers. But later in the day Bill Balfour said not so—only, if he began advertising himself, he would do for himself—and later still in the day Eddie Hartington[19] said: 'That is what he will do, of course.'

17. Sir Alfred Zimmern: Montague Burton Professor of International Relations at Oxford University.
18. Leslie Hore-Belisha: Minister of Transport, 1934–37; Secretary of State for War, 1937–40; Minister of National Insurance, 1945.
19. Marquess of Hartington, 10th Duke of Devonshire, 1938: Under-Secretary of State for Dominion Affairs, 1936–40; for India and Burma, 1940–42.

Vera telephoned after breakfast to say Chaim was returning at once from Paris on account of a letter from Coupland, warning him that there were last minute changes in the Report. No doubt those frontiers we have heard of. How thankful Vera and I were that we had insisted on Chaim's return! He also said he had seen Blum, who had told him he wouldn't have Arabs on the Lebanon frontier—and would say so! We may have saved the situation!

May 30th Edgar drove me to Chaim's. He had just landed from Paris in response to Coupland's letter. He is to see Coupland tonight. Ben-Gurion, Dov Hos, and Arthur Lourie were there, besides Vera and self. We discussed what should be done, although still quite in dark about what Coupland will say. Unaminous agreement that there *must* be contiguous frontier with Syria, and Huleh. Blum can be counted on for this. The others present wished to include Haifa among the essentials. I combated this, and clearly had Chaim's approval. Chaim (who was in fine form, and getting on quite well with B.G.) said there was no doubt the Jews could wreck the Report if necessary. Nothing can be forced through without their acquiescence. But the result might be a stoppage of immigration for several years—possibly involving the ruin of the Yishuv. A terrible responsibility, but Chaim evidently favours taking it, rather than agreeing to impossible frontiers.

May 31st Went up to Zionist Office at 11 a.m. for a conference. Present: Chaim — Ben-Gurion — Katznelson — Lewis — Arthur — Brodetsky — self—later on, Peter. Chaim told us he had decided to refuse a frontier which leaves Huleh, Tiberias and the adjacent colonies and Safed outside. All agreed to this. It was also decided that if agreement were after all reached on frontiers, another *sine qua non* is 'effective occupation' during interim period, which might be anything from two to five years. There *must* be a big immigration during that period, to build up an Army. The talk was very unanimous and very serious. It is a great responsibility to wreck this Scheme, and Chaim is in his heart so tremendously pro-State—as is Peter, also Lewis, also (I think) Ben-Gurion. But on the other hand, by standing quite firm about N. Galilee, we may get it!

Did some shopping. Tea at House of Commons with Walter in his room. I told him about Palestine—he said Anthony—Swinton—Halifax[20]—were our key men in Neville's Cabinet. He thought Delbos[21] and Pierre Cot[22] were the right line of approach to the two former. I telephoned to Chaim from

20. Edward Wood: Viceroy of India, 1926–31; Secretary of State for War, 1935; Lord Privy Seal, 1935–37; Lord President of the Council, 1937–38; Foreign Secretary, 1938–40; Member of War Cabinet 1939–45; Ambassador to U.S., 1941–46; succeeded as Viscount Halifax, 1934. Cr. Earl, 1944.
21. Yvon Delbos: French Foreign Minister, 1936–38.
22. Pierre Cot: French Minister for Air, 1933–34, 1936–38.

Walter's room. He told me he had just seen Coupland again, and told him we should stand firm on N. Galilee.

I went to a cocktail at Sybil Colefax's. Talked there to Harold Nicolson, who spoke about leadership of National Labour. We agreed it would have to be Malcolm. But Harold thought Ramsay had better hang on for the present.

June 2nd   Met Victor Lytton in St James's Square—urged him to go and see Billy about the Potash Concession, which must be left in Jewish or British hands.

Fourth of June[23]   A lot of chat with Buck on telephone in the morning. He had decided to lunch alone with Malcolm MacDonald before the group meeting, to talk the question out together. I thought Buck's own attitude most dignified—thinking more of the work than the position. It seems almost impossible that MacDonald would have *time,* with his Departmental work. But he *must* lead in the House of Commons, if he can and will.

June 9th   Went to Zionist Office, where found several listening to an account by Chaim of a dinner at Archie Sinclair's, where were James de Rothschild, Jos. Wedgwood, Victor Cazalet, Amery—and Attlee. . . . Winston seemed to have inveighed against Partition. Winston in his most brilliant style, but very drunk, fulminated against H.M.G. and in favour of Zionism for three hours. Chaim oddly impressed by this performance, and anxious to exploit it in some undefined way. I pointed out that these people were in no sense a team—that they knew little or nothing about the subject— and that Partition must not be made the cat's paw of English politics, as might easily happen in the present undefined state of personal relationships following on changes in personnel. They agreed, reluctantly, but Chaim asked Lewis and me to get the reactions of some others of the guests at the dinner. After lunch (which I had alone with Chaim at the Carlton), I met Lewis and Ben-Gurion in the House. We saw Victor, who *more* than con- firmed my impressions of Winston's state, and wild talk. Victor did not think anything useful could come of the dinner. But it had this advantage— that some of the Jews (probably Ben-Gurion and Brodetsky) had to face the question of their own attitude towards Partition. We are at the 11th hour now. After dinner, at a small meeting at Henry Melchett's B.G. declared he would fight for Partition under our minimum conditions—e.g. full sovereignty—all N. Galilee—access to Haifa—and (he adds), at least some *token* rights in Jerusalem. This is very important.

June 10th   L.N.U. Executive. Spent whole afternoon and evening in Buck's house—confabulating on Foreign Policy with members of the Group, who

23. The principal annual celebration of Eton college was held on 4 June.

will I think form a Foreign Affairs Committee—namely, Harold Nicolson, Alfred Zimmern, Major Church,[24] Commander King-Hall.[25] We were pretty well agreed, although the ideas of Sir George Schuster,[26] who was invited to join us for a while, were not acceptable. Zimmern is to prepare a Memo. His mind and Harold's are very clear. King-Hall is a 'live wire', and I think very genuine. I think there are possibilities, but the group is still terribly in the air. There seems to be a hitch in Central Southwark.

June 14th Chaim came here about 10. He talked about the next step—expressed himself as more fed up than usual with his colleagues—I could not help laughing at his description of life in the office yesterday. I drove with him to War Office, where he was going to see Creedy[27] about strategic frontiers. Then I went to Office, where I found things much as he described them. Neither Ben-Gurion nor Brodetsky has any sense of proportion or of tact. Their idea is to ask for everything as a 'minimum' requirement. Fortunately they do not even agree on that. Lewis is all right, as always, when there is something to do. I scolded them a bit, and we set to work on final draft of Chaim's letter.[28] I left them to it, and went off to House of Commons to attend a luncheon in honour of Ramsay MacDonald, about to depart on a long holiday. Harcourt Room quite full. After lunch, Buck inadvertently let out to me the fact that he, Lord Swinton, Anthony, and 'one or two more' are dining with Billy tomorrow night to discuss the Report! I should think this will be decisive. Walter *not* of it. He is in Scotland. I went back to the Office to make sure Chaim's letter is ready for posting tonight. Final draft quite good.

June 17th To tea in House of Lords with Buck. Got from him full list of Billy's guests two nights ago. Coupland, Anthony, Lord Zetland,[29] Lord Swinton, Malcolm MacDonald, and Buck himself. I am sure they discussed fate of Negev. Billy told Jos. Wedgwood, whom I met later, that the soldiers must be consulted about that. This makes Chaim's visit to Creedy very timely. Re National Labour Party, Buck and I discussed Central Southwark machinery.

June 18th Very cold. Started writing a book about Mamma and others.[30]

24. Major A. G. Church: Labour M.P. for Leyton, 1923–24; for Central Wandsworth, 1929–31; treasurer of the National Labour Organization.
25. Commander S King-Hall: Journalist and broadcaster; Independent National M.P. for Ormskirk, 1939–44; founded the K-H Newsletter, 1936.
26. Sir George Schuster: Banker and company director.
27. Sir Herbert Creedy: Permanent Under-Secretary of State for War, 1920–39.
28. To Ormsby-Gore, setting out the minimum requirements of a Jewish state as regards territory and sovereignty.
29. Marquess of Zetland: Secretary of State for India, 1935–40; for Burma, 1937–40.
30. Eventually published as *Family Homespun* (John Murray, London, 1940).

June 21st Went to a Political Committee at L.N.U.—More and more unreal. Then to National Labour Office . . . Settled that I should go to Central Southwark as soon as possible, and hold some little meetings.

June 22nd The Palestine Report was signed this morning. The motto for the week in my Palestine Calendar is—'I will say to the North—Give up, and to the South—Keep not back.' May it be a good omen. But—I have seen the Report (Savoy Grill about midnight)[31] and there is one thing which may wreck all, for it is recommended that immigration be limited to a maximum of 12,000 for five years. Walter will work at last moment to change that, in Cabinet, to *no* immigration for one year. I would do what I could to get that accepted, difficult as it would be, but I really believe Palestine would be the better for it—the other idea is out of the question.

The day was very full. An L.N.U. Office Committee in the morning. Lunch at Pinoli's, where Bakstansky[32] made a good speech. Shopped. To Zionist Office at 5—where heard Report was signed—but they knew very little more. Ben-Gurion very gloomy—I fear he is beginning to play politics. Chaim is in Paris. . . . At supper we saw George Antonius, who had rung me up this morning, just arrived in London. If he had known what document was in Walter's pocket! The boundaries look to me all right. Haifa is all right. Jerusalem a British enclave—Mandate in perpetuity. Peter's Works and Potash Works to be safeguarded. Nothing in all this that cannot be adjusted by negotiation—provided this immigration idea does not spoil all. Treaties are to be concluded. This will take a long time. We are only at the beginning of our troubles!

June 29th Cabinet will discuss Palestine Report tomorrow. I fear Peter's Works will be a difficulty—but I remain pretty hopeful. 'Le vin est tiré.' Lewis came here late, and we discussed and re-discussed, situation and tactics. Ben-Gurion will now stand or fall with Chaim.

June 30th Spent morning writing a speech on Fascism. In afternoon went with Vera to a WIZO[33] Garden Fete in Regent's Park. At 7.30 met Walter at Club. Cabinet had preliminary discussion of Report today. Final will be on Monday, when Walter will not be there.

(1) H.M.G.'s statement, accompanying publication, will be non-committal—accepting recommendations only in principle;

(2) Haifa will remain in British hands, say for 10 years;

(3) No concessions re Jerusalem;

31. The report was issued to the public on July 7th.
32. L. Bakstansky: General Secretary of the Zionist Federation of Great Britain and Ireland from 1938.
33. Women's International Zionist Organization.

(4) A great mess (in my view) about the Mandate. British will relin-
quish part? I did not fully understand in short time at disposal.
Walter's view was that nothing is yet lost—but it will be a stern
fight. But in present state of Jewish opinion we cannot have a
stern fight. Cabinet did not forbid Billy to give Chaim the Report—
but there was no promise. It will be published on July 7th. Roosevelt,
who has asked for it, will not get it till the day before.

Went to Savoy, to dine with George Antonius! We were in the midst of
Palestine discussion when Walter joined us.
George said:

> Commission had missed opportunity of settlement. He thought 'extremism'
> on either side out of question, i.e. the National Home could not be
> crystallized—nor could Jews become a majority. He thought partition
> would drag in Ibn Sa'ud[34]—who would not tolerate accretion of Abdullah's
> power. He was convinced it would never work.

Walter brilliantly explained British point of view, which is that Nationalism
runs so strong in the world today that it grinds to powder any alien element.
It would be the same in Palestine. Therefore (as in Ireland), the only hope
is in separation. Then Walter had to leave us. I explained to George that
the Irish analogy dominates the British mind. Separation has rid them of
the Irish problem. They are passionately anxious to be rid of the Palestine
problem too.

George explained his own position in Palestine. He does *not* run Arab
policy. He was affronted that it could be supposed, considering the mistakes
they have made. He never withholds his advice, but often the Mufti does
not consult him for weeks together. He hates and despises Wauchope to such
an extent that he recently refused to dine at Government House. He called
him a 'political crook'.

July 1st God! What a day! Went to Zionist Office and found Chaim
raging, after a telephone talk with Boyd (Billy Gore's secretary) in which
he learned he was not to get the Report till Monday—i.e. three days before
publication. I have never seen him so angry. 'They shall not strangle us in
the dark' he cried—and said he would show the British Empire what were
the consequences of antagonizing the Jews. Then Wauchope rang up. Chaim
had sent him a very plain-spoken letter about the last Report of the Palestine
Administration to the Mandates Commission—and on the telephone he
absolutely refused to see or speak to him here. Agitated by these two events,
he was talking to Ben-Gurion and myself, when the Colonial Office rang up
again, and Billy himself came on the line. For a quarter of an hour they
argued—we, of course, could only hear Chaim's end, and see his face. I
never saw such an expression on it before. He made seeing the Report a

---

34. Ibn Sa'ud: King of Saudi Arabia.

question of confidence—and finally warned Billy that H.M.G. could not in future count on the cooperation of the Agency. I do not blame him—I blame Billy for the folly of denying Chaim this Report. Especially as I know that the Cabinet, though unwilling, did not forbid it being shown him. Why antagonize Jewry?

I left the Office—came home—rang up Walter—told him what had happened—and begged him to speak to Neville. This he did—though exactly what he said I do not know.

Home. Lewis talked to me. And Chaim—to say he had just received a hand-written, hand-sent letter from Billy. I saw it later on. Very friendly— but too light in tone for the occasion—chiding Chaim for going off the deep end, saying the Viceroy had not seen the Report, etc. Chaim will not answer for a day or two. Much now depends on the destiny of the Negev—Shertok has cabled he believes it goes to the Arabs—but I believe he is wrong. If he is right, then today's events will greatly harden Jewish resistance.

Dined at Club with Walter . . . General Dill has sent the Cabinet a very serious military report of what must be expected if the Report is accepted.

July 2nd Lewis rang up and told me that we had a summary of the Report from Moshe in Cairo—and that Chaim and Ben-Gurion were intensely relieved by it. This greatly altered the importance of tactics here.

July 4th . . . Arthur Lourie told me (and showed me) summary of Report received from Moshe—and told me it had already been communicated to Palcor[35]—and thence to U.S.A. and other papers. On return to London, and when dining at Chaim's (only Lewis there), I found Chaim knew nothing about this—Ben-Gurion had done it on his own. This perturbed us greatly. We rang up office, where B.G. and Arthur still sat decoding endless streams from Palestine—and asked just *how* it had happened. Arthur said B.G. was determined *not* to implicate Chaim, equally determined to break the details of the Report gently to the Yishuv. He may have been right or wrong in this judgment (tomorrow will show), but he was certainly wrong in acting at this juncture alone. He did not seem inclined to come to the telephone—nor did Chaim want to speak to him—but Chaim gave me leave to get him on the 'phone and tell him what I thought. This I did. He said twice he was very sorry—believed he was right, but now thought he had perhaps been wrong. I hope the rash act itself will not matter much—but isolated action *must* not be taken. Walked home with Lewis, speculating on the great events now unleashed.

July 5th Went to Central Southwark and there addressed my first meeting—of seven women and two old men!

35. The Jewish Agency's news service.

July 7th   Telephoned for to come to Zionist Office by 10.30. Found all in an uproar—Ben-Gurion especially—news had come through that H.M.G.'s statement on Report would also contain statement that immigration for next eight months will not exceed 8,000 for all categories—thereby departing from 'absorptive capacity'. A wire had come from Jerusalem, showing Moshe knew this—and desired a protest—but he did not suggest a break with the British Government. Ben-Gurion was all for this—he spoke really like one demented, at a conference held between Chaim—Brodetsky—Lewis—Goldman[36]—Stein—Dov Hos, and self. No-one took so extreme a line—but the statement as drafted by us yesterday was now no good. There was a desire to see Billy Gore—in hopes this immigration restriction might still not be announced—although, as it had been given to Press that was unlikely. Still, resumed contact with Billy seemed important—but Chaim would not be the first to propose it after his letter. They asked me if I would go. I said yes, if Billy would see me, but I should not agree to saying anything which could lead to a break with H.M.G.

I rang up Colonial Office. Billy had gone to Cabinet, but I sent a message in there. The hour of waiting for a reply was occupied partly in listening to Ben-Gurion fulminating—in the course of it he referred to the 'bloody British'. I said nothing—but Lewis afterwards told him how far this showed loss of self-control in front of me. He was terribly upset—it began to bring him to his senses—and he rushed into the room where I was and apologized in the most affecting way. Meantime, I was drafting a letter to Billy in case he did not see me. I had got so far as explaining the harm done to relations by the immigration policy, when a message came that Billy would like to see Weizmann at 4 p.m., and if he would not come, then me.

Weizmann had gone to the War Office. Lewis, Ben-Gurion, Arthur and I went off to Carlton Grill, met him there and lunched and gave him this message. He said he would go. I gave him my unfinished letter to Billy, which I believe he showed Billy later on.

Lewis and I went and sat in St James's Park and talked matters over—as a result went back to Office, and with Brodetsky's help started drafting a new statement—on assumption that Billy would not withdraw immigration policy. This proved correct, and our draft was approved unchanged by whole conclave, including Henry Melchett, and much precious time thereby saved.

Chaim's account of Billy was that he seemed on verge of a breakdown. Said that he himself intended to resign at end of Parliamentary Session—he was badgered and abused on all sides and could no longer carry the burden. He professed amazement that the Jews objected to the 8,000 figure—and said it could not now be changed. He added that 'it was said' that the Mandate had brought on Great Britain the hostility of the Arab world, and not secured the friendship of the Jews. Chaim told me privately that when

36. Dr Nahum Goldman: Representative of the Jewish Agency at the League of Nations; later, President of World Zionist Organization and World Jewish Congress.

Billy said this, Chaim realized that it was the Colonial Office speaking, and that the core of hostility is not in Palestine, but there. He considers this very important. Nevertheless, he told Billy that personal cooperation with Wauchope had become impossible.

While Chaim was recounting this interview to us at the Office, a call from Jerusalem came through at 5.30. Chaim and Ben-Gurion spoke to Moshe—got his approval for our line of statement. Heard that all is quiet in Palestine so far.

July 8th   Report out. Favourably received by whole press. Spent morning and afternoon at L.N.U. Committees, everybody asking what I thought. I said 'A basis for negotiation'.

July 9th   Lunched with Victor Cazalet. Present: Chaim—Henry—Lewis—Ben-Gurion—Brodetsky—Lourie—Archie Sinclair—Major Nathan.[37] Chaim had now read Report, and found a new point of alarm in indefinite occupation by British of the four towns [Haifa, Acre, Safad, Tiberias] in the Jewish area. This shows the bad effect of his new-found distrust of British—only too readily reflected in all his followers, even to some extent Lewis.

Re Debate in House of Commons, it was settled to avoid a vote if possible. The letter to Billy was agreed upon—but a further proposal was seized upon that Chaim should see the Prime Minister, and Victor offered to sound the ground. I would have stopped this—but could not—and my fears were right. The P.M. has refused—on ground that he does not want to see the Arabs. This has done great harm again—Chaim is being thrown back on himself.

Dined at home and went on reading Report.

July 11th, Sunday   The whole day at Zionist Office, drafting with Lewis a letter from Chaim to Billy setting forth the vital points for negotiation re territory and sovereignty. Got Ben-Gurion's alterations and improvements to the draft. Only home (with Lewis) in time for supper with Edgar. Afterwards, Lewis and I went to Chaim's to show him the draft. He approved it on the whole, but decided not to send it to Billy tomorrow—but to await communication with Palestine and U.S.A. The latter is unaccountably silent. They are probably reading the Report. That has now been done thoroughly by Lewis and Ben-Gurion, and partially by Chaim. In the two latter opposition to it hardens—and partially so with Lewis, who considers it 'shoddy' under its crust of fairness. Chaim is now quite obsessed with that distrust of British goodwill which burst into flame on July 7th. This is serious for the negotiations which should be undertaken immediately, in my view, with H.M.G., so that Chaim may know what to say to Congress about the chances of amendment to the vital points. He went this afternoon to

37. Major H. L. Nathan: Labour M.P. for Central Wandsworth, 1937–40. Cr. Baron, 1940.

Churt to see Ll.G.—who talked in the same irresponsible manner against the Report as Winston did against the Government on June 9th—though not for the same reason! However, it may be that strong criticism of the Report in the House of Commons will do no harm. On the other hand it may. I am against Chaim interfering with advice. He wants to see Walter, Malcolm, the P.M., etc.—but I do not know what he can say to them in his present mood except express distrust of British intentions.

Lloyd George told Chaim a thing very interesting to me, namely that the Cabinet Minutes of November 2nd, 1917, reveal Nunk as saying that the 'natural evolution of the National Home' would lead in course of time to a Jewish State. Lloyd George said this in evidence before the Commission, and asked them to include it in their Report—but they refused.

July 13th Went to Zionist Office, where Henry Melchett retailed a most interesting talk he had with Billy Gore in House of Commons Smoking Room last night. An amazing spilling of beans on Billy's part! He says H.M.G. thought Report rotten in almost every respect—greatly disliked publication of the Map as it stands—agreed with most of the Jewish points. He revealed that the Report had only put in about the temporary Mandate for the four towns in order to wrap up the British intention to keep Haifa. Admiral Chatfield[38] had pitched in a terrific Memo about Haifa—he must have it always for the British Navy. (If so, then why not say so? It's no good trying to fool Jews—and then telling one of them what you are doing.) Billy expressed his contempt for the Administration in no measured terms— and said it was almost as bad in Kenya and Ceylon! On the whole, Henry came away convinced that Billy will concede easily almost all the Jewish points except Haifa. *But* he said he did not want to see Chaim, or give this information in a usable form before Congress—as he must await the Mandates Commission of the League. This sounds not unreasonable, but it alarms me—for if you take off 25 per cent of this conversation for Billy's irresponsible garrulity—and another 25 per cent for Henry's optimism, the 50 per cent which remains is not authoritative enough to make it safe for Chaim to say anything to Congress about H.M.G.'s intentions—and without that he may not be able to quiet their justified doubts about such vital points as transfer, etc. So after this talk with Henry, Lewis and I finished the final draft of the letter to Billy which has been on the stocks for three days—and still put the case for an interview.

July 19th To Zionist Office to hear Chaim's account of his interview with Billy this morning. Billy appears to have agreed that all the main Jewish points would be favourably considered. Followed discussion of pros and cons of Chaim sending him an aide memoire to prevent misunderstandings which might prove fatal at a later stage. Ben-Gurion and I in favour of

38. Admiral of the Fleet Chatfield: First Sea Lord and Chief of Naval Staff, 1933–38; Minister for Coordination of Defence, 1939–40.

this—Lewis against, thinking that with Billy's rabbit-like psychology, it might frighten him, and start a bargaining in which we should lose most of the ground won today. But on the other hand, that ground must be tested some time or other, and Ben-Gurion strongly felt he ought to have certainty before facing Congress. So on the whole the pros have it—though I think it a doubtful question—and Chaim himself is rather more than doubtful. But we decided to make a draft in any case.

July 20th Had some talk alone with Ben-Gurion about the Congress—probable currents there—and Jabotinsky's[39] intense personal jealousy of Weizmann. I do not believe J. himself would incite to foul deeds, but I trust no mad Revisionist will make an attempt at Zurich! Chaim himself said to me today that if he is ever 'bumped off' it will be by a Jew, not by an Arab!

Palestine Debate in House of Lords went on from 3 to 7 and then was adjourned! Peel made a pro-Arab speech—Lord Dufferin,[40] speaking for H.M.G., a very tactless one—Lord Samuel, who stole Henry Melchett's place in the Debate, made kind of 'Brith Shalom'[41] proposal which will bring on his head the wrath of Jewry. The Archbishop of Canterbury made a valuable contribution in saying the Jews ought to have the modern suburbs of Jerusalem.

Henry Melchett, restraining a white heat of emotion with great dignity, made a very fine speech. I went out thrice from my place near the Bar—first on to the Terrace with Buck, when we had some discussion of the position in Central Southwark. I told him it was time now that I, or somebody else, should be adopted. Then with Henry after his speech. He was limp with the effort, and very bitter against Samuel—not only for his speech, but for making it in a full House.

July 21st I was in the Speaker's Gallery from 3.30 p.m. till 12.30 a.m., with one interval for dinner, with Victor Cazalet and the Melchetts in Harcourt Room, listening to Palestine Debate. The Government had a very rough passage—the Report no passage at all, for Lloyd George and Winston persuaded the House to defer judgment on it till after Billy had presented it at Geneva. After that, a Select Committee will be set up. This means that H.M.G. has not yet got the backing of Parliament for its approval of the Report.

It also means a great deal more delay, and God knows what the terms may be at the end—or what may have happened in respect of immigration

39. Zeev Jabotinsky: Leader of the Revisionist party; founder of the New Zionist Organization, 1935; he stood on the right-wing of Zionist politics.
40. Lord Dufferin: Parliamentary Under-Secretary of State for Colonies, 1937–40.
41. Brith Shalom (Covenant of Peace). This organization held that Arab-Jewish understanding was a *sine qua non* for the establishment of the National Home, and to attain this end they were prepared to consider and propose far-reaching concessions. Their partisan activities often caused the official Zionist leadership acute embarrassment.

in the meantime—nor what the Jews will now do in Zurich. In my view it makes acceptance of the principle of Partition very much less likely. In fact, from the Jewish point of view, I look on last night's performance as a disaster—although it does great honour to Parliament and its sense of responsibility. What a difference in the tone and knowledge about Palestine from the debates of some years ago! I set down these views now, just because I have not yet found any Jew who agrees with me—except to some extent Ben-Gurion.

July 22nd Lunched with Walter at Club—he agrees that our hopes for Palestine settlement have had a set-back, but Partition still holds the field. But *what* Partition? I fear we may lose Galilee, or part of it—in which case the whole thing goes.

He thinks Billy mishandled things, and is annoyed at him for giving in. Henry Melchett told me this morning that Billy told him that was Neville Chamberlain's doing. Neville said to him on the Bench, 'I will not have a Party Vote on Palestine—you must get out of it as best you can.'

Michael dined, and we played a little bezique, but soon Namier came fresh from Manchester, to talk over situation. He agrees the Debate was a great misfortune, and I hear the others are coming round to that point of view—and feel they have done their work too well in pointing out defects in the Partition Scheme. I *am* glad Chaim did not address the Parliamentary Committee!

July 23rd Chaim is now in Paris. He is there seeing members of the Mandates Commission, and telling them Congress will agree to Partition and they must do the same. I hope he is right about Congress! Went to Zionist Office, where there is little now to be done. Visited some people in Central Southwark . . . Mostly in flats. How awful to live so!

Back to Zionist Office. Henry Melchett there—he was trying to draw a more feasible frontier to satisfy Winston, who, he fears, will want to kill Partition from a purely Imperial point of view. Had some tea with Lewis; dined at home.

July 26th To Henry Melchett's where met Lewis and Brodetsky and Arthur Lourie. Henry had been all afternoon with Lloyd George re Palestine, who advised the Jews to resist everything, and then pull advantage out of the mess! Great indignation growing against Samuel in Jewry. But I fear his suggestions[42] are being taken up, and it will be necessary to *show* why they are unacceptable. Moshe cabled today that the Mufti (now 'in hiding')[43]

42. In his speech to the House of Lords Samuel had proposed that for a given period of time the Jewish population should not exceed 40 per cent of the total population of Palestine; that a great Arab confederation, including Palestine, be set up; and that Jewish development and settlement be allowed in Transjordan.
43. The Mufti had taken sanctuary in the area of the Dome of the Rock.

is proposing a Round Table Conference, at which Magnes[44] and Samuel are to be present. What impudence! Dined at home.

July 27th   Began drafting an 'ideal' Resolution for Congress, just as a guide to what might be aimed at.

Dined at home. Chaim rang up from Paris to discuss situation . . . Chaim is far less alarmed than I am about Partition idea being in jeopardy, but is impressed with the necessity of working. He asked me to write to *Times* saying Jewish State is the evolution of the Balfour Declaration. Sat up late making a very bad draft.

July 28th   To Zionist Office where, with Lewis, I made a quite different, and much better, draft of my letter. Yesterday Walter went through with me my draft Resolution. Worked on that amended draft with Lewis—we sent our joint product to Henry, of course keeping Walter's part in it secret.

July 31st—Hotel Dolder, Zurich   Lewis picked me up at Roland in a taxi; we lunched at Victoria and at 1 p.m. started for Croydon, and took big Swissair plane which brought us here 5.30 without a halt. Dropped Lewis at Dolder Waldhaus, and came myself to this vast luxury hotel where I joined Chaim and Vera. He had been in Geneva for opening of Mandates Commission. Orts[45] means to keep them sitting till they know what this Congress decides. This makes Zurich more important even than we supposed. Chaim is extremely hopeful—says the calculations are that 70 per cent of Congress will be for Partition. All Palestine except Mizrachi[46]—all Eastern Europe—but not America. Warburg[47] and Wise were at Geneva, swearing they would never agree!

August 1st—Zurich   Lewis and I went down to Eden Hotel to find Ben-Gurion and learn the latest currents of opinion (nearly the whole Congress is now in Zurich, potted about in the different hotels). Ben-Gurion had the most incredible piece of news—he came fresh from two and a half hours' talk with Ussishkin,[48] and reported that he would withdraw his opposition to Partition provided he were made President of the Congress and that there was a Declaration made about the rights of Jewry to all Palestine. Lewis and I found this hard to believe—Ussishkin has been so uncompromising and has made so many public speeches in opposition. But apparently he feels himself

---

44. Judah Leon Magnes: American Zionist leader; Chancellor of the Hebrew University, 1925–36; President, 1936–48; ideologue of Brith Shalom.
45. M. Orts: Chairman of the Permanent Mandates Commission of the League of Nations.
46. The religious parties.
47. Felix Warburg: American banker and philanthropist; a non-Zionist but a generous supporter of the Zionist cause.
48. Menahem Mendel Ussishkin: Veteran Russian Zionist leader; had led the anti-Uganda faction in 1903, and now emerged as leader of the *nein-sagers* in 1937; generally considered as the iron-man of the movement.

F

a sick, as well as an old, man, and his ambition to preside over Congress once is overwhelming. It is only charitable to suppose that reflection is also showing him that there is *no* alternative. Nevertheless, I do feel as if the image of Nebuchadnezzar has feet of clay. I looked on Ussishkin as immovable as the Assyrian god-king he so resembles. But, if true, it is a great relief, for with him the spearhead of opposition is broken. Ben-Gurion asked me to put the proposal to Chaim; he did not feel quite sure he would be willing, and did not want to seem to be putting pressure upon him. I was quite sure Chaim would be more than willing, if he could be brought to believe the fact—and so it proved. Lewis and I went to Baur-au-Lac Hotel, where we were trysted with Chaim, and put the suggestion. He laughed—was sceptical —said he would be only *too* pleased—we telephoned to Ben-Gurion to come and convince him—and so the affair is arranged. Only I cannot yet believe Ussishkin will not go back on it.

Lewis and I then went through Chaim's speech with him once. There are doubtful questions: ought he to give his real opinion of what Arab nationalism is really worth? I think he will *not* have the speech typed, but will trust to the inspiration of the moment. Therefore I am very anxious not to interfere, or suggest too much.

Chaim and Ben-Gurion left. Lewis and I talked to one or two people— Lewis very nearly converted the South African Delegation yesterday—they telegraphed to Kimberley asking for a free hand to vote as they pleased. If Ussishkin comes over, they will certainly follow. I wonder what the Americans in that case will do. We walked most of the way up to Waldhaus Dolder, where dined pleasantly on a terrace overlooking the lake and lights of Zurich—fine after a pouring wet day. Talked of many things, and Lewis evolved a new argument. If we do not have Partition now—and if by a miracle immigration were still permitted—the struggle would come when Jews were 49 per cent in Palestine. It would be fierce and bloody, for it would be for life or death—and Partition would be bound to come *then*. We walked in the pinewoods before coming in.

August 2nd—Zurich Chaim proposed Ussishkin for President of the Actions Committee today. This is almost universally acclaimed as a fine gesture on Chaim's part, but some think it doubtfully wise, as it is held by no means certain that Ussishkin will really drop his opposition. I agree with Chaim that the whole thing is much less important than they think it. I told Lewis that in my view the danger is now abstentions. If I were an anti-Partitionist (and there are plenty of them), I would now work for that, as a Vote against Partition now seems highly improbable. The majority *for* is today estimated at 75 per cent—I suspect this of being optimistic.

Chaim addressed the General Zionists this afternoon. I hear he was very good, but I was not there. Chaim returned to hotel for a stroll before dinner with Lewis and me. He said he had never known a Congress so unpoisoned by personal intrigues. The issues are too grave. Lewis and Leon Simon[49] dined with us—the latter a typical anti-Partitionist, hankering for agreement with the Arabs. What agreement *can* there be between 49 per cent and 51 per cent. After dinner we drove down to Zurich—were joined at Baur-au-Lac by Chilik Weizmann[50]—Sacharoff[51]—J. Cohen[52], and we walked with Chaim to the Histadruth Party meeting. Big room in Tonhalle, crowded and overcrowded with Halutzim—men and women—all young—the eager, bronzed, earnest faces would have made a great scene for Rembrandt. Locker[53] in Chair, Ben-Gurion delivered a long (over-long) speech in Hebrew—I understand all in praise of Lewis and me. Then Chaim spoke in Yiddish for some half-hour—very simple—very fine indeed. I could follow nearly all. He told them there *must* be Yes or No. Not much applause, but they were evidently deeply moved. Ben-Gurion hopes for a united Labour Front—bar some 20 Marxists. We left them at it about 11.30 p.m.

August 3rd—Zurich   Spent all day on Chaim's speech—and preparing the Press résumé.

Before dinner Henry Melchett and the Blumenfelds arrived. Delightful to have Henry here—so gay and cheerful. At 8 we all went to the formal opening of the Congress in the Tonhalle—Vera and I in our best evening gowns—I wore the 'carcanet'. We had best seats in the gallery, but dreadfully bad acoustically, and could hardly catch the drift of Chaim's speech in German. It was, however, only formal. Hall packed out and boiling hot. He mentioned me, and there was a wonderfully cordial response. Henry too, got an ovation.

We came back to the hotel and had sandwiches—followed by David Ben-Gurion and Moshe Shertok, who disapproved of some phrases in the Press résumé. These took a long while to alter, and in the end did not amount to much. The Jews are too Talmudic!

August 4th—Zurich   The day of Chaim's great speech. The birthday of the Jewish State, as it will prove. We went to Zurich after breakfast—Vera had the first box in the Theatre, and I a front place in there.

After formalities, Chaim went to the Tribune. I will not try to reproduce what he said. He spoke for two hours. It was not a speech—it was an inspired utterance. He will never rise to these heights again—we shall never

49. Leon Simon: Author and Hebraist; member of Zionist Commission to Palestine, 1918; Director of Public Savings at the General Post Office from 1935.
50. Weizmann's brother.
51. Yechezkel Sacharoff [Sahar]: Private secretary [but acted as bodyguard] to Weizmann from 1933.
52. J. Cohen: Weizmann's personal assistant in Hebrew University and Sieff Institute affairs.
53. Berl Locker: Member of Executive of Jewish Agency from 1931; in charge of political work of the movement in London, 1938–48; Chairman of Executive of Jewish Agency, 1948–56.

hear the like of it again. I do not know how much he got from the audience—
which was swept by gusts of Hush-Hush-Hush-ing when occasionally some
few were driven to a burst of hysterical applause. Looking back on yesterday,
when Lewis and I were preparing a few poor bones of the skeleton which
he brought to glorious life, I think one of the greatest moments of privilege
of my life should be that when he came out to the balcony where we were
working—apologized for interrupting—and said: 'Children, I shall probably put in a few words about the Messianic hopes.' To have been near him,
and perhaps a little help to him, in the days when he was preparing this,
is an unforgettable thing. All felt like this. I sat next him on the drive back
here—he never asked for the compliments he usually wants after a speech—
and all words seemed too poor. I asked him whether he knew this morning
that he would be able to do this—he answered he knew some parts would
be good. The Blumenfelds and Sacharoff, also Lewis, Chilik and Anka[54]
were at lunch with us in the Restaurant. Henry came in after. He felt his
title to fame was that Chaim had mentioned him by name in this speech.
Chaim went off to rest, though not *yet* tired. We all went back to Zurich at
4.30 for resumed session to hear Ussishkin, who had accepted the Presidency,
but made a violently anti-Partition speech—very ineffective, poor old fellow.
A tragedy, that. So ends a great day!

August 5th—Zurich   The Histadruth came at last to the end of its Party
Meeting this morning, and decided unanimously to give powers to the
Executive to negotiate—but on condition that the proposal is brought not to
this Congress—but to another to be specially elected. This practically amounts
to a Referendum. I do not quite know how it will work. Lewis and I soon
adjourned to Baur-au-Lac, where we worked at the translation till it was
finished, dining with Henry, as was also Kaplan. He has been working at
the finance of the Partition Scheme, and finds that the Jewish State could
not make ends meet without the four towns proposed to be left under
Mandate. Unfortunately the same may be true of Jerusalem, without the
Jewish suburbs.

Chaim came down into Zurich to fetch me back. Very hot night, but
felt happy to have made a good job of his great speech—as I hope we have
done.

August 6th—Zurich   We all, including Henry, dined with the Werner
Baers[55]—out of doors on the balcony—a wonderful hot night. After dinner,
Chaim launched into reminiscences of Herzl—the naiveté through all the
greatness—the simple faith—combined with his belief in the great of the
earth. Chaim once asked him why he always made Sir Francis Montefiore
Vice-President of the Congress? 'Er öffnet mir die Pforte der Könige', he
replied. 'Was brauchen Sie mit den Pforten der Könige?' Chaim asked him.

---

54. Weizmann's sister.
55. Swiss friends of Weizmann.

He was utterly amazed when he first met Russian Jews—Ussishkin etc. He had never imagined civilized, cultivated men. His ideas, too, were simple— when Norddeutscher Lloyd were selling old ships, he wanted to buy them, to bring the Jews to Palestine. Forty years this week since the First Zionist Congress. Truly, the Faith that has moved mountains.

Lewis would not admire him—but we all felt that but for him we should not all be here in Zurich tonight, discussing the real practical beginning of the Juden Staat. And old Ussishkin is by way of being against it. Who could have thought it!

August 7th—Zurich   Sabbath—so no Congress till 9 p.m. Stiflingly hot day. I drove in the morning to Eden Hotel, by request of Ussishkin, for a talk with him. . . . I stayed an hour. Ussishkin talked most of the time, in his bad Russo-German. I think I made no impression at all—to adapt the Talmud proverb: If the stone falls on Ussishkin's head, woe to the stone; if Ussishkin's head falls on the stone, woe to the stone! I was the stone. But the old boy's best argument is simple: how can you honestly make a Treaty for a part of Eretz Israel without tacitly relinquishing your historic claim to the rest? He thought A.J.B. would have been against. I told him No—'there is a tide in the affairs of men . . .' He rejoined that Smuts[56] and Lloyd George were against. When I left, agreeing to differ, he spoke of my work for Zionism, and said that he would not have discussed this matter so with any other Goy.

Lunched with the usual lot here—quiet afternoon—read a novel in the pinewoods. . . . The evening session consisted of two speeches—one from Grossmann,[57] very violent against Chaim, and basing his attack on the minutes of Chaim's talk with Billy on July 19th—confessedly purloined from Zionist Office somehow. Arthur Lourie suspects a Revisionist called Bach. We must be more careful. It was idiotic of Grossmann to read the thing out—he would have been far more effective had he used the contents to question Chaim—a sort of 'J'accuse'. *Did* you insist on the Negev? etc., etc. instead of roaring and yelling. There are no orators in Congress except Chaim.

August 8th—Zurich   Heat wave goes on. It was awful in Basle whither I motored this morning with Chaim and the Blumenfelds (who left us there) to the celebration of the First Congress in 1897. Ussishkin presided—he is among the eight or ten survivors. Those who were there spoke; Chaim, too, though he was not at the First Congress because he could not scrape together the money to come. His speech was good, though his voice so weak that I doubt if it could be heard. He never liked Herzl, and his tribute was less

---

56. Jan Smuts: Boer general and British Field-Marshal; member of Imperial War Cabinet, 1917–19; Prime Minister of South Africa, 1919–24, 1939–48; a firm Zionist.
57. Meir Grossmann: Leader of Jewish State Party; this was the remnant of the Revisionist party which did not secede from the Zionist Organization in 1935.

fulsome than the others. He said one illuminating thing: speaking of his attitude to Jewry as a whole, he said: 'Er wirkt *für* uns, und nicht *mit* uns!'

August 10th—Zurich   Chaim made quite a good polemical speech to wind up the Debate on the Resolutions.

He has been in wonderful form, privately and publicly, all through—no whimsies.

One of his stories: talking of the people we nicknamed the 'Prontras'—of which there were many in the Congress—who could make up their minds neither way—of a woman who needed good weather for lifting the potatoes, and cold to dry the land: 'We must pray for a warm frost', she said.

August 12th—Strachur[58]   And yesterday morning I was in Zurich! Before leaving London I got a wire from Chaim to announce a two-thirds majority. It could not have been better! I found the transition from one world to another too sudden—but am getting acclimatized now.

September 2nd—Balbirnie   This morning got two letters from Chaim written from Cannes—the first since Zurich. The second enclosed one from Billy complaining very unpleasantly about the publication of the notes of his conversation with Chaim of July 19th—the document used by Grossmann at the Congress (see this Diary of August 7th). Chaim very worried—sent a draft reply, I thought not nearly stiff enough, and too apologetic. (Miss May[59] told me the text of it over the telephone from London—I got the original of Billy's letter direct from Chaim). I asked Miss May to hold up Chaim's draft. I prepared an alternative draft and sent it off to Chaim at Cannes. Billy's letter to him seemed to me peevish, undignified, and giving the incident far more importance than it is worth—the letter of a badly frightened man, especially in its allusion to his own position in the Government.

September 7th—Caponflat   Lewis told me the history of how he was excluded from the Executive. Not a very pleasant story. He is taking it very well—does not refuse to go on serving. But the position is very difficult.

September 8th—Caponflat . . . After the children went to bed, Lewis and I walked up the hill. After dinner, being alone, we had a long talk about the situation—undoubtedly Chaim could have fought for him and did not. Brodetsky is very jealous, but he and the others will certainly expect that Lewis will go on working as before, provided I do. Of course I shall, but am determined that he shall not be exploited. At the same time, he *must* be associated somehow with the negotiations with H.M.G.—otherwise the

58. Strachur, by Loch Fyne, opposite Inveraray; the home of Lady George Campbell [Aunt Syb.], Mrs Dugdale's aunt.
59. Doris May: Weizmann's secretary in London.

Jewish team will be too hopelessly weak. The question is *how?* I read to Lewis the Billy-Chaim correspondence. He thought my draft reply 'harmless' but not very skilful. I agree—and am only thankful that he thinks it harmless. Poor old Lewis. He is at his best here . . .

September 13th—Hotel Beau Rivage—Geneva Sacharoff met me at the aerodrome here. Found Chaim in his sitting-room with Shertok, Goldmann, Katznelson. He had just had an hour's talk with Walter and felt reassured—but perils beset us of the whole Partition Scheme being postponed. The Mediterranean situation is very delicate—and Walter told Chaim that Anthony is awaiting with anxiety the Italian reaction to the Nyon Conference.[60]

After dinner a conference in Chaim's room. Present: Shertok, Agronsky, Katznelson, Goldmann, Harry Sacher and Ussishkin. Chaim related his talks with Walter and others here today. Shertok gave a depressing account of affairs in Palestine—economically quite at a stand-still, and eleven bad cases of Jewish reprisals—for the first time approved by public opinion. Ussishkin then gave tongue, saying that Chaim's conversations were not in accord with the Resolution of Congress, and urging that Jewish policy should still be the old Mandate. All were against him, Chaim arguing powerfully that you cannot turn the clock back. If ever there were a case of 'There is a tide in the affairs of men,' etc., it is now. But, except Chaim, I do not think that the most astute of them, not even Shertok, realize the dangers of delay in the present state of the world, and of British policy. I feel every hour that passes before negotiations for the Jewish State begin is an hour wasted.

September 14th At 5 p.m. Anthony made his statement about Palestine to the Council, but Walter had been unable to get me a ticket. Chaim saw the Italian 'observer' this afternoon, who made to him the important statement that Mussolini would recognize, and be friendly towards, a Jewish State. All returned here at 9.30 to hear the report of the Council from Agronsky . . . who brought the text of Anthony's statement, which was an utter surprise, in that the announced despatch of a 'further body' to Palestine before negotiations begin—whether in London or Jerusalem. He also pinned H.M.G. definitely to Partition. This, in Chaim's view, is *the* important point, and gives the Jews an ace of trumps. H.M.G. will now require their cooperation, as they will hardly get that of the Arabs. Nobody liked the idea of a fresh Commission to Palestine, but much will depend on its composition, of which no hint was given by Anthony. Chaim will not negotiate with it if it be a Colonial Office body. But this it can hardly be! Chaim

60. The Nyon Conference (10–14 September) had been convened to devise counter-measures against Italian pirate submarine raiders in the western Mediterranean. The nine convening powers decided to initiate naval patrols in those areas most prone to attack, the main burden of decision and action resting with Great Britain and France. In the event these proved most effective.

will also make clear that no frontiers *less* than those proposed by the Royal Commission will be acceptable, and no partition of Galilee. Only *with* Galilee did he recommend the Resolution to Congress.

We talked together of dangerous lack of *young* leaders. Moshe Shertok the best brain, but he lacks the magnetic quality of leadership. Henry is also a coming figure for the Galuth [the Diaspora]. Chaim said the history of the past 20 years had been made by the partnership between himself personally and the Yishuv. But the weakness of the Palestine Labour Party is that it is a collective movement, and does not encourage the development of personality. Ben-Gurion leads it, but apart from Moshe, his successor is not visible.

September 15th—Geneva   Chaim breakfasted with Malcolm MacDonald, who however was not able to throw any light on the obscure points in Anthony's speech. It seems clear that it is a purely Colonial Office product. Chaim then visited Sir John Shuckburgh, who told him that he is to be chief of this Commission. They had some very friendly talk, discussed the personnel—Chaim suggested Coupland for one—if he cannot come Shuckburgh suggested Maurice Carter—they agreed that Martin would be the best secretary. The only objection to these people—as Shertok pointed out—is that they will be very wedded to the Report of the R.C. Chaim then went to see Orts, who was very stout that the Permanent Mandates Commission will not allow anything to be done over the heads of the Jews which goes against the Balfour Declaration. Next he visited Delbos, who was rather sore that the British had not consulted the French. Anthony had exchanged speeches with Beck (the Polish F.M.) before yesterday's Council—but he knew nothing of the proposal. We all lunched together in Chaim's room, and heard all this. Shertok still gloomy about the Commission—he thinks it will be subjected in Palestine to terrific pressure from the Administration. However—at any rate the position is clarified by today's interviews.

September 18th—Fisher's Gate[61]   Came here by train before lunch. Buck and all his family. . . . Buck much perturbed by Neville Chamberlain's desire to make friends with the Fascist Powers, as evinced in last week's Cabinet. Walter had given me a hint of this. We discussed whether Buck should resign if Abyssinia is recognized, which is the *sine qua non* of Italy's friendship. Buck thinks Anthony must be the key man. *I* think National Labour could not stand for that. But it would throw us into the arms of the Liberals.

September 19th—London   Pouring wet day. Played bezique a lot. . . . Came to London by car with Buck after dinner. Talked foreign politics all the way. He would be ready to barter recognition of Italian possession of

61. The De la Warrs' home in Withyham, Sussex.

Abyssinia for Mussolini's word to renounce Balearic Isles and aid to Franco. At least, he argued in that sense, but is clearly undecided. We reckoned up Cabinet pros and cons, but it all hangs on Anthony. Buck said Lord Zetland was passionately anti giving in to Musso. Of course, as usual, it is all a question of where to make the stand.

September 24th—London . . . Edgar and I dined with H. G. Wells—Moura[62] was there and the Weizmanns. We talked, among other things, of 'greatness'. H.G.W. doubted its existence. I said 'What about Shakespeare?' He branched off to say that there was a great affinity between Shakespeare and Defoe, Dickens and Charlie Chaplin! These three latter he thought must be Jewish—or at any rate non-Aryan. He was sure about Defoe, suspected it of Dickens, whose art was very like Chaplin's in its use of pathos. He talked a good deal of nonsense—but he has the art to conceal a good deal of his immense self-conceit. Sometimes he says interesting things—amid a lot of rot—as for instance that a man seldom produces great art if he has lived always in his own class and circle. You have to move from one to another. Chaim's great distinction of mind and profound natural modesty shone out in contact with Wells. It was a very brilliant evening, in a perfectly appointed setting. Moura was charming—she is the perfect type of a cultivated European.

September 28th—London . . . Had tea with Chaim, who is shattered by the Andrews murder.[63] A code wire from Palestine announces that the Civil Administration has refused authority to the Military to look for proofs of the Mufti's responsibility—not for this particular murder probably, but for terrorism. Chaim is considering writing to Billy to say that it is useless to begin negotiations in this state of affairs—and perhaps to demand Wauchope's resignation. This must be considered. It may be that Billy will take action—but I doubt it. There was a very strong leader in today's *Times*.

September 30th—London Lunched alone with Chaim at Savoy Grill, and spent p.m. at Zionist Office. There was the first meeting of a Committee set up by the Executive—a 'working committee'[64] really to direct the London policy this winter, when Chaim and all members of the Executive except Brodetsky will be away. I am on this committee—the first time I have ever accepted a position on any Zionist body—but it seems to me silly to refuse now that my advice is so much sought, and Lewis would not have worked without me as things are. Henry Melchett is chairman. The members are: Lewis, Harry Sacher, Perlzweig and myself, besides Brodetsky and other

---

62. Moura Budberg: a close friend of Vera Weizmann.
63. L. Y. Andrews: Acting District Commissioner for Galilee. He had been shot down and murdered by Arab gunmen outside the Anglican Church in Nazareth on September 26th. The murder was the prelude to the renewal of violence in Palestine.
64. The committee was officially known as the London Political Committee.

members of the Executive who may be in London. Chief business today: the terrorism in Palestine, and what, if anything, should Jews do? Negotiations will be hopeless in this atmosphere, and no moderate-minded Arab would dare to speak for fear of his life. The Mufti rules the country—and by terror. But Chaim cannot refuse to let negotiations begin, or the partition scheme might break down altogether. He will lay a letter from Bernard Joseph[65] giving a terrible picture of affairs, before Sir John Shuckburgh tomorrow. His relations with Billy are still clouded by the Grossman affair.

Word came from Palestine that Billy has telegraphed out: 'Terrorism must be stopped at all costs—await your proposals.' Rather late in the day! Meanwhile, as far as we know, Wauchope is still on leave in Scotland.

October 1st—London   Today after lunch, Lewis telephoned me that the Mufti had been deposed, the Arab Higher Committee dissolved, and several leaders arrested in Jerusalem! ! Better late than never. Andrews has not died in vain, but his blood is on British hands—especially Wauchope's and Billy's. This changes the whole situation—makes Partition a certainty, and may I think also lead to the formation of an Arab State under Abdullah. Moshe spoke to me on telephone. Said his alarm now was that the Administration and Colonial Office might sabotage settlement by delaying it. Chaim had gone to see Shuckburgh, determined to urge opening of negotiations as soon as possible. Chaim himself came to tea with me at the close of this interview—Shuckburgh's view had coincided with his own, and he talked of the Commission going out in November. There is a water-survey just begun, of the Negev and Transjordan. It might take a year, and be used as an excuse for delay. Shuckburgh was alive to this. He said if the Arabs would not negotiate, their territory would just be administered by H.M.G.

Today opens a new chapter. Pray God the Jews do not triumph too openly—that the effect of the Arab agitation is what we have always hoped and prophesied. Anyway, H.M.G. has gone too far now to draw back.

'*The horse and his rider hath He thrown into the sea.*'

October 19th—London   Chaim rang up before dinner. He had seen Billy today, and was happy at the way things are shaping. It must be the aim of our Zionist Office committee to keep M.P. friends from saying much—and from throwing more cold water on the partition policy . . .

October 20th—London . . . Lunched with Walter at Carlton Club. He came from Cabinet, and thought dead-lock in non-Intervention Committee complete. But I see by evening papers that Musso has climbed down a bit. I expect he is in great straits, and now is the time to call his bluff everywhere. Walter said the French Government had not thought out at all what

---

65. Bernard Joseph: Legal adviser to Jewish Agency; first Minister of Supply in Israel.

their policy should be. At Geneva they told us they would have to open the frontier. *Now* they ask us to support them by action of some sort. This quite new request runs counter to all British policy. Walter thinks it would probably be against the interests of the Spanish Government to open the French frontier. No *more* stuff would get in, and it would involve acknowledging Franco as a belligerent and letting him blockade the ports and stop food ships.

October 29th—London   Billy Gore announced today that Wauchope will resign after one short return to Palestine. Enormous relief!

November 2nd—London   To lunch with me came Kenneth Lindsay[66]—Sir Alfred Zimmern—Commander King-Hall—Harold Nicolson—invited by me as a nucleus of a Foreign Policy Group, to try to work out some principles of foreign policy for National Labour. The result of two hours' very interesting talk was quite barren. There was very little certainty or agreement as to what are basic questions in the present welter of world politics. For instance—has the time come to proclaim that Democracies and Dictatorships are not talking the same language about even the binding nature of Treaties or respect for International Law, and that therefore there is *no use* entering into Conference with them. Or should Britain go on trying to bring them round Conference Tables? There was some agreement that cooperation with France is the basis of everything at present. But that is hardly worth stating as the policy of National Labour! Nor the other point—that it would be a good idea to make a Trade Treaty with U.S.A.! We are to meet again next week. Walter said when I told him tonight that it all sounded very like a Cabinet discussion—only rather more conclusive! He admits himself privately terrified—not so much at the 'drift'—but at the state of our defences. It does not seem that the Cabinet discussed at all what British policy is to be at the Brussels Nine Power Conference[67] which opens to-morrow!

November 9th   The National Labour Group came to lunch again. It begins to emerge that we are all 'Anthony's men'. This may not be without its importance, later on.

November 10th—London   In the evening went down to Sevenoaks to talk about Palestine to a Drawing-Room Meeting of goyim. . . . Did not speak very well—it is so difficult to change the key to suit non-Jewish audiences.

66. Kenneth Lindsay: M.P. for Kilmarnock Burghs from 1933; Parliamentary Secretary to Board of Education, 1937–40.
67. The Nine Powers were those who had signed the China Agreement at the Washington Conference in 1921–22. The conference at Brussels was intended to devise solutions for the present Sino-Japanese dispute; it met without the participation of Japan and failed in its task to inaugurate negotiations to end the war.

November 12th—London . . . To tea—the Readings—Lewis—to meet
Henry Melchett, who came bursting from an interview with Billy Gore
today. Billy had told him he would *like* us to begin now gradually to work
up to an open demand for the Jewish State to become part of the British
Empire. There is a *great change*. British policy begins to shape itself round
the Eastern Mediterranean—friendship with Turkey etc. Billy did not say
this, but I know it is so, from remarks made by Walter. This brings Haifa
into the centre of the picture, makes it necessary for the British to get rid
of the Mandate, so that they can make a naval base, 'and garrison it with
2,000,000 Jews' as Walter said to me the other day. But this cannot yet be
openly said by them. We must make a very careful programme for educating (1) Jewish public opinion, in Yishuv and Galuth; (2) British public
opinion. It immensely enlarges scope of this winter's work. Billy told Henry
that tendency is to make Jewish State smaller—British Mandate larger—than
Committee's Report. British want to keep coastal strip round Acre, and the
Negev. This ought to reconcile the Jews to Acre, but the aim now must be
to make them see that British and Jewish territory is *one,* in the end.

Billy said that the French treaties for Syrian independence are not likely
now to be ratified. He is satisfied that neither Iraq nor Ibn Sa'ud are at all
interested in Pan-Arabism—only the Syrians, and the Mufti Party, who are
'small beer'. They are terrified of the Mufti getting away to Rome (though
I think they may be wrong in fearing that). They believe now that Italy is
at the back of all the existing trouble, and financing it. If only they had
believed these things when we told them 18 months ago, *how much* would
have been saved! Billy (of all people!) thinks restoration of law and order
must come first, before politics are talked, and before the Commission goes
out.

November 23rd—London   Dined at Club with Walter . . . He told me
that last week Anthony launched an attack on the policy of the Peel Report
in the form of an F.O. Memo., with annexes, and covering Memo. from
himself. This might have been taken straight out of any Arab Nationalist
paper—advocates no partition, Jewish minority for ever, etc., etc. The basis
is not, as I supposed, hostility of Germany and Italy—Walter had so far
heard nothing of that—but the Arab Kings. Chapter and verse in the
annexes giving recent evidence of their violent opposition—especially Ibn
Sa'ud! Anthony is prepared to wipe away all H.M.G.'s policy in past years
as if it had never been! !

This flabbergasting document has been before the Cabinet, but discussion
adjourned till next week. Billy has said to Walter it would be for him a
resigning matter. I think Neville might hesitate to have his Colonial Secretary resign on such an issue as this. The House of Commons would certainly have something to say to it! *There* lies our best hope. As far as one
can see, the Cabinet alignment is not very good. On our side would be

Billy (a broken reed), Walter, Ernest Brown,[68] probably Kingsley Wood,[69] who is attentive to the House of Commons. On this issue we cannot count on the Service Ministers—they want peace in the Middle East, so long as Britain keeps her hold on Palestine. Anthony's policy is really the 'palliatives'.[70] And to think this is the *first* discussion of the Peel Report that the Cabinet have *ever* really had. A year too late!

Walter feels that the Jews at this moment can do *nothing*. The opinions of the Arab Kings have very likely been instigated by tendentious enquiries. But even if we could disprove them—Walter thinks the battle must now at last be joined, and won—or lost—in *Cabinet*. It should have been fought out there long ago. If we win, the Jewish State will at last have driving power behind it. If we lose? I said that the 400,000 of the Yishuv would tear down Government House with their bare hands rather than consent to the palliatives. Walter said: 'Yes, and what then? They are helpless.' I do not agree—but we are as yet far from that. Walter thinks it would be fatal to both Jewish and British interests if any hint should leak out of this Cabinet division. It is not hard to keep the secret so long as there is nothing to be done. Walter will tell me if and when there is. His own idea at the moment is to drop the label of 'State', and perhaps be forced to agree to going on with the Mandate, ostensibly as it is, but to do internal reorganization on cantonal lines—*but* giving the Jewish 'canton' all that really matters —viz. control of immigration and police. But that, too, is looking ahead. Oh—if only Zurich had been more whole-hearted for the Jewish State! Anthony can argue that the whole policy was founded on *consent,* and that neither side has given it.

Billy told Walter that he thought the author of this attack is Rendel[71]— head of Middle Eastern Department—and a Papist. Walter told me that Anthony is a very tired man—obsessed with the notion of the weakness of Britain, and unable to endure the thought of a disturbed Middle East on the top of everything else. It is (he thinks) easier to ignore the Jews than the Arabs. We shall see! Walter thinks that if the German-Italian protests were really made, it would do our cause good.

As for Billy, it is a pity that he was thinking of resigning and quitting the House of Commons anyway. He must be a Peer before long. If he were a bit more of a careerist, he might fight harder.

---

68. Ernest Brown: Minister of Labour, 1935–40; Secretary of State for Scotland, 1940–41; Minister of Health, 1941–43; Chancellor of the Duchy of Lancaster, 1943–45.
69. Sir Kingsley Wood: Postmaster-General, 1931–35; Minister of Health, 1935–38; Secretary of State for Air, 1938–40; Chancellor of Exchequer, 1940–43.
70. These were a series of proposals recommended by the Peel Commission in the event of partition not proving acceptable. They envisaged a political high level of immigration of 12,000 per annum for the coming five years, and severe restrictions in land sales and settlement.
71. G. W. Rendel: Head of Middle Eastern Department at Foreign Office, 1930–38; later held ambassadorial rank in a number of European countries. Knighted, 1943.

November 24th—London   In view of what Walter told me yesterday, I urged Arthur Lourie to prevent despatch of the anti-partition Memorandum, now being prepared . . . I could not explain, but took responsibility. It would be unfortunate if Colonial Office got the impression of weakening and indecision just now.

November 25th—London   Received from Walter following letter:
'I saw Billy today at the Carlton, and had a word with him. He is writing a paper on the subject I mentioned, which will come before my Committee in due course. I asked him whether he would like Chaim to return. He said: No. But he thought that if I could tell someone who would tell some-one who would tell Weizmann to go down to Egypt and have a talk on affairs with Miles Lampson, it would be of use. He (Chaim) must not know anything of the subject we were discussing—and all the more so, since naturally anything Chaim says to him (M.L.) will immediately reappear in London as a telegram from the Ambassador. But a conversation between the two on the weather and prospects and so on and such like would probably do good, and in any case be useful. The impressions gathered by Chaim in Paris would probably be a peg. But I don't think Chaim should appear despondent or frightened. If you found it necessary to give some source to indicate why you were giving this advice, it might be that you could state that there was an impression, in spite of everything, that the Middle East was really deeply averse to the proposed changes, and that you had this from reliable sources, and that Chaim might, without obviously doing so, explore this ground. M.L. seems in a considerable state of nerves anyway.'
I went to L.N.U. Executive and then to lunch at Horse Shoe with Arthur Lourie, with whose help I wrote a code wire to Moshe for Chaim. It was not well drafted, and late at night, after talking to Lewis, I got Arthur to wire en clair not to act on it, and prepared another to go tomorrow. This runs: 'Shertok: Instead of previous message take to Chaim the following equally secret quote Try on some pretext to see British Minister Cairo and attempt to discover what he thinks about present Middle Eastern attitude to H.M.G.'s Palestine scheme, taking care to say nothing which might increase possible misgivings on his part Stop Very urgent and important. Baffy'.

November 27th—London   Lewis came, and talked over some points to make to Walter. Chief, that a return to the 'palliatives' meant denying in-dependence to the Arabs as well as immigration to the Jews.
. . . Walter came about 10.30 p.m. and stayed till 1 a.m. Part of the time we talked about the Palestine situation. His mind runs on his scheme of the Cantonization *label*—as a way of getting over what he calls the 'two stiff hurdles' of the League and the Arabs. These hurdles are interconnected in his mind, i.e. the Arabs have friends in the League. Not only Iraq and Egypt, but de Valera. These can block partition, unless it is negotiation *by consent,* i.e. consent of both Jews *and* Arabs. Therefore we shall not get

Arab consent. Therefore the best way to get what we want is to cantonize the country, giving the Jewish canton control of immigration and police, but keep the British flag flying over all, and British troops on the border.

I see this point. It is far too late to make it—but that could be met by saying that we had always hoped for consent, and failed to get it. But the idea of a Jewish State is in being—and working. If the other plan is to replace it, we ought to begin to back-pedal on the State—but Walter was firm that I must not write anything to Chaim. To begin with, the battle in the Cabinet is not yet begun, and it may not be necessary to compromise at all. Walter thinks the pieces on the board are set right for the present. He is in touch with Billy—I with him—and Chaim will obey any directions I send, and after Christmas, if advisable, I will go to him.

November 29th—London   Wrote a bit of *Family Photographs*. Lunched with Rob and Hannah. . . . Shopped—went to Zionist Office for a Political Committee. Dr Goldmann told us how he has gathered from Bova Scoppa in Geneva that the Italians are likely soon to urge that they *and* the British shall together guarantee the frontiers of the new Jewish State—they will probably soon propose this to the Jews, tempting them by promises to call off the Arab opposition. I wrote this to Walter tonight, and also said to him that I thought his cantonization idea (we call it his 'Hindenburg Line') COULD NOT even be put to the Jews unless they were guaranteed absolute control of immigration—absolute control of Police—absolute freedom of land sales—and absolute freedom from British Administration—perhaps a Jewish Deputy High Commissioner. Even so, I don't think it will do.

December 2nd—London   L.N.U. Executive—as much a bear-garden as usual. Gilbert Murray[72] is quite unfit now to chair it. . . .

December 8th—London   . . . A filthy, cold, sleety day. Went to Political Committee at Zionist Office. In the middle Henry Melchett telephoned to say that 'a prominent Cabinet Minister' had just told him that it would be a good thing if the Jews would display a desire to preserve a British connection, as there was an acute division of opinion raging in the Cabinet at present on the fundamental policy. So that cat is to some extent out of the bag! They were much agitated, but not knowing all, did not take in the full extent of the danger.

I found out from Arthur Lourie that the person who leaked to Henry is Hore-Belisha!

December 9th—London   Lunched with Walter at Club. He told me that the Palestine policy was discussed yesterday. They decided that they could not at present go back on the announced policy—therefore they will proceed

72. Gilbert Murray: Regius Professor of Greek at Oxford University; Chairman of the League of Nations Union.

to appoint the Commission and send it out shortly. But a very grave discussion turned on the wording of the *Statement* which will be made at the same time. They take that so seriously that it is not even referred to a Committee, and the final draft will be submitted to the full body next week. But I think it will probably show the muddle-headedness of our opponents. It will probably say that H.M.G. stands by its policy (e.g. the White Paper)—but the White Paper contains all we want! In the first draft there was a paragraph that the Jews could not be condemned to be a permanent minority. They took that out, but so long as the other part is left in, surely that does not matter. But it shows the new spirit, and that is alarming. Walter put it to me this way: he said it was like the Gallipoli Expedition— the orders were 'to try and force the Dardanelles'. Winston took that to mean: 'Go on—heads down and force the Dardanelles!'—but the others interpreted it to mean: 'Have a crack at the Dardanelles—but if you can't do it, never mind—it wasn't a very good idea anyhow, and we will try something else!' And *that* is the spirit in which the Commission will go out. Well, thank God we are warned! The Jews must not give any excuse for the negotiations to break down.

Neville knows *nothing* about Palestine, and is all in favour of delay. They contemplate perhaps a twelve-month delay. Well, we may (if advisable) be able to do something to shorten that too.

I have urged Chaim not to make any plan of campaign until I come. I sail from Marseilles on January 4th. Victor Cazalet is coming also.

Walter thinks the Jewish State has receded—but that land for Jewish settlement will not be stinted. He took the line in Cabinet that control of immigration is the vital point, everything else secondary. But *I* think we must have sovereignty.

December 11th—London To see Victor Cazalet to arrange about our journey. He told me that Billy had told him yesterday about the Cabinet and Palestine—had said that the only people who supported his policy there are Malcolm and Walter. He also complained that he was hampered by lack of enthusiasm on the Jewish side. I enjoined upon Victor to say nothing about all this at present.

Lunched at Club with Walter who was horrified at Billy's indiscretion, especially in giving Cabinet names.

December 15th—London Got a letter from Chaim dated December 8th, saying that Palestine is full of rumours that the Foreign Office and the War Office want Partition to be proceeded with very slowly—not for two years. How *do* these things get round? He is much worried, of course—says 'the economic structure will not stand it for too long, although in my opinion it is better than what people make it out to be.' He also says 'the activities of the various peace-makers are on the increase, and moves are made from various sides. I'm certain that the more definite the Government will be

Blanche Dugdale with her children, Michael and Frances

The Rt. Hon. Walter Elliot, C.H., M.C., F.R.S., M.P.

Lord Balfour with Dr. Chaim Weizmann in Tel-Aviv, 1925

about Partition, the easier the Arabs will come to terms. I hear it from Egypt and from other sources.'

Harold Nicolson and Kenneth Lindsay lunched here. We mainly discussed the question of National Labour leadership—which Buck wants decided at the Conference when he comes back from Australia in March. *There* the vote would undoubtedly go to him. But Kenneth and Harold do not think the leader has yet arisen—neither Malcolm nor Buck possess all the necessary qualities. Malcolm is not a leader at all. Buck is, but they do not trust his judgment. They are all for postponement, and I think I agree—but Buck is determined to force a decision.

Took a lift in Kenneth's car and joined Lewis at Athenaeum. He suggested getting Amery to put a Question before the House rises, asking when Commission is going out, and if Billy's answer is unsatisfactory, raising the subject on the Adjournment and asking for a Select Committee. This Leo would probably agree to do—it was his suggestion in July. It would get the question of policy out of the Cabinet into the open.

I put it to Walter when I dined with him tonight—and found him very averse to doing more than putting down a Question on the last day—to be answered in February—this as a sort of reminder to the Cabinet that the eye of the House is on them. He thinks that now they will come to no decision themselves before Christmas—but, so long as they make no public announcement to the contrary, H.M.G.'s partition policy stands—and it will become more difficult to recede from it—and if there is increasing Jewish unrest in Palestine it becomes more obvious that they must do something. The subject was on the agenda for tomorrow's Cabinet—but has been taken off—Walter will find out from Billy tomorrow why—but thinks it is probably because the Foreign Office and the Colonial Office have not been able to agree upon a draft statement of policy.

Meantime, he is obviously very nervous of me inspiring any action on my inside information—even though the leakages are now very widespread. Lastly, he thinks that the question of the policy is too important for the House of Commons to be allowed to decide it, and that a Select Committee would not therefore transfer the battle to any ground where we could direct it. It *must* be fought out in the Cabinet, as he said at the beginning.

December 17th—London . . . Went to L.N.U. Conference,[73] and was waiting for the Refugee Resolution to come on, when a telephone call from Arthur Lourie reached me to say that Henry had had a talk with Billy this morning, and had urgently summoned Lewis, Brodetsky and me to Mulberry House. I went there at once. After tea Henry recounted from Billy's own mouth the whole story as I knew it, with the addition that the Defence Services have lost interest in Haifa, and are turning their attention to Cyprus instead—largely because they think it will in any case be so long before

73. The L.N.U. Annual Conference had opened at Conway Hall, London, the previous day.

G

they could begin to fortify Haifa that they cannot wait, in the present state of Mediterranean affairs. Also Billy was much more pessimistic than Walter—represented himself as fighting a practically lone hand in the Cabinet—described 'most of his allies' as 'liabilities'—though I do not know whether he named them—gave no hint of what he said two days ago to Walter that 'Neville is on our side'—and generally gave the impression that he was fighting with his back to the wall, and more or less suggested that Chaim should come home at once.

I resisted this—it seems to me far more important that Chaim should stay in Palestine, so as to be in touch with Moshe and Ben-Gurion when I come out, than that he should fly home just when everybody of importance leaves London for a month. Probably he will have to come back about the end of January—but not before. We settled that I should write tonight and tell him about Billy's talk with Henry—and add that we think there ought to be some expression of Jewish desire that their new State should be connected with the British Empire. It was also decided that Lewis and Arthur Lourie and I should study a memorandum of a new plan for partition sent us from Palestine by Ben-Gurion the other day, and see whether on the basis of that we could work out a policy which should command enough Jewish support to be presented to H.M.G. as our scheme.

December 19th—Sunday   One of the foulest days climatically of this specially foul winter. Spent most of it at Zionist Office with Lewis, Arthur and Miss May working on our Federal Scheme—the B.A.L. Scheme as Lewis calls it, in distinction to the D.B.G. Scheme (David's),[74] though in this case B (Baffy) had little to do with it beyond formulating and modifying. The ideas came from Lewis, but it did not somehow fall into pattern until Arthur Lourie yesterday suggested the Federal (instead of the Cantonal) pattern. After that, in a curious way the thing seemed to take shape. If, by chance, we were making history, this ought to be recorded.

. . . After dinner, Henry rang up to say 'he had never been so much disappointed in his life' as by our memorandum—that it in no way fulfilled Billy's requirements—that what was needed now was a tremendous Jewish demonstration, demand for British connection on lines of Southern Rhodesia, etc., etc. I was sorry, but not impressed—for I know that the conditions do not yet exist for such a demonstration—they must be created—I think our scheme *might* focus them. However, of course, I said to Henry that he must work out his ideas himself and send them also to Chaim.

December 20th—London   Lewis lunched alone with me. We agreed that Henry's tactics are wrong—no good rushing things—what we are suffering from on the part of H.M.G. is too much delay—the Foreign Office attack has been repelled—but the danger now is that the Report scheme will die

---

74. Mrs Dugdale had rejected the Ben-Gurion scheme on the grounds that where it departed from the Peel proposals it was all 'in disfavour of the Arabs'.

of inanition. Wrote these views to Henry, and took the letter by hand to his house. Also wrote some account of all this to Chaim.

Dined with Walter at Club and told him all that had happened since we parted just before the meeting in Henry's house. He agreed with my views, but said he was doubtful whether demonstrations of loyalty to Britain were the right tactics—H.M.G. rather look on Palestine as a liability—and specially the Jewish part of it (everyone in this affair seems to look on their friends as 'liabilities'!) and a better way would be to convince Neville that the Jews might help him to find a solution. Walter would be in favour of Chaim's adopting something like our Federation Scheme (if he and the others agree), and sending it, quite personally and unofficially, to Neville as well as to Billy, in such a way that it could be withdrawn if it does not find favour. This before his return in February, if at all possible. Walter evidently considers the scheme is on the right lines. I told him I thought I ought to see Billy myself before I go out (much as I dislike the idea, for I despise him, and think him responsible for most of this mess). Walter agreed, but did not seem very hopeful of bringing it about, and I would only do it through him. He says Billy is very anti-me—thinking me more Zionist than the Zionists. This may be true, but he does not realize that I am also a far warmer supporter than almost any of them of the policy of the Report—and that I have at present far more influence than anybody else with the Zionist Executive. However—I can do no more—but I should welcome instructions of some sort—for these hysterical confabulations between Billy and Henry only make things more difficult.

December 22nd—London   Got following letters from Walter—

'I have had a talk with Billy, and set down the notes to give you time to chew upon them.

(1) The Draft[75]: This has been gone over by six Ministers and agreed. Billy thinks it will do, though he has had to weaken in other places in order to retain the position of the Commission as an objective technical body.

(2) The Draft will be published about January 5th. The Commission will go out as previously mentioned.

(3) Billy has agreed to the Draft, and therefore thinks no good purpose would be served by contesting it tomorrow (i.e. in the Cabinet).

(4) Billy says I am not a liability but a help, and that only Malcolm and I know anything about it.

(5) He considers the position of the Zionists to be weak because of (i) the Foreign Office and the departmental drive against them; (ii) the Arab Kings' opposition; (iii) Jewish opposition—*Jewish Chronicle,* Brandeis[76] and Wise anti-partition; Herbert Samuel.

---

75. Of the proposed Government statement of policy on Palestine.
76. Louis Brandeis: American jurist and Zionist leader; justice of Supreme Court, 1916–39.

(6)   These persons being active and in touch with the Departments, he thinks Chaim should return about the end of January. This for the purpose of meeting and influencing persons such as Horace Wilson,[77] Kingsley Wood, F.O. men, such as Vansittart.[78]

(7)   He does not want to see you, on the ground that it is much easier for him to give me a message to give you to give Chaim than to give you any himself.

(8)   His fear is briefly that the opposition to Partition will win, and then the Jews will find they have got, not *all* Palestine, but nothing.'

Meanwhile, the present Cabinet and governing circle is another Pharaoh which knows not Joseph. The Jews, he feels, have still completely in their minds the Pharaoh of A.J.B., Lloyd George, etc.

Dined at the Club with Walter. I saw the Statement. All right on the surface, but as Walter says, riddled with traps and dangers. He thinks our opponents in the Cabinet are getting ready for a Hoare-Laval coup, but will put everything off as long as they can. He said I must make Chaim realize that the Balfour Declaration is no more—and that all we have is 400,000 in the Yishuv, and a few friends outside. We must make it suffice! Also, we have now *time*. Walter evidently thinks our Federal State scheme may come in very usefully.

December 23rd—Merevale[79]   Before leaving London I settled, by telephone, with Lewis and Arthur to cable to Moshe—on following subject, which I forgot to record yesterday—namely, that Walter at my suggestion, spoke to Billy about the psychological importance of estimating the next immigration on e.a.c.,[80] not politically. Upon which Billy said he would enquire of the Palestine Administration what the numbers on an e.a.c. basis would be likely to be. I think it very improbable that Moshe will be consulted if Billy does this—but it seemed sufficiently important to take no risks, so Arthur wired a warning to put the estimate low.

December 30th—Bridgnorth . . . Before lunch Arthur Lourie telephoned from Zionist Office, to say there was an article by Easterman in today's *Daily Herald* giving an accurate account of the Cabinet position on Palestine, saying the Balfour Declaration is dead, also Report of Commission, and the Jews are in danger of being in a minority for ever. Brodetsky wanted to organize protest meetings all over the world against breach of faith on part

77. Sir Horace Wilson: then chief industrial adviser to the Government; Permanent Under-Secretary at the Treasury, 1939–42; Chamberlain's chief adviser on most matters, including foreign affairs.
78. Sir Robert Vansittart: Permanent Under-Secretary at the Foreign Office, 1930–38; chief diplomatic adviser to the Government, 1938–41.
79. Merevale Hall, Warwickshire, the home of Sir William Francis Dugdale, Edgar's elder brother.
80. Economic absorptive capacity, see entry for 18 Jan. 1937 ft. 1.

of H.M.G. Lewis and I, of course, both felt this should not be done on basis of a mere newspaper article in an opposition paper—but we drafted the following, and after half-an-hour telephoned it to Lourie for despatch:

'Instruct all Zionist leaders to draw attention of H.M.G.'s Representatives in their respective countries to *Daily Herald* article of December . . . and to express anxiety evoked throughout Jewry. Stress adherence to idea of Jewish State, and Jewish resistance to possibility of permanent minority status being imposed on Jews in Palestine. Put your communication in form of anxious enquiry, but do not let it become indignant protest doubting good faith of H.M.G. because far-reaching accusations on basis of newspaper article would be resented by Mandatory Government, and do harm.'

Arthur Lourie did not think Stephen Wise would act on this, if phrase about Jewish State were left in—so he probably took it out in the version for U.S.A. How incredible it seems that people should be so blind to the dangers ahead! This article of Easterman's will do good, if it opens the eyes of some! Lewis sets store by the meeting of the Actions Committee. Yes indeed! If it only closes our ranks! Lewis thinks Ussishkin, Wise, the greatest dangers.

December 31st—Bridgnorth   A lot of Palestine talk with Lewis—going over points to be emphasized—the importance of remembering that we cannot have the Report *and* the amendments to it. Lewis truly said that H.M.G. has only so far envisaged the difficulties of implementing the Report—not the difficulties of devising or carrying through any *other* scheme.

Saw the New Year in alone with Lewis—the others having gone to bed.

$\mathbf{1938}$ *January 2nd—Sunday,* London   Packed. Lunched at Horse Shoe with Lewis and Arthur, and received their last commissions. Had tea with Eva Reading. Found Eva much oppressed and over-worked, and terribly worried over Henry. He is very ill, and knocked out for quite three months. He nearly died of a clot on Christmas night. She asked me to tell Chaim (1) that Mrs Warburg is taking up Felix Warburg's place as the non-Zionist leader and ought to be cultivated now; (2) that No. 77 is in need of re-organization (nothing new in that!). She suggests making Bakstansky General Secretary.

January 4th—SS. Mariette Pacha   On Calais boat found Rob, Hannah and Robin Hudson, with whom we travelled as far as Paris. On boat also Anthony and Beatrice Eden. A few words with him; he said Neville had suggested putting Palestine under the Foreign Office—but he (A.) had refused. I wonder when. Thank God he did!

January 10th—Weizmann House, Rehovoth   We were in Jaffa roadstead when I woke up . . . After five minutes in Palestine one feels the old, familiar sense of springing, growing *life,* which 'the troubles' have in no way quenched. But what a humiliation for British rule that these same 'troubles', which began on that very day of April 1936 on which Edgar and I landed from Cyprus, are still going on, and this very night on the wireless we heard of the murder of Mr Starkey, a British archaeologist, on the Hebron road.

We picked up the pilot outside Haifa about 2 p.m. I was watching the quay for friendly faces, when on the deck beside us stood David Ben-Gurion and Moshe Shertok! Oh, the joy!

Tea—and I gave them a sketch of how things have been going in London. Ben-Gurion asseverates that 75 per cent of the Yishuv are pro-Partition. I told him the time is come when that must be publicly proved. He wants Chaim to go to U.S.A. in February, and organize a big demonstration pro-Jewish-State there. This may be a good plan—but I think Ben-Gurion over-estimates importance of U.S.A. opinion on H.M.G. I felt at once the advantage of my coming—we get an exchange of *atmosphere.* Victor joined us, and we drove here, along new coast road, safest in Palestine, but we had two armed guards in the car. Arrived soon after 7—a most joyful reunion. Vera showed off this truly *lovely* house. I gave them Walter's present of a cushion, and my own—A.J.B.'s silver box, which I had inscribed —and it gave real pleasure. After dinner much gossip . . . and then some 'politics'. Chaim very 'inspired'—professing faith that *nothing* can prevent the setting up of Jewish State. But—I told him—the time has come for *testimony*. It will not do to wait any longer, for demonstration must be made by the Jews. He considers the F.O. very ill-informed. Lampson in Egypt gets his information from his Oriental Secretary,[1] who is brother-in-law of Antonius. (This is important news to me.)

January 11th—Rehovoth A glorious day—sun everywhere, and I felt hot in a linen dress. Chaim took Victor and me all over the Institute . . . We all went down to the experimental farm of 20 dunams, where a careful rotation of feeding crops has been worked out, to support three cows and 60 head of poultry. Also there are fruit-trees. Off this a man and wife, working (between them) 10 hours a day, made a profit last year of L.70. This farm is visited by hundreds of people from the settlements; all will be copied, with variations for soil and water, all over Palestine.

This house is surrounded with armed guards, and there is always another car with armed guards with Chaim's when he goes on the road, which he does as seldom as possible.

January 12th—Rehovoth Smilansky came, talked most interestingly of desire of Arab farmers for a joint delegation to London to beg for removal of Mandate trade restrictions[2] . . . When they were gone, Chaim gave out his reflections—based on reports he receives from all surrounding countries—and on what I have told him from London. He remains unimpressed by Arab nationalism. It will only last while they have *not* got a State—and they know this themselves. The F.O. is throwing away the substance for the shadow. German and Italian intrigue will *not* stop with elimination of the Jews—it will find other food, and H.M.G. will merely alienate the Jews. The Arabs calculate now that if they can gain time—put off partition for five years—they will kill Jewish work. These are his convictions—the only message he has for the world just now—but he cannot give it. If he spoke his mind, he would turn all Jewry against H.M.G. He is disinclined to come to London and stand on doorsteps asking to be heard. H.M.G. has not cared to consult him. He would come, I think, if he were sure Neville and Anthony would listen to what he has to say. He spoke to us with fire and bitterness. I did not press him to decision. He *must* come, or we cannot fight for him. I must see if we can get assurances that his visit will be

1. W. A. Smart: Oriental Counsellor, Cairo Embassy, 1929–45, Knighted 1942.
2. They claimed that the administration's tax and customs policy crippled trade with other countries and forced Palestinian products into English markets.

useful. This mood also makes my hope of a great speech from him in Tel-Aviv less likely. Unless he feels inspired he will do no good. It is not that he will not fight to the end, but at the moment he is disinclined for tactical moves. We dined alone, the four of us, and talked of these matters all evening. Vera, as always in a crisis, very sensible.

January 13th—Jerusalem   Peter Rutenberg called at Rehovoth on his way to Jerusalem, and picked up Victor and me. A most lovely day—and all seemed so peaceful, even in what is the dangerous part of the road, among the Judaean Hills—only a good many police about. Victor alighted to speak to a group of three British Police—one turned out to be one of his own constituents! Arrived at . . . Rehavia about 11 (Vera went to King David Hotel). . . . to Va'ad Leumi for a moment, to receive their greetings—then had some political talk with Moshe, David, and Leo Kohn. Urged a Mass Meeting in Tel-Aviv, pro-Jewish-State. David very averse—I think he fears to commit himself to advocating partition, and falls back on asseverations that the great majority of the Yishuv are for it. I argued vehemently, saying we must have *proof* at the English end. Lunched with the Shertoks—afterwards read this Diary to Moshe and David—and again urged a Demonstration Meeting. Made a little more impression on David, I think, after he read this Diary. He said if Chaim wanted a Meeting, of course he could have one. It seems to me that the Statement [containing the terms of reference for the Partition Commission] required some kind of public pronouncement from Chaim.

January 14th—Jerusalem   We went to tea with Nebi and Hadassah Samuel.[3] Nebi is coldly logical anti-partitionist—thinks Jewish State cannot exist—cannot deal with Galilee Arabs, and yet without Galilee is nothing . . . So he is quite content to have no constructive alternative, except a sort of cantonization, which, like all such schemes, seemed to me the worst of both worlds. Victor was greatly upset—he has become a most passionate 'Ja-Sager'.

January 16th—Rehovoth   Victor related horrifying talk with Tegart[4] about the rottenness of Administration, especially police. Chaim had some secret reports of Mufti's activities and other things still more secret. The state of affairs passes belief! I again dwell on thought of Jews having to proclaim their own State! Meanwhile they buy land on frontier like mad. Today, 4,000 dunams approximately 1,000 acres in the North. The spirit is indomitable, and when one contrasts it with the cringing, vacillating blindness of our policy . . .!

3. The Hon. E. H. (now Viscount) Samuel, elder son of Viscount Samuel: Deputy Commissioner for Migration in the Palestine administration, 1934-45; and his wife, Hadassah.
4. Sir Charles Tegart: Member of Council of India, 1932-36; in Palestine from 1937 to advise the administration on police organization; erected Tegart's wall along the northern frontier.

January 19th—Rehovoth Back to Rehovoth[5] for tea. Chaim read us a draft letter to Billy, asking to see Anthony and P.M. and tell them his views before he speaks to his own people. A fine and dignified letter. It goes with Victor, who leaves us by air tomorrow. He has been a most charming travelling companion, and absorbed knowledge like a sponge. I am sure he can do much for us.

January 20th—Rehovoth Victor left. At 11.30 I went to Tel-Aviv. Met Dov Hos, who drove me to the Port. An extraordinary achievement—20 months ago, when I was here, it had not even been thought of! Now a mole, a harbour full of big lighters, locally built, and a huge warehouse for the oranges. Seven steamers waiting in the roadstead. It has been too rough to load for a week—serious at this season. This port has employed 1,000 men in building, working night and day. No wonder the Jews are proud—it is perhaps the biggest single achievement. The Administration continues to discourage it in every way! After dinner, taught Vera bezique. It was settled that Weizmanns and I return to London together on *Marietta Pacha,* leaving Haifa on February 9th.

January 23rd—Rehovoth Chaim, Vera and I left for Jerusalem at 9 a.m. A car full of armed guards behind, another in front on way home. There was shooting on road about an hour after we passed. Meeting of *Va'ad Leumi*—Chaim spoke twice, I once, and many others. Feeling in favour of Jewish State overwhelming. All speeches in Hebrew, but Moshe kept me au courant with written notes. Lunched at King David with Vera; Chaim with his sister, where we picked him up after. First Vera and I called on Captain Wingate.[6] He told us that Ibn Sa'ud's London Representative had wired to Ibn Sa'ud, in answer to a question, that he understood a joint memorandum from all the Arab Kings on the subject of Palestine would be acceptable to H.M.G. This confirms Chaim's conviction of F.O. intrigue against policy. Wrote to Walter about it. Moshe will see that the letter goes safely. Lucky for us that Wingate's fanatical Zionism gets the better of his sense of duty as Intelligence Officer. He is clearly one of the instruments in God's hand. Home before dark. Chaim was visited at the Institute by a man he knows who said he was an emissary of an emissary of the Mufti, who (he declares) wants to see Chaim. Chaim asked for a letter from emissary No. 1, which is clearly the right thing to do to begin this. The man said this would be forthcoming.

January 27th—Haifa Left Jerusalem about 8 with Baratz[7] and J. Gordon.[8] Car again stopped for permits near km. 5. Reached Rehovoth soon

5. Mrs Dugdale had been on a two-day tour of Galilee.
6. Orde Wingate, later Major-General: Served in Palestine, 1936–39, where he organized the Special Night Squads against the Arab insurgents.
7. Joseph Baratz: Palestine labour leader; farmer and author; a founder of Degania, the first collective settlement.
8. Joshua Gordon: Chief aide to the Political Department of Jewish Agency.

after 9—and soon set out again with Chaim and Vera, escorting cars etc., also J. Gordon, for Degania. Rain ceased in Galilee, and I never saw more superb views on Lake Tiberias of the Hermon massif covered with snow. All Degania drawn up to meet Chaim, and we lunched, like Louis XIV, in full view of some 300 people. Tea at Nahalal the same—speeches in both places. Chaim told them that he need not stay in London half an hour, for all he had to say there was that nobody could impose a solution which had not the goodwill of the Jews.

January 30th—Rehovoth   Wet, windy and cold, again. Unlucky, as the High Commissioner came to lunch with Mr Bickersteth, his P.S. Wauchope seemed in good spirits, and told Chaim he would still be here on March 15th. But Bickersteth whispered he was to leave on March 1st, but they hadn't told him yet—which seems odd! A Mrs Scott (née Walter) came too. In the morning Sacharoff drove Vera and me to a Meet of Hounds about 10 miles off. Hounds arrived in a van, and were put into an orange-grove, and found a jackal at once, and streamed after it across a sandy lane where we were standing. Field about eight people—all British of course—Master in pink. Queer Meet—all mixed up with camels, donkeys, etc.

February 1st—Rehovoth   Heard from Walter, Billy is pressing Neville to see Chaim. Changes at F.O. will shift Rendel from Middle East Department. Chaim remarked that his grandfather used to say: Never wish for the death of a goy, lest you get a worse one in his place!

February 3rd—Rehovoth   Spent day in garden, working at my speech for tonight. After tea, we drove in to Tel-Aviv—five cars, bristling with rifles. Three hundred Haganah guarding route, as all Palestine knew Chaim was travelling. We dined with one of his sisters—and then on to big hall in Exhibition grounds. Nearly 4,000 people . . . I spoke first—quite well—great reception. Moshe translated. Chaim in Hebrew for an hour—I am told very fine. Tremendous enthusiasm. This meeting is my doing, and I am very glad.

February 4th—Rehovoth   To Jerusalem, with Vera and Sacharoff, stopping en route to visit Crusaders' Church at Abu Ghosh—shown by charming old French monk. The Roman Well is *in* the lower Church—water flowing clear and deep. The most unspoilt Christian monument I have seen in Palestine. Did a little shopping; then to Va'ad Leumi, where Ben-Zvi[9] and the rest of their Executive presented me with a beautiful Hebrew Bible, bound in chased silver, made here with inscription for me. I was deeply touched, and said so.

9. Yitzhak Ben-Zvi: President and chairman of *Va'ad Le'umi* (National Council); President of Israel, 1952–63.

After dinner the guards on this house were invited in for supper and a sing-song. Fifteen of them—grand boys, and their Hebrew singing a joy. But it was the old Yiddish songs which really cleared the trouble off Chaim's face for half an hour.

February 6th—Continental Hotel, Cairo. We flew from Lydda—Chaim, Vera, Sach. and I, starting at noon. Cairo by 5 p.m. . . .

February 7th—Rue de Menasce, Alexandria We all went to lunch with the Lampsons at the British Embassy. Lord Newton and Hilda Legh— another English couple, young Mr Shuckburgh, and the Oriental Secretary, Mr Smart, and his wife, who is sister to Mrs George Antonius. So Miles Lampson has an adviser in heart of Mufti's camp. Chaim had a talk with Miles before lunch. At lunch I sat between Miles and Smart. Came away certain that Chaim was right when he said the 'smell' comes from this milieu. Miles made no secret that he wants a 'stand-still' in Palestine for five years if need be, in hopes of something turning up, or present troubles dying down. Of course, I repeated what Chaim had already said, that till there is decision they will never die. I urged Miles to realize that things will not stand still in Palestine. They will break at any moment. I also said that, though I would never think a stand-still policy the right one, he should at least urge the other half of it—namely to close the Transjordan-Syrian border to the bands. To this he warmly agreed, adding that he knows nothing about Palestine, but judges of general situation. He was impressed by Chaim's knowledge—and he is an honest man; Chaim may have set him thinking. He turned me over to Smart to answer my questions about El-Azhar College. Smart says this body has only with difficulty been kept quiet. No doubt about Smart being our enemy!

February 9th—Alexandria Slept very late. Got wire from George Antonius asking me to lunch with him at Union Restaurant. His wife there, and very peculiar conversation ensued—she is a violent Arab nationalist, and revealed desire to have things come to a real show-down with arms between Jews and Arabs, when she supposes the Jews would be swept off the face of the country. George greatly deplored this talk, and tried to stop it, but I begged her to proceed. George indicated that no negotiations with Arabs other than the Mufti and party would avail Chaim anything. I indicated that it was useless to expect any negotiations on basis of permanently restricted immigration. George said he would never use the word 'permanent' but if there could be a truce to immigration for ten years the violence would stop at once (i.e. the Mufti could and would stop it?). I said I did not think the Jews would agree to political restriction even for one hour. So there is the old deadlock. I asked him to account for the fact that there are hundreds of thousands of dunams for sale to Jews, if only they had the money to buy. He said it was the same as the British firms who traded with Germany during the War. Mrs Antonius added that they could only sell their land to Jews. I asked why, if so passionately attached to soil, they had to sell their land to anybody? Answer came there none. A depressing conversation. One significant remark slipped out about Smart. I mentioned that he had made no secret that he wanted a stand-still. George (who realizes the economic difficulties of going on as we are) said: 'I am afraid my brother-in-law is not a very good Arab.' I said: 'I hope he is not an Arab at all. Isn't he a British official?'

February 11th—SS. Mariette Pacha   After tea Chaim held forth to us in fighting spirit. He refuses still ever to consider our 'Hindenburg Line'.[10] His campaign will be to buy more land, occupy it and hold it. This if he gets no satisfactory certainties in London. Sacharoff, who of course agrees 100%, said: 'We shall want some months, and half a million pounds.' I said: 'You will get the first.' Chaim: 'We shall get all the money we need.'

February 12th—SS. Mariette Pacha   A nasty rough day—none of us up to much, and Vera kept her cabin all day. Sacharoff at work translating two reports from Chaim's agent in Syria. After tea he showed me a verbatim of Nuri's conversation with Mufti and his friends on Nuri's return from London. Certainly authentic, for one of them is peaching, and why should Nuri lie to his intimates? From this it appears that Billy has encouraged Nuri to believe that H.M.G. will give them part of Galilee. On reading this I felt sick at heart. No wonder Chaim is in fighting mood. He will confront Billy with this document, and ask him to deny it. I think we have there enough dynamite to blow Billy out of the water if we choose, and I think I do so choose. Though that is secondary. I also think that our possession of these Reports may be invaluable. Moshe put them into Chaim's hands in Alexandria. 'Confound their politics . . .' One can hardly deny when Chaim calls it a 'conspiracy'.

February 17th—Roland Gardens   Talked to Walter on telephone for some time. He was inclined to belittle the importance of Billy's talk with Nuri. But he gave me the impression (not for the first time) that H.M.G. do contemplate trying to barter part of Galilee for other things. He likened Billy's treachery to Coupland's talking to Chaim about Galilee before the Report was published. This is no analogy—H.M.G. was not *then* bound to that Report.

Went to Victor's, where had quarter of an hour's talk on Palestine with General Haining[11]—very nice, very intelligent, very well-informed.

February 19th—London   Was to have walked with Walter, but there was a sudden Cabinet at 3 p.m. Differences between Anthony and Neville as to

10. See entry for 29 November 1937.
11. General Haining: Commander-in-Chief, Palestine, 1938–39.

whether to begin talks with Italians *now*. Dined with Walter at Club. Another Cabinet tomorrow. Anthony may resign. Walter thinks he should not do it on this issue of beginning talks with Italy, but should consent to begin, and make withdrawal of troops from Spain the test and breaking-point. I think Walter is wrong, and that if Anthony sticks to his guns he will crystallize a vast amount of feeling here, and be the rising star. Neville will probably let him go, and face the storm—if storm there be. But it would be a great mistake to seem to restore Mussolini's prestige now. Impact of Europe with a vengeance! Very bad atmosphere for proper consideration of our affairs. Walter is of opinion Chaim's right tactics are not to worry about what Billy said—or did not say—to Nuri, but to remember that England is virtually at war already, and convince Neville—if he can—that the Jews are better allies than the Arabs—or conversely (say I) the Arabs less formidable enemies.

February 20th—Sunday, London Sunday Despatch has facts pretty accurate, including Anthony's resignation. Colin Coote telephoned at breakfast-time to ask what I know, and to aver Walter will be sunk if he does not go out with Anthony. Next, Victor from the country—very agitated, very pro-Italian. Next, Diana De la Warr arrived, very worried about what to do, if anything. She stayed most of the morning, and by my advice, rang up Malcolm MacDonald, and told him she was sure Buck would stand by Anthony, whatever Anthony does. Malcolm replied he was in close touch with Anthony—nothing decided yet. . . . Victor Lytton had telephoned Anthony to assure him of L.N.U. support.

. . . Dined at Dorchester with Chaim and Vera—after dinner David Ben-Gurion and Arthur Lourie came in. In the course of the evening came (1) telephone from Victor in country asking for news; (2) about 10.45 telephone from Colin to say Cabinet had met again at 10 p.m. and Anthony and Bobbitty had resigned—so far none of the others, and he (Colin) felt doubtful now whether they would! I *cannot* believe it! Obviously some of them *must*—to wit Malcolm MacDonald—and I cannot think Walter would not. Colin thinks tomorrow already too late, but I don't agree there. Colin says: If they don't, what a triumph for the Dictators—Mussolini has forced the resignation of the British Foreign Secretary, *and* got his way! Colin thinks, by the way, that there will be a strong reaction in the House tomorrow, and probably some of the Junior Ministers will resign.

Chaim *really* depressed for first time—especially at rumour that Halifax succeeds Anthony. But anyway, he predicts this opens era of triumph of 'petit bourgeois' politics for some time—fatal for Palestine policy. *I* think, on contrary, it may mean that the forces of righteousness have a leader—but I do not see clear how things will work out for Palestine. Chaim talks of returning very shortly, as he does not think he will get much hearing here just now—and of preparing Palestine for war. He is worried about its power of being self-supporting in food—wants to plant soya beans etc. So ends the week-end. To think that *yesterday morning* none of us had any idea of all this!

February 21st—London Colin spoke about 9 a.m. and said he had seen Walter late last night, and Walter was not resigning. Colin begged me to do what I could, both on public and private grounds, to alter this before too late. Walter himself soon rang and asked me to lunch . . . [I] told him that if his decision was irrevocable, we had better not meet today. But he said he would like to talk it over. Next Bob Boothby, to ask me what Walter was doing—to say Walter was the key man, and did he understand this? Bob quoted Winston a lot. Winston feels this is the fundamental choice. Are we to seek to preserve peace by going *with* the Dictators—or our own way? Next Colin again—to beg me to make Walter understand about his being the key man. Next Diana, to say Buck had wired to Colin for news, from Singapore. Colin had drafted a wire advising Buck to wire support to Anthony, and put off other steps till he gets home. . . . Went up to Zionist Office, where found poor Chaim, biting his nails figuratively in despair and idleness. Lewis pro-Neville, rather, on account of his dislike for the League. With him, worked a little on a draft letter of Ben-Gurion's re immigration schedule.

Then to Club, to meet Walter for lunch. His line was: (a) Anthony went on a point of procedure, and it was not enough to justify upsetting the Government at such a crisis; (b) Walter feels his own responsibility, and will not upset Government unless he sees his way to another. But he admits (in fact he urged on Cabinet) the danger of trying to run this country on a Government which has not the confidence of the moderate Left. He seems inclined to wait and see whether Neville's policy bears fruit. I told him that was equivalent to supporting Neville with the *arrière-pensée* of perhaps carting him later on. This is not fair on Neville, and will blacken Walter's own name with everybody, for ever. Of all the pleas I used, this seemed to make the most impression—but I left him very uncertain whether I have made any impression at all.

February 22nd—London Got the following letter from Walter when I woke up—written in House of Commons last night:—

"I have listened with the most intense concentration to Neville's two speeches, and to Anthony and to Bobbitty. Each time, as I am away from the argument, and pressed by you or by Colin, I feel I must be wrong. Each time, as I re-hear the facts and the reasons, and consider again the case, I am convinced I am right.

'I wish with all my heart I felt otherwise. I am not blind to the position which would come to me if I had lined up alongside Anthony last night or tonight. All I can say is I think it would be dishonest. Perhaps I should discard reason—go upon instinct. I cannot do that, unless I have some overwhelming instinct which will take charge. But no such instinct is apparent. The P.M.'s speeches said clearly and unmistakably we are entering into conversations, not an agreement. The terms of that agreement must include a settlement in Spain on terms as previously defined by Anthony and accepted by the League. These terms, it seems to me, meet my requirements. I cannot see—I cannot possibly see—that one can do more than await the Agreement.'[12]

To League of Nations Union Emergency Committee—full, but only Government supporter there was Victor.

February 23rd—London . . . Victor Cazalet had tea-party at House to meet Chaim. Met there Sir Harold MacMichael.[13] He looked an efficient 'White Man', with pleasant manners. Long talks with Mr Denman[14] and Archie Sinclair on the crisis. Denman holds with Neville.

Dined with Rob and Hannah Hudson—Colin Coote—Rob Bernays— Thelma Cazalet-Keir—the Louis Spears[15]—and Victor later. Only the one topic! Mrs Spears yelled like a peacock, and spoiled the talk much. Rob Hudson argued that Anthony was committed to the talks beforehand—and the whole argument of the Nevillites turned on proving that he resigned owing to personal quarrel. Brendan Bracken was also there—very bitter against Bob Boothby, who had made an anti-Winston speech. I feel they have all lost sight of the big issues in these personal suspicions. Anthony has lost much sympathy by coming to the House yesterday and making signs of assent and dissent during the debate. That was a mistake—but what does it matter? Neville's policy is ruining our relations with France, U.S.A., and I think very likely the Empire. I think Bob Bernays is becoming very uneasy. The ship shows small cracks already!

February 25th—London There came to lunch Chaim and Vera—the Philip Bakers,[16]—Bob Cecil—Sach. Chaim arrived straight from Billy, and told the whole company at lunch about his interview, Nuri Pasha bit and all. He was in one of his great moods, and the indiscretion did not strike me till later. I must write to Philip not to use the information. After the guests left, David, Lewis and Arthur came here, and Chaim repeated it all again, and Arthur made notes. Then Chaim left and the others stayed on, and expressed dissatisfaction and inconclusiveness. It is always so when

12. Extracts from this letter have been published by Sir Colin Coote, *Companion of Honour*, (London, 1965), p. 156.
13. Sir Harold MacMichael: High Commissioner for Palestine and Transjordan, 1938–44.
14. R. D. Denman: Labour M.P. for Central Leeds, 1929–31; National Labour, 1931–45.
15. General Sir E. L. Spears: Conservative M.P. for Carlisle from 1931. His wife, an American, was Mary Borden, the novelist.
16. Philip Noel-Baker: Labour M.P. for Derby, 1936–50; Minister of State, 1945–46; Secretary of State for Air, 1946–47; for Commonwealth relations, 1947–50; of Fuel and Power, 1950–51.

Viscount Peel, Chairman of the 1936 Royal
Commission on Palestine, arrives at 10 Downing
Street for a Cabinet meeting

General Sir Arthur Grenfell Wauchope.
High Commissioner to Palestine and
Transjordan, 1931-38

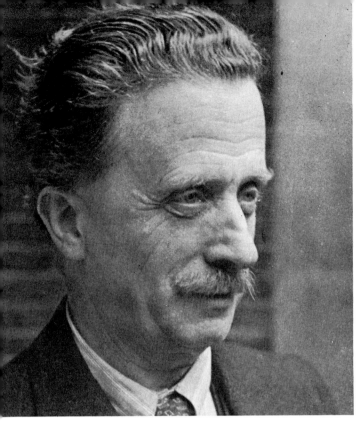

Berl Locker, who directed Zionist political work in London

David Ben-Gurion, Chairman of the Zionist Executive and Jewish Agency, 1935-48, and Prime Minister of Israel, 1948-53, 1955-63.

Chaim talks alone! I promised to draft a letter trying to clinch something out of it.

March 3rd—London   L.N.U. Executive—more like a mad tea-party than ever, but it is clear they will give no lead.

March 4th—London   Walter told me today that the other subject of difference between Neville and Anthony was the reply to the U.S.A. who made a tentative proposal for a Peace Conference including the small European States.[17] N. thought this no good, and snubbed it—Anthony would have got them to begin to play on any pretext.

March 9th—London . . . Lunched at Club with Walter. Very important talk. On public affairs he told me the F.O. had launched a fresh attack on Palestine policy—this time centering on basis for the Immigration Schedule due on March 31st. Went to meeting of Zionist Actions Committee. Sat by invitation at Executive table, between David and Chaim. Chaim came straight from interview with Lord Halifax, and in a statement of an hour and a quarter gave a brilliant resumé of situation, and expressed his doubts about cooperating with the Commission. They drank it in. Chaim also spoke about need for reorganizing the London Office—leading up to his intentions about Lewis.[18] He gave some offence to Arthur, and others of office staff—his real butt being, however, Brodetsky.

March 10th—London   To League of Nations Union Executive for short time. Then to Zionist Office. Chaim came in after seeing Prime Minister at lunch, took Sacharoff and Arthur and me to lunch at Savoy, and told us about his interview, which lasted 50 minutes. Neville kept saying to him: 'Why do you worry so much?' 'Why are you so uneasy?' 'We are committed to partition.' Chaim said: 'To what partition?' He told Neville his fears that Palestine might be a pawn in the talks with Musso. The P.M. very vehemently and categorically promised that it would not be mentioned at all. I wonder? Rendel, our great enemy at the F.O., has gone to Rome with Lord Perth.[19]

I spent all afternoon alone at Zionist Office, drafting a letter from Chaim to Halifax and the P.M. . . . Dined at Dorchester with Chaim, Vera and Walter. Most lovely evening. Chaim very tired, but greatly relieved his interview with P.M. is behind him. What feats he has accomplished in this

17. At the beginning of January Roosevelt proposed convening a world conference to discuss the underlying causes of international tension, in particular questions of disarmament and raw materials. He later linked this proposal with the Italian negotiations and expressed concern at the British idea of granting *de jure* recognition to Italy's conquest of Abyssinia.
18. He wished to appoint Namier Political Adviser with the authority of a member of the Executive.
19. Sir Eric Drummond: Secretary-General to League of Nations, 1919–33; Ambassador to Italy, 1933–40; succeeded as Earl of Perth, 1937.

H

three weeks! He told me that in his talk with Lord Halifax he felt, for the first time, that if he knew him better, there might be something of the quality of understanding that A.J.B. used to display.

Walter amplified to me what Buck said yesterday about Halifax.[20] I think he is very startled. He said Lord Palmerston had come among us again. It all seems a very odd result of getting rid of Anthony!

March 12th—London   Walter rang up early, to say Cabinet at 10.30 . . . Rob Bernays asked me to lunch, to meet Walter, who came from Cabinet. Nothing can be done about Austria.[21] But what about Czechoslovakia? Cabinet in close touch with the French (who at present have no Government!), and have taken Mr Attlee and Archie Sinclair into their confidence, with result that there will be no demand for a Foreign Affairs Debate. I would have wished them to send for Anthony to join Cabinet as Minister without Portfolio, and perhaps take in Winston too—in fact begin to form a Ministry of National Concentration. But the time for that does not seem ripe. The Italian conversations will go on at fullest blast. Whatever one thought about their beginnings, it is clearly right that they should go on now. The attitude of Italy to the Austrian coup still seems obscure—but we must try to detach her. It will take all of us all our time to hold The Brute.

March 13th—Sunday, London   On Palestine, we heard the new Schedule[22] to be announced in a day or two. A very poor reward for Chaim's three weeks here—though Walter says it represents a victory over the F.O. who wanted a complete 'stand-still'.

March 14th—London   To Zionist Office to finish drafting Chaim's letter to P.M.—Chaim himself very depressed—wondering whether, as things are now, he ought to be in London or Palestine. But that particular question was settled by his interview with General Haining, who said the new frontiers would be largely settled by himself and Sir Harold MacMichael.

After dinner, a huge procession with bands marched down Hyde Park shouting 'Chamberlain Must Go!'

March 19th—London   All day at National Labour Conference, which continued to show much vigour and independent thinking. I drew from Malcolm MacDonald a repudiation of some shocking statements by Mr Lennox Boyd[23] about 'ridiculous guarantees' for Czechoslovakia, made in a speech yesterday.

---

20. That 'Lord Halifax will count in foreign affairs.'
21. German troops had crossed the Austrian frontier at daybreak on Saturday, 12 March.
22. For the period, April-September 1938: 650 labour certificates were released; 350 more were held in reserve.
23. A. Lennox-Boyd: Parliamentary Secretary to Minister of Labour, 1938–39; of Aircraft Production, 1943–45. Cr. Viscount, 1960.

March 20th—Sunday, London   Went to Zionist Office. Found Committee sitting, listening to reports from Vienna. It is desired that someone go there to make them feel that they are not utterly forsaken—and if possible influence the Germans to certain clemencies. It was decided to ask first Sir Wyndham Deedes[24] and then Lord Lothian if they *would*—it should not be a Jew, and it should be a person of influence. I told Lewis and Berl Locker at lunch that I would go if anybody thought I could do any good—but I did not feel I could go quite alone.[25]

It was settled that we are to re-start the Political Committee, and David wants me to be Chairman in Henry's continued absence. I said yes.

March 21st—London   Lewis and I went to see Wyndham Deedes and ask him to go to Vienna. With characteristic quickness this really saintly man said that he would go at once to talk to the Foreign Office about it.

March 22nd—London   Went to Zionist Office after lunch, to say goodbye to David, returning to Palestine, and to arrange about running of Political Committee with Arthur. I want to get it on a basis of Minutes, properly circulated, Agenda, etc. . . .

March 28th—London   Namier rang me up and asked me to come home in time for an Emergency Committee on newspaper report that the Italian talks *are* concerned with keeping the *status quo* in Palestine.

Walter reassured me on telephone about Italian talks, as far as he knew. However, at Palestine Committee we took a lot of steps. Perlzweig happened to be seeing Lord Halifax this afternoon, and mentioned the matter, and got another categorical assurance from him . . .

April 8th—London . . . to Zionist Office where talked over things with Lewis, Arthur and Locker. To Inter-Aid Committee. Walked away with Sir Wyndham Deedes, who goes to Vienna for us next week. But he will not be able to get the Zionists Stricker and Friedman out of Dachau. They helped Schuschnigg[26] with money for the plebiscite.

May 6th—London   Went to see Leo Amery and tell him some of the things in Chaim's recent letters. He confirmed Simon's [Marks] impression that there is only one man in this Cabinet, and that is Neville. Where he is interested in anything, it moves—but he is interested neither in Billy nor in Palestine problem. How to make him so?

24. Sir Wyndham Deedes: Chief Secretary of the Palestine Administration, 1920–23; an old friend of Weizmann.
25. She did not.
26. Kurt Schuschnigg: Federal Chancellor of Austria from July 1934 until the Nazi occupation of Austria in March 1938. Following Hitler's ultimatum to Schuschnigg on 12 February, Schuschnigg decided to hold a plebiscite on 13 March by which the Austrian people would decide whether or not to accept Hitler's terms. This was the act which led to the German occupation of Austria.

May 16th—London   While I was in Chair at Zionist Political Committee, news came on telephone that Malcolm MacDonald is the new Colonial Secretary. I think this is probably the best appointment that could be made from the Jewish point of view.

Walter rang up while I was out—so I saw in the evening papers the other appointments. He is Minister of Health in place of Kingsley Wood, who goes to Air. Thumbs down for Lord Swinton—and Neville has a twinge of gout. No wonder!

May 19th—London . . . League of Nations Union Executive. Harold Nicolson[27] gave an interesting account of what Henlein[27] had said to the group of M.P.'s whom he met. He tried to minimize what he had said in his speech about Czechs having to give up their alliance with Russia etc., declared he had been misreported etc., and that the Sudetens knew they could not insist on that sort of thing. He wants a plebiscite in the German districts—not an Anschluss with Germany but Autonomy. Then he wants a Minority Statute for the Czechs and German 'islands' respectively, and also for the Czechs in Vienna. He professes to desire liberty for all political and *racial* minorities! He declares there are three ways of settling the Sudeten question:

(1) —and preferably—by direct negotiation between himself and Benes.
(2) by intervention of England, France, *and* Germany.
(3) by Germany alone—i.e. War.

One of these three ways *must* be taken!

Much of this was evidently for British consumption. They tried to make clear to him that British opinion would not stand for the least infringement of Czech independence. Harold's opinion is that Henlein is not a very tough guy, nor yet very intelligent—probably just a mouthpiece of stronger people. Philip Baker said this was borne out by the fact that Henlein's party had never let him enter the Prague Parliament!

May 22nd—London   Pottered about all morning at Fisher's Gate—papers all report great tension in Europe.[28] Told Buck again that a Government of National Safety becomes an urgent necessity. Drove up with him after lunch, and left him at Treasury. Came home, arranged flowers, . . . and heard nothing more till about 11 p.m. when Bob Boothby rang up. Anthony Eden is with him at French House. He told me extraordinary things, which I swore not to repeat to anyone but Walter. Baldwin has been in closest touch with Anthony all the week—advising him what to do. Baldwin is of opinion that the country will not stand Neville's Government much longer, and that if things go on as they are, not one of the present Cabinet will have the least chance of getting back. Anthony must come forward very soon. Baldwin

27. Konrad Henlein: Leader of the Sudetendeutsche Partei.
28. During that weekend there had been rumours of German troop concentrations along the Czech border. In response the Czech Government ordered partial mobilization. It later transpired that the rumours were without foundation.

advises him to go to the House tomorrow, and sit there for the next two days—in case it is necessary for him to speak in the Air Debate on Wednesday. Bob had a list of the Government of National Safety in his pocket, worked out between him and Anthony. He read it to me over the telephone. I can't remember it all: Anthony—P.M.; Lord Halifax—Lord President; Archie Sinclair—F.O.; Winston—Supply; Attlee, Dalton,[29] Morrison[30] all in somewhere; Malcolm—Colonies; Shakes Morrison—something; Buck—War (Anthony won't have Hore-Belisha at any price!); Walter—Health.

June 24th—London . . . went to Zionist Office where was Chaim, immensely happy after an interview with Lord Winterton,[31] whom he had never spoken to before. He put several ideas about Evian[32] into his head—notably to tell the Germans that if they want to get rid of the Jews, they must leave them some of their own money. As for Palestine, Lord Winterton had told him that he was 'sick of the Arabs', and that he thought H.M.G. had behaved very unfairly in not implementing partition.

June 28th Dined at home with Edgar and after dinner went to see Chaim who was alone. He gave me an account of his most extraordinary day: (1) He saw a man who will help him to get the Daniel Sieff Institute in on the Oil Refinery now being started in Palestine. (2) By an extraordinary series of coincidences, he got in touch with one Ginsburg—a Turkish Jew, the Ataturk's[33] dentist and *homme de confiance*. Through him, Chaim may get his hand on the political and economic development of Turkey—and *immense* possibilities. (3) A telegram from the U.S.A. urging Chaim to go to Evian. As I sat alone with him, listening to the weaving of his great thoughts on all these mighty affairs, I felt that they are right who say that the Jews are all-powerful (and yet—*how* impotent!). But it would be terrible if the power and the influence were under evil direction. But when one is with Chaim one feels the infinite nobility of soul—the vast intellect—and knows that here is one of God's greatest instruments. But was there ever a man more full of human weaknesses, as well as human power of suffering? In Chaim there is *everything*.

July 11th—London . . . Dined with Chaim and Vera. Eva Reading came in after. Terribly depressed by her own first impacts with anti-Semitism. It

29. Hugh Dalton: Labour M.P.; Minister of Economic Warfare, 1940-42; President of Board of Trade, 1942-45, Chancellor of Exchequer, 1945-47; of Duchy of Lancaster, 1948-50.
30. Herbert Morrison: Labour M.P.; Minister of Supply, 1940; Secretary for Home Office and Home Security, 1940-45; Member of War Cabinet, 1942-45; Lord President, 1945-51; Foreign Secretary, 1951. Cr. Life Peer, 1959.
31. Earl Winterton: Chief British delegate at Evian conference.
32. The Evian conference, 6-15 July, was convened on the initiative of the U.S. to provide solutions for the European refugee problem. Thirty-two countries participated. But no striking decisions were taken at Evian; the conference became the occasion for much sophistry and speechifying, but little action.
33. Mustapha Kemal: President of Turkey.

is terrible for her, brought up as an English girl, and she sees it affecting her children. Chaim treated her with all the deep wisdom of the ghetto. He spoke almost wistfully of its shelter in the old days. Now that shelter is only found in the Yishuv. Would to God I could help these people! But I can never touch the depths of their affliction. Even Jimmy de Rothschild, with all the staff of the Ritz bowing and running to serve him, told me with panic that on the golf course at Hoylake (?) this morning they found a swastika, and 'Down with the Jews' painted on a putting-green.

July 14th—London   Edgar and I went to Terrace of House for a great tea-party of Victor's, previous to inauguration of the *Eva Reading*—a Jewish motor-boat manned by Jewish sea-scouts, about to start for Palestine. We all went to the Speaker's Steps to see it. I never thought to see the blue-and-white flag of Zion float on a craft in the River Thames—from the Terrace of the House. A good augury!

I said so at a meeting where I spoke tonight in Whitechapel. About 300 Delegates from Synagogues and Friendly Societies. I made a good speech . . . I got a tremendous reception. Barney Janner also spoke well. Went with him after to Bloom's Kosher Restaurant off Whitechapel Road, and then for a stroll through the deserted 'Lane', and he told me many interesting things about East End Jewish customs. These are the good Jews of England—it is like a breath of fresh air to go among them.

July 15th—London   Last night Chaim imparted to me the latest development of his 'apocalyptic' programme—namely to call in U.S.A., probably in October, a Conference of world Jewry under auspices of (say) himself, Einstein, Blum! This is the answer to the wretchedly inadequate results of Evian. If the negotiations with H.M.G. are successfully over by then, such a Conference will be a tremendous pro-British demonstration. If not—then not! Chaim says he cannot leave the destinies of the Jewish people in the hands of Mr Woodhead and Co.[34] at this hour—nor even in the hands of Malcolm MacDonald. I told Walter on telephone, by Chaim's request. I thought him impressed and rather alarmed. Chaim is right. He gains initiative this way.

July 26th—London   Went to House of Commons and listened to nearly all of the last Debate on Foreign Affairs for four months. A great triumph for H.M.G. as there was practically no criticism—I can't think why the Liberals raised it at all. But the peculiar thing was that nobody (except little G. Mander[35] just a little) perceived or mentioned the incredible thing that

34. Sir John Woodhead: Chairman of the Technical Commission sent to Palestine to propose frontiers for the Jewish and Arab states; the other commissioners were, Sir A. Russell, Mr A. P. Waterfield, and Mr T. Reid. See entry for 14 September 1937.
35. Geoffrey Le Mesurier Mander: Liberal M.P. for East Wolverhampton, 1929–45; Parliamentary Private Secretary to Sir A. Sinclair, 1942-45. Kt. 1945.

Nevill has done today—appointed Lord Runciman[36] to go to Czechoslovakia as a sort of adviser or mediator.

Had a long talk with Walter about it on Terrace after House over. We agreed (1) it brings England back on to the map of Europe for good or evil, with a vengeance and decisively. (2) Whether Runciman succeeds or fails, things cannot be the same again. (3) Neville is probably too stupid to perceive the implications of what he has done. (4) He has completely regained the initiative over Anthony. If Runciman succeeds it is Neville's doing (he did not consult his Cabinet). If Runciman fails, Anthony was in the House today and never said a word.

September 6th—London   I left Caponflat yesterday morning, and met Walter in Caledonian Hotel before lunch. . . .

World situation—chances of war and peace about 50/50. French have told us they will accept Runciman's verdict![37] Walter says that makes him (for the moment) the second most powerful man in the world. Hitler, alas, being Number One. Who would have thought a year ago that nobody knows or cares where Anthony Eden is, and that all eyes should be on Runciman!

As for Palestine. Sitting in Princess Street Gardens, I read hastily a long document issued by Malcolm MacDonald to his colleagues. Obvious from it that the Peel Plan will probably be greatly reduced—that no frontier will be forced upon the Jews—that probably Chaim will be confronted with the hideous decision of advising acceptance or rejection of what Walter called for short 'a Tel-Aviv concentration camp'—the alternative to acceptance being most likely a continuance of the Mandate with all its restrictions on immigration, thus accepting a permanent minority status. What a terrible decision! I am not sure whether the present leadership could survive it. Walter is, of course, passionately anxious that the Jews should accept any territory in sovereign power—however small—provided it backs on to sea. He says we must all realize the old policies, the old promises, are broken and gone—since the Zurich Congress last year Jewry is broken—Austria and now Italy.[38] They must establish themselves somehow—make Tel-Aviv a second London—live in streets, not fields, if need be—but *live,* not die. Make a City-State like Venice. Do not think of shattered hopes—think of getting out of present Hell—and so on and so forth. Wonderful stuff—but is it possible to bring them to it? Will it indeed be necessary?

36. Viscount Runciman: President of the Board of Trade, 1935–37; Lord President of the Council, 1938–39; was sent to Prague as an unofficial mediator between the Sudeten Germans and the Czechs.
37. His first report indicated arrangements whereby the Sudeten Germans could receive satisfaction within Czechoslovakia. Later during the crisis, when it became apparent that Hitler would accept nothing less than self-determination, Runciman re-drafted his report to recommend Hitler's wish.
38. The Fascist Grand Council decided upon a programme of anti-Semitic legislation during the summer of 1938.

Dined alone with Chaim at Addison Crescent,[39] talked till midnight,
picking up all dropped threads. Two things are going well: his idea for a
big Jewish loan, and Jewish relations with Turkey. This may be a very
important card in the future.

September 7th—London This morning *The Times* threw out the suggestion that the Czechs might consider ceding the Sudeten territory outright!
This is an amazing suggestion from a responsible paper at such a moment.
Can H.M.G. be behind it? Buck spoke on telephone—highly agitated. I
have always thought (I mean earlier this summer) that it might have paid
the Czechs to do this, together with a big plan for exchange of populations,
in spite of the obvious difficulties—but *now,* under threat, obviously quite
impossible.

September 14th—Redcliff, Whittingehame[40] Perhaps one should write
down *now* the prediction which I heard while at Strachur, that the European war will begin on September 16th.

The first post brought a letter from Walter in London, written yesterday.
He says:

'Well, there's Nuremberg[41] over. It is clear that the first Government
contention was right—that the steps taken to secure that the final
Nuremberg speech would not kick over the bucket would succeed. The
bucket was not kicked over; therefore the steps taken were adequate.
Apart from that, the only difference is that yesterday was the 12th September and this is the 13th. The real situation is not changed at all.
Mobilization in every country is in fact still proceeding. We are not under
any illusion in the matter. The Nuremberg speech could have been made
by a leader who was preparing to accept terms. It could also, have been
made by a leader who was preparing a coup, and didn't want to give any
plans or dates away. There is a good deal of evidence for the latter view,
of course.

'I was much interested in your report of L.N.U. attitude as to intolerable pressure being put on the Czechs.[42] That can only be coming
from the Czechs, and it does make me sympathize with Runciman in his
efforts to get these very obstinate people to *do* something. So far the net
results of the Runciman mission have been a handful of postmasters. . . .
That's not to say, of course that G. Dawson wasn't one of the biggest
fools in Christendom to blow off Secession as a public statement in the

39. 16 Addison Crescent, W.14, Weizmann's London home.
40. The home of Lord Traprain, afterwards 3rd Earl of Balfour, on the Whittingehame estate.
41. 12 September was the last day of the Nazi party rally at Nuremberg. It was generally
      accepted that Hitler would then make public his solution for the Czech problem.
42. Mrs Dugdale had received this information from Jan Masaryk [Czech Minister to Great
      Britain, 1925–38; of Foreign Affairs, 1940–48]. He described the pressure as 'inhuman'.

midst of the Tug-of-War. Runciman gave him a good solid slamming from Prague, and so did H.M.G.'

. . . The six o'clock News had nothing much. But the Third News gave the startling information that Neville has decided to fly to Germany tomorrow to see Hitler.

September 15th—London Here before breakfast. Rang up Walter first. He said Neville's journey was a sort of last chance—no very settled plan. (But I have a fear it will lead to their pressing the Czechs to agree to a plebiscite.) Walter thought the danger is that people will expect magical results, and be proportionately disappointed. Spoke also to Colin, who on the whole thought Neville was right to go.

Chaim trysted Lewis and me to lunch at the Carlton Grill, where we sat till past 3 p.m. hearing resumé of two talks he had had with Malcolm MacDonald—one on the 13th, the second last night at his own house, from 9.45 p.m. till 12.30 a.m.—the two of them alone.

First talk mainly concerned with Security Measures—*very* satisfactory—more Jewish supernumeraries, more troops, Tegart flying out tomorrow as member of General Haining's Staff, and police to be under (his) military orders.

Second talk: future policy. Both agreed that nothing they said should be binding, or to be quoted against them. They arrived at ground of agreement on one or two points:

(a) The whole situation largely due to bungling, and ineptitude. Responsibility for it lies on Palestine Government *and* H.M.G. This is the first time any Minister has ever admitted such a thing to the Jews. (I should say that M.M. took the initiative in talking throughout this conversation.)

(b) The Mandate was, and is, workable. Although Chaim seems to have admitted this in principle, he pointed out that it could only be *if* conditions in Palestine were quite different from what they ever have been.

Malcolm said he remains a Partitionist, even from Arab point of view. He warned Chaim of difficulties ahead. He pooh-poohed Arab opinion in Palestine and Transjordan—even in Syria and Egypt—but took graver view of Ibn Sa'ud's opposition. Ibn Sa'ud is not our dependent. He controls the Mecca routes, etc., etc. If Chaim could get from him some such declaration as he once got from Feisal,[43] the Arab trouble could be disregarded.

Chaim asked what made Malcolm MacDonald think that Ibn Sa'ud would really be a formidable opponent to British policy in Palestine? Would

43. King Feisal of Iraq, 1921–33: Leader of the Arab revolt, 1916–19; represented the Arabs at the Paris peace conference; signed an abortive agreement of cooperation with Weizmann in January 1919.

he throw away British friendship? Would he bring his desert Arabs out of the desert, where they are formidable, to attack modern troops elsewhere? Fifty thousand Jews would 'beat him to a frazzle'. Face Ibn Sa'ud with a *fait accompli,* and he would accept it. It seems that M.M. did not deny this.

Speaking of the present situation and its repercussions, Chaim said: 'If it is War—then the Jews will once more count for something. If it is a real Peace, then the Jews will count for something. It is only while the kind of *"peace"* which we now have persists that the Jews count for nothing. If peace is kept at the price of betrayal of Czechoslovakia, there will be War in six months.

They are to meet again on Saturday, when Chaim and Ben-Gurion spend the afternoon in Malcolm's house in Essex. I am glad Ben-Gurion goes, for he is firm against prolonging the Mandate. He has become sadly anti-British.

Malcolm indicated that if the Mandate (or another in a different form) were renewed, there would be a return to 'absorptive capacity'—to be interpreted 'for a year or two' in a very 'conservative spirit'. This alarmingly bears out Walter's warnings (see September 6th). Malcolm does not yet know what is the Commission's Report. Chaim spoke to him again frankly about our knowledge of the 'Harris Plan.'[44]

Lewis was anxious that Chaim should 'cash in' at their next talk on Malcolm MacDonald's admissions about the Administration, and ask for the removal of Keith-Roach and Crosbie.[45] I felt doubtful about this, and later, after further talk with Lewis, telephoned Chaim suggesting that Professor Coupland might be asked to suggest it. It is true that these men (especially Keith-Roach) have deliberately sabotaged the Peel policy, and are virulent, open, anti-Semites.

Walter dined here alone with me. Extraordinary revelations on European situation, especially French attitude. He told me of the wonderful timing of Neville's flight. He had conceived the idea before Hitler's speech, and no doubt talked it over with Neville Henderson[46]—but it might be called 'Plan Z'—only to be operated in desperate resort. It became plain from the telegrams on Tuesday afternoon (13th) that the situation was deteriorating. Neville wired to Hitler *before* consulting Cabinet or telling the French. There was no leakage. At one time he thought of wiring to Hitler from the air, but abandoned that idea. They were quite prepared for a refusal. That would probably have meant War. We should have sent out the Mobilization Order. It seems quite likely that if Neville had not come Hitler would have entered Czechoslovakia on Tuesday night. Whatever comes of it—certainly Neville has stolen Hitler's carefully built-up effects for this week. The eyes of the world are on him tonight, and not on the Fuehrer. Apparently he is

44. Yet another partition plan concocted by the Palestine administration.
45. Two high officials in the Palestine administration. Keith-Roach served as Commissioner of the Jerusalem district; Crosbie, as Commissioner of the southern district.
46. Sir Neville Henderson: British Ambassador to Germany, 1937–39.

going to tell Hitler that if he wants England's friendship he is not going the right way about it. He may summon Runciman to meet him. He may propose Runciman as an arbitrator—either side to accept his award. He may do worse things! But it looks like a *détente* of two or three days any-how—which may be an eternity. Parliament will probably be summoned next week, just to hear Neville's report.

September 12th—London   Chaim observed that he thought Benes[47] more to be pitied than himself if things go wrong with Palestine. For Czecho-slovakia *is* a State, has been a going concern for 20 years. I think Chaim is coming round to the idea of a Federated Palestine—undivided—with an in-dependent Jewish State as one of its parts. This reminds us of the plan worked out by Lewis, self and Arthur Lourie last December[48] just before I went to Palestine, which we could not persuade anybody to look at then.

September 17th—London   A day of suspense. Walter spoke to me before the morning Cabinet, knowing then nothing—and rang up after lunch to say Cabinet was resuming. I lunched with the Weizmanns. Vera came back last night from Paris. Chaim saw Jan Masaryk last night—he said: 'We have nothing more we can sell now.' He was far more confident about Russian help than Walter was, and said the Czech and Russian General Staffs were conferring even now. Every indication seems to be that the Czechs will not allow anybody to settle their destiny. I stayed most of the afternoon playing bezique with Vera—a soothing occupation—and then came home, lest Walter should ring up, which he did about six, saying we could dine together. He only said over telephone that nothing is definite, and that the French Ministers are coming to London tomorrow. He said that the French seem to be 'coming round' a bit.

He came at eight. We dined at Scott's and went to an excellent film *The Rage of Paris*. Gradually, at dinner and after, I heard bits and pieces of what happened today. Neville full of his journey—Hitler's appearance—'the commonest little fellow I ever saw', etc. Hitler announced that what he wanted was 'self-determination'. I asked whether Neville had enquired what he meant by that. Walter said no; he answered that the Cabinet had not empowered him to discuss this subject. I have the impression that Neville has today been pressing the Cabinet to let him discuss it. I gather that the Egerland[49] was mentioned, and the Czechs *might* give way on that—so it is said. But I can hardly believe it—it is a leak in the dam, and once you let the water in anywhere, where can you stop it? I think they came to no conclusions today—they are waiting on the French—and above all on what Russia will do. If Russia moves, we shall all move—because the Left everywhere would insist on Russia not being let down.

47. Eduard Benes: Foreign Minister of Czechoslovakia, 1918–35; President, 1935–38.
48. See the entry for 19 December, 1937.
49. Czech border district.

Runciman gave them a description of the Czech Government in his precise little way. Benes—a man of very agile mind—'more honest than he appears at first sight to be'. Hodza[50]—'intelligent, but very limited'. The rest—'very mediocre, very mediocre indeed'—'the calibre of one of Franklin Roosevelt's Cabinets let us say'.

September 18th—London This day began by my being wakened to hear Buck was on the telephone. He was here before I had finished breakfast and stayed till 11. He was in a state of mind. Told me, what I had not realized from what Walter said, that the Cabinet virtually authorized Neville yesterday to propose to the French to negotiate on 'self-determination'. Buck felt he ought to have made clear yesterday that he reserved his position. He spoke to Lord Winterton (who is one of the dissident group) from this house, and told him his scruples. Lord Winterton replied he thought the group had made their position quite clear to Neville yesterday. Walter later confirmed this—he is one of the group—the others being, besides Buck and Lord Winterton—Oliver,[51] Duff-Cooper, and (Buck believes, though he said nothing yesterday in Cabinet) Hore-Belisha. But what a position! They are going to resign if 'the terms' are not to their liking—e.g. they would sell the Egerland, but no more. I told Buck then and Walter later that this is a hopelessly weak position. Buck said to me: 'Tell Walter that if he goes I will.' I replied I would give no such message. Later he modified it to: 'Tell Walter that if he goes he will not go alone.' I urged Buck all I could to *go*. For one thing (though I did not say this) he will count for nothing if he stays; if he resigns, he may help to make a nucleus.

After dinner we[52] settled down to a game of poker, in midst of which Lewis rang up and told us three very interesting things:

(a) The French Ministers are *still* here and after a morning and afternoon session decided to meet again at 9.30 p.m.—but kept the British Ministers waiting till 10.18.

(b) Jan Masaryk told Seton-Watson[53] this afternoon that the Czechs would not agree to any plebiscite, anywhere. (I think he does not know that Benes had agreed to losing the Egerland).

(c) There was a letter from Benes to Chamberlain and Daladier[54] on the tape tonight, saying he would not agree to any solution settled over his head.

It all looks to me like War.

50. Prime Minister of Czechoslovakia.
51. Oliver Stanley: Minister of Transport, 1933–34; of Labour, 1934–35; President of Board of Education, 1935–37; of Board of Trade, 1937–40; Secretary of State for War, 1940; for Colonies, 1942–45.
52. Mrs Dugdale, Walter Elliot, Colin and Denise Coote.
53. R. W. Seton-Watson: Masaryk Professor of Central European History at University of London.
54. Edouard Daladier: Prime Minister of France, 1938–40.

September 19th—London   Lunched at Carlton Grill alone with Chaim—who was deeply pessimistic about general situation—predicted abandonment of Czechs and all pledges, consequent decline of France as a great Power, and war and Bolshevism all over Europe very soon. Spent p.m. at home. . . .

I wrote all this before tea—when I expected the American, Mr Ben Cohen (a friend of Felix Frankfurter), whom I had never seen before. As he entered the room, I heard Archie Sinclair's voice on the telephone. From him I first heard the news of how H.M.G. had *unanimously* given away the Sudeten districts where the majority was 75 per cent German. During his visit, Colin spoke, and added that he heard there had never been a more harmonious Cabinet—that there is to be an exchange of populations—that they expect the Czechs to accept it—and are only doubtful whether it will be good enough for Hitler. To finish this part of my miserable experiences, after dinner at Chaim's, I spoke to Seton-Watson, who said that Jan is heart-broken, and that the Russians have said they cannot move alone. And while Malcolm MacDonald was with Chaim, he got a message saying the Czech Cabinet had sent an interim reply—which is more acquiescent than refusing. So that is that. There is neither honour nor courage anywhere it seems. I have not heard a word from Walter. On Sunday (only yesterday) he told me that he had made it plain that if he had to choose between giving in altogether and War, he would choose War.

Seton-Watson said no doubt this guaranteed State would have to be disarmed—and the Germans would have the Skoda Works almost at once.

Chaim, Vera, David Ben-Gurion and I dined together, and Vera and I played bezique (in a sort of way) while Malcolm MacDonald was with the other two from 9 till 12. Then he left—we did not see him—and Chaim told us the gist of the conversation. They are going to sell the Jews also—give up Partition, for fear of the Arabs and the Germans and the Italians. This is what it amounts to—wrapped up in words, of course—and it will be some weeks before the Report is made public. We are all stunned. Ben-Gurion's first reaction—and mine—was that the Jews will fight, physically, rather than go back to the Mandate as it will be. Chaim said nothing much.

September 20th—London . . . Talked to Walter. After some discussion, decided he should come to dinner tonight. Spoke also to Archie Sinclair, to apologize for not believing him last night. I asked if I could do anything to help; he said: Try to get Anthony into the open—he is the only leader for the former Government supporters. This is not my job—I do not know Anthony well enough. I told Colin, however. I urged Archie to press for a meeting of Parliament—even if it does give Neville a majority; their plan of making all this a *fait accompli* without summoning Parliament is an abrogation of Parliamentary Government, as well as all else. I said this to Colin, who warmly agreed, and said he might even get something like that into *The Times*.

Then I wrote to Buck, resigning membership of the National Labour Party. Then, before posting the letter, I spoke to Harold Nicolson. He had dined last night with Buck and Walter. He said Walter had been very 'persuasive'—had told him that he (Harold) was a 'sentimentalist'. Thinking it all over in the night, H. concluded that there was little in Walter's arguments. *The Times* leader this morning finished him. He said to himself: 'If this what supporting the Government involves, then I am not for it.' I gather he is writing to Buck also to resign membership. He is in touch with Anthony—could not disclose to me his attitude, but said 'he has not dissapointed me.'[55]

After I talked to Harold (or it may have been just before) Seton-Watson rang up. He had been in touch this morning with an English friend (Mr Griffin or Griffith) in Prague. So far (12 noon) the Czech Government had not sent a reply. They are said to be preparing counter-proposals. But the feature of this morning's situation is the enormous influx of *German* refugees out of the Sudeten area *into* Czechoslovakia. So many as to be a serious embarrassment to the Administration. Seton-Watson was told of further steps the Czechs are taking. Firstly sending out leading men into all foreign capitals to be their spokesmen if the worst comes. They will not be put in Schuschnigg's position in that respect. The Director of National Art Collections is putting together and despatching abroad materials for first-class exhibitions of Czech Art and culture.

Seton-Watson feels like me about the summoning of Parliament.

Before lunch, Chaim spoke to me. He wants a conference tomorrow morning on his talk with Malcolm last night. He is going to see Jan at 7 p.m. tonight. Jan is ill in bed today. Little wonder!

Lunched alone. Lewis came about 3, and stayed for tea. He foresees the early break-up of Europe as we know it, and widespread Bolshevization. France irretrievably sunk to position of Sweden—an ex-Great Power.

As for Palestine—he favours Chaim warning Malcolm MacDonald that he is not going to be disposed of in a gentlemanly way—not led to the altar of sacrifice conversing amiably like poor Benes. He will not enter into talks on any such basis as MacDonald's conversation last night. This is the right policy, I think, but must not be operated before we see the Woodhead Report. But from now on there should be more reserve in talks with Malcolm MacDonald—and none should be sought by the Jews.

While Lewis was here, Seton-Watson rang up to say he had seen Jan. Latest from Prague—that the Government has refused the terms, but is preparing others to put forward. Also that the Czechs will fight. Rumours from Berlin that they seem flustered there, and much against negotiations. Will they march tonight, I wonder?

Walter dined with me—and argued his point of view with the usual plausibility. He admitted that when he said to me on Sunday night that he

55. For Nicolson version, see N. Nicolson, ed., *op. cit.*, pp. 334–55.

preferred war to surrender, he did not know 'the terms' were so stiff. But he still feels them to be within the bounds of that for which he would not ask the British to shed their blood. To use his formula, he will fight for Prague, but not for Carlsbad—because he does not believe that at the end of a bloody war you could demand that Carlsbad be restored to the Czechs, but you would Prague. He affirms that he *can* pull himself up somewhere on this slippery slope of concessions to Hitler.

While he was here, Chaim rang up to say Jan had told him that Benes' answer will be received here tonight. It is a refusal—but an offer to negotiate cession of territory on an 80 per cent basis of Germans. This, if true, of course strengthened Walter's argument that it is a question of degree. Lewis, who rang up still later, was quite horrified when I told him. He said: 'Then they are selling themselves.'

Well, I think considering I spent all day indoors with my bad foot, I have amassed a good deal of information. *Personally,* I am happier than last night.

September 21st—London   A Conference at the Zionist Office this morning. Present: Chaim, Ben-Gurion, Lewis, Berl Katznelson, Berl Locker, Brodetsky, Arthur Lourie and self. Chaim reported on his talk with Malcolm on Monday night, expressed his opinion that the Partition Policy has been abandoned by H.M.G. (as he believes) at the bidding of Hitler and Mussolini. He spoke solemnly of the need for the Jews to return to their traditional policy of relying on themselves alone—not on Babylon—not on Assyria—not on Egypt—and now, not on the British Empire. Though, to him, Chaim, reliance on Britain had hitherto been as the 'Rock of Gibraltar'. But now his policy would be uncompromising hostility to Britain—to work, silently at first, towards arming and preparation, which in time (he knew not how long) would enable Jewry to pursue its own policy in the Middle East. In the meantime, a break with the British was not possible—but he personally would not negotiate again with Malcolm. Chaim was called away, and left the room without saying anything more. Ben-Gurion expressed general agreement, but vehemently urged that Chaim should not break off with Malcolm. Ben-Gurion then said that Chaim had given no indication whatever of withdrawing his confidence from Malcolm MacDonald on Monday night—in fact his last words had been that he looked on MacDonald as the best friend—it would be as injudicious as impossible to break with him without another interview, and it would be very bad to continue negotiations without Chaim, as it would give the impression that the Agency and he were not of one mind. I was asked to put these considerations to him, and another conference was fixed for Friday morning.

Then Chaim and I went to the Carlton Grill, where we lunched with Peter Rutenberg, who arrived yesterday from Palestine. His account of the utter breakdown of law and order there passed even what I had imagined. He burns with indignation, and the intention of rousing Malcolm and public opinion here. There was on him still the reflex of Palestinians to whom the Czech crisis is not all-absorbing. Also the habit of hope—which Chaim has quite lost, and me very nearly. Before the end of lunch, Peter had realized something of our mood. I came home, and took up my post by the telephone. Before long Seton-Watson rang up—gave me my first certain news that the Czech Government has surrendered to the terms—and told me that they did so on the official intimation made by the British and French Ministers in their visit in the small hours today that unless they gave in, unconditionally and at once, French support would be withdrawn. Seton-Watson asked me to spread this news, in the faint, forlorn hope that public opinion here might be so roused as to influence Neville before he flies to Godeberg tomorrow.

I thereupon called up Archie Sinclair, and told him. He said that he had written to Downing Street asking again for meeting of Parliament, but was sure there would be no change in the refusal given to Attlee. I also spoke to Colin; he said he would talk to Geoffrey Dawson, but had no hope. The best hope is that Hitler may overplay his hand when he sees Neville tomorrow, and demand even further concessions. He hears that this is not impossible. Also he hears that Neville is very disappointed at the lukewarm reception given to his peace efforts! ! He had heard of growing discontent in France, and of the possibility of the fall of the French Government. As for Cabinet gossip—he had heard that Walter had not let out one word of protest at the terms, and Oliver Stanley's had been the only voice raised. But I always take these stories with more than a grain of salt unless they come from the horse's own mouth. Colin talks of the Cabinet—and especially of the group of whom we had such high hopes a few days ago—as 'the rubber stamps'.

September 22nd—Mersham-le-Hatch   Lunched at Club with Walter. Long talk. As far as I can understand, his attitude is that he would fight rather than force the Czechs to give up Teschen and Grosser Schutt. Why? Because if Hitler demanded those, Walter would be convinced (which it seems he is not as yet) that Hitler was out to dismember Czecho. This seems to me an idiotic position—but I record it. He professes himself so satisfied with what H.M.G. have done up to now, as being in the *Czechs' own interests,* as well as in the interests of peace, that he would not shrink from proclaiming on any platform how chivalrous we have been.

I cannot understand him. But anyhow, I believe now he will resign rather than submit to the next demand.

September 23rd—London   Walter met me at the theatre—*Banana Ridge.* We laughed heartily. Came out—papers selling everywhere—'Chamberlain flies home'. Walter gave a gasp, and said: 'This is the last play you will see for a long time.' From the Savoy he rang up somewhere, and heard that although Chamberlain flies home tomorrow, he is seeing Hitler again tonight.

So it may be there is still a chance. But Walter told me Chamberlain had reported this morning 'very unsatisfactory', and that the thing is that Hitler is determined to occupy Sudeten territory at once. Terrible as it is, my mind is at peace once more—the Cabinet will surely stand firm, and the horrors of the past week can surely be forgotten until the time comes (if it ever does) for historical recriminations.

I dropped Walter at Admiralty House towards midnight, after we had had something to eat at the Savoy, which was full of people—calm and full as usual. Also Whitehall was quite quiet tonight. Telephoned to the Weizmanns on getting home. They were up, and I went round. We sat for an hour—listening at first to the Voices of the World. A German telling atrocity stories about Sudetenland—a Czech reciting all the mobilization instructions (for they ordered full mobilization this evening). Chaim said Lord Halifax had sent for Jan about 6 p.m. and told him Britain had advised this, and would stand by them. Jan (apparently) said he had heard as much before. Lord Halifax repeated that he had sent the word to Prague. The most extraordinary story, though, is from Jan through Israel Sieff—Jan called yesterday on the Runcimans. Lord Runciman said he thought it right that the 80 per cent German territories should go back. Jan said: '80 per cent—but it is 50 per cent!' Runciman: 'Nonsense.' Jan: 'But I have the written proof of it.' Whereupon Runciman broke down, and said: 'Then they have lied to me, and deceived me, too.'

The future is all dark. Walter said: 'Perhaps God is doing all this so that the Jews may go back to Palestine. I believe that will be the result.'

September 24th　　Woke to read rumours of fresh demands to be made by Chamberlain on Czechs! When I spoke to Walter at 10, he knew nothing—nor of course would he commit himself to any line of action or of resistance. The telephone calls this morning included one from Bob Boothby, for the first time since the crisis—he got back from Geneva last night, where he talked with Litvinov.[56] Litvinov said the Russians had been incredibly badly handled by France and England. Bob was of opinion that even now, today, war might be averted by a firm Anglo-French-Russian declaration.

About 6 p.m. Seton-Watson rang up. He said that at about 4 p.m. Lord Halifax asked Jan to come to the Foreign Office, and handed him Hitler's new terms—he wants 'all the booty' of the surrendered areas, and a plebiscite in certain others under German supervision. 'Utterly unacceptable,' Seton-Watson says. The Czechs *could* not, even if they would. Halifax told Jan that Chamberlain was convinced that if Hitler got this he would ask no more, but proceed to discuss a general European settlement. Jan replied that he was very credulous.

September 25th—London　　Walter telephoned to say he was going out to

56. Maxim Litvinov: Soviet Minister for Foreign Affairs, 1930–39.

I

Oliver Stanley's before Cabinet. He would not say anything more. From that much I try to gather faith.

10.20 a.m.—Hannah telephoned. Buck De la Warr had just spoken to her, but had said no more than Walter. Her impression was not unlike mine—there is no reason to lose faith. She said Derrick had some good names on his letter[57] to the P.M.

. . . 12.20 p.m.—Bob Boothby . . . He, too, realizes that Czechs *cannot* accept. Says this Cabinet must be hurled from power, whatever happens—being, as Winston says, unfit to conduct either a peace or a war. I agree, and only pray that Walter may make such small reparation as is in his power by resigning today—or by forcing repudiation of Hitler's terms. Bob shares my sense that the tide of feeling is rising in our favour.

. . . Lunched alone. About 3 p.m. Seton-Watson came with draft of a letter or statement. We discussed draft, and possible signatories, till he had to go to Czech Legation. Then Namier arrived, and I went on working at the letter with him till 5 p.m., when he left. . . .

Seton-Watson came back at tea-time from the Czech Legation, with the certain news that Jan is instantly to deliver to Lord Halifax the uncompromising NO of his Government. Seton-Watson saw Jan for a moment between his return from Chartwell (Winston) and his visit to Downing Street—or the F.O., I am not sure which, for I believe the P.M. had asked to see him. Jan has his tail up for the first time for days. We worked on at the statement. Round about 6, Walter rang up. He *said* that he had no news—but he gave me the feeling that the Rubber Stampers are changing back into Men—and he hinted that Lord Halifax is coming over to them. Cabinet sit again tonight, when the French Ministers arrive—and they will all be in session next door while the Old Brutes[58] are seeing the French. So *that* idea has got across. Directly after, Namier rang up to say, from a sure source, that the French Cabinet, after a terrific row this afternoon, has reached agreement and not split. Which must mean that it is standing firm. And the Czech NO must be decisive.

. . . After dinner, Rob Bernays rang up, just back from Geneva. Dizzy with the impact and horror of London. Having seen Litvinov, he is full of the criminal clumsiness of the way the Russians have been handled.

I think an awful retribution is preparing for the Cabinet. If there is really a firm stand taken today, and if by some miracle it is still in time to stop war—then *what* an indictment of the policy of surrender, and the rage and humiliation of the nation will vent itself (and rightly) on them. If, as seems almost inevitable, there is war, Neville could no longer unite the nation. Bob Cecil thinks that the War Prime Minister would and should be Winston. Bob wants a predominantly Conservative Government, and would therefore include some Rubber Stampers, but of course none of the Old Brutes nor

---

57. Sir Derrick Gunston: He had sent a letter to Chamberlain together with Boothby and others demanding 'no more pressure on the Czechs'.
58. i.e. Neville Chamberlain, Sir John Simon and Sir Samuel Hoare.

Halifax. I said I felt that *none* of the present Cabinet had shown themselves fit to govern in peace or war. The Rubber Stampers had committed the crime of accepting responsibility without power. They should have resigned. Bob, standing on his own doorstep to bid me goodbye, said: 'Do not judge them too harshly; resignations are difficult and unpleasant things to carry through.'

What splendour, what courage, what nobility of soul! If he were only twenty years younger!

About 11 p.m. I talked again to Chaim on the telephone, and told him my prediction of retribution. He said: No, that is bad psychology. If we have peace, the relief will be so great that people will forget their wrath, and only remember that they have been somehow saved from war under their present rulers.

September 26th—London Michael, Edgar and I dined at home and listened to the English resumé of the speech delivered by Hitler at 8 p.m. tonight. The speech of a maniac—the only ray of hope being that he seems to be sticking to October 1st for attack. That gives us four days more—perhaps. Spoke to Chaim, and Colin, who was the first to tell me, about 11 p.m., that the Foreign Office have put out a very good, firm, declaration tonight. But will it not be too late to save us? The Cabinet seem to be unanimous at last; Colin says the French Ministers went back to Paris very satisfied about that.

The late news told of Territorials called up and volunteers needed for Air Raid Wardens, and for digging trenches in the Parks. Michael says he does not think he will take on A.R.P. work until he sees whether he ought to join the Army. No indications have been given yet to people like him.

September 27th—London Walter spoke at length on telephone for first time for some days. Appeared certain that Neville will have a great reception when the House meets tomorrow, and that there will be no question at all of enlarging base of Government or changing leadership. I was imbued with the belief that there ought to be a Government of National Concentration immediately, and that the participation of Labour would be much easier if Neville were no longer P.M. I spoke to Philip Baker, to try and get confirmation of my views—but failed, except so far as he personally was concerned. He said that he had never heard discussion in the Labour Party of that sort of question so far, so could not express any view.

When I went out at midday, there was a long queue at our Public Library, getting gas-masks. Edgar and the servants got theirs today. I had no time. Talked to Stew about stores and arrangements.

Went in a 'bus to tea with Chaim. Trenches were being dug in Kensington Gardens, as in all the Parks, for Air Raid Shelters. At Chaim's saw

Meyer Weisgal[59] just landed from U.S.A.—en route for Palestine. Chaim asked him whether there were many Zionists in America who would come over to fight for Britain in Palestine or elsewhere. He answered confidently: 'Countless thousands.' We have had no time to discuss Zionist Policy at all . . . But here is a card in Chaim's hand.

I then went off to the Caledonian Club to meet Walter. There was Cabinet at 9.30 so we only had an hour and a half together. He is, I am sure, genuinely sure that the main line of Cabinet policy has been right. Says he is content to have had 'responsibility without power'—that any P.M. has the right to have, and to choose, his camarilla of advisers—that 22 men cannot all have a say—that their power consists in resignation etc. I think all this *unutterably* wrong.

I did not hear the P.M.'s broadcast—but was home to hear the repetition on Third News—*most* lamentable in tone. I only hope it may complete the conversion of my friends to my point of view! . . . Is the man mad? And then it was translated into German, so that Hitler would be sure to understand that Chamberlain had said tonight that he would not fight for a small nation![60] Good God!

September 28th—London   Before breakfast, Derrick Gunston on telephone, wild with bewilderment and grief at the P.M.'s broadcast. Bob Boothby the same shortly after—and, as he said he was going to ring up Walter, I asked him (rather bitterly) to ask Walter why he had not told me last night what the P.M. had said when we met at dinner. This shortly brought Walter himself on to the line—professing to think the broadcast of little importance, but very grave, and warning me that things were not good—the Dominion Governments much less solidly behind us than they were on Monday, etc. Still—he said Neville's speech today would be all right.

Went to a meeting in a House of Commons Committee Room at 11 a.m. A queer meeting, which grew out of a plan formed two or three days ago of inviting all people and organizations interested in (what used to be called) the Peace Movement, to coordinate themselves. About 100 people turned up—several Opposition M.P.'s—Norman Angell[61]—Victor Gollancz[62] Seton-Watson—a lot of Youth Movement.[63] Far from negligible meeting. Atmosphere of *indescribable* tension. We sent deputations with our views to the leaders of the Parties before the fateful meeting of Parliament this after-

59. Meyer Weisgal: American Zionist leader; Weizmann's personal representative in U.S.A., 1940–46; until 1969, Chairman of the Executive Council of the Weizmann Institute; now President.
60. This was Chamberlain's notorious statement about 'digging trenches and trying on gas-masks here because of a quarrel in a far-away country between people of whom we know nothing'.
61. Sir Norman Angell: Author and lecturer; Nobel peace prize winner, 1933.
62. Victor Gollancz: Publisher; founder of Left Book Club.
63. Of League of Nations Union.

noon, and decided to meet again at 8 p.m. We separated feeling that by that time war might be almost upon us.

I lunched with Chaim, Vera and Michael Weizmann[64] at Carlton Grill, and went back with Chaim to the Office (for Palestine, see lower down). Then home for tea to meet Edgar and listen on wireless to the P.M.'s speech relayed—for of course I could not get a seat in the House, which has never been so packed. Then we heard of the invitation to Munich, and of the amazing ovation given by the House to this news. Of course, one's first feeling was of incredible, almost stunning, relief. But when Walter rang up ten minutes later, I had already begun to wonder and doubt. He was still under the intoxication of the House of Commons scene. It was difficult not to be too unsympathetic—and even that contact with one person over the telephone made me understand why no voice of criticism, or even question of policy could conceivably have been raised in the House of Commons *today*. Later I understood this even better when I went to the L.N.U. for the adjourned meeting, and saw Archie Sinclair, Philip Baker, and other M.P.'s, who had not felt enthusiastic themselves, but had met the impact of the enthusiasm. They were like men who had been bruised. Violet Bonham-Carter,[65] hard as steel, took Archie Sinclair, her leader, to task in front of us all for having said nothing. He and Philip both assured us that it would have been *physically* impossible, but Violet was implacable. Parliament, on which we had set such hopes, had failed her. She would not even join in a very critical resolution, because it began: 'While sharing the universal relief . . . '. This meeting is worth recording in some detail because the first thoughts of people came tumbling out—and time will show how much of what is feared—hoped—expected—will come true. I made some notes of phrases and conclusion—but forget who said what:

The Four Power Pact to be concluded at Munich wrong and dangerous without Russia. Both Russia and Czecho ought to have been invited.

Musso will expect heavy payment for his intervention—and will get it in Spain.

Germany's road to the East is now cleared. This is only a first instalment of Danegeld.

This is the first time a British House of Commons has acted like a Fascist Parliament.

Now Palestine. This morning Malcolm MacDonald sent for Chaim at a moment's notice—told him that in the event of war Palestine would be put under military law—the troops would have to be removed to Egypt—enrolment of Palestinian Jews had begun—but MacDonald intended to announce that immigration is stopped. Chaim and Lewis, who went with

---

64. Weizmann's youngest son.
65. Lady Violet Bonham-Carter: Eldest daughter of H. H. Asquith; member of Executive of L.N.U. until 1941; president of Woman's Liberal Federation, 1923-25, 1939-45; of Liberal Party Organization, 1945-47; governor of B.B.C., 1941-46. Cr. Baroness, 1964.

him, protested strongly, and when Chaim got back to office, Lewis and I drafted a letter, which was sent at once, recapitulating. It said that this announcement—quite unnecessary, because in war ordinary immigration would stop in any case—would alienate Jews from Britain in proportion that it pleased the Arabs. Malcolm MacDonald must now choose between friendship of Jewry and of Arabs.

Later Walter told me he had advised strongly against saying anything about immigration—and he would have told Chaim he would let in fighting men. The incident passes, with the other changes of this extraordinary day—but like them, it does not leave things as it found them. It reveals MacDonald's true bias. Also, if in fear of war they begin recruiting the Yishuv—that, too, cannot be undone.

I told Walter today that it leaves me still his implacable political enemy. If we are saved it is in spite of H.M.G.—not through them. As they left the House of Commons, Winston shook Neville *by the hand,* and said: 'By God, you are lucky.' (Walter told me this.)

September 29th—London   Bob Boothby talked—told me there would be activity today among the groups round Winston. Nobody could oppose Neville just now, but the Government must learn that, if they stay in power a few months more, these must not be wasted like the past three years.

Colin spoke—wanted to make sure I had not been carried away by Neville last night!

Walter spoke—had been with his colleagues to Heston to see the P.M. off. He was a little more sobered, but still seemed utterly confident that the country is utterly behind him and his friends. I am *sure* it is not so. The tone of the Press shows reserve. I heard two men in a 'bus grumbling that H.M.G. had given in again to the Germans, who need a lesson. Walter said to me that I was only English in one thing—my serene confidence that if we fight we win—a certainty he does not share!

Lunched at home, went to meeting of Emergency Committee as constituted after said meeting last night. Lytton came in, and gave us an account of Focus Club[66] Lunch. Lord Lloyd, Winston, Harold Nicolson, Spears—many others, including many M.P.'s. It was decided there that a letter should be despatched to the P.M. at once in Munich, demanding: (1) no further pressure on Czechs; (2) measures of resistance to be concerted with Russia. This to be signed by Lloyd—Winston—Sinclair certainly; it was hoped also by Attlee and Eden—but I suspect that Eden is running out.

Our Committee decided to write a factual leaflet of which 1,000,000 copies to be distributed in next 24 hours. This will cost £250. I did a bit of telephoning after dinner to help finance, and got £30 from the Wedgwood

66. A group, first organized in 1935, whose original aim was to coordinate the various campaigns against Nazi Germany. It soon developed into a platform for Churchill's activities.

family. . . . We heard the French Left are perplexed and dismayed by the apparent unity of backing Neville got in the House last night.

Dined at home with Edgar. Was horrified to hear on Third News that Czechs have made further concessions—it is hinted under British pressure. Spoke at length to Namier after this, who said that, if true, it is fatal that the Czechs give way, however lofty their motives.

September 30th—London   Came down to breakfast to read that in Munich honour died. Even poor Edgar was shaken and appalled. Colin and Bob spoke to me, confirming that in their view for the time being all is lost. They had both met Walter at 'The Other Club' last night, where there seems to have been a very distressing scene, and Walter said in public many of the things he has been saying to me in private in the past two weeks, and which I hoped he would never say to anybody else.

Presently he spoke to me. I asked him if he thought he would agree to these terms. He said he thought probably so, but did not want to commit himself now, but must study them and decide whether in his view they go beyond the Anglo-French Agreement. . . . I said that I thought that for both our sakes, and the sake of our past and our future, we had better pull down the shutters between us just for the present, and would he let me decide when I thought we might pull them up again. I told him I had heard what passed at 'The Other Club', and I begged him to do like me, and at present only consort with the people he is working with and agreeing with.

He agreed to all this—much moved—promising not to keep me five minutes in ignorance if he cannot follow this line of humiliating surrender. Then I rang off.

To L.N.U. Emergency Committee. Arrangements go on to get out large numbers of the Facts leaflets prepared last night. A statement, drafted by Norman Angell, was going round six or seven leaders of all parties for signature. I was asked to take it to Leo Amery, and I found him just departing for Birmingham, to speak in his constituency. His line was not quite that of the statement, so he could not sign, but he told me he was going pretty far. I did not realize quite what courage it requires for a Conservative M.P. to go against the tide *tonight*. The scenes of the P.M.'s return, and all along his route from Heston to the Palace and No. 10, seem to have beggared description.

Nevertheless and nevertheless—I was speaking on the same platform as Eleanor Rathbone[67]—Pritt[68]—Bob Boothby—at a protest meeting at Friends House. There were 2,000 people, even tonight, and the enthusiasm was great. Bob spoke very bravely—*his* boats are burned. I did not speak badly. Bob came back with us to Chaim's for a drink. We discussed chances for Monday's House. Bob has some hopes, but I can't find out so far how many

67. Eleanor Rathbone: Independent M.P. for Combined English Universities from 1929.
68. D. N. Pritt: Labour M.P for North Hammersmith from 1935.

Conservatives are standing firm. I fear Eden is ratting. Will Neville go to the country? Dare he in a few weeks' time? On the other hand, dare he not? Much may depend on what happens in Europe. It looks tonight as though the Poles are marching in [to Teschen].

Here ends the day of utmost humiliation.

October 1st—London   I dined at Chaim's for a Palestine conference (see below). Present: Simon Marks, Israel Sieff, Harry Sacher, Ben-Gurion, Katznelson, Locker, Lewis, Chaim, Vera and self. About 10 p.m. Jan Masaryk came in. We all rose, and Vera and I kissed him. He sat down, and talked for nearly an hour—discursively—a little excitedly, of course. But the story he told—the black shame of the story he told! Some I knew— but there were touches. For instance, the day he was sent for to be told that Britain had no objection to their mobilization, the 'high official' (it *must* have been Halifax) added: 'For God's sake do it quick!' And three days later they were sold—the fortifications for which poor people had pinched themselves to provide £50,000,000 were handed to their enemy and ours. Then again, Chamberlain was shown in Munich a bogus record of telephone conversations between Jan and Benes—plotting to bring down the present Government! ! Jan tackled Alex Cadogan[69] about that. He seems to have registered embarrassment. I fear there can be no doubt that telephones are tapped, and people's movements watched, here in London. Jan affirms that when the French Ministers were here they spoke with two voices—Gamelin[70] telling the truth about the Army, and Bonnet[71] telling lies (which he had been well paid to tell) to the Inner Cabinet.

We asked Jan what *he* thought the underlying reason for what was done. He shares Chaim's view that it was fear of Bolshevism. He says Chamberlain has said to someone today that he thinks he has shut Russia out of Europe for good. I must say Jan is a master of vigorous phrase: About John Simon: 'I would not let my dog lift his leg in his left eye.'

Re Palestine: Chaim and the Palestinians hold the view that the turn of the Yishuv to be sold to the Arabs is very near. We cannot yet resist by arms—we can only work by every means, fair and foul (all is *kosher* now) to buy land, bring in men, get arms. And in two—three—four years we will bring the Jewish State into being. The Marks and Spencer brothers were rather middle-class in their timid reactions—*défaitisme*—but their first reactions are often so. The lesson of the Czechs reinforces the lesson to trust only ourselves. One could not press it on Jan—but *the Czechs ought to have fought.*

October 4th—London   Bob Boothby early on telephone, saying threats

---

69. Sir Alexander Cadogan: Permanent Under-Secretary of State for Foreign Affairs, 1938–46.
70. General M. Gustave Gamelin: Chief of Staff of National Defence, 1938–40; commanded the Allied forces on the western front until May 1940.
71. Georges Bonnet: French Foreign Minister, 1938–40.

were used after last night's Debate,[72] to him, and he thought others, that if they vote against the Government (who have now brought in a Vote of Confidence), the Whip will be withdrawn, and candidates run against them. This shows the Government was frightened last night—but the men are both angry and shaken. . . .

October 5th—London   Colin rang at breakfast-time, to tell me that the Winston group was meeting this morning at Brendan Bracken's house at midday. They had decided to act together, and the question was: should they vote against the Vote of Confidence or abstain? Colin felt they *must* only abstain, owing to the wording of the Motion—but he feared Winston might advise the more extreme course, and Colin urged me to talk to Leo Amery to get him to use his influence the other way. I felt this rather impertinent, but telephoned to Leo, who did not resent it at all, but gave me an account of his attitude, and quite agreed. Lunched alone. Found message from that angel Gardenia Gunston that there was a front row ticket for me in Ladies' Gallery! ! Met her in Lobby—oh, I forgot to say that in the morning Colin passed on a strong rumour that Oliver *has* resigned but been persuaded to withhold it for the present! I have no idea if this is true, but told Gunstons, with view to urging him to come out into the open. This message had been passed on to Anthony, who said that he could say no more to Ministers.

Went up to Ladies' Gallery, where met Violet B.C. and a friend. Stayed till dinner, and heard Winston. A great and *terrible* speech. Dick Acland,[73] just back from Prague, seared and searing, with what he had seen and heard. I fear atrocities begin. He had *seen* a young woman with swastika branded on her chest. Oh, the shame of it—and that row of grinning fools on the Front Bench. They had another bad day today—and when I came out, there was Benes' resignation! Chaim on telephone wondered whether this Government of ours will not *have* to break up—or be broken up. He himself had seen Malcolm MacDonald today, who had made a statement in the House to say the Palestine situation is 'deteriorating'. MacMichael is flying home to be consulted. About what? Chaim says he spoke very plainly to Malcolm. I shall hear more tomorrow.

October 6th—London . . . Talk alone with Chaim, who had seen Malcolm, who professes that he is trying to stand firm under renewed pressure of Cabinet and Arab Kings. I said to Chaim we must listen to him, work with him but never trust him, or one of them, ever again. Chaim agreed. He is putting out a statement tonight that Jewish Agency can never agree to

---

72. The Commons debated the Munich settlement from 3–6 October. Apart from the Liberals and the Labour party, some thirty Conservative M.P.'s opposed the agreement and they registered their opposition by abstaining from the vote. Nevertheless, the Government carried the motion of approval by 366 votes to 144.

73. Richard Acland: Liberal M.P. for Barnstaple from 1935. Later Sir Richard Acland, Bart.

Minority Status. But what can we do? At present? It is obvious that Palestine is next on the list for sale. Heavy-hearted, I came home. Colin rang up, told me Neville had made a wonderful speech. Spoke to Bob, who told me only 17 of our lot had abstained. But they were good men. Passions running very high.

October 7th—London This morning had this letter from Walter. It was written just before the Division yesterday:

> 'I shall have to do what I think I ought, as I see it. My responsibility for this is very simple. I did not know enough or work hard enough, three years ago, or even two, at the problem of armaments. But, being in the Cabinet, I am responsible for the fact that I am weaker than Germany. It is no use resigning—that does not get me out of my responsibility. The Munich terms stick in my throat as much as ever they stuck in Duff's.[74] That fearful timetable is a great crime and scandal, for which those of us who accepted it will be justly condemned, and I believe some day will be justly punished. Of course it is true that Neville had no authority to sign such terms (although Halifax on his own responsibility had proposed a similar timetable to our Ambassador that week). That does not get me away from my desperate question—if I could rub out that agreement, and get us put back to Tuesday night, would I do it? In the present state of our forces—French and British—I cannot say that I would. Therefore, I accept the Munich terms. Therefore, re them, I do not, and cannot, resign. I saw Colin, and explained this to him, very briefly, today. The next question is the future. It seems to me clear that the only thing to work for is the reconstruction of the Government on the widest possible basis. That may be impossible—you may say that you must have us all away. I quite understand that. I think you would be justified. But that, the future alone can tell. On business. I am, as of course you are, very anxious and disturbed about Palestine. I saw Malcolm today. His view is that it will have to be reviewed by a Cabinet Committee, on which he hopes to have me. There is, therefore, so far as I can learn, no danger of immediate sweeping decisions such as must naturally be in your mind in the present catastrophic state of affairs. I shall be away most of next week. I have told Malcolm that I am of course at his disposal if he wants me before.'

Dined at Chaim and Vera's. Lewis—Leo Amery—Wyndham Deedes—Bob Boothby—and self. Besides much talk on general situation, much important Palestine discussion. Chaim (not joking) argued that now the Jews might do better within an Arab State for the time being, than under British Administration. Immigration, arms, etc. would be a matter of backsheesh. Land would be harder, and German-Italian meddling make things difficult.

74. Duff Cooper was the only Minister who resigned in protest at the Munich settlement.

Chaim may be prepared to go into conference with Arabs under H.M.G.—on condition no arbitrary limit to immigration. Amery said, and all agreed, best would still be Partition *à la* Peel. But Chaim considers that Malcolm has practically told him Partition is given up. It was decided that we must try to strengthen the Palestine Parliamentary Committee.

One does not yet measure the full *dégringolade!*

October 13th—London . . . I had a lunch party at home—Vera, Chaim, Harold Nicolson, Bob Boothby, and Noel Coward,[75] who had never met Chaim before. He was, of course, spell-bound—as he told me when he gave me a lift after lunch. Chaim talked mainly of Turkey. Ever since Dr Funk's visit[76] he has been approached by Ataturk's emissaries about the Jewish loan. Ataturk does not *want* to fall into German hands. Bob explained that the Funk trade agreement is not really new money. There might still be a hope! If we could keep Turkey, we might call halt to Hitler in the Eastern Mediterranean—a sea line such as Britain could hold. It is indeed our Hindenburg Line. If that goes, all is gone. Can we make this Cabinet understand—or act? The fate of the British Empire hangs on it, and it may be that this key is in Chaim's hands. Apocalyptic times indeed! Noel was dining with Anthony Eden tonight, and will tell him . . . Later Chaim told me on telephone he had talked to Malcolm MacDonald about it, who instantly began to make an appointment for him to see Lord Halifax. Victor Lytton (to whom Chaim had talked about it yesterday) intends for him to see the Governor of the Bank of England. Can we save Eretz Israel through this? Anyhow, for the first time in these three weary weeks there seemed to be a gleam of hope, a bit of constructive possibility.

October 16th—Sunday To Church at Crown Court, with Edgar. Fine sermon from Moffett[77] on Romans XIV. Felt fortified.

October 17th—London Was in Zionist Office before lunch, drafting a letter from Chaim to Malcolm MacDonald about conditions for a Conference with Arabs. Returned to Zionist Office after lunch, to hear his account of the Kettner[78] lunch. Lord Halifax emphatic about coincidence of Jewish and British interests in the Bosphorus. Chaim said: 'Yes, and right down to Alex.' Halifax full of protestations about good faith, which I don't particularly trust. Malcolm (after Halifax had gone) full of ideas about this Conference, and also keen to meet Chaim's views. I don't trust either of them.

75. The actor and playwright.
76. Dr Funk: German Minister of Economics and President of Reichsbank; he had been on a tour of the Balkan countries and Turkey.
77. Rev Dr Joseph Moffett: Minister of Crown Court Church from 1917 until his death in 1962; received Dutch and British decorations for his work among Dutch refugees during the Second World War.
78. The restaurant in Soho; he had met Halifax there for lunch.

October 18th—London   Went on to meet Walter at Club. We dined on oysters at Drivers, and walked about the City for over two hours. On Palestine—they will set up a Cabinet Committee tomorrow, on which Walter will be. Malcolm's ideas are as follows: The Woodhead Report is split in three—that is to say, four commissioners, three opinions. Malcolm wants to get it out before Parliament meets, but Walter and I agreed it should not be while the extreme state of lawlessness continues. Tonight the rebels are barricaded in the Old City. They will have to be starved out, probably. Malcolm wants to announce the Conference[79] simultaneously with the Woodhead Report. He wants to say it is to last three weeks, and if it has not come to agreement then, H.M.G. will decide. This is (I think, and so does W.) that it will amount to its not agreeing—especially as I now know that H.M.G.'s solution will be—namely *Zones,* and in the Jewish Zone the Jews will control their own immigration. We must let H.M.G. impose this—it suits us, we could not get a better bargain under present circumstances. That is H.M.G.'s 'short-term' policy—i.e. for a year or two. What their 'long-term' policy may be they are probably not very clear— but let the future take care of itself! Size of 'Zone' an unknown quantity— but they will suggest not more than Sharon and Emek. The tussle will come on Galilee. In my view, we must take anything we can get—but I can no more control the Jews than Malcolm and Walter can control Neville. With Neville, Walter advises Malcolm to keep talking about America. If we can think up any new, intelligent ways of keeping up American Jewish pressure—so much the better.

October 21st—London . . . I lunched alone at Horse Shoe with David Ben-Gurion, and had a quiet talk in which I told him all that Walter had said to me on Monday night. He was not displeased with the Zone idea, but said it must all depend (a) on the size of it; (b) on what arrangements were made for the Jews in other Zones; (c) on autonomy in Jewish Zone. He is more and more sure Chaim ought not to go to Constantinople just now; he will be needed here if the Cabinet Committee is sitting, and he thinks the other will provide a wild goose chase.

October 25th . . . Lunched at Club with Walter. He told me the Cabinet Committee on Palestine had its first meeting yesterday. The P.M. in the Chair—Halifax, Malcolm, Zetland, Hoare, Simon, Walter. Showing that the Big Four are taking a hand. They discussed for a long time the pros and cons of the conference, and came down for it, although Walter was not the only one to perceive objections.

Policy is: mention Woodhead Report in King's speech, and say some action will be taken. A little later announce conference. And the policy of time-limit, etc. stands. . . .

---

79. An Arab-Jewish-British conference; eventually met at St James's Palace in February 1939.

October 28th—London   In the morning, Captain Wingate came here to talk over his ideas for a Jewish Defence Force, and how to get them across here. I wrote to Bob Boothby, asking Winston to see him. He had wonderful stories of his Jewish Squads, and their value, and also of the hostility of the Administration, and how it has infected General Haining.

October 30th—London, Sunday   Dined at Chaim's. Chaim is going to Constantinople on November 15th—having now received a message from the Turkish P.M. to that effect. I am still vague (and so is he, I think) about what he is to do there.

November 1st—London   Wrote letters. Lunched alone with Chaim at Carlton Grill. He really wanted to find out what was in my mind about Constantinople. I could only say that I was afraid that in attending to what was not strictly his business, he might be unable to deal with his own affairs. I know Walter holds this view, and does not think that a Jewish Loan would give Chaim any particular pull with H.M.G.—it would only mean that some good Jewish money would be sunk in Turkey. However, I talked it over with Walter this evening, and we agreed that I can say no more to Chaim.

November 8th—London   Lunched alone with Bob Cecil. As always, thrilling to talk to—the robust common sense of the old days. We discussed the lamentable failure of the opponents of H.M.G. to cohere. Anthony has accepted to speak for L.N.U. at Queen's Hall, but will not appear with Archie Sinclair and Attlee as co-speakers. This seems to show that his objective is to be P.M. of the Tory Party. Bob suggested to Violet Bonham-Carter a Lib.-Lab. pact in the constituencies—but she nearly bit his head off. However, he perseveres in other quarters. He, too, is convinced that Neville will not take vigorous measures about rearmament because that nullifies the appeasement policy, in which he *really* believes.

Dined with Chaim and Vera, and Moshe came in later. The Woodhead Report is in their hands today, and Chaim says it is much worse than Walter led us to expect. For the first time, an official document suggests doing away with the Balfour Declaration. Although Malcolm's statement to Parliament will do something to soften the impression, it will be a great blow, an immense encouragement to the Arabs, and Chaim says he cannot possibly enter into a conference now, unless another Ministerial statement disavows the worst parts of the Report. That I think finally kills the conference idea—but it also upsets the future programme as sketched out by Walter.

Is nothing *ever* to go right?

November 11th—Merevale   Armistice Day! And the news of the pogrom in Germany,[80] as bad or worse than I dreaded and expected.

80. On the night of 9–10 November a planned pogrom against German Jewry was carried out in retaliation for the murder of a German diplomat in Paris.

November 14th—London   Morning chiefly at Czech Refugee Committee, and then went on to the Zionist General Council meeting in Anglo-Palestine Club. Saw very many friends. . . . It was better to be among them all, though so tragic—one's spirit finds rest. . . .

November 15th—London   L.N.U. Refugee Committee. Went through a memo. to be presented to the P.M. . . . but there is no doubt that the German pogrom is going to have far-reaching political results. A wild campaign of anti-British hate has broken out in Germany. It looks very much as if Hitler were trying to pick a quarrel. Anyway, 'appeasement' lies in ruins, and when Chaim went to see the P.M. this afternoon with the Anglo-Jewish Deputation, Neville said as much. Chaim demanded an immediate Children's Aliyah [immigration] of 1,500, and a large number (I forget the exact figure) of the trainees in Germany. Neville said that if Malcolm agreed, he did. Altogether a better day—and when I went to dine with Chaim, Vera and Shertok, all were happier.

November 17th—London . . . Lunched at Club with Walter who gave me to understand that H.M.G.'s idea is to receive refugees 'in bond'—and consult U.S.A. and other Governments about permanent settlement and loan. I hope it will turn out so. Wrote to Bobbity Cranborne suggesting he put this in a speech.

There came to tea here: Vera, and Victor Cazalet, just back from five months' trip to Antipodes. He brought with him a most extraordinary young American Jew—name of Ruskin—who has made a lot of money and has been financing Hagana, but keeping himself entirely out of the limelight. He has now had a sort of vision that Jewry must cash in on this world-wide wave of sympathy—make a *coup d'état* in Palestine, proclaim a State, trust to world sympathy. He is *not* crazy, and has thought the matter out. Vera and I arranged that he should meet the Palestinians tomorrow at Victor's. It may all be impracticable. It *may* be the signal. Who knows?

November 18th—London . . . Went after lunch to Victor's, to meet Vera, Moshe, Locker and one of the Hagana. Mr Ruskin there (he sent a beautiful bunch of violets here this morning). He exposed his extraordinary scheme. Their faces a study! Locker purely critical. No one made any comment, but Moshe came up and whispered to me that it was not a subject to be pursued any further, except 'unter vier Augen', and he wanted him to talk to Ben-Gurion, who was ill in bed today. Whereupon I gave a hint to break up the meeting. Vera and I decided (with Ruskin's full approval) that he had better not see Chaim. Ruskin does not want to meet anybody while he is here. He has a most un-American urge to remain in the background—which is very disappointing to dear Victor's impresario nature. But Ruskin is right. This is all dynamite—or nothing!

November 24th—London L.N.U. Executive. Lunched alone at Dorchester with Mr Ruskin, who has now seen all the Histadruth leaders. He considers that Moshe and Chaim speak with one voice, and are definitely discouraging to his plans, as premature. Ben-Gurion takes the same line, but Ruskin notes how much thought he has given to the subject, being able unhesitatingly to answer every question on strategy and the like.

December 1st Went to Zionist Office for a talk with Locker and Lourie . . . The tide runs strong against us. We feel it in sorts of ways. It is almost impossible to get any pro-Palestine letter into *The Times* just now. Then we have gathered that H.M.G.'s post-conference solution includes prohibition of sales of land.

December 2nd—London Spoke to Walter on telephone about prohibition of land sales. He said he had heard of this from me for the first time—but did not exclude the possibility. He is sure there is going to be a terrific clash of policies in the New Year.

Then I went to lunch, and a long talk, with Mr Ruskin at the Dorchester. He has been away for a week in Paris and the Hague, and returns with his plans incredibly advanced. I begin to believe that November 18th—the day he came here with Victor—may be a memorable date. His activities are now two-fold. The organizing of a huge Refugee Loan, in conjunction with Wolf, a Dutch Jew new millionaire, is genuine, but a screen for the *real* thing. He felt he owed it to me to tell me this—but I shall make no more enquiries, and at present the others do not know that I know. But in this week, Ruskin has arranged for a force of 15 planes—the training of pilots—mostly near his home in Chicago—and *other* things against *The Day*. Dov Hos is in consultation with him over all this, and must probably go to U.S.A. I wonder what Chaim will think! When he left, he surely thought it all moonshine. Will he approve? Ruskin does not wait for his approval, which he thinks cannot formally be given. But he flies to Paris on December 7th to meet Chaim on his return from Istanbul—and thence to Jerusalem for one day, to meet the Executive!

December 6th—London . . . to House of Commons, where Victor and Miss Rathbone were forming a Parliamentary Refugee Committee.

December 11th—London . . . Chaim returned. I had a high temperature, but went to supper with them. He had not signed the protest about the 10,000 children,[81] as he sees Malcolm tomorrow, and thought he should speak to him first—but he is absolutely prepared to make this a test case of going into the Conference at all. I am sure this is right—as things are going we shall gain nothing from the Conference, and there could never be such

81. On 8 December Lord Dufferin had announced that the Government would not allow 10,000 Jewish refugee children into Palestine without Arab consent.

advantageous ground for breaking as this. Chaim is all up on his toes. 'Our backs to the wall now,' he says. *Pourvu que ça dure!*

December 12th—London . . . After lunch to Zionist Office where Chaim reported to us his interview with Malcolm this morning. It seems to have been lively! Malcolm offered to take the children *here*, but without guarantee that they should go on. Chaim refused. He said to Malcolm 'We shall fight you from here to San Francisco, and when I say fight I mean *fight!*' Malcolm: 'Do you mean I am to go to the House of Commons on Friday and announce that you will not come to the Conference?' Chaim: 'No— we shall have saved you that trouble.' Again he said: 'No Palestine—No Turkey.' He believes he has brought back something to bargain with. He sees Malcolm and Halifax again on Wednesday. Moshe will be here by Thursday—then we decide. I *think* H.M.G. will give in. For the first time they are up against the Zionist will. Of course, there may be Jews who would still make their Conference (Samuel and others), but the Yishuv will be solid as one man behind Chaim.

December 15th—London   To Zionist Office—Heard the account of Chaim and Namier's interview with Malcolm last night—Namier put him through it, and at the end was more than ever convinced that we have nothing to gain by going into this Conference. But I think Chaim is weakening.

December 16th—London   To Zionist Office for a Conference. But Chaim spoke to me beforehand in a *most extraordinary* manner—about 'a cloud' between us. Also declared that Vera had said to him that I had told her that Namier had criticized Chaim as being 'weak' with Malcolm. There is not one word of truth or substance in this, and I was terribly upset that Chaim should be ready to swallow an allegation that I was making mischief between him and Namier. But what can Vera have said—and *why?* Why Chaim's sudden unmistakeable suspicion and hostility towards me. All this like a bolt from the blue! At the Conference it was decided not to break on the 10,000 children, but to issue a statement, which Stein will prepare. Chaim's violent animosity against Lewis burst forth in black rage.

On going home, I wrote both to Chaim and Vera, saying I must make it clear for Lewis's sake that he never made any such remark as that attributed to him. I also told them that I thought we had better not try to meet until after I come back from Scotland. I told Chaim I had advised Lewis to withdraw from trying to work with Chaim. It is obviously no good. All this nearly did me in. I begin to despair of ever feeling well.

December 20th—London . . . Had talk with Lewis, who had had long talk with Chaim. This miserable misunderstanding had better be left behind. I feel too ill to care about anything much.

1939 *January 10th—London* . . . to Zionist Office, where had a long happy talk with Chaim. Happy because all clouds between us have rolled away. The political situation re Palestine is more hopeful than before Christmas. Malcolm's Conference does not look like materializing—the Arabs cannot agree among themselves even to form a delegation. Meantime every week's delay is in our favour—the Jewish position in Palestine is not deteriorating either economically or morally. There is very little unemployment at the moment, for all the orange-picking is being done by Jewish labour this year. Land is being bought—a few settlements founded—in fact the country is not so bad as some parts of the world—at present. Apart from the authorized trickle of legal immigration, there is now a well-organized importation of men and other things.

January 15th—Sunday, London . . . to tea with Chaim and Vera. He told me he thinks of retiring after the next Congress, becoming an Elder Statesman, living at Rehovoth and running his Institutes. It may be the best thing possible, and prolong his life for ten years. But who knows what may happen between now and August?

January 16th—London . . . home to tea—then was rung up by Peter Rutenberg, this moment arrived from Palestine. He has been very active there, pinning the moderate Arabs to our side by the usual methods. Fakhri Nashashibi is earning his keep by staying in Jerusalem and shouting aloud that the Mufti and his friends do not represent Palestine.

January 18th—London Dined at Club with Walter whom I had not seen since before Christmas. Today was Cabinet. He told me (re Palestine),

(1) That the General Staff circulated a memorandum a day or two ago about Middle Eastern strategy—in which they insist that they *must* have a peaceful, friendly, Arab world. The Jews are not even mentioned. They evidently discount them as a force. This is all bad from one point of view, coupled with the fact that Lord Gort[1] had refused to make an

1. Field-Marshall Viscount Gort, V.C.: Chief of Imperial General Staff, 1937–39; Commander of British Expeditionary Force to France, 1939–40; Governor and Commander-in-Chief, Malta, 1942–44; High Commissioner for Palestine, 1944–45.

K

appointment to see Chaim—on the ground that he is too busy. This may well be! But it is very unfortunate—as it is more and more clear that the soldiers' view will soon dominate all others.

(2) The Cabinet is divided into 'Husseinis' and 'Nashashibis'—that is to say those who think peace with the Mufti the most important, and those who say that it is impolitic to ignore the moderate party, who are not unfriendly to Britain, and *might* come to an understanding with the Jews! In fact H.M.G. is in a cleft stick over that. So much the better, so long as it draws things out—and of course it will be best for us if the Nashashibis do not come, but stay in Jerusalem squealing against the Conference.

Then, as regards general situation:

(1) War expected in March.

(2) It *might* break out against Holland.

January 26th—London   Home to lunch—went shopping; then to Chaim's who says that the Arab delegation is starting for London without any Nashashibis. Good! The Egyptian Delegate has a German wife, and everything that passes at the Conference will certainly be reported to Germany. Gestetner,[2] however, has 'a line' on Nuri Pasha, and will attend to the necessary financing thereof. This is more important: Jewish (non-kosher) immigration reaching pretty high figure now—perhaps 20,000 per annum.

January 27th—London . . . I went on to lunch with Walter at Club. Important talk on Palestine. Malcolm has circulated to Cabinet Committee a memorandum for discussion on policy for Conference (if this takes place). Points: No Jewish State—No Arab State—No stoppage of Jewish immigration, but a ten-year proviso that it shall not exceed 40 per cent at most, or even less (they would like, of course, to find the minimum which they think there is a hope of the Jews accepting!)—Restriction of land sales outside certain areas, but no real 'zoning'—An Advisory Council on basis of parity. I think Malcolm intends to sound Chaim as to whether the Jews would voluntarily restrict their own immigration for a period!

I told Walter I did not think there was a chance of the Minority quota being acceptable to Chaim and Co., even if it is not called minority status. He did not think, however, that there was any hope of getting that altered. He referred to the backing of Samuel and Bearsted[3] and Gerald Reading.

He told me one very interesting thing. Malcolm referred to the spiritual argument of Zionists. Neville said he simply could not understand what was meant—but Halifax saw the point. Inskip swallows whole the military arguments for placating the Arabs, and takes the line that as the Jews are utterly dependent on Britain they must take what they are given.

It seems that Malcolm has telegraphed to Lampson, inviting the Nasha-

2. Sigmund Gestetner: Managing Director of office equipment firm of same name.
3. Viscount Bearstead: Chairman of Shell; prominent Jewish non-Zionist leader.

shibis as a separate but official Delegation, if they care to come. This, of course, may bust the whole Conference with the Mufti Party. I hope it does! Walter has a scheme of his own for offering the Arab Kings the right to maintain some sort of guard in Jerusalem. I don't see much objection to this personally, if they feel they are getting something that way.

Walter hinted that if the Jews do not agree to terms, immigration might be stopped altogether. Personally, I would rather face that possibility (I don't think it could be carried through) than *agree* to be a minority for ten years, even though in practice it might be difficult to become a majority in that time.

Lewis to tea, and then I went to see Chaim. They consider that the cards fall well for us. But we all feel that war is so likely in a few weeks that it is hard to take plans seriously—and how many changes and chances even this Diary has recorded in Palestine affairs!

February 1st—London . . . Dined with Chaim and Vera. Gerald Reading and Peter there. Most interesting discussion on Conference policy. Chaim outlined his speech at opening. It will be on lines of his statement to Royal Commission brought up to date. Cleverly he persuaded Gerald that the Non-Zionists need not make a statement of their own. Chaim will say that, although not at one on every point, they all agree on principle of immigration to Palestine. Gerald begged him not to throw too much cold water on other possibilities. Some disagreement later between Chaim and Peter about bargaining on numbers in next five years. Going home in the taxi Peter urged me to *prevent* bargaining at all. Our demand should be for absorptive capacity—nothing less, and the numbers must be forced upon us. Also to try to make Chaim talk of the *Jewish people,* and *not* of Zionists.

February 5th—Sunday, London To Chaim's in the morning. Lewis came, and we went over the speech, Lewis suggesting a few small changes. Chaim saw Malcolm yesterday, and showed him another wire from our people in Cairo—following up one of some ten days ago, which I forgot to mention here. The first one is how Miles Lampson tried (in vain) to put pressure on the Jews of Cairo and Alexandria to accept the Arab demands; now it seems that Mr Smart has been doing the same to a Press Conference. I told Walter about the first wire a week ago, and he agreed that it was very unwise of Miles. Yesterday Malcolm asked Chaim to leave him the wire about Smart that he might 'report' it. But these wires and other indications have determined Chaim to ask openly whether the policy of H.M.G. is to give all away. He said so to Malcolm yesterday; of course got no definite reply though he looked very uncomfortable. We shall have to break Mr Smart! Ambassadors may come and go, but Oriental Secretaries remain. We heard all this when we lunched at the Cairo Embassy just about a year ago.

February 7th—London . . . to Chaim to hear about the opening of the Conference in St James's Palace, which went well, and was a fine sight.

The Nashashibis were not there, and Malcolm told Chaim he had sat till 4 a.m. persuading them not to come, because if they did, the Mufti people would not. This seemed to us a very extraordinary attitude on the part of H.M.G., but Walter (with whom I dined at the Club) tried to argue that it was right, because without the Mufti there would be no Conference.

February 8th—London Dined at home, and afterwards I went to the Savoy Grill to join the Weizmann family awaiting Chaim's arrival after his statement to the Conference. He had spoken for two hours, and evidently it was very good. Shalom Ash[4] came with him, and was very enthusiastic. Chaim satisfied, and not too tired. Some of his points: 'You have to placate the Arabs because you have got the Jews—but I say nothing about either the ethics or the sportsmanship of that policy' . . . 'The Arabs are trying to run before they can walk—they attained statehood too easily through the expenditure of British blood and treasure.' . . . 'The Peel Report was given a second-class funeral in the Woodhead Report' (and that is all he said about the Woodhead Report) . . . and said: 'There is some advantage in having an old history—everything that happens to us has always happened before.' Of the position of the Jews in the world now he said very little, except to remark that he had read an account of the Lincolnshire floods in the paper last week, where it recorded that children got separated from their parents for *several hours!* Lord Halifax was there, and spoke warmly of the speech. There will be no press report in full—he used the privacy to speak by name of certain people, including Miles Lampson.

February 11th—London . . . Lewis came to lunch. He had heard Chaim's reply to MacDonald's statement of the Arab case yesterday, and said it was first class. MacDonald had talked a lot about the 'natural right' of the Arabs, and how the Jews had been let in without their consent. When he had done, there was a short interval, the British Delegates left the room, and there was a brief discussion as to whether MacDonald should be answered at once. Some of the Americans, and the English Lords, were for waiting and Chaim himself said he would like a little time to prepare. But Lewis and the Palestinians felt he should be answered at once, and Ben-Gurion made a reply which was quite good. Chaim, listening, became inspired, and said he would like to add something. He asked, à propos of 'consent'—by whose consent are we in India—or Egypt? Then he quoted the word 'restitution' from A.J.B.'s Albert Hall speech,[5] and asked: 'Is

4. The Jewish author.
5. On 12 July 1920, Balfour spoke before a mass Jewish audience at the Albert Hall. He enunciated the principle of self-determination, and he pleaded for unity and discipline within Zionist ranks and the difficulties this would entail for a politically inexperienced people. He also touched upon the Arab question. 'It will require tact . . . judgment . . . above all sympathetic goodwill on the part of both Jew and Arab , and he hoped that the Arabs 'will not grudge that small niche, for it is not more geographically . . . being given to the people who for all these hundreds of years have been separated from it.'

our presence in Palestine an act of restitution, or is it not? If not, why do you not tell us we have no business there? If it is, why do you not tell the Arabs so?' Malcolm MacDonald felt that he had to reserve his reply! All the dialectical honours fall, so far, to the Jews—but they know that that is a barren triumph.

I went to tea with the Weizmanns and found Chaim satisfied, and I fear too optimistic about the lasting impression.

February 13th—London . . . Lunched alone at Carlton Grill with Chaim, Lewis joining us later. Chaim once more went over his points for this afternoon's meeting. Stephen Wise also speaks for U.S.A., and that concludes the Jewish case. Chaim has determined today to ask to meet the Arabs. They will not meet the Jews, but the request is good tactics. On Wednesday or Thursday, H.M.G. must make its proposals. If they are unacceptable, the Americans will probably walk out—but this is being kept very secret, as we consider it a trump card.

. . . Later, Lewis came here, after the Conferences, and said Chaim had spoken for an hour, answering Malcolm, and quite magnificently. Such weight and dignity, and consciousness of a united Jewish people behind him. Malcolm, in his reply, said H.M.G. had only 'suggestions' to put forward. This may prevent the American gesture of walking out. But Chaim thinks that perhaps the Jewish case has impressed them, and caused them to modify their original intentions.

February 15th—London   Chaim told me on telephone that the Conference had a meeting on strategy yesterday—very unsatisfactory from our point of view.

Dined at Club with Walter. I gather that the proposals Malcolm puts forward are stiffer than will be the ultimate idea of H.M.G.—Malcolm evidently reckons on the Jews bargaining. Walter said that Nuri Pasha is the most extreme of the Arab Kings [*sic*]. All the others would compromise. Antonius keeps harping on the McMahon Letters.[6] The Lord Chancellor said that he could make a much better case out of them on our side than is made in the memorandum prepared by the F.O.!

Reverting to Palestine, Malcolm is really impressed with the Arab case. A change has come over him since he met them. No one in the Cabinet seems to think U.S.A. opinion matters as much as Arab 'friendship'. Because the three big Democracies are working together, in the closest collaboration, inspired by the fear of a World War—and in this (so Walter thinks) Palestine immigration is a small matter. He admits that he *may* be wrong.

I wrote so far when I came home about 10.45. At midnight I spoke to

6. The correspondence between Sir Henry McMahon, British agent in Cairo, and Sherif Husein of Mecca, July 1915–March 1916. As a result of the conference the letters were published and can be examined in Cmd. 5957. The Arabs argued that the correspondence 'pledged' Palestine to them; the British and the Zionists disputed this interpretation.

Chaim on the phone. Malcolm put forward H.M.G.'s 'suggestions'—no decisions—at this evening's session. Limitation of immigration for a certain number of years—on principle of absorptive capacity—but not to exceed a certain proportion of the Arab population. Council on parity principle. At end of period, immigration figures to depend on Arab consent!! This was evidently an Aunt Sally, for he withdrew it at once when Chaim declared he could discuss nothing on that basis. The Jews asked why the Arabs were not there. Answer came there none. Chaim reserves his reply till Monday—four days hence—though there will be a short session on Friday. Chaim appears relieved that the proposals were not worse. He sees symptoms of a change for the better in the Foreign Office attitude, from something R. Butler[7] said to him.

February 16th—London I learn from Lewis and Moshe that Chaim's account last night was optimistic, and Malcolm MacDonald did not withdraw the veto clause. Lewis thought Chaim not firm enough. The fact is that his genius lies in exposition. He is not a very good debater. He saw the P.M. today—Malcolm, Wise and Ben-Gurion also present. The P.M. seemed impressed by Chaim's anxiety about the economic position of the fellaheen after these three years. The P.M. said British position much stronger now—and all the strategic considerations might weigh much less in a few months' time. This is a very different tone from Malcolm's! But I am still sceptical that none of this will make a difference.

February 20th Went to Peter's office after breakfast. Found him strong for an immediate break—arguing that we have nothing to lose, and that H.M.G. will probably run after the one who breaks first.

Then to Zionist Office—to discuss matter with Lewis, David, Moshe and Leonard Stein. The latter of course against a break. He is the chief of the O.T.I. (Lewis' name for the 'Order of Trembling Israelites'!). The others were sure a break must come—question of *how* best tactically. Moshe put forward the plan (which will, I think, be adopted tomorrow unless the unexpected occurs) that after hearing Malcolm on Land Sale Restrictions, Chaim should say he can see nothing further to discuss, and leave it to H.M.G. to make the next move. But no spectacular walking out, no communication to the Press, who can draw their own conclusions that there is a deadlock if they hear no further date for a meeting has been arranged.

Then to tea at Chaim's, he just back this morning from Paris.

Much talk pro and con—and agreement on Moshe's plan—but I am not sure of Chaim's attitude. He is very unwilling to break, and may easily take a line of his own.

7. Richard Austin Butler: Under-Secretary of State for Foreign Affairs, 1938–41; President of Board of Education, 1941–44; Minister of Education, 1944–45; Chancellor of Exchequer, 1951–55; Lord Privy Seal, 1955–59; Home Secretary, 1959–62; Foreign Minister 1962–63. Cr. Life Peer, 1965.

February 21st . . . At 10.30 to see Peter Rutenberg, who had heard things had not been well handled at the Conference yesterday. Malcolm had scored a number of debating points, and although Chaim said that he saw no object in continuing discussions on basis of H.M.G.'s suggestions, nevertheless Malcolm had been suffered to go on for another hour on the subject of orange production! However, on going up to Zionist Office, I found that no further meeting with the Jewish Delegation had actually been arranged, and the Conference does seem to be dying on our side. Lewis very critical also of Chaim's handling yesterday. Went with him and others into Chaim's room. There is at the moment no very firm direction with regard to the policy or the tactic of the break-off. Chaim looked, and is, tired.

February 23rd   Dined hurriedly at Club with Walter, before he went off to his Cabinet Committee Meeting on Palestine. He knew about the Ibn Sa'ud cable.[8] (I heard later from Chaim that it was to H.M.G., and that he did not wish his son to know about it! This showing how he is compelled to seem to 'play the game'.) I could not help saying to Walter 'I told you so'. I warned him the Jews now have their tails well up. Then went to Chaim's, where were Moshe, David and the two Berls.[9] They gave me an account of today's meeting with the Arab States—all there except Transjordan. They were very indignant with Malcolm's handling—giving out that the subject was the Constitution—taking Iraq as a model, and trying to spring the subject on the Jews without warning, in front of the Arabs. Chaim seems to have done very well, and it was decided that tomorrow he tells Mr Butler that they must in future ask to see H.M.G.'s suggestions in writing as he will not give unconsidered opinions on such subjects.
    Played some bezique with Vera before leaving.
    I fancy H.M.G. begins to see that they can't just sell the Jews, as they had intended to do.

February 25th   Went to Peter Rutenberg's office and we had an hour's talk.
    He said Chaim was 'all broken to pieces' at the moment, but must be preserved in leadership as 'there is no other Weizmann'.
    I then came home and had an hour's talk with Lewis before lunch. He is much more violent against Malcolm, and the whole idea of this Palestine State than Peter—but of course entirely at one with him that nothing must be done now to prejudice later status. Nothing other than parity of numbers on the new Councils will satisfy him. He said that the criticisms of Chaim's conduct of the negotiations were widespread—far too weak, many points going by default, and a subservient manner.

February 26th—Sunday   Went to Zionist Office before lunch, and heard the Jews had decided to break, after hearing from Malcolm in private con-

---

8. Ibn Sa'ud had apparently cabled the Government 'not to antagonize the Jews'.
9. Locker and Katznelson.

ference yesterday what H.M.G.'s terms were. My faint hopes that Walter might persuade his colleagues to return to parity were shattered on hearing that Malcolm had refused parity in deference to Arab wishes. It is a complete sell-out.

Lunched with Lewis at Horse Shoe, and spent afternoon at Mount Royal Hotel with him, David, Nahum Goldmann and Brodetsky, drafting the statement to be read out by Chaim on Tuesday, breaking off. They also decided that, in view of the terms, and the leakage of them which had already occurred (from Arab sources) in today's Press, and the fact that Arab demonstrations of joy had already occurred in Palestine today, it would be impossible for the Jewish delegates to be present at H.M.G.'s official luncheon tomorrow. Jewish public opinion would misunderstand it. Chaim was away all day at Simon Marks' where he rested and slept. He spoke to me on the telephone just before dinner, and I told him all the foregoing. He was rather taken aback, especially about the luncheon, saying 'Is not that rather rude?' I tried to explain how far the situation had moved beyond such considerations in the past 24 hours. He said that he had just received a message from Malcolm that he was going to ring him up at 10 p.m. I begged him to get the *Stimmung* of the Jews before he spoke, which he could do by going to a reception at Miriam Sacher's which began at 8.30.

Came home and rang up Chaim to try and find out what happened tonight. Simon Marks answered me and said Chaim could not speak. Lewis rang up a little later, and I told him. He telephoned to Chaim's and Chaim spoke to him himself in Russian, and said that Malcolm was there, also Gerald, Simon and David Ben-Gurion. Lewis very upset at having been left out of this hastily summoned conclave, and considering it rather sinister.

February 27th Went to Zionist Office in the morning, and heard that Malcolm had come to Chaim's last night in order to explain that the version of H.M.G.'s proposals which had been put as an Appendix to the Meeting with the Jews on the 24th had been circulated *by mistake* to the Arabs. They had, of course, published in Palestine that H.M.G. is giving them an Arab State. This is far from true, and bad as the proposals are, they do not warrant this interpretation. Malcolm was in a great stew, put the blame on his officials, etc. Chaim pointed out that whosoever's fault it was, the Arabs would now say they had been cheated (as very likely they have been! !). The Panel[10] met at 12, and I waited at the office in case I was wanted. Thus I was present when just before lunch Malcolm telephoned to Chaim. The news came in from Palestine in the course of the morning of horrible bomb outrages in Haifa and Jerusalem. Almost certainly Revisionist work. Chaim told Malcolm in response to his question that he heard some at least of this was retaliation for previous murders of Jews, and not caused by the Arab demonstrations of joy. Malcolm then went on to beg Chaim not to break

10. The Panel was the main deliberative body of the Jewish delegation during the conference.

off—Chaim answered with reserve, saying that Panel was now deliberating. I warned Chaim then that Malcolm's game was to detach him from the others. Chaim agreed that this was so.

I dined at Club with Walter to discuss affairs. In the afternoon, the Jews had met H.M.G. again, and Chaim's statement had been read, but the break is not yet complete—they gave in to H.M.G.'s request for a small informal Conference tomorrow, to discuss new proposals.

Walter and I had a rather heated talk. It boiled down at last to this. He thought Chaim's statement was a negotiating document, and believed its points might be met. I said that if H.M.G. brought tomorrow not only new proposals, but a new man to talk about them, the Jews *might* go on. But Malcolm had earned nothing but their contempt, disgust and hatred, and they would not believe his word. Let Lord Halifax come instead. And let there be a *public* statement that there can be no Arab State. Walter promised to pass this on. We parted at 10.30 p.m. I went to Chaim to report, and told Peter also from there on the telephone. They both approved, but Chaim was sceptical whether anything will come of it.

February 28th   Nothing came of it! I was at the Zionist Office all morning when the Executive was discussing (a) whether to break off, (b) how to break. Pandemonium—the Yeshiva[11] at its worst, and nothing really decided.

Dined with the Weizmanns: Brydde Amery, Victor Cazalet, Colin Coote, a French industrialist and Flora Solomon.[12] Victor gave an account of the Duke and Duchess of Windsor, with whom he dined last night in Paris. They seemed extremely happy, but he said the conversation was very inane and dull, with endless repetitions of the same stories, and went on till 1.30 a.m. The Duke said that if the P.M. had not gone to Munich at the time of the crisis, he had intended to do so, and expostulate with Hitler! !

March 1st . . . When I got to Zionist Office I found that Chaim had just telephoned to Malcolm to say that *The Times* this morning had 'put the lid on it' saying that H.M.G.'s proposals remained the same, but the Jews were feeling a little more cheerful! Malcolm then begged Chaim to receive him at his house this evening after dinner, adding that he knew he was not 'persona grata' with the Jews. This, no doubt, was said because Walter had got it across to him that Lord Halifax had better continue the negotiations— a plan which broke down because Lord Halifax got 'flu . . .

There was discussion about receiving Malcolm, but it was finally decided to do so, against the advice of Lewis and myself.

March 2nd   Early to Zionist Office. As usual found them professing absolute decision to break today. David Ben-Gurion quite hysterical, but Dr

11. Hebrew: literally a 'sitting'; but also used to describe a meeting or religious seminary.
12. Flora Solomon: A close friend of Vera Weizmann.

Wise seemed very sensible. The Palestinians, headed by Ussishkin, came in to say goodbye to Chaim. I think they really are going home! Lewis and I spent the morning drafting a *Note Verbale* to be left with the P.M. this evening, which does announce the intention of recommending the Panel to break. I lunched with Lewis and left him and Stein to finish the draft.

. . . After dinner Lewis rang me up, in great wrath and depression; reported that Chaim, Wise and David had seen the P.M., and been again persuaded not to break. I cannot make out if they left the Note Verbale or not. I spoke to Peter later and he thought they had not. It makes me sick that they do not know their own minds!

March 3rd After tea Lewis rang me up at close of this afternoon's meeting of Conference, and later on, Chaim did the same. It really looks as if there *is* an improvement. H.M.G. has at last promised a document stating policy by Monday, when we also produce one. Moreover, on the Minutes of today will stand recorded that unless the Arabs agree to reasonable safeguards for the National Home, the whole scheme of an independent State falls through. They will certainly *not* agree, and I think Malcolm will be in a hole to explain away to them some of the assurances he has given them. So now we shall see in a day or two whether there *is* any basis for agreement.

March 4th Dined at home with Edgar. Walter came to see me about 10 p.m. . . . I told him the Conference developments. From what he said it remains clear to me that they work towards terminating the Mandate, that they will restrict land and immigration meantime, that they will not give the Arabs an independent State nor in any way relax control. This Walter said all along. There seems to have been division in Cabinet about talking about an independent State—the Lord Chancellor[13] very sensibly saying that much previous trouble had come from their ambiguous phrases in documents. Walter told me two new facts of importance:

(1) The U.S. Ambassador[14] told the P.M. that Roosevelt would not interfere against anything H.M.G. chose to do. This was reported at last Wednesday's Cabinet.

(2) Nuri Pasha is back in Baghdad. He is reported in a Foreign Office telegram as saying that he is astounded at the patience of the Colonial Secretary—that the Jews will not get all they want, nor will the Arabs get their State, and that there will be an interval of three to five years before they get anything. This appears to imply that the Arab States are satisfied with the arrangement that H.M.G. intends to impose, and will not support the Mufti's extreme demands.

13. Lord Maugham.
14. Joseph Kennedy: American Ambassador in London, 1937–41.

This, of course, would be a success for H.M.G. I feel sure Galilee is excluded from the Jewish Zone. This will make trouble.

March 6th   I went to Addison Crescent, late to hear the news. According to Chaim there was advance. Malcolm said there would be no independent State without consent of both parties—he also said he would like to work towards a Federal solution. Chaim wants Galilee a mixed canton—he thinks it is the only way we shall save it. The Arab States want to meet the Jews again tomorrow evening. It looks to me as if the Mufti is going to be thrown over by all—but all the issues are still obscure, except that H.M.G. does not mean to leave—which the Jews are at last beginning to believe!

March 8th   Talking to Walter on telephone after breakfast, he told me that he did not think the Jews would get the satisfactory answer to the letter[15] I hoped for. He also told me that there had been a message from Roosevelt saying that though he would stand by H.M.G., he expected some anti-British demonstrations if this policy goes through. I then told Walter that whatever happened it would not have been organized here. I was in the room when Dr Wise came in for a few last words with Chaim before going to the U.S.A. and Chaim's injunction was: 'Do not make anti-British propaganda.' And Wise agreed.

Went to Zionist Office. Found a quite new calm and cheerfulness, everybody having made up their minds that there will be no real improvement—the Arabs were quite moderate and reasonable last night, but nothing much emerged.

Lunched at Carlton Grill with the Weizmanns. Walter joined us after, and Chaim had a few minutes' talk with him. Walter of course dwelt on the impression Chaim had made on Halifax and the P.M., and urged him to use it. But—*à quoi bon?* H.M.G. think they have got what they wanted—an understanding with the Arab States. Dead Sea fruit—but it has not yet turned to ashes in their mouths. At lunch Chaim made a wonderful phrase about Malcolm: 'He is like a commercial traveller trying to sell you a parcel of rotten goods, and begging you not to open the parcel!'

He [Walter] told me that Cabinet had decided this morning (his the only voice raised against it) that in five years they propose to make Jewish immigration dependent on Arab consent. They will, at the same time, make the State dependent on Jewish consent—thus hoping to put each in the power of the other, and induce agreement within the five years. It is a most filthy trick, seeing that life is in one balance and imaginary constitutional privileges in the other—more filthy than even I had imagined possible. He said he had considered resignation but had been convinced that this was the best plan. A very distressing talk. I asked whether a cable from Roosevelt

15. To MacDonald, setting out their conditions for continuing the conference.

would bring about a delay of six months, if he asked for that. He thought not. They would find out whether or not he was playing politics, and they believe they have had a hint that he will be doing so. . . . On the policy itself, much may happen in five years. But it is closing the safety valves, and blood will be on the heads of those that do it.

March 10th   I tried to persuade David and Moshe not to accept Malcolm's suggestion of seeing him tomorrow. I said it was undignified, once the letter had been sent, to go on talking before we had a written reply. But the Palestinians could not forgo the chance of a talk with Malcolm, without Chaim there! Whatever intentions they may have had about speaking out to M.M. were frustrated by Chaim arranging with the C.O. before he left that Gerald Reading should go too. Chaim is clearly determined that there shall be no break with 'the Lords'. All that the Palestinians could do was to add Brodetsky and Goldmann to the number! David broke out in agony of mind about how the culture and life of the Yishuv would be destroyed—it has been difficult enough to weld it together without the Arabization which he now foresees on the part of the Palestine Administration. I told him that I did not believe this would happen. But it is terrible to see one's own people inflicting such misery on others who have worked as the Yishuv leaders have worked.

March 14th   I dined at Club with Walter. Among other things, he told me that H.M.G.'s statement will not be ready for some days—there is still genuine 'fluidity' about the proposals for a Federal State—and, I imagine, a struggle going on in the Cabinet. Also, he believes that there will be no *real* deduction of illegal immigrants from the number that H.M.G. fix for the next five years. I told him this was a relief to my mind.

March 15th   News in this morning's paper of what amounts to the annexation of Czecho by Germany.[16] Went to Czecho Refugee Committee. People had been in direct communication with Prague. The German troops entering the town—Legations besieged by people seeking asylum, and had shut their doors. Uncertainty about a train loaded with 620 women and children, families of our political refugees, which started for Gdynia from Prague yesterday—no news as to whether it had crossed the Polish frontier. The men here wild with anxiety. The Chairman was rude as usual. It is really unbearable to remain a member of this Committee!

March 16th   Dined with the Weizmanns. Found him in better spirits than since the Conference began. Partly the Rabbi and the Goat, but also relief at being finished at last with these torturing talks, and certain information about the fury of the Palestinian Arab Delegation on several counts: (1)

16. German troops occupied Bohemia and Moravia on 15 March.

that H.M.G. say they are not obliged by promises to set up an Arab State, (2) that the Jews have the veto on it, (3) that immigration is not to be stopped. The Arab States (particularly Egypt) are fed up with the Mufti. On the whole, the Mufti has failed, in so far as he has not united the Arab world, whereas the Jews have never been so united. We start for Palestine on the 27th.

March 19th—Sunday . . . Met Walter at Waterloo . . . he then went to the C.O. to join Malcolm and Butler in drafting Palestine statement. He promised to press in sense desired[17]—thought it might help if he could tell his Committee that Jews and moderate Arabs were in serious negotiation, which would be much helped by postponement. Late at night I got this assurance from both Chaim and Peter. Chaim also told me that in response to his telegram, the strike has been called off. So much for Palestine. Now the rest of our talk. Rumours of Cabinet dissension quite unfounded. Neville's speech on Friday[18] was intended as a *challenge,* and all are quite agreed that Britain must make a stand now. Telegrams have already gone out to Warsaw and Petrograd making enquiries about what they can and will do. There is an immense difference, not only in the attitude of the U.S.A., but of the Dominions, compared with September. Cohesion is appearing. So now—I strive from now on to forget the bitterness left by Munich, but I still think that to unite the nation, Neville must go. He expects war, though, and has looked the possibility of defeat in the eyes. This I cannot do.

March 22nd To Zionist Office where was anger and contempt at the White Paper on the McMahon Correspondence—Sir M. Mcdonnell, the so-called adviser of H.M.G.—a man notorious for his anti-Jewish bias when Lord Chief Justice of Palestine—the selection of documents—the failure to include any Jews in the Committee—all go to show how the scales were weighted. After the Executive meeting, Leonard, Lewis and I drafted a letter from Chaim to *The Times* on the subject.

I lunched at Quaglino's with Dorothy Macmillan and Bob Boothby. Bob full of stories of how H.M.G. show signs of weakening on the subject of a Russian alliance, and how Anthony Eden would oppose them on that, and how about 100 Conservatives would follow. Bob also told me that the story of a German ultimatum to Rumania which caused such a sensation last week, and certainly was the precursor of H.M.G.'s overtures to Russia, was entirely invented by *him!* He went into the Rumanian Legation to arrange about going to Bucharest, and M.' Tilea[19] told him that a week or two ago the Germans had suggested that Rumania might revert more to agriculture—

---

17. To postpone the Government statement and press for martial law in Palestine.
18. Chamberlain's Birmingham speech. It was in the main a defence of his Munich policy, but he also stated that 'any attempt to dominate the world by force was one which the Democracies must resist'.
19. M. Tilea: Rumanian Ambassador in London.

and Bob had then suggested to him to dress up and improve the story for the Foreign Office, and had himself at once passed it on to the *Evening Standard*—thereby no doubt 'making history', and I think doing the country a great service. Provided he has not invented this story too![20]

I dined with Chaim and Vera. The last time I shall ever be in No. 16 Addison Crescent, where they have lived ever since I knew them, and which is to be sold next month. I do not think I shall often set foot in Addison Road again. It is nearly 59 years since I was born there, and I suppose hardly a week has passed when I was in London without my going there. First No. 32—and then the Weizmanns.

March 28th—SS. D'Artagnan M.M.   Left London yesterday morning.

March 30th   The climate gets warmer every hour. Sea perfectly calm. David [Ben-Gurion] reads sociology all day long, and beats Lewis Ruskin at chess after dinner.

March 31st   At breakfast today David talked to me, alone, of course, about his first coming to Palestine from Poland at the age of 19—and how, at once, he knew his life to be harmonized, as the Russian Revolution of 1905 had failed to do for him.

April 2nd   In the afternoon, talking to Lewis Ruskin and me, Chaim had a terrible anti-British outburst, saying he would like to see the Jews of the U.S.A. join with the Isolationists to keep the U.S.A. from coming to the help of the British Empire. I was horrified, but said nothing. Spoke to David about it afterwards, and he reassured me that it was only a passing mood, and that Chaim would never say such a thing in public. I pray, hope and believe that he is right!

April 3rd   The ship berthed off Tel Aviv about 10 a.m. . . .
   . . . for tea to Peter Rutenberg's new house. He showed me all over it— a *beautiful* house: high spacious rooms looking out on all sides, and one of the most beautiful views in this world—and at night looking down upon Haifa as if from Heaven on the stars. Peter's Power House, always floodlit, far below. Dear Peter, a real creator!

I was the guest at their Seder supper tonight. This is the first real family Seder at which I have ever been. Little David asked the Questions—Sandy opened the door for Elijah—here, on Carmel! What a wonderful experience to be as one with these people. The children had provided for me a prayer-book in Hebrew and English, in which they and Peter wrote their names,

---

20. The reasons for Tilea's actions, which led to startling British diplomatic initiatives in eastern and south eastern Europe, have never been satisfactorily explained. A possible explanation here emerges; or perhaps this story only adds another element of confusion to this episode.

and gave me in memory. After leaving, we went for a little drive round Carmel by the light of the Passover moon.

April 14th—Rehovoth . . . a very disquieting telegram about an interview that Moshe and Brodetsky had had with Shuckburgh in which he admitted further negotiations with the Arabs. This led to a talk between me and Chaim in which he told me that he is being urged to give the word to let the Jews occupy some land that they have bought in Galilee, which the Administration is at present forbidding. This might lead to a clash with the British, and Jewish blood spilled. Chaim will see Sir Charles Tegart and General Haining before he decides. I settled to draft a code wire to Namier to try to see Walter and get statement postponed at least till Chaim has written a letter to Butler for P.M. and Lord Halifax.

April 16th—Carmel We left Rehovoth after breakfast (leaving Chaim there) travelling in two cars. The party assembled in Tel Aviv, namely Vera, Hadassah Samuel, Lewis Ruskin, Michael Weizmann, Michael Clark[21] At Haifa we picked up our escort of two armoured cars manned by Jewish supernumeraries—lunched very well in Naharia on vegetables and eggs. The best artichokes I ever tasted! Their vegetables are becoming famed, and the colony prospers.

Then on and on to Hanita,[22] running alongside 'Tegart's Wall' which is a barbed wire entanglement some 18 feet thick, and keeps the bandits out of this part of the country—though our wise Administration leaves the Southern frontier with the Negev quite open! ! Up and up among the carob trees, on the famous road which the Jews made in one night a year ago. But first we had to be let through the gate in Tegart's Wall, guarded by a British Military Post. There I found a boy from Brechin, and we exchanged a few Scotch words, greatly to Ruskin's delight. At the top of a long steep road we found heroic little Hanita. Ghaffirim fully armed at every corner of the stockade, and look-outs on the hill tops. The 80 *halutzim* work literally with the spade in one hand and the rifle in the other. We walked along the hill, among the fruit trees and the corn they have planted in this one year—armed men all around us, for there is often sniping at them from over the Syrian border—to look at the graves of the boys who fell. The wild flowers, and the beauty of the spot, quite incredible. We were among the heroes of the heroic age of Jewish history. We went on to Hebet Sikkum, a still newer colony, also in the heart of the hills, only four months old—there were two boy babies there, the same age as the colony. I was presented there with a little bunch of red flowers, called the Blood of the Maccabees. With them in my hand I listened to Lewis Ruskin telling me in undertones how

21. Michael Clark: An Oxford friend of Michael Weizmann; on 16 May he was shot dead on the road between Rehovoth and Tel Aviv.
22. A newly established settlement on the Lebanese border.

last night in Tel Aviv David and the others had told him how all is ready for the occupation of the new land. It will be carried out suddenly, in a single night, and probably quite soon. The men will not be supernumeraries—they will owe no British allegiance. Whatever happens, they have orders not to return the fire of British troops (but I do not believe that this horror will arise), but they are to do everything to defy that power. I do not know the exact date—perhaps I shall have left the country. Lewis R. told me that they trust me completely—but are anxious not to provoke a conflict of loyalties for me.

What lies ahead?

Back to Haifa by curfew. Three Jews were shot in the Arab quarter by the bridge this morning. And this morning the Ghaffirim found a land-mine on the Hanita road which we went along!

April 18th—Rehovoth . . . we found Chaim just back from an Executive meeting in Jerusalem. They had decided he should wire, not write, to the P.M., and he showed me the draft of a long wire which they are sending *en clair.* The whole point was contained in six words: 'British may have to use force.' The occupation of the land has in fact been decided upon. I do not know the date. If it is forbidden on security grounds, then they will do it, and . . . the leaders and Chaim himself will accompany the halutzim.

While we were dining, a telephone from Jerusalem from Bernard Joseph, informing that this afternoon in the House of Commons Tom Williams[23] asked whether, in view of the international situation, decisions on Palestine could not be put off for six months or a year, and the answer appears to have been that H.M.G. are considering the matter. Could Walter have acted? Anyhow, one must not build too much on this, until we know more; but I believe that if this Statement of Policy is once postponed, it *dies,* and we may be saved after all.

Another wire came in during dinner, from U.S.A., saying Brandeis, Frankfurter, and others are active with the President, and with the French Government through Bullitt.[24]

April 19th . . . Chaim sat on verandah after tea, and talked of earliest days here and men of the First Aliyah, a few of whom are still alive, and what they went through. David and his friends of the Third [in fact, the Second] Aliyah, after Kishinev in 1905—tough pioneers, but already of the Third Aliyah! If only I knew Hebrew, what stories this land would yield up!

April 20th   Home after tea. Two bits of good news:
   (1) General Haining has authorized the occupation of four out of the five new purchases of land;

23. Tom Williams: Labour M.P. for Don Valley from 1922; Minister of Agriculture, 1945–51. Cr. Life Peer, 1961.
24. William Bullitt: American Ambassador to France.

(2) A cable to me from Lewis in London: 'Nothing immediate; situation not hopeless.'

This is an immense relief.

April 23rd—Tel Aviv   A terrifically hot day. Returned to Rehovoth after breakfast, coming back here again alone before curfew. Packed the most of my luggage in the morning. Chaim talked after lunch of politics—earnestly and bitterly. Clarence [?] joined me here in the evening before dinner; I went with him to Jaffa, where I had not been for three years—a city of the dead. Went to house there of his friends the Normans, the Assistant District Commissioner. Very nice, but it came over me with a shock what an utterly different world the British officials inhabit—and how much more at home I feel with Jews.

April 25th   Heat a little less. At breakfast it came over me that I must go to the camp in which 170 refugees arrested after landing from a sailing boat are confined. It is at Sarafand. Leave was got, and after lunch Vera, Michael Clark and I went there. Inside the barbed wire fence they are living, men, women and children, in two big tin-roofed Army garages. They have been there 48 hours, and rest and food have already wonderfully restored them. Their eyes shine; they laugh and gather round. They speak freely—in German of course—of the horrors of their eight weeks at sea, in the power of what is practically a pirate crew, for £200 had been taken from each; but twice the devils put back towards Europe, demanding more, taking even the women's rings and ear-rings. They were starved of food and water, and suffered indescribably. Finally they were landed at Ashkelon—one of the worst and wildest Arab places. Many ran away, and are now scattered over the country, in safe hiding I hope. A good many are in this village and it is said that only one is known to have been murdered by the Arabs. These did, however, inform the police. But within ten minutes of their arrest, the British police had brought them tea, bread, cigarettes, butter, which they had not tasted for many months. In the Sarafand camp the soldiers gave planks for beds, and Army blankets. The Jewish population have showered food, clothes and cigarettes upon them. So there they are, and whatever happens they will not leave the country. I hear that at Haifa there is a similar camp of people who were in still worse plight, so weak that they fell to the earth, and kissed it, weeping. The ones we saw could not say enough of the kindness—I found one man whose child is at Whittingehame. An unforgettable experience . . .

. . . A telegram from Lewis at home: 'Situation deteriorating.' Well, we can do no more.

April 26th   Chaim told me a piece of very important secret information. Within the last week, a Conference lasting two days has been held in Netania between four of the Jewish Agency and twelve very representative

L

Arabs. Our people included Barney Joseph, Golomb,[25] and David Ha-Cohen.[26] The Arabs included the man who killed Trumpeldor[27] 20 years ago, the Mayor of Nablus and others. Never before have Arabs met our people formally in a Jewish settlement. The Conference will be resumed. The Arabs said that if H.M.G. lets the Mufti come back to Palestine, or gives him more power, they will start an Arab Terror against him. Chaim will need about £5,000 for the expenses of these negotiations, which may be continued over months. I may have to get it for him in London through Jimmie [de Rothschild] and Gerald [Reading], if he wires to me that he 'needs books'.

Joshua Gordon came to lunch, and gave me a lovely copper ashtray with the seal of Jehoshaphat reproduced—near 3,000 years old. Joshua told us that the day for occupying the new sites will be about May 3rd—the day I ought to reach London.

In the evening, we went to see 'The Cherry Orchard' given by the Habima in Rehovoth in Hebrew. I was terribly bored. The whole cast came here afterwards to supper.

April 27th—32 rue de Menasce, Alexandria   Before I left Rehovoth David Ben-Gurion and Bernard Joseph came to say goodbye. They endorsed Chaim's message re Netania Conference. B.G. also asked me to talk to Jimmie about the need quickly to establish Jewish fishing settlements along the coast, beginning with Caesarea, which is PICA[28] land. They have *gathered* that the intention is seriously to stop illegal immigration, and one plan is to establish coastguards made up of units of six British and six Arabs. If this is done, the Jews will fight—I must try to stop this mad iniquity. To put the lid on, they propose to give the coastguards a bonus on the confiscated ships! They asked me to try and stop Questions about illegal immigration unless the questioners are prepared to make a *real* row—otherwise it gives the Palestine Administration the idea that no real row will be made.

They said goodbye before lunch, and after lunch I sadly parted with Chaim and Vera, and left dear Rehovoth.

May 3rd—Roland Gardens   Home about 6.30. And so ends my fifth visit to Eretz Israel. Already almost a dream. It is as cold as when I left—people discussing war, as when I left.

May 4th—London   Went to Zionist Office and had long talk with Moshe, telling him all that had happened in Palestine. He told me that early this week the Jews have successfully occupied two of the parcels of

25. Eliyahu Golomb: One of the founders of Ḥagana.
26. David Ha-Cohen: Palestinian labour leader.
27. Yosef Trumpeldor: Formerly an officer in the Tsarist army; killed in a skirmish with Arab marauders in 1920; has since attained legendary status in Zionist folklore.
28. PICA: The organization through which the Rothschilds pursued their philanthropic work in Palestine.

land authorized on April 20th. He wants to go back to Palestine. I said we must have a Palestinian here when the Statement is published and the Debate comes off. Walter warned me on telephone this morning that it *is* coming—but not this week.

May 5th   Had a short talk alone with Moshe, who told me that Rab Butler had said to him that the Jewish point of view was represented in the Cabinet by Walter, who—he understood—was in constant touch with me! Moshe registered amazement. I decided to tell *no one* about this.

Lunched with Hannah. Buck said that if only two or three had left the Cabinet after Munich we might have stopped Hitler! ! Much speculation still as the meaning of Litvinov's dismissal.[29] It *may* mean no change of policy—but it may be very serious. It is *the* question of the hour. In the evening, Walter showed me some of the telegrams. They certainly seem to show that H.M.G. is trying to play fair both by Poland and Russia—quite the contrary of Colin's impressions.

. . . To tea with Victor. Leo Amery there. Told them all Palestine news. Amery deeply disturbed. It was settled that I am to address the Parliamentary Palestine Committee on Thursday afternoon.

Dined at Club with Walter, and he came back here for a cup of tea. He has battled alone in Cabinet over Palestine, and wrote a magnificent memorandum—but has been defeated. The Statement will be out on Monday week—the 15th. That is, unless world affairs intervene. He thinks there is no hope, and perhaps no object, in trying to delay the Statement any more, since we cannot get the policy changed.

May 14th—London . . . Lewis Namier was here. The précis of the White Paper has been gathered from Jerusalem. It is as bad as we thought, except possibly for one thing—*and* there was no mention of the proscription of the Mufti. The one thing is that the restrictions of land sales is at the discretion of the High Commissioner, and therefore elastic and changeable. Namier says we must now concentrate on the Debate, and do all we can to shake MacDonald's nerve. He is weak and pitiable. It might be done.

Dined alone with Chaim in his private room at the Dorchester. He told me all about his interviews since he arrived—chiefly with the P.M. and MacDonald. In the latter he let himself go as never before in his life. The interview *shattered* him. What, I wonder, did MacDonald feel? The keynote for the Debate, Chaim thinks, is *Take it to the Hague Court*. Three times he said to MacDonald: 'Why don't you take it to the Hague, Mr MacDonald?' But he got no reply.

May 15th—London . . . to Zionist Office for a Conference on Parliamentary tactics before the Debate, which will probably not be before next week, although the Statement will be on Wednesday. Labour has asked for two

29. On 3 May Molotov had replaced Litvinov as Soviet Commissar for Foreign Affairs.

days—if we can keep it up all that time, we may wear MacDonald down. The great thing is to break his nerve before and during. I wrote to him today and asked him whether he would see me.

May 16th—London   After breakfast to Zionist Office to take part in Conference on Parliamentary tactics. Into the midst of this walked Jimmie de Rothschild—to say two things:

(1) Chaim must stay in London till after the debate;

(2) Chaim must resign the leadership.

On point (1) all were of his opinion, and I gave mine for yes, on balance. Chaim did not say no—I thought he was reluctantly going to say yes. On point (2) he left himself to the others. It was grand to see how these men answered Jimmie—the scorn, the loyalty to Chaim, the vast sense of responsibility to the People. Jimmie pleaded that an anti-British policy should be led by Jabotinsky, not by Chaim. Poor wretch—we all saw he was gibbering with fear for his own position. He wanted Chaim to rat so that he could rat with him.

May 17th—London   Heard from MacDonald, giving me an appointment for Friday morning! God give me grace!

May 19th   Went at 12.45 to Colonial Office to see MacDonald. He was alone, came forward to meet me, offered a cigarette, which I declined. But he smoked, which he seldom does. I began by saying that I had not come to argue or try to re-state the Jewish case, but had two things to say which I felt I ought to say as it was not right to say things behind people's backs without telling them to their faces. He agreed, thanked me for coming, said: 'Say anything you like.' I then made the point about the consequences of trying to keep out the 'illegals'—he could not enforce that against the confidence of the people, especially as they were prepared to be shot rather than acquiesce. He would have to shoot them or see the law defied. He answered that the whole thing was fraught with difficulties, of which this was only one—the law would have to be administered as seemed best under the circumstances. I said my next point was more difficult to make, and I wished in a way that he had refused to see me, so that I could have written it. He again said: 'Say what you like' and spoke of my courage in coming. I mentioned then how he had broken the love and loyalty of the Jews, which I had thought unbreakable, ruined the fair name of Britain—and I referred to his father, and how he had once helped him to repair a far lesser injustice.[30] At this point, he leaned his arm on the table, hid his face and gave out sounds like groans, and said: 'I have thought of all that.' I said that in

30. See the entry for 1 July 1936, ft. 110.

any case I had no more to say on the subject—returning to immigration: without Jewish cooperation he could not enforce the law; he could only get it if legal immigration was once more on the basis of e.a.c. [economic absorptive capacity]. He said the pressure of immigration would be eased by his 25,000 promised in the White Paper 'as soon as they could be absorbed.' For the only time I answered hotly: '... e.a.c. when it suits you—but not otherwise.' He was going to answer, when I begged him to help me keep my vow not to argue. He agreed. I returned to the point of *honour,* and said he could still do something to restore that by accepting the Conservative Amendment to take it to the League, and not insist on being Judge and Advocate at once. He did not answer this. I said I would keep him no longer, painful to both as the interview had been. I said I had no more to say, shook hands and left. I went to the Dorchester, to lunch with Chaim, Moshe there, and Sach; also Victor. Told them all this.

May 22nd—London . . . Colin drove me to the House. First day of the Palestine Debate. There till 11 p.m., only having a snack about 9 p.m. with Victor who failed to get into Debate today. The high spot was Leo Amery— absolutely magnificent. Jimmie de Rothschild very good. Much turns on what Winston says tomorrow, but I doubt our moving H.M.G. Some of us gathered at Chaim's about midnight, vainly waiting a call from U.S.A. We agreed that listening to these debates is terribly exhausting emotionally.

May 23rd (My 59th Birthday) Went to lunch at Victor's house, where were several, including Eva Reading—but Chaim had been suddenly asked by Winston to lunch with him—as he was now determined to speak, having been roused to anger by yesterday's debate. Victor drove me to the House— my seat was in Speaker's Gallery, as yesterday. It was clear that the House did not like the policy at all—even although the Speaker did not call one of the back-bench dissident Conservatives! Winston spoke just before Inskip wound up—a most magnificent speech, which must have accounted for a good many of the enormous number of abstentions. I did not stay to hear the Division figures (at 7.30) but came home to prepare for my supper party for the Elders of Zion and friends—about 30 in all. Chaim and Lewis were here already when I got in. Presently came the Cootes—Colin with the figures of the Division—majority only 89—on a three-line Whip! We had not hoped for anything so good.[31] Soon the Readings arrived; he had made a good speech in the House of Lords, and reported that the Archbishop had made a very good one. All this put us all in much better spirits than I had dared to hope. At 9.45 we all listened to MacDonald, Williams, Lloyd George and Inskip on the wireless—nothing very new, but I thought Lloyd George good.

31. The Government had an overall majority of 248.

May 25th—London The *Evening Standard* comments on Walter's and Hore-Belisha's absence from the Division, and says that back-benchers are indignant because many of them had strained their consciences to vote with H.M.G. What a testimony from that source.

June 1st—London In Palestine the 'war' has opened with the Administration by Bernard Joseph telephoning to tell the latter that the gentleman's agreement whereby the Jewish Agency consulted them before occupying land was abrogated. Next night the Jews occupied six new settlements in the usual way. Troops and police sent to intercept them were too late. They tried to disarm them peaceably—and to interfere with stockade building— but in a half-hearted way, receiving contradictory orders from Jerusalem, and nothing was done. So the Jews win that first round, but the cablegram 'gathers' that the Administration mean to make this an excuse for disarming some of the Ghaffirs. A dirty trick, which will accomplish nothing. Malcolm threatens retrospective action regarding land sales. But I doubt his daring to do anything to provoke explosions. Illegals pour in—they mean to take them all off the Schedules. Let them!

June 17th—London . . . I dined with Jan Masaryk in the little flat in Marsham Street where he now lives. The Israel Sieffs there too. Jan cooked our dinner with his own hands—a Czech peasant's Sunday meal (with the addition of some wonderful smoked sturgeon). A vegetable soup, and a veal stew with cream and paprika. Czech beer (pre-Hitler) and Chateau Lafite, Jan—as I felt the other night at the J.N.F.[32] dinner—has become though suffering, a great man. But my God! How he is suffering! The whole scene and surroundings seemed unbearably pathetic—if one were not sure he will live to see his country free again. But to be in one room with Chaim and him was a great experience. The talk rolled from gay to grave and back again. The most memorable thing Jan told us was that in the days between Godesberg and Munich, Jan went to see the P.M. and Lord Halifax. The P.M. said to him: 'Some people trust M. Benes—but I happen to trust Herr Hitler.' Jan, telling us this as a fact to be recorded, added: 'I got up and said: "Mr Prime Minister: I am only a servant of my country; I cannot follow you to these heights!"'—and I left him alone, with his Adam's apple working in his throat!' If ever there was hate, it is the hatred of Jan for Chamberlain.

June 18th—Sunday Spent the whole day at Swifts with Victor, going by train to Maidstone, and arriving in time for lunch. There I found the Anthony Edens, Von Cramm, the tennis star, and his cousin, Von Meister (two of the most charming young men, and violent anti-Nazis); also M. Van Zeeland of Belgium, M. Tilea, the Rumanian Ambassador, Mrs and

32. Jewish National Fund.

Miss Ryan, very nice Americans, and, for lunch only, Bob Boothby. Watched a great deal of truly wonderful tennis—Victor and Von Meister against Anthony and Von Cramm. Also played a little backgammon (I forgot to mention another Belgian, M. La Tour, I think)—also some political talk; a little of it alone with Anthony and then Tilea joined. Anthony, like all the rest of us, very worried about the Tientsin situation.[33] The alternative to standing firm is to renounce our interests in the Far East altogether, which is surely impossible. No half measures any good. All turns on the U.S.A., but nobody seems to have much hope in that direction. They will not fight for 'British interests' in China. I suggested to Anthony that we might send part of our Home Fleet to the Far East and ask the U.S.A. to send some battleships to replace them in the North Sea. I don't think it is a bad idea! Anthony thinks we could perfectly well spare *some* ships for the Far East, but he says the Admiralty is the most *défaitiste* of all the offices. Tilea and I urged him to come out into the open and insist on a broader basis for the Government. He said it was a terrible responsibility to break up the Government at such a time—and he did not feel that he knew enough of the facts to put forward any suggestions for different action. I replied that this was not required of him—the first step was to broaden the basis of the Government before any action is taken. He did not dissent—but I am afraid he has not got it in him to make a stand. If only his politics were like some of his tennis strokes down the centre of the Court!

June 23rd—London   To Zionist Office. Chaim told me about his visit to Oxford, where he saw Professor Coupland and Lord Lothian, and there was serious talk about working out a plan for federation, including this time Transjordan and part of Syria. There is, of course, a vast amount to be done before such an idea could become practical politics—but they want to work out details, for it seems to them that the break-down of the White Paper policy must soon be apparent, and then might be the time. Chaim talks of writing to Rappard[34] in Geneva of the idea, while the P.M.C. still sits—for of course the preliminary would have to be the turning down of the White Paper.

July 3rd   Lunched at Horse Shoe with Lewis, Arthur Lourie and Locker. Heard to my great dismay that the P.M.C. failed to get a unanimous Report, owing to Hankey,[35] and so have decided to present no Report at all, but to refer the matter to the League Council in September. This throws our plans for Parliamentary Debate into the melting pot, and it is hard to decide what to do—my instinct would be to leave matters to develop as the atmosphere

33. On 14 June the Japanese blockaded the British concession at Tientsin following the refusal of the British authorities to surrender four Chinese suspected of murdering a Japanese customs official.
34. Professor W. Rappard: Vice-Chairman of the Permanent Mandates Commission.
35. Hankey was participating in the discussions of the Permanent Mandates Commission on the May White Paper.

is not favourable for raising the question again here now. But on the other hand Moshe and David are fighting a losing battle against the extremists in Palestine, and are sorely in need of some external sign of encouragement. But it is doubtful to me whether we could get them that at the present moment. Decided to consult Leo Amery.

Went to spend the evening with the Berl Lockers. Talked over Yishuv situation. I said that if terrorism grows it may be necessary to stage some sort of demonstration (say bringing in an immigrant ship in broad daylight) to let off steam and force an issue. Kaplan thought it could not be practically worked. We were faced with the danger of Jewish terrorism on a large scale. It is the only real danger.

July 4th This morning I decided that I must speak to MacDonald and tell him what his policy is doing to encourage Jewish terrorism. I rang up his Private Secretary and got his only spare ten minutes in the afternoon. The report of the conversation is attached to this Diary,[36] I have sent it to Chaim and to Moshe.

July 6th Dr Nahum Goldmann and Bakstansky came after breakfast to give me the exact facts about the P.M.C.'s run-away at Geneva. I then went to Leo Amery and talked over with him what to do. He agrees no Parliamentary row about it—but advises leakages to Press etc., to stimulate and keep up interest . . . Try to prevent the Opposition from attacking Hankey or accusing him of being slave of Government.

July 13th Came down to breakfast, to read that MacDonald had stopped all legal immigration during the next six months' schedule period. There began a hectic day, partly at the Zionist Office in Conferences, partly with Peter, partly telephoning to Amery and others. We heard in the afternoon that the Opposition intend now to raise Palestine on Thursday on the C.O. Vote.

Walter had no idea last night that MacDonald meant to do this. The Cabinet were not consulted. Query—Was the P.M.? I think MacDonald may have over-reached himself this time.

July 19th . . . Home to prepare my speech for Palestine Parliamentary Committee, which met at 6 p.m. under Jos. Wedgwood's Chairmanship. I spoke first, to my great chagrin worse than I have done for some years. However, Moshe followed, and was very good. A good meeting, about thirty, many of them Conservatives. They will mostly abstain and (we hope) be in the House and remain seated. Had some food with Victor, in the House.

36. Not found.

July 20th We were going to the Buckingham Palace Garden Party, but it was cancelled, owing to the rain, so I got to the House of Commons for the Palestine Debate soon after Tom Williams opened. Stayed till close at 11 p.m. It went very well for us, Victor made a first-class speech, Malcolm spoke twice, utterly failed to meet his critics, and was obviously rattled. He made a monstrous attack on the Jewish Agency, hinting that they were organizing illegals in order to defeat the White Paper. But the worst thing he said was: 'If I were an Arab I should be passionately against Jewish immigration.'

But his day is nearly done, unless I am much mistaken. Walter told me this morning that the Cabinet want a Memo. from him explaining what he means to do next, and has re-constituted the Palestine Committee *pro tem* to report on this. Walter will be on it.

July 23rd . . . The Cabinet Palestine Committee has been re-constituted and is to meet on 28th to consider a Memo. which the Cabinet has instructed Malcolm to prepare, to indicate his ideas of how to carry out his policy. I think he will find it embarrassing, and all indications point to growing realization on the part of the Cabinet that he is getting himself and them into a mess.

July 24th . . . Hannah Hudson rang me up, in great agitation. The newspapers (all except *Times*) full of a story about Rob having proposed, in conversation with Dr Wohlthat,[37] a £1,000,000,000 loan to Germany. I promised to go to lunch with them. The great question was, would the P.M. throw him to the wolves, or uphold him. Colin told me on telephone that he had heard on good authority the former. I found Rob and Hannah themselves expected this, though when I saw the written report of Rob's conversation with Wohlthat (which he had sent to the P.M.) I saw nothing in it to criticize, and when Rob came in to lunch, and I found the P.M. had sent him no message the whole morning I could not believe he would do such a caddish thing as throw him over without any warning. However, we had no certainty, and though Rob had not been indiscreet or wrong in his talk to Wohlthat, he was very foolish in giving an interview yesterday to the *Daily Express* and the P.M. might well have been incensed by that. Also Rob is unpopular. Buck was also at lunch and gave Rob excellent advice about what he should do and say if the P.M. did throw him over. However before the meal was over the Messenger brought from No. 10 the draft of the P.M.'s answer to the Private Notice Question, supporting Rob most generously. Beaming smiles and relief on the part of both Hudsons! There was nothing wrong with Rob's talk with Wohlthat, except that *he* (W.) must have leaked to the Press, and it is a lesson not to talk to Germans. But

37. Dr Wohlthat: Göring's Commissioner for the German four-year plan. According to the press, the proposed loan was to have been the basis of an ultimate settlement between the two countries.

I know that neither the Cabinet nor Neville had anything to do with what Rob chose to say, and it will be very unfair if people insist on suspecting them.

August 10th—Strachur   Found a lot of letters. Two from Walter. One dated August 4th about meeting of the Palestine Committee; he says 'federalism has now come so far forward as the final goal as to monopolize the picture, even to the extent of blotting out the proposed constitutional arrangements.[38] For the rest, nothing likely to cause clashes is to be expected in the immediate future, and if your friends keep their heads all may yet be well.'

August 19th—12 Rue St Victor, Geneva   Dear Sach met me at the aerodrome, with a bunch of pink roses. He brought me here to the Bigards[39] large and luxurious house, lent to the Weizmanns. So here I am again, with my *other* people, and in the atmosphere which is also home. Bless them.

Then a bath, some gossip with Vera, and well dined at the Eaux Vives, David Ben-Gurion, Moshe, Bernard Joseph, Sach, the Weizmanns and me. The band, out of compliment, played some lovely Hebrew tunes.

Then to Congress, held in the theatre. Vera and I in a box, greeted by innumerable friends, and heard a good many speeches, all in Yiddish, no Hebrew this time I am glad to say. All solid against White Paper, except one lamentable one from Rabbi Silver[40] condemning illegal immigration. This was very ill-received by Congress, but will be nuts to Malcolm!

August 20th—Geneva   This has been a fearful day, much of its trouble arising out of Silver's speech. After breakfast, Chaim, Vera, Sach and I drove quietly down to Congress. Then Ussishkin called Berl Katznelson to the tribune, where upon the Mizrachi Party set up a fearful row, stamping their feet and shouting 'He shall not speak'. After some minutes of this uproar, Ussishkin rose and said that he understood that this demonstration was not against Berl, but against the Chair. (Arthur Lourie had come into our box, so that Vera and I could understand the Hebrew parts of ensuing scene.) However, only about half-an-hour passed before the Mizrachi consented to let Berl speak. He did so in Yiddish for over an hour. I followed him with difficulty, but perceived that parts of his speech were moving and beautiful, as Berl's thoughts always are, but even at the time I was horrified to hear him denounce Rabbi Silver in very rude and unmeasured terms, and declare that illegal immigration was the chief weapon for fighting the White Paper. Chaim has been most anxious *not* to have pronouncements, or even allusions to that delicate matter, and although Berl is not a member of the Executive

38. Those contained in the May White Paper to establish a Palestine state.
39. Swiss friends of Weizmann.
40. Rabbi Abba Silver: At various times between 1928–48 head of Zionist Organization of America, American Zionist Emergency Council and United Jewish Appeal; chairman of American Section of Jewish Agency.

he *is* a Labour leader, and Chaim's position was made very difficult, also (as he thinks) by the insult to Silver on the eve of Chaim going to U.S.A. When Berl sat down the whole Congress rose (with a few exceptions) and cheered him to the echo, thus endorsing it all, and Chaim's temper was not improved by David, to whom he said 'Not a helpful speech', and D. impulsively answered 'The best Zionist speech yet made here.' So, when we four got into the car to drive to the Eaux Vives for lunch, we found Chaim more angry than I had ever seen him, his eyes looked like small hard stones, and remained so all the afternoon. We all three tried to pour oil, but Chaim declared this was a conspiracy on the part of Labour to force his hand about illegal immigration, and that he would not give way to it. He would not make a winding up speech after this, and would not join the new Executive. Vera, as always in a *great* crisis, was extraordinarily sensible. We drove home for the siesta, I went to my room, and read a book about Goya. At 4 p.m. we assembled to drive to Congress, only to find that the political discussion was put off till 7.30[41] . . . Chaim angrier than ever at this. I ran across Kaplan, and told him how things stood, asked him to find Moshe and send him here. At 5 p.m. Moshe appeared, Vera and I had tea with Chaim and him. Moshe argued as tactfully as possible, that no harm had yet been done which Chaim and he could not put right in their speeches, but Chaim remained firm that he would *not* speak, or join the new Executive. Finally I suggested that Moshe should go and fetch David and Berl himself and (I think) Kaplan too, and talk things over with Chaim. Chaim very grumpily consented, and Vera and I went upstairs and played bezique for over an hour, while this Conference went on below. Then Chaim came up: he had not changed his attitude. Vera went with him into their bedroom, where she tried to reason with him further (but I think by that time it was no good) and I went down and found Sach and we discussed the affair in all its bearings, agreeing that Berl *had* expressed the feeling of Congress, though too violently, and that although it *has* made Chaim's position difficult, Chaim should have insisted beforehand on a Conference of the Party leaders, to decide what *was* to be said, or not said, about illegal immigration in the speeches of responsible people. Not to do that was like leaving a heap of gunpowder lying about, and trust to the common sense of people not to go near it with lighted candles.

August 21st—Geneva   Internal affairs better—external worse. Chaim was still Achilles sulking in his tent till evening, when he came to the Political Committee, and made a fine speech there. . . . For the first time a note of immediate reality was struck in a speech by Kurt Blumenfeld,[42] who advised turning at once to emergency decisions. They ought to elect a new Execu-

41. The Mizrachi were creating chaos with the timetable of Congress. They were pressing for changes in the voting system and refused to allow the proceedings to continue until their demands were met.
42. Kurt Blumenfeld: President of German Zionist Federation, 1924–33; director of Jewish National Fund.

tive, and discuss the raising of Jewish legions, and then all should return home.

August 22nd—Geneva   Day of deepening mystification as far as outside world is concerned. At breakfast the Swiss papers gave us the news of a Russo-German non-aggression Pact. The truth and meaning of this were debated all day, in conversation, but I have no doubt it is a great blow. At lunch time I told Gershon Agronsky (with whom I lunched in Hotel Bergues) that I predict a new Government in England before the end of the week, with some other P.M. than Chamberlain. By the end of the day various people had been in communication with London. We know Parliament is summoned for Thursday morning at 10 a.m. We are still in doubt about the nature of the Pact. It appears that if either side commits an act of aggression, it is denounced! Does it mean anything, or nothing? In any case, a great blow to British policy.

Congress now fully alive to situation, and will try to elect a new Executive tomorrow, and disperse on Thursday. Moshe leaves early tomorrow for Palestine, flying to London for twenty-four hours on the way, where he hopes to see the War Office people, and offer a Jewish legion to serve in Palestine or adjacent countries, and to do our best to raise a U.S.A. legion.

He dined with us at Eaux Vives, and said good-bye. I felt very sad. Not only because I love him and shall miss him, but because it felt like the first of the War good-byes. . . .

August 23rd—Geneva   A cable had just arrived from Dov Hos in Palestine, saying there had been a Conference of Army Chiefs there, including General Wavell.[43] Their decision was to leave off harrying illegal immigration, to evacuate those in the Concentration Camps, in order to leave these free for suspected persons who are to be interned. Dov advised sending an emissary from here to London, on the very same errand to the War Office on which Moshe had already decided to go. This makes his errand far more likely to succeed. But what a comment on MacDonald's Palestine policy! ! Sach came to fetch me to join the others at lunch: I could not forbear telling him. He nearly went off his head with joy, but his first reaction was grand and very like him, the true spirit of the Yishuv: 'Thank God we have kept our hands clean.'

Chaim has decided that we start for Paris on Friday by car. He wants to get over the frontier. Once in Paris we can see how matters stand. We *ought* to be there by Saturday the 26th August.

August 24th—Hotel du Golf, Divonne-les-Bains, France   Thank goodness, we are in *France*. But only just in time, for the frontier is closed!

Nothing going on at Political Committee till 4 p.m. when they hurried through the Resolution. I was there when about 6 p.m. Joseph Cohen came

43. General A. P. Wavell: Commanded British forces in Palestine, 1937–38; Commander-in-Chief, Middle East, 1939–41. Cr. Viscount and Field-Marshal, 1943; Earl, 1947.

in and told me to go up to Rue St Victor and pack, for Chaim had heard the frontier might be closed any time, and he decided to leave Switzerland tonight. I packed in about an hour, and Vera and I dined together at Beau Rivage. Then to Congress, to hear Chaim deliver his farewell speech.

Never shall I go through a more moving scene. Who can guess the thoughts that filled all our minds, these 600 Jews from all quarters of the world, some of them already cut off from wives and families.

A Committee has been sitting all day, arranging (or trying to arrange) for their transport home, though only the Palestinians, the English and the Americans can be said to be going 'home'.

Chaim had a word for each, especially the Palestinians and the Poles. He spoke very simply and in Yiddish, said the Jews would stand by the Democracies. Then in Hebrew, he said 'au revoir'. The Congress stood (except Meyer Grossmann! !) and sang the Hatikvah. Chaim embraced old Ussishkin and David Ben-Gurion as if he would never let them go. David flies back to Palestine tomorrow.

I came out utterly overcome, and found Sach the same. We all drove back to Rue St Victor, packed the luggage on the cars, the Weizmanns and myself in their Rolls with their English chauffeur, Bishop. . . . and the bulk of our luggage in the Bigard's car, lent by him with his Swiss chauffeur. So we had meant to travel, all the way to Paris. We left Geneva about 10.30 and reached the Swiss frontier here about 11 p.m. and found the French frontier had been closed half-an-hour before! ! We had visions of returning to Geneva, and perhaps staying there for days or weeks. But Chaim persuaded the French officer to let us British through, as Allies returning home. He would not let the Swiss chauffeur through, except as far as this hotel and then return. However, Chaim has hired another car, to join our convoy and carry our luggage to Paris.

The world, so far as I know, is not yet at War. Danzig we believe to be already declared German. Chamberlain seems to have made a firm speech in Parliament and D.O.R.A.[44] will be in force tonight.

What a nightmare. And what an experience to have been with them all, the Jews, through the Twenty-First Zionist Congress.

August 27th—Paris, Hotel Plaza. Sunday   I went to the British Embassy Church at 10 a.m. Found the service was at 10.30, so sat for a while under the browning chestnuts, bordering the Place de la Concorde. Many young couples passed, twined together, pale as death. Certainly 'ce n'est pas gai' to be in France during mobilization.

August 28th—10.45 a.m., Paris   Chaim saw Blum this morning, who says Britain is doing the most with regard to Italy. Blum also said that he does not believe in the possibility of 'another Munich'. He thinks there is just a ghost of a chance that Hitler may recede a little, may propose something that

44. Defence of the Realm Acts: emergency war regulations.

might end in negotiations. He believes that councils are very divided in Germany, and that is our only hope. France and England are solid and prepared. Spain will certainly remain neutral. Japan will not go on Russia's side. Italy still on the fence. If Hitler does *not* recede, war seems probable on Wednesday.

We leave Paris in an hour from now.

August 29th—London   A day of vague optimism in the air, I fear not justified by events.

I had a telephone talk with Walter after breakfast. He said there was no truth at all in the stories of dissension in the Cabinet over the reply of Hitler. The long sittings to deliberate its terms on Saturday and Sunday were meant as an insult to Hitler, who had said he was going into Poland on Saturday; we refused to be rattled by this, and so far he has not gone in. Till he does there is a glimmer of hope. Daladier did not consult H.M.G. before writing to Hitler.[45] He *should* have done this. We are doing all we can about Mussolini, but nobody knows his attitude if war breaks out. He is violently against war. I told Walter that Europe does not believe we are earnest so long as Chamberlain is P.M. It may be that the refusal to enlarge the Government *before* war breaks out will be on a par with Sir E. Grey's refusal to say Britain would come in in 1914.

. . . Lewis and I then went to Zionist Office and drafted a letter from Chaim to the P.M. offering Jewish cooperation. This was approved after many re-drafts, by Brodetsky and Locker. The difficulty was to define the Jewish attitude to the W[hite]P[aper] without spoiling our effect, or giving anything away. The Jewish attitude is precisely that of Ulster in 1914, but nobody would agree to the letter using that analogy, and perhaps they were right, though the British mind would understand it. However, Chaim signed the letter, and sent it to Downing Street by hand tonight.

August 30th—London   Talked to Walter, but before Cabinet met to consider Hitler's answer, though he seemed to think it may open the way to some sort of talking, which we agreed, is the dangerous time. Talked to Bob Boothby, who said Parliament is watching H.M.G. as a cat watches a mouse and he did not think the Cabinet would be allowed to wobble. He was bitter that Winston is not taken into their counsels at all.

August 31st . . . with Brodetsky to Zionist Office. In taxi he talked about Chaim's studied neglect of him, and his unhappiness at 77, the fifth wheel of the coach, which of course is rather what he *is*. But Chaim is a *bad* team-driver. They all feel some grievance. I was today appointed formally by him a member of the Political Bureau which is to run the London work, Brodetsky, Lewis and Locker the others. We had our first meeting, and

45. He wrote to Hitler on 26 August that nothing need prevent a pacific solution of 'the international crisis with honour and dignity for all peoples'.

discussed necessity of getting the Zionist work scheduled as of National Importance, otherwise we British subjects cannot devote ourselves to Malcolm on this subject.

September 1st—London   War broke out this morning between Germany and Poland. When I emerged from Holborn Tube Station on my way to the Zionist Office about 11 a.m. I saw the posters 'Danzig proclaims return to Reich—Germans bomb Polish Town'.

I felt a sort of relief that the waiting is over. At Zionist Office merely talked about what Chaim should say at the interview he seeks with Mac-Donald. He saw him later in the day, all very courteous and correct. MacDonald will have a conference with War Office and Foreign Office about position and activities of Jewish Agency, as soon as may be.

Just before midnight Colin rang up. The Government is being reconstructed. Winston is making very heavy terms . . . He does not believe Chamberlain can last a week. Oh, why has he been suffered to exist all this year—Why did the clay feet of the idol not crumble before it was too late?

September 2nd   This has been a dreadful day. Walter spoke after breakfast and asked me to lunch. I asked him why we were not yet at War with Germany. He replied that we were in close touch with the French.

Walter came late to Club, happy about the way his evacuation [scheme] goes but saying there were rather more tears today when the women began going, and leaving their husbands. As to the declaration of War, he said that the French cannot do it without their Parliament and it took time to assemble that. I accepted this explanation, which I expect was all he knew, and it is true as far as it goes. He had got me a ticket for the Members' Gallery. I went there when the House met at 2.45 and sat through two hours of Emergency Bills . . . later Bob Boothby came up and beckoned me out. We went for a drink and he told me there was an awful commotion going on behind the scenes. Greenwood[46] and Winston had both been offered to join the Cabinet, both had refused. Greenwood because he would not serve under the P.M. and Winston because there were to be no other changes. Bob said he could never prevail under those circumstances and would only ruin his value later by defending the Government. He must stay out, but if that happened, Anthony, Bob himself, and others, would go off and join their regiments. I agreed that unless Winston could bring in some of his chaps (Amery a key man) he had better stay out. Bob raved against the P.M. and his gang. We felt the honour of Britain vanishing before our eyes. Thirty-six hours now since Germany invaded Poland, and we have not yet honoured our pledges! I went back to the Gallery. It was now 6 p.m., the House was filling up, the Ambassadors came in, etc. All was set for the P.M.'s entry. Then the Speaker rose, and said he must adjourn the

46. A. Greenwood: Labour M.P. Minister of Health, 1929–31; without Portfolio, 1940–42; Lord Privy Seal, 1945–47; Paymaster-General, 1946–48.

sitting 'for a short time'. We waited for an hour and forty minutes. Ministers went out. I believe there was a Cabinet. I don't know yet what exactly caused the delay. Then, at 7.40, the P.M. came in. He read his first Statement. Then Greenwood rose. When he said he spoke for his Party, Amery shouted 'Speak for Britain'. I saw the P.M. turn round, as if stung. The House was with Greenwood. The P.M.'s second (impromptu) speech was made by a dithering old dodderer, with shaking voice and hands. Surely he can never face the House again! It was a bitter hour.

September 3rd   The shame is over. We were at War with Germany at 11 a.m. today and France at 5 p.m.

After breakfast we heard that the P.M. would tell us this on wireless at 11.15 a.m. Stew, Catherine,[47] Edgar and I heard the announcement, sitting together in the Pink Room. We stood up for the National Anthem. Then I said 'God protect us all, and those we love.'

Walter picked me up and brought me to lunch at House of Commons. The Harcourt Room saw Lloyd-George, Miss Stevenson,[48] Bob Boothby, Archie Sinclair lunching together.

They had little news. Colin had names of what (proved later) to be some of War Cabinet. We rather felt that, thus composed, it cannot last long. Last night's performance in the House has gravely shaken old Neville. Walter told us the true inner history of those dreadful two hours. All the time of waiting had been taken up by frantic telephone calls to Paris, telling them we could not wait any longer, they insisting that we must. Their mobilization and A.R.P. both required that they must wait another day. Our cabinet met and it was agreed that Neville should say we would declare War at midnight. Ministers (as I saw) returned to their places, and the Ambassadors were ranged in a row. Neville dallied, and when he came Ministers heard him make a quite different announcement to what had been authorized. Walter at once realized there was still a hitch with the French. As soon as the House rose Ministers gravitated to (I think he said) the Chancellor's Room, and said *this would not do*. I think they then all went over to Downing Street, for Walter told me he left there at midnight, and it was then settled to send an Ultimatum to expire at 11 a.m. today.

. . . But even so, it was touch and go, and the House was on the eve of a terrible scene. Winston very nearly rose and moved a Vote of Want of Confidence, which he would probably have carried. Perhaps the real hero of the hour was David Margesson[49] when he got up and moved that This House do now adjourn. The familiar voice and figure saying the same thing he had said every night for the past five years worked by force of habit. If there had been more speeches a terrible disaster might have occurred. I

47. Mrs Dugdale's parlour-maid.
48. Lloyd George's private secretary; they married in 1943.
49. David Margesson: Government Chief Whip, 1931–40; Secretary of State for War, 1940–42. Cr. Viscount, 1942.

saw one of the most fateful dramas in the whole history of Parliament!

I left them and went to Zionist Office. There a long consultation with Lewis, Locker and Katznelson (who left Marseilles and came here for a few days) on pros and cons of raising Jewish legions for General Service or Palestine Service. It will certainly be for General Service, Chaim is clear on the point. Tomorrow we have to draft a Declaration for him to Jews, also a private letter to H.M.G. Lewis and I went to Dorchester Hotel to talk to Chaim about this, and there heard King to People on 6 p.m. radio.

September 7th To Zionist Office. Belisha has vetoed the formation of Jewish Legions for the present. It is equipment, not men, whom we need just now. But I think we shall go on enrolling.

September 14th . . . I lunched in L.N.U. Canteen. For the last time! The L.N.U. vacates to Grosvenor Crescent for smaller offices in St Martin's Lane. Only seventeen of the staff retained. Seventeen years since I first went there as head of their Intelligence Section and made it. Another big chapter closes.

September 15th Zionist Office. Drafted letter to MacDonald asking for admission to Palestine of 20,000 Polish children. Poland is nearly gone now, and the plight of the German Jews will be a bed of roses compared with the 3,000,000 Polish Jews when that happens. In spite of all anxieties and worries I come home of an evening to my dear pretty house, and its household of devoted friends and servants, feeling oh how lucky! What *can* one do to deserve it?

September 18th To Zionist Office where Chaim told me privately that he had information about an anti-Hitler plot in the German Army, and that he was certain that *we* could get more news, through Zurich, Brussels, Amsterdam and our contacts there. He was anxious to pass this on to the Foreign Office, it might help to melt what we call the 'glue' in which Jewish efforts to help are smothered, and we think we have located the glue-pot in the War Office. Hearing that Chaim's information is shared by Sir Wyndham Deedes, I suggested asking the latter to come round, as all this story seemed queer to me. He came, I found the facts as stated, names should not be written even here, but it seems a very serious plot. But of course it can hardly ripen while German arms are triumphant. The Foreign Office knows about it, but Chaim's point is that *we* can open to them fresh sources of information.

September 20th Chaim dined last night with Winston, Brendan Bracken and Colin and Professor Lindemann[50] also there. The latter, like Winston,

50. F. A. Lindemann, 'The Prof.': Professor of Experimental Philosophy at Oxford; Churchill's scientific adviser. Cr. Baron Cherwell, 1941.

M

sleeps in the Admiralty. Winston professed himself satisfied with the prospects of the War at sea, and with the hopes of Italy, Yugoslavia and Turkey remaining really neutral for the present, and their coming in on our side. About Palestine he was keen for a Jewish Army for and in Palestine, appointed Brendan his liaison with the Zionist Office and said that what Chaim wanted to further these ideas should be done.

September 30th Went to Zionist Office where found Chaim just returned from the Colonial Office, where MacDonald had asked him to come to say that the 2,000 certificates from Germany had been granted. This no doubt at the insistence of the Foreign Office and our first concrete victory over MacDonald.

Home to tea. Then to Dorchester to dine with the Weizmanns in their private rooms. Present: Lewis, Colin, Brendan Bracken. To the latter Chaim put the points which we want Winston to carry through in Cabinet. (1) Permission to erect an Arms Factory in Palestine; (2) Permission to bring here at once 200 Palestinians to train as officers to form cadres of a Jewish Army. Brendan took note of this. We are to prepare a Memo. for him. At dinner talk on general situation, about which both Colin and Brendan were gloomy, dwelling on our inferiority in equipments, guns, machines of all sorts. We might get even by May. Question—How long does Hitler mean to hold off from attack?

October 6th Zionist Office. Moshe arrived from Palestine, quite green after a fearful crossing from Havre to Southampton, but a sight for sair een.[51] It is only about six weeks since we said good-bye to him in Geneva—I knew not for how long! He brought a vast budget of news, the half of which I have not heard, but we have already begun to deal with the gravest part of it which brought him over, namely that MacDonald is trying to go on with the land-restriction part of the White Paper. Already Chaim has spoken to Oliver Harvey,[52] and I to Brendan and I think we shall scotch that.

October 12th . . . to Zionist Office where Moshe reported on a talk with MacDonald, who evidently wants to go on with the White Paper if he can. I wrote to Brendan Bracken and reported this. Installed myself in Lewis's room at Z.O. where I hope to begin to build up an Information Department.

October 30th . . . Chaim goes again to Switzerland to see Willstaetter,[53] at desire of H.M.G.

51. Scottish dialect: 'A sight for sore eyes'.
52. Oliver Harvey: Private Secretary to Eden and Halifax, 1936–39, 1941–43; Minister at the British Embassy in France, 1940; Assistant and Deputy Under-Secretary of State at the Foreign Office, 1943–47; Ambassador to France, 1948–54. Cr. Baron, 1954.
53. Richard Willstaetter: Nobel Prize for Chemistry. 1914; friend and scientific collaborator of Weizmann. Weizmann went to Switzerland to collect information about German secret weapons, particularly new forms of gas.

November 2nd   To Zionist Office where we discussed further progress of the campaign to save the forty-three.[54] Attlee is speaking to Hore-Belisha on the subject. If we vanquish MacDonald on this, without a row in the House, I really think his downfall is near. If we do *not,* we are now convinced that this is the opening of a campaign against the Hagana and the Agency.

November 5th—Great Swifts, Cranbrook . . . Captain Wingate arrived to dine and sleep. Edgar saw the likeness to T. E. Lawrence, was rather scared by his fanatical earnestness. He is a very forceful character.

November 14th   Morning Yeshiva at Zionist Office spent in discussing the opening of the Parliamentary campaign against MacDonald on the grounds of the forty-three. Lewis and I lunched at Dorchester with Chaim, and Lewis went in the afternoon, and saw several of our M.P. friends, and Barrington-Ward.[55] But at 6 p.m. Chaim went off to the War Office and saw General Ironside[56]—and Lo! The walls of Jericho began to fall. He said he had already telegraphed to Palestine, to reduce the sentence, and revise it after six months. He called it 'savage and stupid'. As for the Hagana, he said: 'Wauchope told me all about it long ago.' Chaim said: 'I could raise you a brigade tomorrow.' Chaim came away convinced that we have in Ironside a friend who will see us through. He said: 'The idea of condemning one of Wingate's boys to imprisonment for life. They ought to have given him a D.S.O.' Chaim thinks that we have really begun now to smash MacDonald. Anyhow the first 'goat' is gone! (See story of Rabbi and goat!)

November 15th . . . At 6 p.m. the whole Yeshiva adjoined to Dorchester, where, with the addition of Captain Wingate and Mr Gestetner, we heard David Ben-Gurion's account of the interview which Chaim forced him today to have with MacDonald. (Lewis gave him a cake of Palestine soap with which to wash his hand after MacDonald had shaken it!) He returned saying he felt as if he had swallowed a frog. I think MacDonald must have felt he had swallowed red hot iron. David warned him that if he tries to disarm the Jews there will be bloodshed, and the guilt on H.M.G. He gave no sign whether or not he knows Ironside's orders to reduce the sentence on the forty-three.

At Yeshiva this morning I suggested we should try to get Palestine transferred to the Foreign Office. Chaim said that Eddie Devonshire had suggested to him that it should be transferred to Dominions Office. Either would have advantages, but D.O. has no machinery of administration. We

54. Forty-three members of the Hagana had been arrested while training and charged with illegal possession of arms.
55. R. Barrington-Ward: Assistant editor of *The Times*, 1927–41; editor, 1941–48.
56. Field-Marshall Sir E. Ironside: Governor and Commander-in-Chief, Gibralter, 1938–39; Chief of Imperial Staff, 1939–40. Cr. Baron, 1941. Ironside had met Wingate in Palestine in 1938 and had been profoundly impressed with his Special Night Squads.

should pursue the idea. Eddie told Chaim he was ready to resign at any moment, on the Palestine policy. Chaim dissuaded him.

November 20th—London . . . To Zionist Office. Discussed the offensive to be opened against MacDonald on two accounts, illegality and inhumanity, of his present interpretation of the White Paper. This offensive all the more necessary because Col. Meinertzhagen[57] told Chaim today that MacDonald is asking the War Office to consider what they will do with Palestine after the War if there is a big Jewish Army there.

November 27th—London . . . I went to Zionist Office after lunch. Found Berl Locker returned from Palestine. He just saw David at Brindisi. Heard that the birds say MacDonald wants to close the Port of Tel Aviv. I hope he tries. That would bring matters to a head. Otherwise the trumpeting goes on in. The C.I.G.S. recommends not making a public offer on a Division *yet.* That is a set-back. The idea of jurists on the White Paper also recedes. Drafted some other ideas as an *aide-memoire* for Chaim when he sees Lord Halifax on Wednesday. . . .

November 29th Zionist Office. Discussed draft letter to Gen. Ironside about offering a Jewish Division, which was finally approved. In the evening to Victor's Yeshiva at Dorchester, where was Captain Wingate. Back to Zionist Office where a discussion on draft on Chaim's Memo. for Lord Halifax on the Colonial Office policy. Dorchester again at 6 p.m. Moshe reported on cable from Palestine, asking our views on a suggestion of Palestinian Labour Corps for French front. Chaim thought it fishy, Captain Wingate passionately convinced it is a clever trap either to prevent further Jewish service, or to reproach us with refusal. It certainly is odd: we know that man-power is not needed in France at present.

December 1st—London Zionist Office. Chaim reported his talk with Lord Halifax with whom he had left our Memo. and definitely invoked his aid against MacDonald and asked for a Cabinet decision on Palestine policy. Moshe also reported on talk with the Labour Leaders, who are going to the P.M. on the subject and will tell him that they will ask for a Parliamentary Debate if the White Paper policy is pursued. So the boats are burned, 'to gain or lose it all'.

December 3rd—Sunday Spent all day at Oxford. Harold Stannard met me at the station (he is on the Chatham House Staff, housed now in Balliol) and in his room there I met Mr Beeley,[58] working on Survey for Middle

---

57. Colonel R. Meinertzhagen: Chief political officer in Palestine, 1919–20; a militant Gentile Zionist.

58. Sir Harold Beeley: Principal adviser to E. Bevin on Palestine affairs from 1945; Secretary to Anglo-American commission on Palestine, 1946; Ambassador to U.A.R., 1961–64, and 1967–69.

East affairs. A harmless young man, who knows nothing whatever about Palestine, never having been there, but an Orientalist who has met a few Arab propagandists. Much imbued with the dead-alive atmosphere that radiates from Chatham House. But I was happy to find that Institution in a bad way, and suspicious that the Foreign Office wants to kill it . . .

December 4th Zionist Office all day. Locker saw the Labour Opposition leaders, who had been to see the P.M. on Palestine. Chamberlain said little and seemed embarrassed and ill-informed. They got the assurance that the land legislation would come before the War Cabinet before it was enacted, and that they would get another talk with the P.M. before anything is done. I do not think that MacDonald would face the music in the House of Commons, and we know that Halifax has written to him. I think we are getting him down at last. . . .

December 5th . . . Chaim had a very satisfactory talk with Brendan on Winston's attitude. But Brendan told him that Winston is terribly worn, and is not sleeping. Brendan wonders whether he will hold out.

December 6th Zionist Office. Chaim talked to Lewis and Berl Locker and me about the Will he is making before he goes to America. He means to bequeath Rehovoth House (after his children's death) to the Jewish people, together with about £70,000, out of which it is to be kept up, either as a sort of 'Chequers', or as a Museum, with 50 dunams, never to be built over. The two big rooms at all events to be kept as they are. The trustees to be the Jewish Agency and Keren Kayemeth [The Jewish National Fund]. A fine idea.

December 8th . . . I spent all day at the Zionist Office. Chaim met General Wavell (commanding in Middle East) by chance, and is to have a talk with him. Moshe thinks it a pity that he should appear in London before the question of the Jewish Division etc. is more forward. Lewis and I are not so sure. I think there is the Finger of God in such meetings. It is interesting his being here: it can hardly be on leave. Armageddon approaches perhaps.

December 9th . . . I dined at East India Club with Walter. He told me that there is now to be a weekly meeting of Ministers. They meet three members of the War Cabinet, Neville, Lord Halifax and Lord Chatfield, and are encouraged to discuss everything, though of course they do not decide on new constitutional developments.

December 13th . . . Zionist Office. Read aloud to them their 'Yeshiva Minutes' in Book of Bosh[59] style, and very good. Great success. They all

59. The Balfour Book of Bosh. This was a compilation of remarks, often unconsciously humorous, made by members of the Balfour family during the years 1890–1920. The Book was circulated in typescript form within the family circle.

roared with laughter, and nobody the least offended. Jews have a Balfourian sense of humour.

December 19th . . . Lewis and I drove to Dorchester to say good-bye to Chaim and Vera. We reached Dorchester about 6 p.m. before Chaim had got back from last interview with C.I.G.S. He came in well satisfied. Among other things he had heard that the C.I.G.S. believes more than ever that the War will go down there, and he might in the end send a whole Army. He spoke of 14 Divisions.

While Chaim was telling us this, and in good spirits, a letter was brought him, by hand from Lord Halifax. He began to read. Lewis went and looked over his shoulder, and at first glance said 'This is bad.' It was a cold, stiff re-statement of the White Paper position, stating that the land legislation could neither be modified nor postponed. This was a severe blow to Chaim, and we felt bitterly that it should have been dealt (knowingly) within twelve hours of his departure for U.S.A. when the *aide-memoire* to which it is a reply has been in Lord Halifax's hands for two or three weeks. Vera and I felt, at first go off, that it made his tour in U.S.A. impossible. We telephoned to Moshe to come at once, Locker was summoned as soon as Moshe arrived, Victor turned up, and we held a Yeshiva in his room with Vera, without Chaim who was upstairs with his chemists. All felt he must go to U.S.A. Money must be obtained to keep Palestine going. He can do no more good with the Foreign Office along the lines pursued recently. He must attack on a new front, American Jewry, Roosevelt, etc. It was a great blow to Moshe too, who came here at the first alarm of land legislation and now returns to Palestine for a short holiday with nothing done. But it is a good thing he is going, as communication is so difficult. While we were conferring Chaim rang up Butler at the Foreign Office who professed to know nothing about the letter, but at once went to speak to Lord Halifax and presently rang again to say that the letter was 'not meant to distress' Chaim whatever that may mean! Possibly it means that it is merely a re-statement of position, dictated by MacDonald and does *not* imply that they mean to start land restrictions. But that remains unclear.

I went off to Carlton Grill with Walter. Re Palestine he said he had all this time been struck by the discrepancy between my reports and Chaim's talks with Foreign Office and their own cables to Arabs, which resist the pressure to make further concessions when War ends, but stand firm by policy already announced—i.e. the White Paper.

December 20th To Zionist Office. Yeshiva only consists now of Lewis, Berl Locker and me, with occasionally Brodetsky as today. We felt the miss terribly of Chaim and Moshe, departed at such a depressing moment. However, we worked away at their instructions about the Halifax letter, sending it to the Opposition Leaders, Churchill, Amery, with covering letters. . . .

December 27th—Bridgnorth . . . Lewis had heard by telephone from Berl in London that the birds have told us that MacDonald has communicated with MacMichael, asking his views on whether the Arabs should be told to ask that the constitutional part of the White Paper should be implemented now. This seems the lowest depth of intrigue that MacDonald has yet sunk to, and cannot be justified by any excuse of national interest at this juncture. We had a long talk on whether this information could be acted on by us in any way. It is not easy, but when Lewis goes back to London we may be able to convey it to the Opposition Leaders and Winston.

December 28th . . . In the afternoon Brendan unexpectedly rang up from London. He spoke very cryptically and in some excitement, and asked us whether we could catch Chaim by cable before he spoke in New York. I answered that no doubt the office could. Brendan then said it was very important that Chaim should know as soon as possible that the whole of our affairs were changed for the better. He (Brendan) then said that 'the little rabbit [Malcolm MacDonald], you know who' was 'finished' (or words to that effect). Winston had spent five hours talking to him (he did not say whether alone or in War Cabinet, but Lewis and I concluded alone, probably one evening). Brendan then asked us to prepare at once for Winston a Memo. on the Land Question. So we prepared a cable for Chaim, saying 'Donald (my code word for Brendan in the private code I arranged for Chaim) desires inform you situation radically improved' signed 'Baffy'. We then rang Brendan again, got his approval of this cable, and his instructions about the Land Memo. Then we rang Berl, dictated to him the cable, and asked him to send by passenger train tomorrow, a selection of Memos already existing in Zionist Office.

We feel that, making all allowance for possible optimism on Brendan's part, the instruction for cabling to Chaim must mean that Winston has taken a strong line, and that MacDonald will not be able in future to have his own way.

December 31st—Bridgnorth   So the year ends with a turn for the better so far as the affairs of Eretz Israel are concerned.

'The Lord shall reign on Zion's Hill'. . . .

1940 *January 2nd—Central Hotel, Glasgow* . . . I waited half-an-hour for Walter and John Boyd[1] in the Malmaison Restaurant, where we three dined together . . . Walter told me that Winston had sent in long Cabinet Memo. on Palestine (it was probably this that took 'five hours' to prepare. See December 28th). This Memo. had caused the despatch to Lothian to be suspended by cable until the Cabinet should have discussed it. There has been one discussion, when MacDonald divided the White Paper policy into three parts—(1) Immigration, on which he said there was no dispute; (2) Land, on which he said he would bring forward proposals in a fortnight; and (3) Constitution, which he said would not be operative for five years. This shows that either the information recorded on December 27th is inaccurate, or he is grossly deceiving his colleagues.

This accounts for Brendan's request for a Memo. on Land.

January 4th—Strachur Heard from Lewis, who had seen Brendan in London. Brendan said 'there has been a change of heart. MacDonald had had "a thorough trimming" but we must not crow over him—nothing must be known about his defeat.' Winston had pointed out the reduced majority over the White Paper, and had reminded his colleagues of the fact that he had opposed it. Now no important legislation or administrative action is to be taken in Palestine without the War Cabinet. MacDonald had finished by admitting the wisdom of what Winston said. Bracken added 'that of course MacDonald would be against us as much as ever, but that this decision had clearly trimmed his wings.'

January 14th—Sunday . . . The chief gossip since I left still centres around the Hore-Belisha affair,[2] and speculations as to what the P.M. and he will say in the House on Tuesday. I talked to Colin Coote about it on the telephone. He says it is a Horace Wilson decision (like everything else apparently) and the Generals did not do it, but have been used by those who

1. John Boyd: Solicitor in Glasgow, a lifelong friend of Walter Elliot; Professor of Mercantile Law, Glasgow University, 1946–57. Kt. 1961.
2. Hore-Belisha had resigned as Secretary of State for War on 5 Jan.; he was replaced by Oliver Stanley.

were determined to do it. Whatever Hore-Belisha's defects, Colin thinks it was done in a most disastrous way and time. The offer of the Board of Trade was made under conditions Belisha could not accept . . . Belisha has had a most *enormous* 'fan-mail'. Nobody knows what he will say on Tuesday. Certainly the Wilson gang have made a most formidable enemy. But it will probably blow over in *this* House of Commons.

. . . It is a pity Sir Horace Wilson cannot attend to the Civil Service instead of trying to run high politics.

January 16th   Brodetsky and Berl saw MacDonald yesterday, but he only talked about refusing permits to Jews from Germany, for fear they be spies. A Yeshiva at which we discussed this and whether to cable for one of the Palestinians to come here. This was decided on and I am glad for Brendan rang me up this evening to say things looked ugly again . . .

January 17th   Walter said on telephone this morning that he thought Brendan's scare was because the Cabinet yesterday had before it the Memo. on land policy which MacDonald said he was going to prepare before Christmas, and it is very strongly for going on. However, at the Yeshiva we decided to strengthen our line in every possible way. . . . All day at Zionist Office . . . Victor's Yeshiva at Dorchester, Gestetner there and Orde Wingate. The latter very adverse to training Jewish officers in Palestine. Clearly he wants it here, where he might get General Ironside to give him the running of it. That would be all right, but I do not think that all other considerations ought to be sacrificed to it.

January 19th   I dined at Carlton Grill with Walter . . . he told me that the boundaries within which MacDonald wants to permit land purchase are those of the Woodhead Report.[3] We expected as much (or as little). Also manufacture of munitions will be forbidden, not out of ill-will, but for lack of machine-tools. Walter wondered whether we could get some Jew to dismantle a factory in America and send over machine-tools to Palestine which H.M.G. could not otherwise get! Only so can we get the thing started.

January 29th . . . Berl Locker telephoned that he and Lewis must see me. I bade them come, and . . . they told me that someone has come from Palestine, bringing word that a ship with 730 (illegal) halutzim on board had been arrested, at the western end of the Dardanelles, coming out of the Black Sea, and brought by H.M. Navy to Haifa, where she arrived on January 23rd and awaits orders from London what to do with the refugees who are still on board. Moshe sent us a message to see Winston about it. I said that this was a matter on which it was our primary duty to see Malcolm. Lewis and Berl objected that in an official interview their warnings about

3. Presumably Plan C of the Report which restricted the Jewish area to the coastal plain between Tel Aviv and Zichron Ya'akov, approximately four hundred square miles.

the effect on Palestinian opinion if the refugees are not allowed to land would sound like threats. What they wanted to know was whether they would be allowed to land, or be deported to some distant concentration camp (say Seychelles, Hong Kong, Singapore). I volunteered to go and see Malcolm alone, and this was agreed to. I telephoned, and his Private Secretary got me an interview for tomorrow morning at 11 a.m.

January 30th Went to Colonial Office. MacDonald said at once that he intended to let the refugees land. We arranged that he was to cable to the High Commissioner to tell this to the Jewish Agency at once. I dictated a full account of the interview as soon as I got back to the office, and will only say here that I thought the atmosphere changed. It was arranged that we were to have another talk soon about the whole situation, he to propose the date. I dined with Walter at the House of Commons and told him all this and consulted him about what I should say. He suggested the following line, starting from what I said to MacDonald today, that it cannot be anybody's duty to try and make water run up-hill.

Jewish immigration. No pressure that MacDonald could apply could equal the pressure of Gestapo outside. It will go on until that pressure is released. Statesmanship is to take account of facts. See Ireland. MacDonald put the finishing touch to the reversal of Unionist policy.[4] I grew up with that, I have seen its failure, I see the price we have to pay for its failure. Our ships run the gauntlet of German submarines every day all the way to the Bristol Channel. But it is inevitable.

Recognize the inevitable. Be constructive. Work now for Federation. Let us be definitive. The Jews cannot live without Sharon, Emek, Galilee.

Arabs: Ibn Sa'ud is the one that counts. What does he want? Surely, like all desert dwellers, money and wheat. Does he want to see the sand cover Palestine once again? Does he want to see Tel Aviv sand-dunes once more? Does Britain want it? Will it bring peace to Palestine?

The Jews are talking to the Arabs. They are talking to Philby,[5] for what that is worth. It is not too late for MacDonald to take a hand in the greatest work for the Middle East. Today, he and I sit, just for once, outside the story. Tomorrow, we might fight one another again. We are both British. We seek the same end. It is not too late.

Then Walter told me that MacDonald put in lately a second Memo. against the Hagana, proceeding from the assumption that it is a subversive organization. If he gives me a chance on that, to take the line of gentle irony. What is the idea does he suppose? First to destroy the British Empire, and then take on Germany and Russia? An ambitious programme indeed.

4. MacDonald negotiated the Anglo-Irish settlement of April 1938. By it the Government renounced its naval rights in the southern Irish ports of Berehaven and Queenstown, and gave up its naval base at Lough Swilly.
5. H. St J. Philby: Indian civil servant; chief British representative in Transjordan, 1921–24; Arabian explorer and adviser to Ibn Sa'ud.

If in fact he has heard stories of bombs, is it not more likely that they were actually for self-defence?

If only God gives me power to get some of this across!

February 7th   Zionist Office. Brendan had asked Lewis for a redraft of the Memo. on Land which we prepared for Winston at Bridgnorth. This we did. It may be that the conference of the four Ministers is to be held at last. There has been a long and mysterious delay. Every week that the White Paper remains a dead letter is so much to the good. For everyone who comes from Palestine . . . speaks of peace spreading, and the Jews buying more land, especially in the outposts of Galilee . . .

February 13th . . . felt very seedy and drowsy . . . I staggered out to the Carlton Grill, where met Lewis, Moshe, and Brendan Bracken. The latter told us that Winston has been defeated by MacDonald in Cabinet on the White Paper, and the restriction will shortly be promulgated, as Walter warned us. It was a great blow. When Brendan was gone we decided: (1) to tell the Opposition leaders and get them to go to Chamberlain, threaten a Debate, and ask for a judicial opinion on legality; (2) to wire to Chaim, who can get judicial opinion in U.S.A. It is all that is left for us to do just now.

February 14th . . . I dined with Walter at the House of Commons, and learned: (1) that the boundaries of the land purchase areas are not yet decided, and (2) that they are telling Lord Lothian to inform Chaim about the decision. This seems to show that they are anxious about the way he will take it, and strengthens the feeling which has been growing in me all day that he ought to come back to England at once, and announce the reason why he cuts short his tour.

February 15th   Went to Zionist Office where the Yeshiva decided to cable to Chaim in above sense.

February 21st . . . We were all greatly perplexed by a letter from Mr Attlee to Berl Locker, saying he and Greenwood had seen MacDonald who assured them that no disturbance of the status quo is contemplated and that they would be given due notice of any. In view of what we know from Walter from Brendan and from the birds, this is a lie. I gave the letter to Walter with whom I lunched at the Chandos,[6] and I hope he will try to see Mac-

---

6. At the beginning of the war, Mrs Dugdale together with Lady Violet Bonham-Carter arranged to hold weekly luncheon parties at the Chandos restaurant, then a modest establishment on the corner of Trafalgar Square and William IV Street. Certain close friends and relatives could come as they pleased, each paying for himself, and other guests were occasionally brought. This institution was dubbed 'the Venusberg' because Mrs Dugdale and Lady Violet were jocularly supposed to use it to seduce young men into divulging valuable disclosures.

Donald about it. Berl went to see Tom Williams and try to persuade him that we are not panic-stricken for no cause.

February 22nd   Heard something of what passed between Walter and MacDonald yesterday, but am somewhat puzzled. It appears that MacDonald quite realizes that the Labour leaders intend to make a fuss, but I do not know whether he admitted that he tried to cheat them into thinking that nothing is imminent. But anyhow this afternoon Berl and Moshe persuaded them to write to the P.M. as suggested yesterday, so I think that we can do no more here.

February 26th—London . . . After lunch went to the Zionist Office and there learned that the blow has fallen. MacDonald informed Moshe and Berl this morning that the Land Regulations would be promulgated in Palestine tomorrow. He showed me the map. It is as bad as we expected, but I think now the worse the better. Lord Lothian has been told to inform Chaim and a cable has come from Jerusalem saying that they have seen the map etc. They will put out their own statement, we spent this morning drafting the one to be given to the British Press tomorrow. It is a great blow even though we expected it. We heard by telephone from Tom Williams that Major Attlee was 'furious' at the way Labour leaders had been tricked into believing nothing was imminent. We have also heard by telephone from Williams that Attlee and Greenwood saw the P.M. this afternoon, but after an hour's hot argument they did not prevail. So it looks as if there is nothing now to do except to prepare for the Debate.

February 27th   A very strange day! Went up to the Zionist Office as usual, and worked on draft statement, in preparation for a Press Conference we had called for 3.30 p.m. Soon after 11 a.m. Archie Sinclair rang up and asked Lewis to come and see him at noon. After Lewis had gone, the Colonial Office rang up Moshe, and said the publication was delayed until 6 p.m. That was our first hint that anything had gone wrong with their plans, and we did not like to attach any importance to it. Then Lewis returned from Archie, who told him that far from things being as Tom Williams had said last night, the P.M. had promised the Labour leaders and himself to take the matter back to the War Cabinet this morning. This at the end of an hour's very hot discussion. (Greenwood said later to Berl that there had been nothing like it since Munich.) The P.M. was quite unprovided with arguments and seemed to know very little about the matter. It appears from what Archie said that they told him they would 'break the political truce' on this, as it was a matter of major policy, on which they had a right to be consulted. We also heard that when the Labour leaders saw MacDonald yesterday, they roundly accused him of having 'deliberately deceived' them.

After Lewis' return, we put off our Press Conference (we afterwards heard that MacDonald had had to do the same for one which he had called at midday). We four (Lewis, Berl, Moshe and self) lunched in 77 off smoked salmon sandwiches and pickled cucumbers, not liking to go far from the telephone. We finished our Statement, and had it roneod for release at any moment. Later in the afternoon Berl saw the Labour leaders. We did not go home till after six, when it was evident that no publication could take place today. But unfortunately the text of the Government's Statement seems to have leaked from Palestine to U.S.A. and got published there. All we could do was to cable Chaim that there is a delay here.

I dined at House of Commons with Walter and told him all this. He said that to have held it up even so far is a miracle. He thinks H.M.G. has got itself into a fearful jam, and that whatever happens the events of today will leave their mark against MacDonald and his policy. Walter seems never to have realized that MacDonald had 'been so foolish' as tie up his land ordinances with the White Paper. If he had brought them in as a War measure of administrative necessity, nobody (except the Jews) would have said a word against him.

February 28th Yesterday's hopes were a good deal dashed by the news which came to Lewis through Brendan about midday, that H.M.G. propose to put the Land Regulations into force at once, and at the same time circularize the Members of the League Council about it . . . It did not take us long to realize that this is a clever trick which makes matters worse for us; it is not likely that any of the neutral States will upset a *fait accompli* which will please Hitler as much as MacDonald.

I went to a public lunch at the Dorchester, where Lloyd George was speaking on 'Dig for Victory'. There I saw Tom Williams and told him. Locker had meantime seen Attlee and we found the Opposition determined not to agree to this trick. There will be a Debate next week, so we have all the lobbying, etc. to do. Leo Amery came to our Dorchester Yeshiva. It was decided there to call the Parliamentary Committee, etc.

February 29th To L.N.U., got them to pass a resolution condemning the Government's trick over Palestine . . .

. . . to see Watt about my book [*Family Homespun*], which he is offering to Faber and Faber. Then to Zionist Office, worked on draft by Moshe of a letter to *The Times*. Dined at home. The Debate will be on Wednesday next. Lewis heard from Brendan that Winston was at the Palace when the War Cabinet took the decision about the League and thinks it idiotic. Lord Halifax is supporting MacDonald, but the P.M. is uncomfortable about it all. The Nine O'Clock News told of mourning in Jerusalem, processions of protest in Tel Aviv and Arabs dancing and singing in the streets of Jaffa.

March 1st Walter told me it could not have been the War Cabinet which took the decision; it must have been an *ad hoc* meeting of Ministers.

March 5th   My pamphlet[7] out, also the map of the Land Regulations. The whole office worked feverishly all day to get these things circulated to M.P.'s in time for tomorrow's Debate. I lunched with Gestetner at Carlton Grill; he is charming and so helpful. It was his firm who prepared the map, which we only got on loan from the Colonial Office for two hours.

Victor gave a dinner at the Dorchester for Conservative M.P.'s, there came Oliver Locker-Lampson,[8] Mr Lipson,[9] Mr Strickland,[10] Sir P. Hannon,[11] Sir Joseph Lamb[12] and Leo Amery, all sympathetic, but all except Leo and Victor very doubtful of voting against H.M.G. on a Vote of Censure in Wartime. That shows what we may expect tomorrow. Moshe and Lewis were at dinner. Berl and Bakstansky came in after, all these had been at a Palestine Parliamentary Committee, and a Labour Dinner, both which I understand went very well.

March 6th   The Debate. A bitter day. Dear Victor's sincerity the one bright spot.

March 7th   Went to Zionist Office. Moshe away ill, the others there, we discussed the question of a House of Lords Debate, before I went to see the Archbishop at Lambeth by appointment. Last night we should all have shuddered at the bare idea, today there seemed another side to the matter. To me it seems vital to show the Jews that they still have friends, that there is still honour in Britain. So much depends on who would speak. Talked to the Archbishop about it, he said he would like to talk it over with Bob and Lytton. He was very nice, called me 'valiant' and after hearing about MacDonald said he would be unhappy if I ever spoke of *him* in such terms, or had cause to, so he would make his position quite clear. He must be of independent judgement, the land clauses were not to him quite the same as the White Paper etc. I said *of course,* he was the head of the Christian Church and that was enough for me. He said 'Yes and some people would say that as such I must not concern myself with politics'. I only smiled.

March 14th ... Drove with Chaim to Zionist Office where he gave us an account of U.S.A., the need for reorganizing Zionist forces there, which no-one can do but himself, and how much MacDonald has caused pro-British feeling to collapse. It is evident to me that the first result of MacDonald's policy will be to diminish the importance of London as a Zionist political centre, and to enhance that of U.S.A.

April 7th   Went to Dorchester for half-an-hour before lunch to see Chaim

7. Apparently refers to *Documents and Correspondence relating to Palestine August* 1939–*March* 1940, (London, 1940).
8. Commander Oliver Locker-Lampson: Conservative M.P. for Handsworth from 1922.
9. D. L. Lipson: Independent Conservative M.P. for Cheltenham from 1937.
10. Captain W. F. Strickland: Conservative M.P. for Coventry from 1931.
11. Sir Patrick Hannon: Conservative M.P. for Moseley, Birmingham, from 1921.
12. Sir Joseph Lamb: Conservative M.P. for Stone, Staffordshire, from 1922.

and Vera, he off tomorrow for a short visit to Switzerland, where he will see Willstaetter and will consult him about an invention which a German refugee chemist has laid before him for converting salt water into fresh. This invention, if sound, would transform the world, not only Palestine. Chaim thinks it could not be patented, but could at the outset be given to one Government, he thinks only Britain or America. As things are, he may prefer America, but we must think the matter over carefully if it turns out to be practical. Chaim would certainly not hand it over now to Britain without a *quid pro quo* for Palestine.

April 9th   The War *has* begun. In the course of last night the Germans invaded Denmark and Norway. There was little about it in the morning papers, but when I dined with Walter at the Club this evening he told me that some of the French Ministers flew over here for consultation today. Some kind of naval battle is going on in the North Sea. The Navy has been told to retake Bergen (it is still obscure to me how it happened that the Germans were able to occupy these Norwegian ports today without interference).[13] . . .

Against all this developing situation the ordinary Zionist Office things were at a standstill.

April 10th . . . I went to the luncheon at the Dorchester and heard Lord Halifax speak. He said two things of importance: (i) That even if Norway negotiated for peace with Germany, the Allies would consider it done under pressure, and come to her aid as promised . . . (ii) That our attitude to Russia would depend entirely on Russia's attitude to Germany . . . I then went to Zionist Office. There was news from Jerusalem that Ben-Gurion is resigning from the Executive on account of differences with the majority about the right reaction to the White Paper. He wants to break with H.M.G. Whether right or wrong, the effect of disunity now would be serious. I sent him a wire imploring him to consider this.

April 19th   Zionist Office. Heard that Ben-Gurion is coming to London for a few days soon, and has put off his resignation.

April 22nd—London   I was invited to Seder at the Lockers. Twelve people. The youngest only six, too young to ask the questions, but she stole the Matza. Berl read and sang the service beautifully. My thoughts went back to Pesach last year, and the Seder in Peter's house on Carmel. Then a 'Death Ship' rocked in the bay. But things are even worse this year; Berl said, as he walked with me to Russell Square Station, 'This is the blackest Seder I ever remember.' As always the ceremony moved me much. I wish I were in Eretz Israel!

---

13. On 9 April German sea and airborne units descended on Oslo, Bergen, Trondheim, Stavanger and Narvik. At the same time German forces entered Denmark without more than formal resistance. A British force was dispatched but soon had to withdraw.

April 24th . . . I went to a Yeshiva at the Dorchester with Victor. Discussion of a tragic letter from refugees on the Danube, and also about the Palestine 'atrocities' and how to make all this known. Chaim's bitter, anti-British mood continues.

Then, with Berl Locker, and in Mr Gestetner's car, I went to the far North-East of London, where I'd been invited to a 'Third Seder' by the Hechalutz. About 150 young men and women, mostly East End Jews sprinkled with Palestinian trainers. The room was stifling, reproducing an atmosphere of Chamsin as someone remarked. A fine meal of salad, soup, chickens (from the David Eder farm, where all get their first training), then speeches, not many, Palestinian songs, etc. The true spirit of Eretz Israel, wonderful and moving. What a tremendous thing it is to be welcomed by them to their inmost festivals, to be made part of so great a movement! Gestetner's car waited and brought me home after midnight.

May 1st . . . There is a story that Winston would only have sanctioned the Narvik landings, but allowed himself to be overborne about the others, and suspicion that now, if things go wrong, the Government will make him the scapegoat and go on as before. How is it possible that with this rising and universal feeling that the war is not being vigorously prosecuted that still they are suffered to remain? . . .

Returned to Zionist Office where found David Ben-Gurion, newly come from Palestine by air. He slept in Rome, paid 10/- for a miserable meal. About Palestine he has not so far said much, but when asked how the Jews were getting on with the Army, he replied, 'We have two armies, the Australian and the British. With the Australians we get on very well indeed.' It appears that one British battalion had 100 Palestinians in a Pioneer unit, of whom seven were Arabs. The British objected to eating with these 'natives', whereupon the C.O. decreed that all the 'Palestinians' should have their meals apart! God what fools!

May 2nd A day of great emotions. In the morning at Zionist Office a full Yeshiva with Chaim in the chair, and discussion of whether (as Ben-Gurion thinks) a policy of more active resistance to the White Paper should be pursued in Palestine. He gave his reasons, Chaim countered them, both with utmost dignity and feeling of responsibility. Kaplan also spoke, on the other side of Ben-Gurion, as we all were. B.G. wants to resign from the Executive on this, though not, on this, to go into opposition. But I hope we can dissuade him.

. . . I learned that we are evacuating Norway, the story of it in all the Clubs already. It was a terrible shock, even though I was prepared . . . all took the gravest view of the consequences, especially on neutrals, including Turkey! Provided only that the full story when known shocks this country enough to bring the Government down. If we go on this way we shall *not* win the war.

May 6th A heavy day of work at Zionist Office. At morning Yeshiva Lewis put forward his new idea of utilizing present Government crisis to try to use arguments to show how ill the Allies can do without Jews if war spreads, also risk of bloodshed in Holy Land if present policy continues. He suggests Chaim should see Halifax and Archbishop about this, and work for a transfer from Colonial Office to War Office to eliminate MacDonald from possible fresh effort to come to accommodation. This latter part of project remained in suspense, but Chaim promised both these interviews and desired to be armed with a Memo. on recent events, which we began to prepare. David very contemptuous of whole thing. I fear he means to return to Palestine and pursue a suicidal activist policy . . .

May 7th A terrific day. Zionist Office in morning, worked with Lewis on our new statement of events. Then to House of Commons, where I joined Dorothy Macmillan and we went to Strangers Gallery for first day of the great Debate on conduct of the war. I never saw the House so packed, even for the Munich Debate. But what a change. The P.M. started off, spoke for an hour, a terrible failure, he never held the House for one moment, and dropped brick after brick. Piteous, if there were pity in one's soul for him. Attlee and Archie followed, good, especially Archie, but not devastatingly so. Then Bob Boothby came up and took us down to tea. He reported that there would be no change of Government, that Lloyd George and the Labour leaders were determined not to take charge of affairs at this juncture, that the mess is so great, and the disasters to be expected in the next six weeks so terrible, let those who have sown the wind, reap the whirlwind. That was Bob's story about 5.30 p.m. I could only say that if it were true Attlee had no business to make the speech he did make. We went back to the Gallery and were in time to hear Sir Roger Keyes,[14] in full naval uniform to speak for the Navy. A terrible indictment on the Admiralty. It knocked the House in the very pit of its stomach. Impossible to say what the reaction will be, but never have I seen the speech of a back-bencher change history, as I think this must. The Speaker did not (as usual!) call Amery till the dinner hour and I missed most of him, but hear he was very wonderful. Meantime the Government supporters were feeble indeed. A rot had set in among them after the P.M.

Dined in the House with Harold Nicolson, also there were Violet [Bonham-Carter], Sybil Colefax . . . Walter joined us for coffee. Harold ventured opinion that he does not want a change of Government now, but gradually. Narvik will be a disaster in ten days or so, let Old Umbrella

---

14. Admiral Sir Roger Keyes: World War One hero; Conservative M.P. for Portsmouth from 1934; first Director of Combined Operations Command, 1940–41. Cr. Baron, 1943.

fold up then, but full change over to Labour should not take place until after Holland and Belgium are invaded, and bombing of England begins. What will tomorrow bring forth?

May 8th It has brought forth the fall of Chamberlain and his Government. At least I think it must be so. I was with Chaim and Vera, at the Dorchester, waiting for the midnight news. It gave us the figures on the Vote of Confidence—only 81—almost exactly the same as those which *we* hailed as a moral victory when MacDonald forced the White Paper through the House last May.[15] Walter thought they would fall when he dined with me at the Club earlier in the evening. I feel more awe-struck than rejoicing, the relief to know that the country will be rid of them is enormous, but is it too late? . . . I can write no more tonight, but should perhaps put down now that I think when the King sends for Attlee he will probably advise sending for Halifax. But, horrible as this is, I think he will be more the captive than the master, and anyway we surely get rid of Chamberlain and Sir Horace Wilson.

May 10th When I was awakened by Andersen[16] this morning, with her usual cry of 'It's half-past eight, Madam' I found she had put one of her usual little notes by my bedside. This one ran 'Belgium and Holland were invaded at 3 a.m., Madam'—just as she has so often written something like 'You have lost your gloves, Madam'.

So there it is! Went to Zionist Office where we discussed what to do to repeat and publish Jewish desire to help war effort. Finally wrote a Memo. for General Dill, and a letter to *The Times* from Chaim . . . All day the posters reported fresh bombings, Brussels—Antwerp—Lyons—Nancy—Calais etc. and some incendiary bombs dropped on a village in Kent.

. . . We listened to the news and heard Chamberlain's farewell from Number Ten. Chaim had already told me on telephone that he was going. Leo Amery had spoken with Chaim. He will be in the new Cabinet when formed. Lewis also rang up to say that the Labour leaders had consulted their conference[17] at Bournemouth, who had said unanimously that they would enter Government under a new leader. So it is to be Winston! The one thing I thought he could never be is P.M. Whatever happens now, it is a vast relief to have the old gang cleared out. But let us have no illusions about the War itself. The new men take over a hand of cards so badly played that we dare not expect to win this game of the rubber. Events *must* go against us this summer.

---

15. Then the figure was 89; see entry for 23 May 1939.
16. Amelia Andersen: Mrs Dugdale's personal maid for many years, herself a Dane.
17. They in fact consulted their national executive. Party representatives were gathering at Bournemouth for their annual conference which did not convene until 13 May.

May 13th—London To Zionist Office. Found Chaim and others on the whole pleased. Drafted Chaim's short note of congratulation to Lord Lloyd.[18] Lunched with Chaim and Vera at Dorchester, where Colin joined us, told us some of the Ministerial changes, and that he knew that Walter is one of those who get nothing. Then he talked of how Chamberlain had hoped the invasion of the Low Countries would have saved him, but Labour was adamant. No-one seems to like the present composition of the War Cabinet, but Colin says Margesson got at Winston on Thursday and extracted promises about Chamberlain and Halifax. However, Horace Wilson has been told to go and mind his own business. It is curious how everyone of the Ministers who accepted Munich against the grain have fallen, Oliver Stanley—Buck—Ernest Brown (I think he was one) and Winterton. Buck and Winterton were 'for it' anyway, but it is hard that Neville and Halifax survive and these others are deserted. Duff Cooper reaps the reward of his courage.[19]

May 14th . . . His [Walter's] view of the Debate is that it had nothing to do with Norway directly, only the Government was crushed like a nut between those who remember Munich and the Right Wing who discovered the deficiencies of supply. There has been a reaction. Winston had a bad reception when he appeared yesterday as P.M. He is alleged to have been much disconcerted, and to have said 'I shan't last long.' He is absorbed in the War and is leaving the making of his Ministry largely to Margesson and Brendan Bracken. What a pair! Nobody takes the present War Cabinet seriously, and the appointment of Archie to Air and Anthony to War is taken to mean that Winston intends to run the War himself.

Oliver Stanley was offered Dominions. Winston said to him that he had not enough drive or initiative to carry anything through, but he was a Stanley and might do for the Dominions. He declined!

May 16th . . . Not much doing at Zionist Office. Chaim and Ben-Gurion had a rather unsatisfactory interview with Lord Lloyd, but tonight Chaim had a personal message from Winston, through Randolph Churchill, re-assuring about searches for arms and acceptance of Jewish help.

May 21st The French Army has broken. It appears now to be a question of hours before the enemy is at the Channel Ports.

After lunch went to House of Commons . . . Walter had taken his seat in Amery's old place, I begged him to stay there. Let him mark the beginning of true independence. It might be the beginning of a new career. We were discussing these matters in the tea-room . . . the first breath of the disaster came from Oliver Locker-Lampson, who came into the tea-room and told us the Germans were at Amiens and Arras. Out in the pas-

---

18. He had replaced MacDonald as Colonial Secretary in Churchill's new administration.
19. He returned to office as Minister of Information.

sage we saw Maisky, the Russian Ambassador, who appeared much perturbed and said to Walter 'You *must* get some aeroplanes.' I came home and listened with Edgar to the Six o'clock News, in which Reynaud's[20] speech to the Senate this afternoon, frankly telling that the Meuse bridges had not been blown up, and other tales of ineptitude, or worse . . .

May 22nd   After dinner Berl Locker rang up to say he and Dov Hos had seen both Greenwood and Morrison, and they had been interested in our War Effort proposals. Want a Memo. tomorrow, and told us to remember that things are quite different in the War Cabinet now, they are 'three to two' and the P.M. on our side in Jewish matters.

Is it possible that the Dead Hand is being lifted at last?

May 24th . . . This afternoon Chaim had an hour and a half with Lord Lloyd, who spoke of his fears of Moslem world, but Chaim thinks he 'made a dent' on his mind. The technical and industrial resources will be the line of least resistance. We may however get training of cadres, and if (as Chaim is sure) the Arabs prove unreliable at first approach of War, the rest will soon follow. It was a very friendly talk, and Sir George Gater[21] was there, and Chaim means to go and see him soon.

May 25th . . . to Dorchester where Chaim took Lewis and me into the other room and gave us an account of his . . . talk with Lord Lloyd yesterday. It seems possible that once again, as in 1916, Chaim's genius for pyschology may have had a decisive effect upon the man who matters. Was much upset by Vera blabbing out, before half a dozen people, that Orde Wingate had written eight pages to the P.M. accusing the High Commissioner of being a Fascist. Wingate is an able man but an irresponsible lunatic, and I only hope Lewis is right in saying that such action will do no harm to anyone but himself.

May 28th . . . the appalling news that at 4 a.m. today the King of the Belgians had betrayed his country and the Allies, and without warning, had surrendered unconditionally to the Germans.

Stunned, I went to Zionist Office. There our Yeshiva firstly discussed whether the leaders should disperse, to Palestine, to U.S.A. or stay here. I had picked Chaim up at the Dorchester, and driving with him in the taxi had put the case for his taking Vera and Maidie[22] (who expects a child) and going to U.S.A. . . . He reacted against this at once, on public grounds because he thinks he will be more useful here, both as Zionist leader and as chemist (already he is called in to supply vast quantities of quinine by the Rehovoth process).

20. The French Prime Minister.
21. Sir George Gater: Permanent Under-Secretary at the Colonial Office, 1940, 1942–47.
22. The wife of Benjamin, his eldest son.

Two meetings at Dorchester during afternoon, to hear about a talk between Chaim and Brendan . . . From Brendan Chaim learned that the P.M. is telling Lord Lloyd that no obstacles are to be put in the way of the Jewish War Effort. The walls of Jericho fall, but at what a moment!

May 29th . . . a full Yeshiva in Chaim's room at the Dorchester, to hear his report of talk with Lord Lloyd this afternoon. This opens vistas, the technical help will be accepted immediately, cadres will probably be trained . . . and Chaim launched idea of Palestine as supply depot for the whole Middle East. Constructive work ahead at last . . . Chaim warned him to be careful not to upset the Jews. This made an impression, and there was evidence that he had received at least a hint from the P.M.

May 30th The British Expeditionary Force holds firm, I believe a considerable number are home already. It is said that the French troops are making a diversion for their sake. What heights, as well as what depths, the human spirit can reach!

May 31st All day long the tale of the most glorious retreat in all history [from Dunkirk] was added to. I think that well over 150,000 men have reached England, including several thousand French. Walter tells me that a naval officer perceived that they could be embarked from the beach, and sent word for every kind of craft to come over from every English near-by port, and so they came. But all the guns are lost. Nevertheless, we have not only their lives, but a veteran Army on these shores to mingle with our half-trained troops and help in what may come.

June 5th . . . Went to Weizmanns quite late. Chaim may be made a Chemical Adviser direct to P.M. Amery, Lloyd and MacMillan have conferred, and Palestine is to be made a supply base. Lloyd gives in, but with a bad grace. Question is, how soon can we get a move on?

June 10th Tonight Italy declared war on France and Britain. Duff Cooper in a fine broadcast told the fate that awaited these Wops.

June 17th A black day—for this morning came the utterly unexpected news that the Reynaud Government has fallen. Another, much further to the Right, under Petain,[23] is seeking to make terms with Germany for ceasing hostilities. Does this include the French Fleet and Air Force? All day long there has been silence on this vital question. Well, the British Empire will fight on alone, as the P.M. said, in a short broadcast tonight. But it is a heavy blow.

Jimmie arrived from Scotland before breakfast, and will stay here for

23. Marshal of France; hero of Verdun; signed armistice with Germans in 1940.

the present.[24] He works in Ministry of Information in the liaison between the Ministry and the B.B.C.

June 18th—(Waterloo Day!) To Zionist Office. Discussed plans. Dov Hos returns to Palestine, David goes to U.S.A. Chaim refuses to leave London. I know this is partly for private reasons, but he points out that if the French fight on in Syria and we are one with them there may be political developments with regard to Palestine which necessitate his presence nearer than U.S.A. This convinced Lewis . . . We began to arrange to send archives to Palestine. We cabled to Smuts asking him to press H.M.G. with regard to arming Jews in Palestine. Lord Lloyd saw Chaim and David this morning, proved adamant still against Jewish force, but showed signs that he was being pressed (I met Brendan by chance in the street, and begged him to renew this pressure). Lloyd did agree to stop searching for arms; this is the first little victory we have had!

July 5th Zionist Office. Then lunched at Ivy Restaurant with Bob Boothby. He told me all about an interview he had with the P.M. to whom he had sent a Memo. saying we were not getting on with the War, especially conscription of labour. Winston was very angry, told him if he did not mind his own business he would perhaps have no business to mind![25] He accused Bob of being one of the people 'intriguing' against Neville. He said 'You went to Amery's house the other night. You had no business to go there.' (This shows me Leo is taking a hand. I had heard he was not getting on with the P.M.) Bob thinks Chamberlain flatters Winston. The danger, in his view, is that the Old Gang will be pulled down and, if things are not going right with the War, Winston will fall with them.

July 10th Zionist Office. The Jewish Army seems to be making itself in Palestine. The history of the past eleven months make one wonder how much good it is trying to get things done. Do they just happen when the time is ripe, or does the spadework count? But anyway, it is in the nature of some of us to be always trying to influence events.

July 13th Shopped, last day of Harrod's sale. After lunch Edgar and I went down to Harrow, where the Eton and Harrow Match was played this year, one day, one innings. Eton won by one run, at the ninth wicket, after an agonisingly exciting finish . . . Well if this is the last Eton and Harrow Match we shall ever see (but I don't think it *will* be) it certainly was a worthy ending. I suppose I have hardly missed one in the last forty years!

24. James Fergusson, Mrs Dugdale's son-in-law, had been seconded from the B.B.C. in Edinburgh to London; he lived with the Dugdales for the next three years. Mrs Dugdale's daughter, Frances, and her three grandchildren went to live at Kilkerran, the home of James's parents, General Sir Charles and Lady Alice Fergusson. Kilkerran is situated in a remote valley in south-west Scotland.
25. Boothby, at the time, was Parliamentary Secretary to the Ministry of Food.

. . . Sat for some time on a bench with Leo Amery, who told us that the P.M. was recently asked how the Public Schools were getting on, and answered 'Much as usual, Harrow has Amery, Gort and myself, Eton has the King of the Belgians and Captain Ramsay,[26] and Winchester has Oswald Mosley to their credit.'

July 15th   Zionist Office. Chaim had seen General Haining, who is cabling to General Wavell to get on with the training of cadres of Jewish officers and N.C.O.'s. So the walls of Jericho fall at last, but not much blast of trumpets after all!

July 28th—Sunday   Had to go both morning and afternoon to Zionist Office to work with Lewis . . . David burst out in our room against Chaim's policy, and said he would not attend our Yeshivoth, but go back to Palestine, where he would not openly attack Chaim, owing to the situation, but would work for a Jewish Army in his own way. I did not argue with him.

September 6th   To Zionist Office where all seemed pleased to see me. David Ben-Gurion still behaving like Achilles and boycotting the Yeshiva for no ascertainable reason. Chaim related all that has passed, only about one brick of the Walls of Jericho still stands, and that is a forthcoming interview between him and Anthony. But he has lunched with the P.M. and got his blessing for the Jewish Army on the first anniversary of the War! I suppose that to get what one wants only a year after one first asks for it is not too bad in these days. Also there will probably be a 'Desert Force' (Jewish) destined to strike up at Libya from the south. This is Orde Wingate's idea, and it is hoped that he will train them. A lot of secondary points have now to be discussed, and as Chaim is going soon to U.S.A., I think we shall have to get Dov Hos over from Palestine again.

September 11th   Lunched with David Ben-Gurion in Hampstead, the Lockers there. After a pleasant meal, discussing Christianity etc. B.G. launched into a terrible diatribe against Chaim, and his management of the Jewish Army question. He says he will only cooperate further if Chaim promises never to discuss this with anybody unless he is present. I told him I did not think Chaim could, would, or should agree to this, but I agreed with him that the worst would be if Chaim agreed and then acted otherwise. David thinks the idea of a Desert Force is fatal. It will be used to divert consent to a Jewish Army in Palestine. It is a difficult question, Lewis thinks that we shall never get a Jewish Army trained in Palestine, and that the Desert Force may distinguish itself, especially under Orde Wingate. There are pros and cons, but anyway David is greatly to blame for having sulked like Achilles all these weeks, and then, when it is too late, making his views known in this violent manner.

26. Captain A. Maule-Ramsay: Conservative M.P. for Peebles from 1931; he was imprisoned from 1940–44 under the 18B regulations.

September 12th . . . At Zionist Office the row between Ben-Gurion and Chaim was talked out. Of course Chaim refused Ben-Gurion's terms, and Ben-Gurion is going back to Palestine as soon as he can.

I spent a most interesting afternoon in the East End ... Owing to Jimmie I had been asked in the morning to go to the M.O.I. to see a very nice Mrs Holmes, of the Home Intelligence Dept. who asked me to report what I saw. I am writing this Report, so will only say here that I visited two big 'Deep Shelters' holding about 2,000 each, saw the queues waiting lined up to spend the night, at 4.30 p.m. Saw and smelt the horrible conditions inside. It was like a scene in Dante's Inferno, and something must be done: more deep shelters, better sanitation, coupled with systematic evacuation of certain areas. But the morale, as far as I could see, was perfectly good, and enquiry elicited no sign of anti-Semitism due to present conditions.

September 13th—Friday And yet a Lucky Day. A great Day! For today Chaim met Lord Lloyd, Anthony Eden, and Mr Daggallay of the Foreign Office and heard from them that all our demands are granted. There is to be a Jewish Fighting Force of 10,000 men, of whom three to four thousand to be recruited in Palestine, and national status and recognition granted, as to the Poles and Czechs. The Walls of Jericho have fallen, fallen! I looked in at the Dorchester about 5 p.m. and found Chaim just back from this interview, elated and solemn. He said, 'It is almost as great a day as the Balfour Declaration.' Orde Wingate was there too, radiant. It may be the beginning of a great future for him too. When I got home I telephoned to Lewis. He came here. I told him the great news. We dined alone together and drank to the Jewish Future in a glass of marsala . . .

September 14th At 4 p.m. I went to the Wingate's flat, where was Lewis and Orde explained his scheme for the recruitment, training and future use of the Jewish Fighting Force. He said, without conceit, that no-one could carry out these ideas, except himself, failing himself General Evetts.[27] He lost his temper very badly when he thought Chaim had failed to be straight-forward with him about making an appointment for him to see General Dill, and nearly smashed the tea-cups. Afterwards he apologized, but he is a most ungovernable character.

September 17th Lewis and I had tea with the Orde Wingates. He came back from an interview with General Dill, to whom he put all his ideas about the J.F.F. and discovered that there has hitherto been no fixed intention on the part of the War Office to give him the job of training them. The idea had rather been to send him to the Abyssinian side. I hope he has put this right, for certainly without him the whole thing would be a flop. David

27. Lt.-General Sir John Evetts: He commanded an infantry brigade in Palestine during Wingate's period of service there, and played a considerable part in furthering Wingate's Palestine career, or at least in not disrupting it.

thinks there will be difficulties in persuading the Jews to recruit to leave Palestine for training, just at *this* moment. Certainly only Orde could make them do so.

September 18th   At Zionist Office found Orde Wingate, in an *awful* state of mind at having been ordered off to Egypt without being allowed to fly to Palestine, and demanding that Chaim should get the P.M. to intervene with the C.I.G.S. Chaim of course could not do this, and expressed the view to the Yeshiva that Orde had probably made it more difficult for us to get him by telling the C.I.G.S. that he *is* the only man etc. However Chaim saw the C.I.G.S. later in the day and found that Orde was being sent to Egypt *because* General Wavell asked for him before ever the J.F.F. was decided upon, and I think we shall get him back, provided he does not cook his own goose with his violent temper and so on.

Far more serious was David's attitude. He came to our Yeshiva and talked it all out. He is unreasonable to the utmost, demanding guarantee that the J.F.F. shall fight in Palestine. Chaim rose to his greatest heights in warning him that he is refusing to cooperate in the greatest hour of the Jewish people. It was a sad exhibition on the part of a great and noble fellow, only he has no common sense. Chaim quite exhausted by all this, asked Lewis and me to lunch with him at the Dorchester.

September 26th Morning at Zionist Office. In p.m., went again to Stepney . . . She [Miss Moses[28]] showed me the Hanbury Street Shelter—a scandal.

Came home and in the evening wrote a strong Report to M.O.I. about all this.

September 28th   They [two officials from the Ministry of Home Security] saw the First Aid Post and the Shelter, asked many questions, and were more than encouraging to the workers. Then I took them to the horrible Hanbury Street Shelter, and then turned them on to Miss Moses in her office; she called for her sub-Warden, Mr Rose and between them they gave an account of Stepney, which I hope and believe will bear fruit. Much pleased I drove back with them to Whitehall, and then lunched at the Dorchester with the Weizmanns. The contrast in standards of living a bit too much! Benjy was there, shell-shocked in an aerodrome in Kent, and invalided out of the Army . . .

September 30th . . . Lunched at Vaiani's with Jimmie and Mrs Holmes of M.O.I., a nice person. We talked of the Stepney work, and I decided to do more investigation of the Tilbury Shelter, and of one under Mann and Crossmanns, and another Brewery . . .

28. Mayor of Stepney, 1931–32; wardress of Brady Street Girls Club and Settlement, Whitechapel.

October 3rd   L.N.U. Executive. Discussion of a new Statement of Peace-Aims drafted by Bob Cecil. Dear dear! . . .

In the midday papers the Government changes due to old Chamberlain being too ill to carry on. Well, that is the end of the Chamberlains in politics. The father and the two sons have covered about 65 or 70 years. On the other hand Bobbitty Cranborne is Dominions Secretary: the Cecils do not perish out of the English governing classes!

October 7th   Last night was one of the most trying, up to about one o'clock, since the very beginning. An enormous bomb hurtled past about 9.15 p.m. shaking the house, although it did not touch ground till near Hyde Park Gate, where I hear it did a good deal of damage. Then the racket was pretty continuous for some time, and daylight raids began early. Walter came up to London, and when he rang me up at 10 a.m. I heard the W.O. had been hit, and the Admiralty a near miss. This is the first day they have really got through to London by daylight. Walter thinks the absolute lull of two days ago (which followed on a day when bad weather had prevented our doing anything in Germany) may have been a kind of message; you leave me alone and I will leave you alone. But if so, of course it could not be taken notice of. We were over Berlin again last night. It is our only possible offensive action just now, and if Herbert Morrison gets the shelters etc. tolerable before winter, we shall be all right. But that *must* be done. Night production is slowing down. I think the factory workers should be told they must face danger as soldiers must. But they must be treated as well as soldiers, when not in the line.

October 11th   Chaim told me on telephone after breakfast that the War Cabinet have agreed to the Jewish Fighting Force. A great event, and this is the eve of Yom Kippur [the Day of Atonement] . . .

October 29th   First copy of my book *Family Homespun* arrived from John Murray. It looks very nice and I read it all through in the evening, and was delighted with it.

I went to *The Times* office in the afternoon, to tell him [Colin Coote] and Barrington-Ward about Stepney Shelters, in hopes *The Times* will take up the scandal. In my presence Colin dictated a letter to Malcolm Mac-Donald,[29] telling him the facts I gave, and indicating that if he does not do something in the next few days about City basements *The Times* will give publicity. Felt much better after this. If I can help destroy Malcolm while helping Stepney, what a scoop!

November 6th—7th . . . went down to Stepney, to visit Lady Ravensdale and Miss Moses, and ended by staying the night with the latter . . . There

29. Then Minister of Health.

were traces that my last report had at least stirred up a little dust in White-hall. Officials had been sent down, or were reported coming down.

Home for bath and breakfast, the usual heavenly experience . . .

. . . Victor came with me to the Zionist Office where heard from Lewis how Chaim had had a very unfortunate talk with Lord Lloyd yesterday. He was ill, and very irritable, all his fundamental ill-will to the J.F.F. came out, and he said no Force had been intended, only units in British Army. Chaim said that was not what he had been promised, nor what he would accept. They parted. In the evening Lloyd sent his Private Secretary, Mr Danby, to explain and put things right if he could. Chaim stuck to his guns. So now we are right up against decision at last. Luckily Lord Lothian, who is here, is 100 per cent keen about a Force. It may come to an appeal to the P.M.

November 12th   To Zionist Office where fuss, owing to cables from Palestine where two more ship-loads of illegal immigrants have arrived and are, so far, not allowed to land. Chaim is quite absorbed in his laboratory and comes much too seldom to the office. I telephoned to him, and he came in the afternoon, very cross. The Army arrangements still languish; he has asked to see Lord Halifax to talk to Lord Lloyd and to Anthony Eden.

November 15th   Awful caboodle at Zionist Office about those refugee ships. Lord Lloyd revealed to Chaim that the ones that have arrived in Haifa are only the forerunners of others now at sea. He thinks that the Gestapo are organizing a vast casting out of Jews from the Rumanian ports. This of course altered the situation. Chaim is prepared to acquiesce to Mauritius under conditions, but will try to get the people on the Haifa ships landed, though he does not think he will succeed. Lewis and I agreed, but this led to a painful scene between Chaim and Berl. We have cabled to Moshe, asking him to keep the Yishuv quiet and to send his suggestions.

November 16th—Dorchester Hotel   Last night turned out to be one of the worst, all over London, that we have had since the blitz began. The noise of bombs, planes and guns, usually all three, was fairly continuous all night. No harm done near here however.

November 22nd   At Zionist Office amusing news about the Haifa ships. Dov Hos and the U.S.A. Labour leaders had cabled to Bevin,[30] who had gone straight to the P.M. who had ordered Lloyd not to send the ships away. Great upset at Colonial Office, as they had allowed MacMichael to make a most provocative broadcast about the refugees not being allowed back in Palestine after the War. Also there was the strike, and I don't think he can send them away now, but it will look like yielding to threats.

30. Ernest Bevin: Founder and General-Secretary of Transport and General Workers Union, 1921–40; Minister of Labour and National Service and member of War Cabinet, 1940–45; Foreign Secretary, 1945–50.

November 25th . . . to Zionist Office. In the evening Chaim rang up and told me the affair of the ships has been made more difficult by the arrival of a third one, and an explosion on board one of them which has killed many, and caused the survivors to be landed . . .[31]

November 26th . . . At Zionist Office the ship row boils over. Chaim went to see Lloyd today and told him he was making cooperation impossible, and has asked to see the P.M.

November 27th Zionist Office. There heard Chaim saw Lord Halifax yesterday about the ships, and showed him the High Commissioner's Broadcast. Result: a Cabinet Committee that same evening and orders that all the surviving refugees from the first two ships were not to be deported!

November 28th Morning at Zionist Office. A Yeshiva, where Chaim refused Locker's desire that he should immediately press for landing the people of the third ship. I am averse to jogging Chaim's elbow, but he has made Berl feel that he is not quite *kosher* on the refugee question, and consequently he has lost the confidence of Berl.

December 21st . . . Went to see Chaim. He talked from 3.30 to 5 p.m. without drawing breath, the most extraordinary jumble of thoughts, accusations (of Gestetner and others), of descriptions of his lonely position in Jewry, the faults and failings of his colleagues (e.g. Lewis), in fact of everything under the sun, some of it showing his greatness, some showing his smallness, all of it showing that he is under an almost intolerable strain. When at last he had done, I did my best to disentangle the parts that bear on our personal relationship and explained to him the point at which I thought they had gone wrong, in October or November, when he began to neglect the office for the laboratory, and Vera had let out to me that he thought we were 'bothering' him. I also told him that I must reserve my right to speak of him as I chose behind his back . . . We parted friends of course. But the whole episode has been an experience which I shall not forget.

31. This was the much publicized affair of the *Patria*. The refugees of two immigrant hulks, the *Milo* and the *Pacific,* had been transferred to the *Patria* in preparation for their deportation to Mauritius. On 24 November a third ship, the *Atlantic,* was brought into Haifa. It was decided to transfer these immigrants to the *Patria* also. Before this could be done an explosion occurred on board the *Patria;* she sank and about 250 refugees were killed. The origins of the explosion remain obscure. But it seems clear that an attempt to cripple the ship's engines, with the intention of keeping the refugees in Haifa, miscarried with tragic results.

1941 *January 15th—London*   Wet snow. Zionist Office. Heard about some progress in the Army negotiations, and most sickening and horrible reports sent by Moshe, therefore reliable, about atrocities committed on the refugees who were torn away from Athlit camp[1] and sent to Mauritius. I refused to read the evidence, but Lewis said worse than 'Amritsar'. Lord Lloyd is ill and cannot at present be got at. It was decided that, as a first step, the documents should be shown to Mr Creech Jones,[2] and his advice asked.

January 17th   Zionist Office. Heard Lord Lloyd is to be laid up for a fortnight, which is very awkward, as the question of Sir Harold MacMichael's term of office will be up in March, and after Athlit it must not be renewed.

January 18th   Went with Edgar to the Charlie Chaplin film *The Great Dictator* which is still drawing huge crowds. It is good, but not quite my cup of tea. I do not like Jewish atrocities, even watered down, but the scenes between the two Dictators are very funny.

Then to Dorchester, where had tea with the Weizmanns. Chaim talked to me, alone, about all this dreary quarrelling with the Colonial Office, which takes so much of our time, and (as *he* thinks) absorbs all Lewis's attention, is 'not Zionism'. I most warmly agreed, and said we are *not* enough in touch with the Jewish masses at 77.

January 27th   To Zionist Office. Heard report of interview between Chaim and Lewis with Anthony Eden re Army. Things creep forward. Chaim in despair at the nullity of Anthony. He will, he thinks, never be hostile, but will shrink from the trouble the Jews will give him, and will never understand what Zionism is all about. Halifax, being religious—*does*.

February 5th . . . Lord Lloyd died last night. From the general point of view he is a loss. From the Zionist, a mixture. I do not think he would ever have become a friend. He was too obstinate to change, but he was honest and a good administrator.

1. A refugee camp just south of Haifa.
2. A. Creech Jones: Labour M.P. for Shipley from 1935; Under-Secretary of State for Colonies, 1945–46; Colonial Secretary, 1946–50.

We heard at the Zionist Office that the 43 boys who were sentenced to imprisonment for twenty and ten years for Hagana drilling, have been unconditionally released. Thus Lloyd's last act was a good one.

February 10th . . . I see that . . . I forgot for some odd reason, to record *the* event, namely that among the Government changes that followed on Lord Lloyd's death, Malcolm MacDonald is banished to Canada, as High Commissioner. Walter told me of it first, in guarded language on the telephone—'Sing the Song of Deborah', he said. And it does appear from what Colin said yesterday, that our campaign in *The Times* was the beginning of the exposure of the inefficiency of MacDonald's handling of Shelter problems . . .

March 4th . . . Walter on telephone this morning gave a different explanation of the Jewish Army hitch, after a talk he had yesterday with Captain Margesson. It seems as if the obstruction is much higher up . . . and Walter thinks it unlikely to be settled before Anthony comes home. This of course is much more formidable in some ways, but I prefer a struggle in the upper air, and if it is to end in defeat (which neither Walter nor I think it will) at least it is not at the hands of miserable insects like Shuckburgh and Dounie[3] . . .

March 5th Last night Chaim rang me up and told me he had a letter from Lord Moyne[4] saying the P.M. had decided that the Jewish Division must be put off for six months, the reasons (or excuses?) given are shipping and equipment. It is emphasized that this is not going back on the promise. I am glad anyway that the reasons given are not political. We should nail them to the equipment point and try to make them emphasize the pledge even more. I spoke to Lewis on the telephone and found him bitter beyond bearing.

March 11th At Zionist Office put forward my idea that Chaim should tell the P.M. (or, failing an interview with him, Lord Moyne) that he must tell his colleagues in U.S.A. that he has a pledge that the Jewish force is postponed, but the pledge stands. Lewis thinks this rash . . . I think Chaim will probably follow my line.

March 12th Zionist Office. Last Yeshiva with Chaim. He had quite an encouraging talk with Lord Moyne, who volunteered his word that while the Jewish Division is in abeyance, the Palestine situation shall be kept static, although, he said 'You have no idea how much pressure is being put upon me to implement the third part of the White Paper.'[5]

3. H. F. Dounie: Assistant Secretary at Colonial Office from 1935.
4. Lord Moyne: Colonial Secretary, 1941–42; Deputy Minister of State, Cairo, 1942; Minister, 1944; assassinated by Zionist extremists in November 1944.
5. *i.e.,* the constitutional proposals.

Outside the Zionist Organization's headquarters at 77 Great Russell Street: l to r,
Joseph Linton, Berl Locker, Moshe Shertok (Sharett), Louis Namier, Levi Bakstansky

Professor Selig Brodetsky

Moshe Shertok (Sharett) recruiting in Palestine during
World War II

Sir Archibald Sinclair (left) talks to Malcolm MacDonald at a Foyles Literary Luncheon, 1938

Lord and Lady de la Warr (left) with Robert Bernays: Harold Nicolson is peering over Bernays's shoulder

The irritation between me and Lewis continues, owing to his *défaitiste* attitude.

Dined at Dorchester, where Chaim and Vera gave farewell dinner. They leave for U.S.A. tomorrow . . . A delightful evening, most excellent talk, largely about lectures, good and bad, with reminiscences. But the cheerful note was imparted by 'a miracle' which happened to Chaim this afternoon, when he went to Downing Street to say good-bye to Brendan and without an appointment had a quarter-of-an-hour with Winston, who told him not to worry—'I will see you through.' About the general war situation he found him full of hope and confidence.

April 29th   We decided at Zionist Office this morning that we could delay no longer in pressing for Palestine Home Guard, if necessarily publicly, but the best way would be to get the P.M. to decide it personally. The Labour members of the War Cabinet our best method and Berl takes that in hand . . .

Then I went to see Philip Noel-Baker at his house. He said the Labour Party are going to take up the Jewish Home Guard question, and that we ought to get somebody to speak on it in next week's Debate . . .

May 1st   Zionist Office. Wrote to Mr Lloyd George, asking him to speak about the Palestine Home Guard in next week's Debate.

May 2nd   Pursuant of our campaign about next week's Debate, I went to see Jimmie de Rothschild to ask him to speak. He looked more than ever like a guttering candle in the shadows of his library, where more than half the windows are blocked with canvas (for No. 23 is the only house still habitable in St James's Place, the Dugdales have given theirs up[6]). At first Jimmie said that on no account would he speak, no Jew should speak on such a subject. But I persevered and gradually he calmed down, though not before he had told me that I had lived so much among Jews that I was taking a Jewish point of view, and could not see things in proportion. Surely the oddest remark from him to me. But I still persevered, saying that self-defence is a human right, and I desired that it should not be left to the Gentiles to claim it for the Yishuv. He then half-apologized, and (though Jimmie is too great a gentleman ever to be rude) asked what exactly had been done vis-à-vis the Government. Then he asked to speak to Lord Moyne, who is evidently a great friend of his, and asked him what is being done. This elicited the information that no answer has yet been received to the cable sent to the High Commissioner after Lord Moyne saw Lewis a fortnight ago and more, but that Lord Moyne had sent instructions that 'The fullest possible use' should be made of the Jews in Palestine, and no further consideration paid to parity with Arabs. This was of course very good news

6. The London home of Sir William Dugdale, the diarist's brother-in-law.

O

to me, and we owe it to my visit to Jimmie that we ever heard of it at this stage. It remains to be seen whether Jimmie will use it as a pretext for saying more in the Debate.

May 6th . . . Lewis saw Lord Moyne this morning, and came to Zionist Office quite over the moon at what he had heard. The Jewish settlements are to be turned into 'strongholds' and the urban military police strengthened. At last they have woken up, but I see no such cause for rejoicing. I fear it is only a measure of the danger.

May 12th   Had tea with Hannah Hudson and walked by Parliament Square. The damage to the House and the Abbey is mostly internal and though Big Ben's face has been much dirtied by smoke, he is unhurt . . .

When I got home this evening I rang up Walter . . . He is not only all right but probably did more than anybody else to save Westminster Hall, for he showed the firemen how to get in, from Palace Yard, and as the great doors there were locked, he was 'the foremost man to take in hand an axe'. There was no special House of Commons fire-fighting squad, no one to give directions who knew every inch of the building. How shocking! Walter has written direct to the P.M. about it.

May 13th   To Zionist Office. Lewis came late, having gone to Downing Street to tell some member of the P.M.'s secretariat . . . a bit of information he got through Lola Hahn last night about Hess.[7] She knew it through her Berlin doctor, who betrayed professional secrets to her at the time Kurt Hahn was in a concentration camp, and they were approaching Hess to get him out. Hess is an extreme neurotic, has violent fits of depression, approaches to a dual personality, and had been under psycho-analytic treatment for years. Lewis told this and urged that a psycho-analyst should talk to him unawares (e.g. as a so-called specialist for his broken ankle) . . . I repeated this to Walter when I lunched with him at R.A.C. and urged him to tell David Margesson.

May 15th   A day of Committees with the L.N.U. ghosts. Often I think it is time I left them, lest I become a ghost myself, but then something diverting always happens. Today it was discussion of an idea to set up a standing Conference of representatives of foreign Governments here, to 'keep in touch' with their ideas of a Peace Settlement, and, even more, to influence them to accept ours! This has drawn forth a letter from Dr Benes, which shocked all the ghosts very much, for it said that he thought there would be plenty of time before we could get down to the real Peace Settlement. A number of local wars would have to be fought out first, and a little blood-letting would do us no harm! With such ideas about we settled that we must lose no time in starting our Conference.

7. Rudolf Hess: Hitler's deputy. He had parachuted into Scotland on 10 May to negotiate a peace settlement between Germany and Great Britain.

May 23rd   Walter told me that he thinks that within a few weeks something analogous to the old 'Arab Bureau' must be set up in Cairo. We *cannot* govern the East from blitzed London. This is very important from the Zionist point of view. An Arab Bureau it *must* not be, or we are sunk! Walter advised me to go and talk to Leo about it.

May 24th   Walter . . . said it looked as though Winston had selected Beaverbrook for 'assistant and successor'. The time might come when it would be necessary to choose between Lord Halifax and Lord Beaverbrook as leader. I said that much as I hoped some other might arise, yet if the choice is narrowed to these, give me Beaverbrook. The post-war world requires a tough, rather than a praying-mantis. Walter rather agreed, but made a distinction between foreign politics, in which we must be tough, and home politics, where toughness would certainly not be enough. We must go on with social reform, but also try to preserve the governing classes, for how can we do without them? When the nation desired to unite in the face of supreme danger a year ago, only a Duke's grandson, only a Churchill, could do it!

May 29th—London   Anthony Eden made an extraordinary speech at the Mansion House—of all places—where he hinted that we should be pleased to give Syria 'independence'—what a moment to offer a non-existent place (for what is 'Syria'?) which does not belong to us, when we are about to fight for our lives there and in Palestine! Well, if they are making an Arab Federation, *we* must have a Jewish State.

June 22nd—Sunday   On the 9 p.m. News we heard that Germany had gone to war with Russia. Impossible to imagine yet all the implications of this terrific event. At 9 p.m. the Prime Minister made a magnificent broadcast, focusing thought on the one fixed point, namely that the Russians are fighting for their native land against the Nazis. We must help and forget, for the present, all else but that.

June 28th   Walter lunched alone with me here and we spent the rest of the day at Hampton Court and dined there. He told me that Oliver Lyttelton[8] (of all people) is to go to Cairo as a kind of political chief . . . and Lord Beaverbrook to Ministry of Supply! I suppose he finds he has no power as Minister without Portfolio. The P.M. wants to send Sir P. J. Grigg[9] to Cairo with Lyttelton. But some people, who think the Cabinet Secretariat needs a head, urge the P.M. to put Grigg there. But the P.M. says—'We

8. Oliver Lyttelton: President of the Board of Trade, 1940–41; Minister of State resident in Middle East, 1941–42; Minister of Production, 1942–45; Member of War Cabinet, 1941–45. Cr. Viscount Chandos, 1954.
9. Sir James Grigg: Permanent Under-Secretary of State for War, 1939–42; Secretary of State for War, 1942–45.

must have peace at the centre'—meaning, I fear, that he knows Grigg is not one of his 'yes-men'. He is a complete autocrat now . . .

July 2nd . . . Great flutter in the dove-cotes of No. 77 and a long Yeshiva partly spent in discussing whether or not the Jewish Agency should try to see Oliver Lyttelton before he goes. This turned out to be academic question, as we learned later in the day he is already in Cairo. We decided to cable to Chaim and to Jerusalem that centre of gravity in Zionist affairs shifts to Cairo. We must strengthen our office there, and we think Chaim should return to London. I went to see Leo Amery before dinner, and found him in the garden at Eaton Square and asked him about these appointments. He thinks that Lyttelton may not be much concerned, at any rate at first with high policy. His mind is *tabula rasa* about the Middle East, which as Leo said, wryly, may or may not be an advantage. No doubt Leo would have loved that job!

July 6th—Sunday Dined at 'Chanticleer' with Bob Boothby and Walter. Bob has a little open car and we drove to Greenwich and stood for a long while by the river, looking at it, and the Hospital in the moonlight and sunset. A scene of unbelievable peace and beauty. The tide was full, the rosy sky full, quite full, of barrage balloons, which turned silver to black and mingled with the stars. At last we tore ourselves away, and about midnight drove home by St. Paul's and among the devastated streets and vast gaunt ruins of the great City of London, standing there with the moon turning them black and silver. They are on the scale of our present life, which makes all comparison with the past seem puny and insignificant. But, as we talked, we agreed that all we have yet seen in this island, and all the world has yet suffered, may in its turn seem puny compared with what lies before us next winter and next year. It was an unforgettable experience to see these things and talk of them tonight with these two companions. Whatever happens 'we are the masters of the days that were' and this has been a day.

At dinner we talked of Winston, how the tyrant spirit grows in him, how the people are beginning to feel it, and will not stand it. Bob says he is loathed in the Air Force. They resent being sent to Germany night after night in this weather, where their losses are far too great for the damage they can do. And that (they say) is why the Germans are not bombing us, it is *not* because all their bombers are in Russia . .

July 12th Eton and Harrow Match—at Eton . . . we made mincemeat of Harrow . . . Civilization as intact as this time last year.

July 24th Dined at R.A.C. with Walter. Two of the Russian mission dined with him. One told this story, which the other translated. Hitler stood by Napoleon's tomb at the Invalides and said:

'I am a greater man than you, for I have conquered all Europe, including Greece.'

Napoleon: 'Have you been to Russia yet?'

Hitler: 'Not yet.'

Napoleon: 'Come and lie down here with me, while there is time.'

August 12th—Strachur Spent yesterday in London . . . Lewis to tea, rather depressed about Chaim's unbusinesslike ways. I fear it is true that he is *not* the leader he was, though of course we have no idea of what he may have done for the Zionist public in U.S.A.

September 18th To Zionist Office. Lewis and Chaim both away. Had long talk with Locker and Ben-Gurion, who arrived from Palestine while I was away. Both of them deeply pessimistic about the chances of His Majesty's Government agreeing to a Jewish Army now, after so many postponements. But they are as strong as ever that the claim to fight must not be abandoned. David Ben-Gurion feels that the pressure must come from Palestine now. There is no more political work to be done here he thinks, only publicity and propaganda. It may be that he is right. I shall believe him if the P.M.'s answer to a letter Chaim has written to him is evasive or discouraging. In that case the relations of the Agency with His Majesty's Government would be altered, and it might be that we ought to publish all the records of the Army negotiations of the past two years . . .

September 19th—Fyfield Manor, Pewsey, Wilts.[10] Went to Zionist Office. Found old Lewis returned. A Yeshiva which convinced me that there is little hope of getting H.M.G.'s consent to the Jewish Division under present conditions. The P.M. has practically refused to answer Chaim's letter on the subject. The question is—what next? I am personally in favour of asking H.M.G.'s permission to publish a documentary statement of the negotiations of the last two years. I think that the Jewish public has a right to demand it, and that for its own sake the Jewish Agency should do it. However, Chaim may not take that view, which is shared by Lewis. Ben-Gurion most tiresomely persists in harking back to his disagreements with the Yeshiva last time he was here and makes no constructive suggestions.

October 3rd Heard that Palestine was discussed yesterday in Cabinet (I suppose because of Oliver Lyttelton's visit home), and that the P.M. said that he had never accepted the White Paper, and did not now; that the Jews 'must have territory'. I got permission to tell this *only* to Lewis. The information must make a great difference in our attitude towards H.M.G. on all questions.

10. The home of Rob and Hannah Hudson.

October 5th—Sunday   In the morning I had joined Chaim at Dorchester and had a talk with him. He seems in good spirits, confident about the future of a Jewish State, although I could not tell him what I wrote here on October 3rd. But he smells things from afar. The future of the Jewish force is not so clear to any of us. I think we must press for recognition at any rate of the Jewish Companies in the 'Buffs and Rebuffs'[11] as Chaim calls them.

October 9th   Victor gave a large dinner at the Dorchester to the Parliamentary group, to meet Chaim and the Yeshiva. Some twenty of us there . . . Chaim spoke well, though his account of facts was as Lewis puts it 'rather cubist'. The M.P.s decided to send a letter to Lord Moyne (for the P.M.) about the Jewish Army. Walter, in the discussion, emphasized that we are dealing with 'very high politics' as regards Middle East, the balance of forces so even that it has immobilized the War Cabinet, in which our friends are in majority. But U.S.A. Jewish opinion may tip the balance.

Afterwards the Yeshiva, plus Walter, went to Chaim's room for a cup of tea. Poor Vera terribly sad, the Germans are approaching her home town [of Rostov].

October 16th   News from Moscow very bad, and we had a black afternoon at Zionist Office also, for a letter came from Lord Moyne withdrawing all hopes of raising a Jewish Division outside Palestine. Poor Berl was dreadfully cast down, far more than I, for he and Lewis believe H.M.G. has merely been playing with the Jews all this time, whereas I think there is some substance in the alleged difficulties of equipment. I think too that the P.M.'s promise to Chaim to 'see him through' did not necessarily refer to the Jewish Division.

October 23rd . . . About 7 p.m. Chaim rang me up to report a stormy interview between him and Lord Moyne. Hopes of Jewish Army at an end. Chaim told him that 'the floor is littered with broken promises'. He is very upset. But there is some advantage in knowing where we stand. A new chapter must open in relations of Jewish Agency with H.M.G.

Dined at R.A.C. with Walter and Rob Bernays. We finished the evening at Rob's flat. Intensely interesting on political situation, its dangers, the Peace offensive, Beaverbrook's role in it. All Fleet Street believes he is out to upset the Government by promoting cry that we are not doing enough for Russia (through his press and his men, Michael Foot[12] and Frank Owen[13]). Then he reckons on his own premiership and an agreed Peace. It seems fantastic as well as foul. I merely record it . . .

11. The Palestinian companies were attached to the East Kent Regiment, 'The Buffs'.
12. Michael Foot: Joined staff of *Evening Standard*, 1938; acting editor, 1942–45; Labour M.P. for Devonport, 1945–55; for Ebbw Vale from 1960.
13. Frank Owen: Editor of *Evening Standard* from 1938.

November 10th A lunch in honour of Bakstansky's return from U.S.A. at Anglo-Palestinian Club. Some funny Jewish stories in the speeches, especially one from Berl about the division of labour between the Goy and the Jew who set out together to chop wood, the Goy chops and the Jew says 'Ha' when the chopper falls.

November 20th Dined at Dorchester with Chaim and Vera. Lewis there and John Gunther the American journalist, a *very* nice and intelligent man, also the Orde Wingates. Orde, by our desire, held the floor all night. His description of the Abyssinian campaign, his handling of the natives etc., quite brilliant. He is obviously a Guerrilla leader of genius. But he is so pro-Abyssinian, as to be *almost* anti-British. I suppose it is part of his power to almost identify himself with the bands he leads. Altogether a very remarkable evening of talk.

December 7th As yesterday, only the day was cold and sunny after great gale and rain in the night. We turned on the 9 p.m. news . . . and heard Japan had attacked the U.S.A., while negotiations in Washington still proceeding! I had never quite believed they would. So, the World War now,[14] and no mistake! Best so, I think.

December 18th Chaim spoke heavily today in the Yeshiva about the spread of anti-Semitism and the measure of Hitler's success in that sphere. He has shown the humiliations to which man *can* subject his fellow-men, and the civilized world keeps comparative silence. This is a terrible blow to morality. About Palestine, he feels that before there is a Jewish State the Jews will have to *fight* for one. The policy of the Balfour Declaration is in reality abandoned. But the U.S.A. Ambassador Winant tells him to expect U.S.A. to urge H.M.G. to form Jewish Army in Palestine. How much effect will this have? America is fighting for her life, *not* for ours. How will this affect British attention to her wishes? If U.S.A. had thrown its weight behind a Jewish Army six months ago it would have been different.

December 20th . . . Events suddenly make Indian policy of urgent importance. We must bring India into the War. It is said Amery would grant them greater measure of independence, but is not listened to. If he were to resign he could, in present mood of Parliament, bring the Government down. The P.M. might not carry the country on the cry of Bring India In. Moreover, with his record on India,[15] the P.M. could not do it. In fact Amery becomes a key-man.

---

14. The U.S. in fact entered the war on 7 December.
15. Churchill had led the opposition to the Government of India Act in the early 1930's. He resigned from the Shadow Cabinet on this issue in 1931 and by so doing cut himself off from the mainstream of Conservative opinion.

December 21st—Sunday   Later went to the Weizmanns. Talked to Chaim about Amery. He is seeing a good deal of him just now, and says he is very frustrated.

December 22nd—Merevale   Came here in the morning with Edgar. Train punctual and only half-full, in spite of legends of the horrors of Christmas travel. Found here all the family . . . All the silver on the table (old Clements being here, helping old Hudson!) and a bunch of grapes! One appreciates the amenities now! Nobody has any servants, except very old retainers, giving at the knees, but trying to keep up the standards which we shall (perhaps) never see again. But perhaps we shall! Revolutions come very slowly in Britain.

Christmas Day—Merevale   All to Church and Communion. How I dislike the Anglican Service! Nevertheless enjoyed it. Afterwards we exchanged very tiny presents . . . Lunch, cold tongue and mince-pies. Afternoon spent in listening to the Empire Broadcast and the King, who spoke I thought beautifully, and did not shrink from mentioning the Lord of Hosts.

1942 *January 17th*   Went to the Weizmanns for tea. Chaim has *at last* got the permit to manufacture his toluene,[1] and also the Ministry is now keen on his synthetic rubber process. But it has taken the loss of Malaya[2] to break down the vested interests. A terrible story. I am quite sure now that the vested interests are a far worse menace to this country than any Communism . . .

January 20th   Very interesting discussion at Yeshiva, started by Brodetsky, about position of Jews in Galuth after the War. Berl Locker wants to claim for them special autonomy in education and other ways, in fact a certain acknowledgement of national rights, plus a State in Palestine. Lewis and I both felt that this is impossible, and that any State in Europe would be justified in saying that its Jews must either opt to go to Palestine as soon as possible, or resign themselves to the ordinary citizen's rights where they live. Chaim warned us that effort spent on improving the lot of the Galuth will be more or less wasted labour. Palestine is the only hope and future.

January 26th   Had tea with Gardenia and Derrick Gunston in their flat near Harrods. Derrick full of political situation. Will anybody dare to 'Bell the Cat' in this week's Debate? The P.M.'s position (in Parliament) seems more shaken than I had realized. There are some who would get rid of him altogether! This is folly, but there is a very serious demand that he should give up the post of Defence Minister. But who to? Cripps?[3] Derrick had awful stories of the bad design of the tanks which Beaverbrook has continued to pour out. He says Anthony Eden is almost the only Minister who does stand up to the P.M. . . . If Singapore falls I think it will go hard with Winston.

1. An essential constituent for the manufacture of high explosive—T.N.T.; and also, because of its anti-knock properties, a necessary constituent of high octane aviation gasoline.
2. Japanese forces had invaded the mainland of Malaya in December 1941; by mid-February they had succeeded in capturing Singapore.
3. Sir Stafford Cripps: Ambassador to Russia, 1940–42; Lord Privy Seal and Leader of House of Commons, 1942; Minister of Aircraft Production, 1942-45; President of the Board of Trade, 1945–47; Chancellor of Exchequer, 1947–50.

February 1st—Sunday, London   Walter came to tea . . . He says that all
Bob Boothby's story[4] is substantially true. The P.M. had intended not to
yield an inch to the House of Commons, and only changed his mind on the
evening of the second day of the Debate. Cripps *has* refused, Bevin talks of
resigning; there would be a split in the Tory Party comparable to the Liberal
split in 1916, for many would not follow Beaverbrook. But I think it *will*
be patched up, I hope so; we could hardly afford it with the Japs at the
very gates of Singapore, and Cyrenaica battle swaying us.[5]

I waded out to the Dorchester and dined with the Weizmanns, their son
Michael there . . . It was to have been their very last evening before starting
for U.S.A., but Beaverbrook has insisted on his putting off for a week, as
he can't, or won't, make up his mind whether Chaim's toluene factory shall
be built here, or there. Chaim has been to two meetings of the relevant Committee within the last two days, one presided over by Beaverbrook himself,
and Chaim says it was *pandemonium!*

February 11th . . . Went to the Dorchester at tea-time to bid Chaim and
Vera farewell for the third time, but I think they really do go tomorrow.
'The blessings of God be on your head,' said Chaim to me as he took me
out into the long and so familiar passage leading to the lift.

February 13th . . . Soon after arriving at Zionist Office Mr Linton[6] came
in with the news that Michael Weizmann is missing. We thought of course
it was in the Channel yesterday, where five aircraft of Coastal Command
were among those lost over the battleships.[7] Then we heard that Chaim and
Vera had been caught at Bristol just before starting, and had returned to
London.
   Back to Zionist Office where Lewis and I prepared a Memo for House
of Lords Debate on Tuesday week (Jos. Wedgwood raises it on the Jewish
Fighting Force). I left a note for Chaim and Vera at the Dorchester. Later
Chaim rang me up, and told me there is just a ray of hope. It was not in
yesterday's battle, but engine trouble over Bay of Biscay the day before. He
may have been picked up.

February 15th—Sunday . . . After lunch Chaim rang up and asked me to
come for tea, which I did. Chaim very natural, poor Vera frozen stiff. But
the Air Ministry tell them there is a 'very good chance'. I fear this may

---

4. About Bevin's angry reaction to the decision to establish a Ministry of War production
   under Beaverbrook; and Cripps's refusal to take the Ministry of Supply.
5. By mid-January the British drive in the Libyan desert had been stopped short of El
   Agheila, just west of Benghazi.
6. Joseph Linton: Official of Zionist Organization and Jewish Agency 1919–40; adviser to
   Weizmann; since 1948 has held high office in Israel diplomatic corps; consultant on
   international affairs at World Jewish Congress, London, since 1961.
7. The occasion when two German battlecruisers, the *Scharnhorst* and the *Gneisenau*
   withdrawing from Brest to Germany, sailed unmolested through the English Channel.

only prolong the agony. Berl Locker came in, and Miriam and Simon [Marks], the latter bringing news of the surrender of Singapore—black news indeed! The P.M. on radio at 9 p.m. Missed the target utterly.

February 17th   Zionist Office. Chaim came. They will go off to U.S.A. as soon as Vera feels she can. She is as turned to stone. I went to House of Lords to lunch with Jos. While waiting in Lobby saw Walter, just back from Scotland. He reported the House of Commons very angry and perturbed after the P.M.'s statement. Jos. very depressed at our failure to resist at Singapore. He has written to the P.M. to urge him to send Amery out to India at once as Viceroy. He (Jos.) says Indian Army exists mostly on paper, and that we shall lose the Burma Road!
     . . . I dined at R.A.C. with Walter and Rob Bernays, and we went round to Rob's flat. Spent whole time discussing whether or not they should support Government in Vote of Confidence next week. I was reluctantly compelled to say that unless they were prepared to support an alternative leader (which they do not seem to be) or to think that a General Election would improve matters they must support the Government. *Merely* to smash the crockery is not good enough now, too much like escapism, and too reminiscent of French politics before the debacle of 1940. But it may well be that the House will upset the Government. The P.M. is reported more depressed than ever before, and bearing all the marks of overstrain. But he has not yet given way about a Defence Minister, or indeed anything else. I hear he is bringing Oliver Lyttelton back from Cairo.

February 24th . . . Late in afternoon went to Dorchester, where I saw Victor and Bob fresh from first day's Debate on War. They said House restive and P.M. had baddish reception. He could tell them nothing about Singapore, he is said to be in an awful temper in private life, very sick at having had to discard Beaverbrook, also is said to be biting the carpet. Margesson got the sack without a word, just a letter.

February 25th   When I got to Zionist Office I found all in turmoil over the sinking of the *Struma* which has been in Istanbul last two months with 750 Rumanian Jews to whom Palestine Government refused entry. Finally the Turks must have bid her put out to sea, she blew up, all lost, mass suicide like *Patria* probably? If so MacMichael is a murderer. We sat down to work press, prepare a statement from Jewish Agency, and persuade Chaim to ask to see Bobbitty,[9] which he did this very afternoon, had satisfactory interview, and Bobbitty has asked us for Memo on Administration. Perhaps things at Colonial Office may take a turn for the better under him. I wrote to him on his appointment to warn him that 'He that keeps Israel neither slumbers nor sleeps' and my words came true sooner than expected.

9. Viscount Cranborne had replaced Lord Moyne as Colonial Secretary on 22 February.

March 9th   Had inflamed eye and felt wretched. Nevertheless went to Zionist
Office where much to do re publicity, and tomorrow's Palestine Debate in
the Lords. Felt better as day went on. Went in evening to Hampstead Garden
Suburb Synagogue, where delivered a very good lecture on the Balfour
Declaration to a very intelligent audience of about sixty people. Was met up
there by Henry Melchett's car, which brought me to Claridges at about
10 p.m. Stayed talking with him till nearly midnight, largely on Zionist
affairs, but he also told me the following: (1) It was General Wavell who
insisted on the Divisions which were lost in Singapore without giving battle
being sent there, declaring that with them he could hold Singapore. (2) The
escape of the three German ships from Brest was due to the silence of all
our four radio-location stations on which we had been relying, rather than on
aerial reconnaissance. These stations were jammed by the Bilancourt Station
which we accordingly destroyed a few nights later. But we had not known
that the Bilancourt Station could do this. This secret, so precious for invasion,
was thus given away. Therefore the escape of the German ships was a small
price to pay for the inestimable knowledge; these facts, for some unexplained
reason, are still being withheld from the public here, though the Germans
must know that we know. Randolph Churchill is Henry's informant about
this and other matters. He (R.C.) has been 'sacked' from his M.O.I. job
in Cairo while still here. *He* thinks because of his pro-Semitism, but *I* think
just as much because of his general unpopularity!

March 17th   Zionist Office. Uphill work still, trying to persuade them to
keep on good terms with Bobbitty,[10] who is quite unaware no doubt of how
much he has offended them! . . .

March 18th   To Zionist Office. Chaim's last appearance before he and Vera
set off once more for U.S.A. What a month of martyrdom for both, Vera
has made no effort, so far as one can see, to recover. Chaim then went off to
see Bobbitty for the last time. I gather the interview went well.

March 25th   To Colonial Office in the morning, where had half-an-hour or
more with Bobbitty, first alone, then with Locker. With me he discussed
general situation a little, I explained Jewish psychology on one or two points,
and told him how I thought full cooperation might be restored; it is years
since any Colonial Secretary or High Commissioner has had their moral
respect. He told me one thing which he forbade me to impart to the others,
namely that he tried (and failed) to get the Cabinet to agree to bring these
ships[11] to Palestine, and intern the people there. When Locker came the ships
were discussed. I was satisfied by the impression they seemed to be making
on one another. Locker said to me afterwards that Bobbitty was the only

10. He had come under violent attack in a House of Lords debate over the *Struma* affair,
    particularly from Wedgwood; Cranborne replied in the same vein.
11. News had been received of the arrival in Istanbul of two more refugee ships.

Colonial Secretary he has met who impressed him as completely sincere. We returned to Zionist Office and in the afternoon reported to the others.

April 3rd—Good Friday Went to Colonial Office to see Bobbitty and spent half-an-hour with him. Undoubtedly he is striving with the Cabinet to admit refugee Jews to Palestine, but so far has not prevailed. Consequently pressing him only produces unfavourable answers at present. However, as regards the last lot of small ships, I have hopes that they will be permitted to elude observation and land their passengers somewhere in Palestine. Bobbitty is certainly a great improvement on previous Colonial Secretaries!

April 22nd—London A Yeshiva, mostly spent in deciding against the idiotic proposal of trying to see Sir H. MacMichael (whom Bobbitty has sent for) and telling him what we think of him . . .

May 8th Wearing Zionist Office day, I being rather at variance with Yeshiva on policy to be pursued towards Colonial Office. I would trust Bobbitty to do what he can re 'illegal' immigration etc. in face of an adverse Cabinet policy, but I confess he is not delivering the goods fast enough to prove that I am right.

May 22nd—Fyfield Manor, Pewsey, Wiltshire Word came last night that Bobbitty would like to meet the whole Yeshiva today. So Locker, Lewis Namier, Linton and I went to the Colonial Office at noon. We sat round a table with Bobbitty, and Sir George Gater, and the chief officials. Bobbitty said that after a great struggle with the War Cabinet, he had arranged that 'illegals' who reach Palestine shall not be deported, but released from internment after investigation of bona-fides, and means of support. Refugees who get stranded in Turkey will get visas for Cyprus. This implies the release of the 800 *Darien* passengers who have been interned for fourteen months, and are the worst running sore in Palestine at present. Of course the plan in no way modifies the principle of 'illegal' immigration, it is in fact a peculiarly British way of getting round a difficulty. I did not think any of my colleagues, even Lewis, appreciated what a feat Bobbitty had performed, nor how much we have got the substance of a satisfactory agreement about 'illegals'. Chaim would have understood better, and accepted more graciously. I wrote Bobbitty a private note after I got home to tell him what I feel on the subject.

May 26th . . . Found a letter from Bobbitty epitomizing the conversation of Friday. Berl Locker maddeningly determined that nothing has been gained. Lewis much more alive to realities.

July 6th Zionist Office. Had lunch at Allies Club.[12] In the evening sat on platform at Adolph Tuck Hall, about 1,000 Jews from London and provinces

12. This was not a regular club but a wartime institution established in a large mansion at the Piccadilly end of Park Lane. Officers of Allied forces and exiles were welcomed there.

to say good-bye to Mrs Silverman,[13] who made one of her amazing speeches. Besides collecting £100,000 for J.N.F. she has started a real 'revival' of Zionism in this country — they say there has been nothing like it since the first great wave after the Balfour Declaration. She has done it, I think, not by her own faith and great eloquence, but by digging down to the Jewishness of all these semi-assimilated British Jews. But I daresay it is time she went away. Already (Berl Locker says) she begins to relate as her own experiences, incidents which are in the Talmud ! !

July 26th—Sunday   Lewis came to supper, and afterwards M and Mdme Lipski came in. They have been living opposite in Roland House, for more than a year, but though I knew this I only succeeded in meeting them the other day, at the Club. He was the Polish Ambassador in Vienna at the time of the Schuschnigg plebiscite and the march in, and in Berlin at the outbreak of War, and is most interesting on all that period. One of the things he told us, which I did not know, is that it was the Hungarian Minister in Vienna, a most passionate anti-Nazi, who in all good faith, and an unfortunate hour, suggested to Schuschnigg to hold a plebiscite!

August 2nd—Sunday . . . I dined with Bob Boothby, alone, at the Restaurant which used to be Kettner's, and whose present name I can't remember, but it was very nice, and we dined well off boeuf-à-la-mode and red wine, talked for two hours of war and politics. There are two great questions. (1) What should be attitude towards 'Second Front' weighing all psychological and military factors (and these last none of us know)? (2) Should the Great Beech Tree be cut down, not because we can spare it, but because under its shadow nothing else is *allowed* to grow, that being the nature of that tree? These are matters which every serious M.P. must seriously weigh, and Bob was in his best and most serious mood. He is leaving the Air Force and returning to politics, and Oliver Stanley said to him he was right, for a political crisis is in the air . . . Oliver Stanley is, on balance, for keeping the Beech Tree. Air Chief Marshal Harris[14] assures H.M.G. he can win the war by bombing alone. They want to believe this, and cling to him, so says Bob. Much else—a very interesting evening.

August 5th . . . To tea-party of very large size at Celina Sokolow,[15] to meet Jan Masaryk, just back from U.S.A. He was very pleased at having got a solemn retraction from Eden of Munich Agreement. It is only some four years since I met Jan at Chaim's on that tragic terrible evening when Chamberlain came back with that Agreement in his pocket. If anyone had then said that in four years it would be repudiated, what would we have

13. Mrs A. Silverman: An American Zionist in England to raise funds for the Palestine War
    Appeal.
14. Commander-in-Chief, Bomber Command.
15. Daughter of Nahum Sokolow, the Zionist leader.

felt? Certainly we would not have expected that it would be hardly 'news'! But I am glad the blot is washed out all the same!

August 6th To House of Commons to hear Debate on Jewish Army... Victor spoke well to the brief we gave him. Then I had to go as I was lunching with Frank Balfour,[16] so did not hear Sir James Grigg, who announced the formation of a *Palestine Regiment with separate Jewish and Arab Battalions,* also training and arming of Home Guards. A real step in the right direction, after all these months of struggle. Pray it may not be too late.

October 12th   At Zionist Office. Berl Locker gave definition of two types of Committees, the 'Doing Nothing' and the 'Nothing Doing'. This amused me.

November 1st   Church, by myself. Lunched alone at the Club and finished looking over my speech at Balfour Declaration Demonstration at Palace Theatre this afternoon. Theatre quite full of Zionists, despite awful weather. About 1,600 people. Henry Melchett in chair. Smuts sent me a message, in an entirely hand-written letter, great joy and triumph. Henry read it out. Many speakers, of whom I was the fourth, about ten minutes each. I got a wonderful reception. Was quite pleased by my own speech and delivery.

November 13th Zionist Office . . . Then I went and met Lewis at Allies Club, where we had a long talk about Zionist policy. Told him about a talk I had with Henry Melchett yesterday, when Henry said there are elements in the Cabinet favouring Palestine as part of British Empire, not of an Arab Federation, and that Eden is one of these. Also that Harold Macmillan is going to Middle East after Christmas and wants Chaim to meet him there. We decided Lewis should see Harold soon, and note whether he tells *him* any of this, if not, then somebody is not playing quite straight. We think the time is at hand when we ought to send for Chaim to come back here.

November 15th—Sunday   Before Church listened on radio to the church-bells all over Great Britain,[17] and on way to Crown Court heard St Martin's-in-the-Fields ringing itself fit to burst.

November 22nd ... Frank [Balfour] and I supped alone, and to our amazement heard of Cabinet changes, Cripps out of War Cabinet, to Aircraft Production; Bobbitty leaves Colonial Office and is succeeded by Oliver Stanley. This is a dreadful misfortune from Zionist point of view, the whole thing a great surprise, I am sure Walter knew nothing about it. I suppose that some trouble between Cripps and the P.M. is at the bottom of it...

16. Col. Francis Balfour: The elder of Mrs Dugdale's two brothers.
17. They were rung on the occasion of the British victory at El Alamein. It was the first time they had been allowed to ring since the early days of the war when they might be rung only as a warning against enemy parachutists.

November 28th . . . I began to wrestle with my Z.R. Notes, which must be on the reports received from the Polish Government about the latest atrocities against Jews in Poland.[18] It is an extermination policy now, but what can one do? All protests must be made (Palestine is organizing days of fasts and mourning) but what can be *done?* One or two small things only.

December 2nd   To Zionist Office and then to see Bobbity, installed now in Lord Privy Seal's office, to ask his advice on various points about this atrocity affair. He was most kind and helpful, but it is hard to steer an efficient course, in face of so much indifference, and, I fear, on the part of the Foreign Office, of definite desire to damp down publicity. Jimmie reports obstruction from high quarters, he is working manfully inside the B.B.C.[19] . . .

December 4th   Was at Colonial Office by 10.30 where Oliver Stanley received our Yeshiva for the first time. Locker, Lewis and I were our delegates, Oliver had all his officials. A very polite atmosphere, much stiffer than Bobbitty's however. Locker led us admirably, an excellent and moderate statement about the atrocities, and asking that Jews be given places of refuge inside the Empire, not only Palestine, if they can escape. We went into some details about Bulgaria and Hungary. Oliver asked some questions, putting forward the difficulties, but that may be his habit. He could only promise consideration, but he promised it specially for the children. It is too soon to say, but I fear he is very rigid in mind, and I should not be as sure as with Bobbitty, that he will not be unduly influenced by his officials.

December 7th   A long, heavy day at Z.O. all on atrocity work. Felt terribly 'hadden down' [depressed] by its horrors. But all our plans for protests and so on should mature this week. It is all we can do and how little it is!

December 9th   Weather all this week as mild as milk. Went to Z.O. The Polish Note on Atrocities ready for presentation to H.M.G. Next week publicity will reach its height and then we must work on what to *do* next. Very urgent, rather unpractical telegrams from Palestine, ordering us to take steps of which all the good ones have already been taken. Then I went to lunch at

18. Reliable reports had been reaching England—via Switzerland and Sweden—that the Germans were carrying out an extermination policy inside occupied Europe, particularly against the Jews, but also against other peoples. Eden reported to the House on this topic on 17 December. When he had finished the Members rose and stood in silence. This was an unprecedented act. Lloyd George later said: 'I cannot recall a scene like that in all my years.'

19. For some time now reports had been coming in about German atrocities against Polish Jewry. The Foreign Office's directive to the B.B.C. at this time was to ignore these reports as their sources (mainly from the Polish Government) were considered suspect. Sir James Fergusson, then a commentator on the Overseas Service on Nazi propaganda, put together on 5-7 December a report based on German evidence garnered from the B.B.C.'s monitoring service since July, confirming, even boasting of the deportation of Jews from occupied territories to the East, though of course not revealing the fate that awaited them there. This report was received rather sceptically at first.

The Rt. Hon. Malcolm MacDonald
hurries to 10 Downing Street to
report on his 'snap' visit to Palestine,
August 1938

The Rt. Hon. L. S. Amery,
an invaluable friend to Baffy

Jan Masaryk (left), representative of the Czech government in exile, broadcasts with Anthony Eden

Vera and Chaim Weizmann, outside St. James's Palace during the 'London Conference', February 1939

Savoy: huge crowd to hear Beveridge on his Report [on the Social Services], an admirable speech. Whatever happens, that Report makes history and is a high peak in British thinking on post-war world.

December 13th—Sunday Alone to Church . . . Communion Sunday. Went straight on to Stepney where joined Miss Moses and went with her to the Service of Intercession at Bevis Marks Synagogue in St. Mary Axe, to which I had received an invitation, a great honour and a wonderful experience. I had never been to a Synagogue before, except for a wedding. I found it less impressive in some ways than I expected (the prayer-shawls are so very like bathing towels!), in some ways far more so. I was unprepared for the ritual when the Ark is opened and the Torah unwrapped, very reminiscent of Papistry. But these are indeed the People of the Book and two thousand years seemed but as yesterday. Once or twice the sound of their sighing was like wind in the trees. The Chief Rabbi preached a very courageous sermon. I wrote an article later for Z.R. [*Zionist Review*] called 'The Winds of God'.

December 14th Most of the day spent listening to Moshe's first report from Palestine.[20] We have seen nobody from there since France fell! It was like the lifting of thick veils of ignorance and very exciting. Some things go well, especially with the Palestine Regiment. The Yishuv has now contributed 19,000 Jews to the Forces! But politically the White Paper is very much alive and its influence is vicious. There is much to discuss and to do while he is with us, for about a month . . .

December 17th–23rd Jimmie and I were telegraphed for, Frances very ill with clot on her lung in the Ayr Nursing Home . . . We were in Ayr before midday. He saw her, but I did not even let her know I was there, for fear of frightening her. We went out to Kilkerran by lunch-time. There I stayed for four nights, spending all my time with the beloved children. The boys realized she was very ill, we concealed nothing. Thank God the news was better every day. Darling Charles was very worried, 'My mind misgives me when I hear the telephone.' I saw Frances on Monday and again on Tuesday before I left. I fear she will be in the Home all the holidays, a dreary Christmas for all. I was reluctant to leave them, but it was not suggested I should stay. Oh the thankfulness! The mere idea of losing Frances was so appalling. And to think of the Jews in Poland! What can one do to show a sense of one's blessings. 'Ten thousand shall fall beside thee, and a thousand at thy right hand, but it shall not come nigh thee.' And *why not*? Came back this morning, feeling as if I had been away for a century! Dined at R.A.C. with Walter. Heard at the Yeshiva that there had been a Deputation to the Foreign Office and that Anthony Eden had promised to try to do something to get children into Palestine.

20. He had arrived in London the previous day.

P

Christmas Day Christmas dinner here . . . Menu—hors d'oeuvres with mussels, roast chicken (from Stew's sister-in-law in Aberdeenshire), cold ham (preserved in wax since 1939 – soaked for a week and very good), with home-pickled peaches out of our store-cupboard. A 'Woolton' plum pudding. Oatcake and cheese. Nuts, apples and two oranges. Drink – a bottle of Vin Rosé and some Drambuie, obtained by me from Skye (£1-14-0) . . .

1943 *January 5th* . . . listened to the Six o'clock News with half an ear. Was about to turn off, when I heard it say ' Colonel Walter Elliot, M.P. for Kelvingrove, fell when getting into a train at Hawick Station this morning, and is badly hurt.' That was all! Felt quite stunned . . . I realized I could put through a call to John Boyd in Glasgow. This I did, but did not in fact get him until I had returned home about 10.30 p.m. . . . John spoke and said Walter had a fracture of the left ankle, and they are taking him to Edinburgh tomorrow, to X-ray the back—but his spine must be all right for he can move his legs.[1]

February 1st—London Zionist Office. Yeshiva in the evening, discussion of H.M.G.'s policy. They will probably announce that they will admit some thousands of Jews into Palestine, but we fear they may also say that the White Paper stands.

February 15th Busy day at Zionist Office mostly about the appeal for funds for Youth Aliyah to bring the 25,000 children to Palestine (if they can be collected) out of the various Balkan countries and Hungary.

February 17th H.M.G. is so slow in all its actions. It is two months since Oliver Stanley agreed to give priority to children for Palestine certificates and to help to get them out. But they treat children's lives as if they were office files.

March 4th Yesterday I lunched with Bob Cecil . . . He talked to me about winding up the L.N.U. He—at seventy-five—is conscious that it and we are getting old. Like other mortal things he thinks perhaps the time comes when its work is done.

March 9th In the morning to House of Commons, to a Meeting to try to coordinate the various Committees working for rescue of Jewish Refugees. Little or nothing will come of this, and the whole idea was so fantastically

---

1. Elliot's accident was in fact far more serious. His right pelvis was torn out of its socket and he did not recover fully until the following October.

unthought out that it was almost funny. There is a good deal more zeal than discretion among most of the people who have been stirred up about this subject. I lunched at the Allies Club, driving there in a taxi with Victor, who was as woolly-headed and active about this project as one would expect . . . In the afternoon to a meeting of the European Sub-Committee of the International Assembly. Topic—what to do with Germany! General feeling, tear it to bits and stamp on the bits!

March 16th A meeting of the Coordinating Committee in House of Commons, very largely attended and interesting. In spite of its beginnings, this may illustrate the truth of John Orr's wise words 'If God loves it, it will grow.'

March 18th Zionist Office, decided we must publicize the fact that the Colonial Office is doing nothing to fulfil their promises about facilitating the entry of children into Palestine, and Lewis and I drafted a letter which Berl Locker signed and sent to *The Times*.

March 20th . . . Sabina[2] left us today, for factory work, and Edgar and I between us are to do as much of her work as we can, i.e. he looks after the silver and his own clothes; I get up at 8 a.m. (instead of 8.30) dust the drawing-room before breakfast, and we wash up the breakfast things after. In the evening I set dining-room table, do some of the blackout, and Edgar (or Jimmie) bring up the dinner and take the dishes down again. Andersen and Stew, with charlady four mornings a week (and lucky to get her) do the rest. This at least is the programme. I wonder whether, having never done a hand's turn of housework for sixty-three years, I shall now do some every day in my own home till I die? Quite likely!

March 25th Meeting at House of Commons of 'National Committee for Rescue from Nazi Terror' as it is now decided to call it. Useful discussion of steps to be taken. I think Victor Gollancz[3] is the driving force and his probably providing the sinews of war. Victor Cazalet in the chair.

April 26th When I was washing up, Jimmie rang up from the B.B.C. to say the Soviet Government have broken off diplomatic relations with the Poles over this affair of the graves in Katyn Wood.[4] Felt stunned and

2. A refugee girl whom the Dugdales had employed as a housemaid.
3. Victor Gollancz: publisher, author, and speaker; driving force behind Left Book Club; chairman of many 'relief for refugees' committees during and after the war.
4. On 12 April the German government announced that its military authorities had discovered, in the Katyn forest near Smolensk, the mass graves of some 10,000 Polish officers who, they alleged, had been murdered by the Soviet political police following on the occupation of eastern Poland by the S.U. in September 1939. The S.U. vehemently denied this accusation and, in turn, accused the Germans. The Polish Govt.-in-exile in London appealed to the International Red Cross to conduct an impartial enquiry. The S.U. interpreted this as an hostile act, and on 25 April severed diplomatic relations with the Poles in London.

appalled. Jimmie rushed home for five minutes and left me the text of the Russian Note. Lewis came here after dinner and we discussed this catastrophe in all its bearings. It is Goebbels first great victory. He will exploit it. As we have done no counter-propaganda (*what* a justification for Jimmie, who has shown great political instinct) it will be difficult to explain now the rights and wrongs without seeming to take sides. The Nine o'Clock News issued a very bad communiqué. H.M.G. ought to insist on the Poles giving an answer which will enable the Russians to resume relations, but Lewis is sure the Poles would never agree to this even if H.M.G. had the guts to try to insist, and that it would lead to a mutiny in the Polish Army. A very bad business, and its repercussions will be more than one can foresee tonight. We settled that Lewis should see Barrington Ward tomorrow and leave with him Jimmie's memorandum, under seal of secrecy as regards authorship. It will greatly help *The Times* to give the right lead.

April 28th   *The Times* had a good leader, referring to its Diplomatic Correspondent, who derives largely from Jimmie.

April 29th . . . At Zionist Office Adler-Rudel[5] just back from Stockholm gave us an interesting account of his difficult negotiations with the Swedish Government which resulted at last in their agreeing to let in 20,000 Jewish children. It is feasible, now we shall see how much there is in H.M.G.'s profession of willingness to help! . . . Then to the Dorchester for an Executive Committee of the 'Terrorists'—Gollancz taking charge. He is a dynamo! I like him . . .

May 11th   Henry sent word to the Yeshiva this morning that he has learned from a sure source, that the P.M. has told Oliver Stanley that the White Paper is *not* to be the basis of the post-war settlement. This, if true, is invaluable information, and I only hope that we shall model our attitude on it when we go to the Colonial Office tomorrow. But both Locker and Lewis are in the mood for a 'shown-down', whereas I think our main object should be to re-start recruiting,[6] and improve relations.

May 12th   Morning spent by Yeshiva concerting team-work for interviews with Oliver Stanley this afternoon, and Lewis and I lunched at Savoy with Henry for same purpose. A 3 p.m. we all assembled at Colonial Office, interview lasted an hour, Sir George Gater and officials there. It ended on a better note than it began. I had persuaded them that we must take advantage of our secret knowledge, which is now precise, that the P.M. told Attlee

5. Jewish social worker; active in organizing relief during the Hitler period; after the war, liaison officer between UNRRA and Jewish Agency.
6. The Jews had closed their recruiting stations in Palestine, a step which Mrs Dugdale strongly disapproved of as she felt it was playing into the hands of the Palestine administration.

(who enquired) that the White Paper cannot be the basis of post-war policy so long as he is in power. No doubt Oliver knows this, though he doesn't know what we know, and the talk ended with cables to Palestine both from him and from us, advising parties to get together.

May 14th . . . on arrival at Zionist Office found a turmoil following on letter from Henry Melchett, confessing that when he took the cable we had most carefully drafted back to Colonial Office on Wednesday evening, he and Oliver Stanley together made alterations in it, without consulting us, and sent it off over Locker's signature. He said the changes were of no importance, but we thought otherwise, for they had added a sentence which implied criticism by us of the Agency in Jerusalem, and certainly destroyed all prospect of agreement. In fact the Colonial Office had pulled a fast one on us! Neither Oliver nor Henry may have realized what they were doing, but what they did was unpardonable. I rang up Henry and told him so. After lunch our Yeshiva considered how to put matters right without un-doing all the good done by the friendly atmosphere of our Conference. We decided to ask Oliver to forward a cable to Moshe, explaining that the final sentence of our first one was not drafted by us. He rang up Namier later at the Club, and consented to do this, and their talk was quite friendly. That is the best we can do, but it seems to me quite extraordinary that Oliver Stanley should make changes in a cable to be signed by somebody else, without insisting that that person be consulted first!

June 6th—Sunday To Church alone, Jimmie being away. On return I got a telephone message from Jos. Wedgwood's secretary that Jos. is dying, and wanted to see me . . . I went off to University College Hospital after, where Jos. is, in a private ward. He was propped on pillows, and very far through, torn with a terrible hiccough. He wanted to give me a message for Chaim, or Shertok. It was this.

He has been thinking about what the Jews ought to do in Palestine. They should go on cooperating until the end of the war, but begin now to organize civil resistance against any attack on their just rights which may be proposed at the Peace Conference. *And they should let the P.M. know, and nobody else* that they intend to resist. When he had got this out I repeated it to him, and asked him whether he meant organize as regards arms. He said, 'Yes—arms—immigrants—work out a scheme.' Seeing that he was very exhausted I rose to go, but told him that the Jews in the Polish ghettoes are fighting back. He smiled radiantly, and said, 'Good. At last! Is it only in Warsaw?'[7] I told him that we had hopes that the Polish Underground Movement had got some arms into some places. He said again: 'Good. Let them fight to the end.' I then approached the bed and kissed his hand. He took mine and raised it to his lips, and said, 'Good-bye. You have been very good to me.' I left, feeling very shattered.

7. The Warsaw Ghetto uprising began on 19 April. The fighting lasted until the 28th, when the S.S. finally succeeded in physically erasing the Ghetto area.

June 7th   Zionist Office. Terrible cable . . . about Bulgarian Jews. Yeshiva decided to take it to Foreign Office and that I should go alone to see Oliver Stanley about it. I had a very satisfactory talk with him, he told me (quite confidentially) that he had decided to ask the War Cabinet to relax all restrictions on immigration into Palestine for Jews who can escape. So, it remains to be seen what power he has, but I think they can hardly refuse such a request to the responsible Minister at this time, and probably none of them want to except Sir John Anderson[8] and perhaps Anthony Eden.

June 16th   I spent the afternoon listening to the Labour Conference, for which Berl Locker gave me a visitor's ticket. With eyes shut it might have been a Conservative ditto, though I think the general level was lower and less progressive, certainly less realistic. I do not think we have much to hope (or to fear) from Labour for a long while to come . . .

July 4th   When I got to the office this morning, Berl broke to me the shattering news that the plane which was bringing Sikorski[9] and his staff and Victor home, crashed last night on leaving Gibraltar and they are all killed.

Such a tragedy is unrealizable. Dear, dear Victor. It will leave an awful gap in our lives. He was among my very nearest friends. To think that it happened last night just while the Weizmanns and I sat surrounded by his pictures and books![10]. I rang up Chaim and told him. Rewrote my Zionist Revue notes, substituting an article on Victor in Palestine, those happy days in Rehovoth in 1938! Cannot believe he is dead!

July 13th   At the Zionist Office we had a Memorial Service for Victor in the Board-Room. Thelma and her husband and brother came, also Miss Rathbone. Speakers were Chaim and myself, Lewis and Barny Janner. It was all very nice. I was nervous of breaking down, but did not, and was not displeased.

July 16th   Zionist Office in the morning. Chaim summoned away by an alarming seizure Vera had after an injection. Luckily she recovered in an hour or two—how awful if she had not, but it was touch and go!

Dined alone at Dorchester with Chaim, Vera in bed, but able to play bezique after. Chaim talked to me about his good talk with Casey,[11] and about his worries over Ben-Gurion, who seems to have gone quite *meshugah* in his dislike of Chaim and distrust of him. Chaim says he will never sit

---

8. Sir John Anderson: Permanent Under-Secretary at the Home Office, 1922–32; Govenor of Bengal, 1932–37; Lord Privy Seal, 1938–39; Home Secretary, 1939–40; Lord President of the Council 1940–43; Chancellor of Exchequer, 1943–45; member of War Cabinet, 1940–45. Created Viscount Waverley, 1952.
9. General Sikorski: Prime Minister of the Polish Government-in-Exile.
10. They were staying in his suite in the Dorchester.
11. Richard Casey: Minister of State resident in Middle East and member of War Cabinet, 1942–43.

with him on the same Executive again. This is a terrible misfortune at this juncture, just when unity is most needed! . . .

July 21st At the Yeshiva this morning Chaim told us that last night Leo Amery told him that a Cabinet Committee is being set up to find a new policy for Palestine! They have discovered at last that the White Paper won't do. Two ideas hold the field. *One* a Jewish State in an undivided Palestine, *two,* in a Palestine excluding Samaria. Amery is to be on this Committee. Sounded by him about partition, Chaim replied he would have nothing to do with it, he had been too badly let down by H.M.G. last time.

October 14th Succoth [The Feast of Tabernacles]. Office closed, but we had a Yeshiva there . . . Chaim saw General Smuts for an hour this morning. They have not met for twelve years! After Chaim had given him a survey of the situation Smuts said, 'Your attitude has changed very much.' Chaim replied, 'You and I started from opposite poles. You began as an enemy of the British, I as their staunchest friend. But it seems they do not want my friendship or that of my people. Hitler has won this war as far as the Jews are concerned.' Smuts said, 'I assure you Hitler will not win this war as far as the Jews are concerned.'
He promised to bring Chaim to see the P.M. but said he must have time to look around. He asked Chaim whether he thought of going to Palestine. Chaim said he could not go there with empty hands, and in any case would not now go while Smuts is in London. Smuts said 'You are right.'

October 20th Yeshiva this morning discussed cables from Berl and Moshe urging Chaim to come to Palestine at once. He will not, and we all agreed that the centre of gravity is here, while Smuts is here. Also he will not face Palestine empty-handed and he will not sit at same table with David Ben-Gurion. He asked us whether, if partition is suggested, we would back him in considering it. Lewis and Brodetsky said *yes, on condition only* (said Lewis) that no one knows at this stage that Chaim would even consider it. But it's all very well, he can't keep that to himself. I discovered from Walter (with whom he lunched alone yesterday) that Walter feels sure Chaim *would* accept the idea, though of course he never said so. We gather Cabinet Committee veers that way, but on the other hand the P.M. has never been a partitionist.

October 25th At 5.30 we all went to Dorchester Hotel to hear Chaim's report of lunching with the P.M. which he did today. Long, important, and on the whole very satisfactory talk, which demands some new orientations. It is to be kept very secret. The impossibility of communicating freely with Palestine is most serious. . . .

October 27th I went to the office in the morning, a Yeshiva on cables from Palestine, Ben-Gurion suddenly resigned from the Executive, without warning, though we have known for many months past that he was on the eve of it, having quarrelled with Chaim in U.S.A., though nobody seems to know exactly why. Cables came from Berl and Moshe in Palestine, begging Chaim to come, but the centre of gravity is here, and he has replied suggesting that they send a Delegation to London to be here this winter.

I went to the Dorchester for a big dinner to M.P.'s, Mr Hammersley[12] presiding, to set up the new Parliamentary Palestine Committee, deprived of its chairmen by the death of Jos. and dear Victor. About thirty M.P.'s and Peers, very representative. I sat between Lord Snell and Vernon Bartlett.[13] Chaim spoke, quite magnificently. What a statesman he is! . . .

November 3rd   Zionist Office. Lunched at Guards Club with Bill, Ruth and Ral.[14] . . . Bill's stories of 'Monty' are wonderful. When the King went to Tunisia with the C.I.G.S. they visited Monty's H.Q. and afterwards Sir Alan Brooke said to the King, 'I used to think he would like my job, but I don't think he does now.' 'No,' said the King, 'but I sometimes wonder about mine! !'

November 11th   Zionist Office. Later a big Yeshiva in Simon Marks' room at the Dorchester, to discuss whether or not Chaim should try to influence H.M.G.'s plans for future of Palestine whatever they may be. Harry Sacher strongly held *not*, in view of his responsibilities to the Movement. Lewis and Bakstansky held he should do all he can to get a better settlement beforehand. I inclined to Harry's view, largely because I do not think he will succeed in influencing things much in present stage.

November 14th   Had tea with Leo Amery in his house, got something out of him about Palestine. I think Partition is in the wind, but *not* the line cutting the Jews off from Galilee and the Emek, of which rumours had reached us from Palestine. More likely Samaria, which would be much more reasonable. Amery took 'Harry's view' (see November 11th) he said that the fact that Chaim had influenced the Jews to negotiate on the Peel Commission proposal had made the Arabs think it was favourable to the Jews!

Dined with Chaim and Vera and told them all this. Chaim very worried by the continuous appeals to him to go to Palestine. Ben-Gurion won't come here. Chaim will not go, he won't leave Vera and she is not fit to travel under present conditions of voyage. Also he says he won't go to fight a madman on his own ground. We uphold him.

November 23rd   To Zionist Office where I heard from Linton and Lewis of a very satisfactory talk Chaim had had with Smuts this morning. Smuts said that the Palestine future will be discussed between the P.M. and

---

12. S. S. Hammersley: Conservative M.P. for East Willesden from 1938.
13. Vernon Bartlett: Independent M.P. for Bridgwater from 1938; journalist and broadcaster.
14. R. A. L. Balfour: Viscount Traprain; succeeded as 3rd Earl of Balfour, 1945.

Roosevelt who are now meeting somewhere in the Middle East.[15] Smuts may joint the party next week. He assures Chaim that the 'Jews will have a show.' I am sure some form of partition is in view!

November 26th . . . This was Chaim's 69th birthday. Wrote to him. Perhaps there will be a Jewish State by the time he is seventy!

December 12th—Sunday Church. Communion Sunday. Good service. Lewis lunched here and stayed some time. Then went to tea at Dorchester with Chaim and Vera. He told me he had had a cable from Smuts (before leaving Cairo) saying 'Your affairs have been discussed, you will receive invitation to Colonial Office'—so, within a few days (or possibly weeks) the crisis will be upon us. I am glad Chaim had already invited the Palestinian and American Delegations here. . . .

December 21st Zionist Office. Busy there. Chaim does not think he will hear anything about the Palestine decisions until the P.M. comes back. He saw Leo Amery yesterday and from what he let fall he is sure it is partition and probably along an acceptable line.

December 26th—Sunday Did not go to church, but to office, for Berl Locker arrived back from Palestine. He brought me a few raisins and two small bananas, which when ripened I shall give to Jimmie, who pines for them! Berl told us something of the state of feeling in the Yishuv, very anti-British and no wonder—it is all the fault of the Administration. Ben-Gurion has gained in influence, he is the leader on the spot. The other news is that just before the P.M. fell ill[16] he had a Press Conference in Cairo, and 'off the record' told about eighty journalists that the time has come to fulfil the promises to the Jews. This is very important, confirming what was privately said to Chaim.

December 28th Zionist Office open again. Yeshiva in the morning, when Berl Locker began his account of conditions in Palestine. A mixture of good and bad, but the most heartening thing the spirit of the colonists, the purchase of new J.N.F. land, chiefly in the 'prohibited' areas (despite the Regulations) and the pioneer settlements penetrating into the Negev.

December 30th Berl went on with his Report, this time on political aspect and Ben-Gurion's attitude. We all urged Chaim to send him a wire, inviting him to come here and sink differences and share responsibility in the approaching time of decision. Chaim said that if we all insisted he would send such a cable, but against his own will, and he would not sit round a

---

15. They were meeting in Cairo in preparation for the forthcoming Tehran conference; Smuts joined them later, on their return from Tehran.
16. He had contracted pneumonia.

table with Ben-Gurion. This was not good enough, and for the time being we left it at that . . .

December 31st Zionist Office. Yeshiva . . . Dined with Chaim and Vera and came home in time to listen to the broadcast, and heard 'O God of Bethel' on a Watch Night Service.

May God keep us all, for except the Lord keep the city the watchman waketh but in vain.

1944 *January 3rd* . . . Chaim yielded to our wish to invite Ben-Gurion once more to come here and share responsibility . . .

January 5th . . . At Zionist Office both morning and afternoon. Berl very worried by Chaim's inability to conceal that he would accept a *good* partition.

January 20th   Zionist Office. Dr Goldmann[1] reported on Zionist affairs in U.S.A. Very depressing. Such low standards both of morality and political sense. Came away with Chaim, who was in despair and said he felt as if he were stifling, and it will be a miracle if the Jews can make, and run, a State out of this material. I said, Yes, but the miracle *will* happen.

January 28th   Chandos lunch . . . Colin saw the P.M. at Other Club last night. He looked well, but said his heart is affected, he cannot walk as he did, but admits to smoking as much as ever. He said the Poles were being very tiresome, and thinks that if only he could get together with Stalin he could put things right in a jiffy. Evidently they have clicked. Speaking of his meeting with de Gaulle, he said that he had said to him that though he (the P.M.) was the representative of a great and powerful country, nevertheless his first thought every morning was 'How can I please President Roosevelt? How can I meet the wishes of Marshal Stalin?'—whereas he (de Gaulle) seemed to have no thought but 'How can I snap my fingers at my powerful friends?'

March 27th   Zionist Office. Long Yeshiva, deciding what Moshe Shertok should say at interview with Ministers. Also reports from good quarters that the Cabinet Committee has suggested alternatives of partition (Royal Commission lines plus the Negev and an international control of water from Jordan Valley) or cantonization. But the P.M. does not desire decisions to be taken at present.

March 30th   Zionist Office. There Chaim told me of Orde Wingate's death in an operational flight in Burma. This is a great loss at this juncture. He

1. Dr S. Goldman: President of Zionist Organization of America, 1938–40.

was evidently a guerrilla leader of genius, whatever he might have been in handling larger bodies of men. I never liked him, and have always wondered whether his influence on the Yishuv would have been as splendid as his friends think, if he had returned to Jewish work after the War. Now we shall never know.

April 6th . . . There was a Memorial Service for Wingate at the office. Chaim spoke, also Moshe and Lewis. Moshe was the best. The hagiology is already far advanced. He will be a greater inspiration to the Jews now he is dead than if he had lived to take a hand in their politics. But they do not perceive that, and think that his work was first frustrated by H.M.G. and is now cut short.

April 7th—Good Friday   To Zionist Office as there was work, then to church at Crown Court. In the evening to a Seder at Miss Moses'. About 100 people, including a lorry-load of American Jewish soldiers. Their two officers and a very nice Free French one sat at the high table near me and plied me with questions about Palestine. Very enjoyable. Then I came out into the moonlit empty streets, for all the Jews were in their houses, remembering how they were brought out of Egypt. From many little slum streets and courts came the chanting of the last Seder Psalm, to the tune of Hatikvah [The Zionist Anthem]. And people say the Jews can be assimilated!

April 14th   To Dorchester Hotel, where Gershon [Agronsky] gave to the inner Yeshiva a disquieting account of the state of affairs in Palestine, the spread of violence,[2] the attraction it has for youth, the difficulties for the Yishuv and Agency in cooperating with the Administration to put it down. It was to say this that Ben-Gurion sent him here so suddenly. Very disquieting.

April 16th   Back to Zionist Office where helped Lewis finish a short article on Crozier[3] of *The Manchester Guardian,* who died suddenly last night. A heavy blow to Zionism. That makes the fourth of the great non-Jewish friends lost in the past twelve months, just when they are needed most. Cazalet, Wedgwood, Wingate, Crozier.

April 20th   Zionist Office. Farewell to Rabbi Fischmann and Schmorak[4] who are returning to Palestine. Their absence will make it unnecessary for the Yeshivoth to be any longer conducted in Yiddish. Chaim's classic description of Schmorak's mind—'It is like an unswept chimney.'

2. On the outbreak of war the Irgun Zvei Leumi, the Revisionist terrorist group, had suspended its operations and had even cooperated to some extent with the British authorities in the general war effort. But at the beginning of 1944 they proclaimed the truce at an end, and, together with the even more extremist Stern gang (an offshoot of the former), recommenced their terrorist activities.
3. William Crozier: Editor of *Manchester Guardian,* 1932–44.
4. Members of the Palestine delegation.

June 4th—Sunday Dined with the Weizmanns . . . Chaim suffering from the shock of an extraordinary story cabled by Moshe from Jerusalem through the Foreign Office. It appears that about ten days ago a German aeroplane arrived in Ankara, with two passengers, one a Hungarian Jew, the other a Gestapo man! They came to make propositions for a bargain in Jewish lives against 10,000 lorries and vast quantities of food.[5]

June 5th Yeshiva twice discussed what to do about the Ankara message.

June 6th *The Day has dawned at last.* The liberating assault was launched during the night at many places on the coast of France. The P.M. has twice spoken to the House, reporting that all goes well so far, better than we dared to hope or expect, and we appeared to have achieved a tactical surprise. The magnitude of the operation by sea and air beggars imagination. Airborne troops have descended in swarms. All day long the radios have given out news. The sound of aircraft frequent over London. Long queues await the issue of the evening papers. How wonderful for Winston, who planned Gallipoli and saw it fail, to have carried through this greatest enterprise of the greatest war!

June 7th . . . Morning at Zionist Office. The letter I drafted for Chaim to send to Anthony Eden about the Istanbul incident has borne fruit. He sees him today. As the idea was also mine, I am very pleased. It is important that Chaim should be in contact with the Foreign Secretary. Lunched alone with Chaim at the Carlton. He was in a charming mood.

June 13th Zionist Office in the morning, where the Yeshiva was filmed in session in the Board Room for 'March of Time'. Chaim pointing to a contour map of Palestine and everybody else looking as if they had never seen it before! . . .

June 22nd Went to the office and we all went off (including Chaim) to the *'March of Time'* film studio, to see the film taken of the Yeshiva the other day. I was horrified by own appearance, but the others thought it very good! Went to investigate damage at the Allies Club. To my delight, found it was only to the front windows and everything else undamaged and in going order. Lunched there and went back to office, where read some of Lewis' Lecture on 1848.[6] It will be very good.

June 23rd Long and busy day there, over the Istanbul story. Moshe cables frantically that we *must* get him here to tell us all about it. He obviously takes it very seriously.

---

5. The full story of this episode can be followed in Joel Brand's *Desperate Mission* (London, 1962).
6. Eventually delivered as the Raleigh Lecture for 1944 at the British Academy.

June 26th Zionist Office in the morning. The Foreign Office is expediting Shertok's arrival so as to hear more about the Istanbul story. . . . Meanwhile the massacres of Jews still go on.

June 27th Saw Locker . . . who told me Shertok has just arrived. He was given very high priorities and was in Palestine forty-eight hours ago. Went back to office and there saw him. Then Agronsky, Locker, Moshe and self got into a taxi and went to the Dorchester. Miss May also coming to take notes. Simon Marks and Israel Sieff joined us and Shertok unfolded his most amazing story, which I cannot here set down. It was arranged he should go tomorrow to the Foreign Office and report all. These are probably deep waters, nothing can or should be done or said without knowledge and approval of H.M.G. All the Yeshiva strongly feels this.

June 29th . . . At Zionist Office. Shertok reported on Foreign Office attitude. He and Chaim are to see Eden. Chaim much impressed by the difference in angle from which Foreign Office and Jewish Agency naturally approach this matter, and with the very great dangers of that situation from Jewish point of view. We thought him unduly nervous about this.

June 30th At Zionist Office. Chaim and Moshe consulted the Yeshiva about the line they should take when seeing Mr George Hall[7] at Foreign Office in the afternoon. I thought Chaim still suffering from quite undue fears lest he should be thought unmindful of Allied interests. His record of thirty years should banish that suspicion. I said this. Chaim much moved, but evidently sunk in deep despair by the story Moshe brought. Harry Sacher was at the Yeshiva, and, as always, displayed the best side of his indolent nature in a crisis.

July 3rd . . . To Zionist Office. There said good-bye to Gershon Agronsky, who returns to Palestine this afternoon. Moshe reported to us on some 'top secret' events concerning some thirty-five people from the Yishuv, who are *operating* in the most wonderful manner. One or two of them are girls. Some day it must all be known. Meantime let it be an inspiration to those few of us who know, and let it set us a standard of courage![8] . . .

July 10th Zionist Office in the morning. Moshe very depressed by talk with Anthony Eden on Friday, who told him and Chaim it had been decided in highest quarters not to follow up the Istanbul story. I never had much hope, it was too fantastic, but at one moment it looked as if it might lead to some sort of result. But anyway it is too late now to save the

7. George Hall: Under-Secretary of State for Colonies, 1940–42; Secretary of State for Colonies, 1945–46; First Lord of the Admiralty, 1946–51. Cr. Viscount, 1946.
8. These were Palestinian Jews who were being parachuted into eastern Europe to help organize resistance among the local Jewish communities.

Hungarian Jews. 'Only a remnant shall be saved'—the prophecy comes true! . . .

July 20th One of those days when one feels one's brain will burst with too many things in it. Morning papers carried—(1) Lord Gort's appointment as High Commissioner of Palestine; (2) publicity of Istanbul story, quite correct as far as it goes. Both these things complete news to our Yeshiva, though it turned out that Oliver Stanley had written to Chaim. The Yeshiva met again in afternoon to discuss what to do, when shattering news came that Vera had telephoned from the place where she and Chaim are staying near Bath, that he is ill. She spoke to David Bergmann,[9] and was very hysterical, spoke of bleeding from the lung and pneumonia. Bergmann goes down by first train tomorrow. If anything happens to Chaim *now* it would be a disaster of greatest magnitude. Anyway, I fear he is *hors de combat* for some time. Thank goodness Moshe is here, but is no substitute.

July 21st News from Chaim that he is not so very ill, needs only keep quiet and not talk. Great relief!

August 1st I went to the Colonial Office at twelve o'clock to see Oliver Stanley by appointment, about the letter I got from Frances ten days ago, reporting the anti-Semitic remarks made by Lord Gort at tea at Kilkerran, on July 19th, the day his appointment as High Commissioner for Palestine was announced. As there will be no other record of this anywhere I shall put it down here in full. Frances' letter was full of horror that a man with this bias should be appointed to Palestine. But she was very anxious that her name should never be quoted as repeating what Lord Gort had said, as her parents-in-law would feel advantage had been taken of a private conversation in their house. I explained this to Oliver Stanley and read him from Frances' letter the direct quotations from Lord Gort. They were the following:
'Lord Gort was here today for tea and he said he was leaving Malta for Palestine. To my horror he proceeded to say he didn't like Jews, that when he saw them in the streets of Tel Aviv he thought they were repellent and Palestine had the worst of them—"the riff-raff of Central Europe". He did say, "Of course I oughtn't to say anything of this sort now." He told my father-in-law that Palestine was in an awful state, with the Jews armed to the teeth with rifles.'
I told Oliver Stanley that I had been doubtful what I ought to do about this letter. I had not even mentioned it to Chaim, or any of my colleagues on the Yeshiva, as I was most anxious they should start on the right foot with Gort, which they are most willing and prepared to do. But I thought he (Stanley) should know. Our conversation was of course very friendly all

9. David Bergmann: Scientific Director of Sieff [later Weizmann] Institute.

Q

through, and he said he was grateful to me for telling him. He agreed that it was most unwise of Gort to have talked in this way at all, to anybody, but he said he was quite sure it did not represent Gort's attitude towards Jewish questions of high policy in Palestine, he had had many long talks with him and was satisfied that he would take a soldier's view and carry out Cabinet orders faithfully. Stanley added, 'Not everybody likes Jews.' I replied No, but if anybody has as strong an anti-Arab feeling as Gort seems to have about Jews in general he would not be suitable as High Commissioner. To this he agreed, but repeated that he did not think that the conversation as reported was Gort's considered view. I said I had been particularly alarmed by the allusion 'armed to the teeth'. Stanley interjected 'That is quite true however'. I went on as if I had not heard, 'Because any repetition of what happened at Ramath HaKovish[10] would be so fearfully dangerous.' To which he made no reply. I then said again that I did not want to impart the information in the letter to anybody. He said, 'Of course if you did I should be bound to tell Gort exactly where and how the information got out.' I said, 'You could certainly mention me, and you could say you know my source.' 'No,' he said, 'that would not do. Gort would have a right to know everything, for it is an accusation, and he might wish to put his side of the story, for after all this is only one part of a conversation, we do not know how it arose, or what the other people said, and so on.' I did not argue this, and he went on, 'No. I should handle this in quite a different way.' I saw the conversation had better now end. We discussed for a little while how and when Chaim had better meet Gort before Gort goes to Palestine—Stanley is very keen that this meeting should take place, observing 'Weizmann could charm a bird off a tree' and then said there was plenty of time to discuss these things, as Chaim is still away, and Gort is going to Malta to say good-bye there, and returning here before he goes to Palestine. He also said, 'Gort gets intensely absorbed in local problems. He used to write me long letters about all sorts of details of Malta administration.'

August 8th   Zionist Office. An accumulation of telegrams and work, and a personal letter from the P.M. to Chaim, presaging the formation, at last, of a Jewish Brigade Group. It may still not be too late for them to strike a blow at the Nazis. Perhaps even on German soil!

September 28th   Zionist Office. Lunched at Club and when I went back to office after lunch, Locker brought into my room transcript of the bit of Winston's War Review this afternoon, referring to the Jewish Brigade and promising Jews should share in occupation of German territory. Talked it all over with Locker and Moshe, who were deeply happy at whole wording of the passage. It is wonderful to be able for once to rejoice with them that do rejoice in that office. Spoke in the evening to Hendon Zionist Society, very small attendance, but it was easy to make a good speech!

10. A particularly heavy-handed arms search had recently taken place at this settlement.

September 29th Zionist Office. Pleasure in the P.M.'s speech marred by news that the outrages of the Irgun in Palestine have broken out again. Moshe was, in any case, going back as soon as he can . . .

September 30th . . . Had tea with Weizmanns, Moshe there. Chaim very upset over the outrages, says the Yishuv must be made to understand that if they continue they will ruin the hopes of a State. Walked for a little in Hyde Park, with Chaim discussed what might be done when Berl goes back to Palestine, as must shortly happen. Chaim thinks perhaps Isaiah Berlin[11] would take his place at the Zionist Office for the crucial period of negotiations next spring. Wonderful if so.

October 4th Zionist Office in the morning. Chaim had seen Amery, who told nothing, but there obviously is a Palestine Partition plan, on which final decision is not yet taken. Chaim says pressure *must* be applied in U.S.A. as well as here. Question—How? He is obviously uneasy about the position, especially with fresh outbursts of violence in Palestine. Ditto Moshe. But this did not prevent a very gay and happy luncheon party given at Savoy by Lewis and me, fulfilling an old promise to give one to Chaim when Pinsk[12] was liberated. Poor Pinsk, what is there left of it, one wonders? Party was— Chaim, Vera, Moshe, Locker, Miss May, Linton. Walked away with Chaim, who was bound for 10 Downing Street. . . . He talked of his Memoirs, of which Volume I up to 1918 is practically ready . . .

October 14th . . . To the Dorchester, to tea with Chaim and Vera. He had heard from a good source the very interesting news that Stalin would view with disfavour an Arab federation on which the Foreign Office is so keen . . .

October 27th Went to the office. Chaim thinks some decision on Palestine is imminent. Brendan Bracken tried to draw him about 'an acceptable' partition scheme. Of course, he said, there was none such, but in his heart I believe he would have liked to make a suggestion!

November 5th—Sunday . . . In the evening Linton rang me up with the dreadful news that Lord Moyne has been murdered in Cairo.[13] Oliver Stanley asked Chaim to come to the Colonial Office to see him this evening (sending his car) and told him it is suspected that the assassins are Palestinian Jews. I fear it may be so, but there is as yet no certainty, and Stanley's manner of imparting the news gave Chaim a terrible shock. Linton, who went with him, reported that he came out of Oliver's room as white as a sheet. It is indeed a dreadful disaster, all the more cruel because it follows on a very satisfactory

11. Sir Isaiah Berlin: Fellow of All Souls College, Oxford, 1932–38; 1950–68; Chichele Professor of Social and Political Theory, 1957–67; President of Wolfson College, Oxford, from 1966.
12. Where Weizmann spent his childhood.
13. By members of the Stern gang. He was suspected by them of pursuing an anti-Zionist policy.

talk Chaim had with the P.M. when he lunched with him at Chequers last week. The P.M. set his mind at rest about rumours of a bad partition and assured him that no decision would be come to without consulting him. We had been very happy about this for the first time in months; and Chaim starts for Palestine on Friday. But this more than spoils all. Chaim will however be more needed than ever in Palestine, for if this murder is really committed by the Stern Gang, the Yishuv *must* now take action against them, which may well plunge the country in civil war. Also there is the risk to Chaim's life. It is a dreadful tragedy.

November 9th . . . At Zionist Office Chaim was rather more cheerful, he has got over the first shock of the news, and the tone of the Press is on the whole very sane and reasonable. He went to see Mr Martin, the P.M.'s secretary, and I am glad to say, told him that Oliver Stanley had behaved to him 'like a brute'. I hope this may percolate. He said 'Colonel Stanley is only half my age, but if he lives to be a hundred he will not have done half what I have in my life-time.' Lewis and I went to tea at the Dorchester, to say good-bye to Chaim and Vera, who leave for Palestine on Saturday. May all go well! If it does then his going there at this juncture may do enormous good. Martin said to him yesterday that the whole Palestine settlement depended upon the lives of two men — himself and the Prime Minister. One must have faith, but it is a solemn thought. They are both seventy!

December 4th Did not know when Michael would turn up,[14] so occupied myself as best I could until at nearly 7 p.m. his voice came through on telephone, speaking from St. Pancras Station. Before eight o'clock he was on door-step. *Completely* unchanged (except that he now smokes a pipe!) He had not been five minutes in the house before I felt he had never been away. He feels the same about us, though he thinks Edgar is looking older. We had for dinner a Whittingehame pheasant (Michael had not tasted pheasant for five years!) and a bottle of Champagne Edgar had been keeping all this time. Talked till midnight. It certainly is pleasant for him to be home . . . 'My cup overflows'!

14. Michael Dugdale had been away for four years, serving in the Near East [including Palestine] and Italy.

1945 *March 5th* . . . Dined with Walter at R.A.C. He has got quite fat, but that will doubtless soon vanish! His account of Russia[1] shows that it is not very unlike what we supposed. They are longing to finish the War and get busy in their own country, quite uninterested in anybody else's except destroying German power to bother them again. The most startling thing was his description of Stalin, who received the Delegation for an hour, and seemed to answer all their questions frankly and with greatest simplicity. Asked about the Free German Committee (von Paulus[2] and Co.) he said, useful now for propaganda, afterwards — pouf! — with a gesture as sweeping them off the board. But Stalin himself struck Walter as a sick man, he knew he was short, but thought he would give an impression of physical strength and energy, but, on this occasion, not so at all.

March 12th Busy day at the office . . . Chaim and Vera returned by air from Palestine, but he not very well and unable to see anybody. But it is good to have them safe back. Linton returned with them, poured out Palestine impressions. He is quite stunned by the difference in atmosphere and outlook. Very natural, but it makes political work difficult.

March 17th . . . Went to the Dorchester and had tea with Chaim and Vera. He in bed with bad inflammation of his eyes, but most eager to talk. Painted a dark picture of psychology of rising generation in the Yishuv, said B.G. is much to blame and is perhaps frightened now of the devils he has failed to discourage. Thinks Moshe lacks 'personality' (I think this is true).

March 20th . . . After dinner Chaim rang me up from the Dorchester to say he had tonight received a letter from Stephen Wise in Washington, written on March 18th, and flown over by a member of the Embassy Staff, to say he had seen F.D.R. who told him that *at Yalta it was decided that Palestine shall be 'handed over' to the Jews!* Ibn Sa'ud cut up rough and F.D.R. tried to placate him, but W.S.C. 'told him off'. There is more in the letter, which we shall see tomorrow.

Is this the turning-point? Has it truly come?

1. Elliot had been to the Soviet Union as head of a parliamentary delegation.
2. Field Marshal von Paulus: Commander-in-Chief of the German forces captured at Stalingrad.

March 25th—Palm Sunday . . . to tea with Chaim, who is recovering. Vera was out. Berl there. I judged it safe at last to tell them about Lord Gort's conversation at Kilkerran in October, for he appears to have changed completely. They were enormously astonished—I almost wished I had *not* told them. Chaim approved very much of what I had done, and said it was perhaps the thing for which the Jews should be most grateful to me. He thinks it most important that Oliver Stanley should have been told, and quite right at the time that the Jews should not. After tea I walked with him in Hyde Park, he poured out things that made him uneasy about the youth in the Yishuv. He said Ben-Gurion was largely responsible and had much on his conscience. B.-G. was nearly killed today in a motor accident and is in St. George's Hospital, but suffering apparently only from shock. It was a very memorable conversation with Chaim. What wisdom and nobility of character! May he live to see his heart's desire. He showed the letter (see March 20th) to Martin, the P.M.'s secretary, and though he said nothing, his manner convinced Chaim that it is substantially true . . .

March 31st . . . In the afternoon visited Ben-Gurion in a Nursing Home, still suffering from his motor accident, and took him S. H. Butcher's *Essays on Greek Subjects* . . .

April 6th   Very busy morning at office, drafting with Lewis an aide-memoire of a talk Chaim had yesterday with General Smuts, for Smuts to take to Chequers, where he is spending the weekend with the P.M. . . . Dined with Chaim and Vera at Dorchester. He will have to have an operation for glaucoma and gives up going to U.S.A.

April 13th   At the office we figured out that although an unmitigated disaster for Britain, the death of F.D.R.[3] may have some compensations for the Jews. He was a friend, but an ignorant and rather wobbly one . . . The Jewish vote in U.S.A. lost importance after his Election. If this unknown Truman (how soon we shall be familiar with his name!) wants to run again in four years' time, it gains in importance. Perhaps. Spent morning drafting condolence telegrams from Chaim and Jewish Agency . . .

April 17th . . . Yeshiva, Chaim sent round a rather disquieting letter from Smuts, suggesting continuation of Mandate, control of immigration divided between Great Britain and U.S.A. Started drafting reply saying Jews would not play on that . . .

May 1st—1 Roland Gardens . . . Interesting Yeshiva on policy of asking for more certificates under White Paper. Ben-Gurion uncompromisingly against, for fear of tacitly acquiescing in it. Locker less extreme.

---

3. **Roosevelt died on 12 April.**

May 4th   Edgar and I dined at Allies Club. When the 9 p.m. News came on there were about forty people of various nationalities standing round the wireless. The Announcer began ALL GERMAN TROOPS IN N.W. GERMANY, HOLLAND, AND DENMARK SURRENDERED UNCONDITIONALLY ABOUT 6 P.M. TODAY. I could hear no more, such a shout went up.

May 8th—VE Day 1   To Zionist Office in morning for a Yeshiva, no staff there. Nothing unusual in the streets in the morning. About 2 p.m. I boarded a 77 'bus to go to Parliament Square. Lucky to get a seat on top, for we progressed at walking pace along the Strand. In Trafalgar Square and White-hall were the densest crowds, and the best-behaved, I ever saw in all my experience of London. Unusually gay and coloured, for it was a warm and sunny day, and the carnival paper hats were many and various and very becoming to most girls. Loudspeakers were on Government buildings all down Whitehall. A 3 p.m. the loud murmur of the vast crowds in Parliament Square were absolutely hushed, to hear the P.M. He was very good. I don't think anyone but him could have got away with 'Advance Britannia!' But he did, at the end there was a mighty roar. The cheering for him when the Commons came out to go to St Margaret's was so loud that I could not hear my own voice, though shouting at pitch of my lungs. I stayed to see them come out. With them walked the ghosts of Victor Cazalet and Rob Bernays.[4]

May 10th   I dined with Chaim and Vera. Benjy there. Chaim recovering, but very low in spirits. He is passionately anxious to see the P.M., says the White Paper position is untenable now the War is ended.

May 17th   At last finished the Zionist Memo to Government, and the covering letter from Chaim to P.M. in which he hints at his own resignation if decision any longer delayed now the War is over. He means this and we all feel the time is come to play the Ace of Trumps . . .

June 11th   Yeshiva in morning, terrible blow in letter from P.M. saying the Jewish Question could not be touched till the Peace Conference. Everyone greatly upset, but there is something odd about this answer. It was sent without Martin's knowledge (Chaim discovered) and Leo Amery whom he saw this evening was much surprised by it . . .

June 27th . . . In the morning, long informal talk between Chaim, Locker, Lewis and self about procedure re his projected resignation, and the means of informing the P.M. beforehand. He will have to write a letter, but also use the best personal channels, which would appear to be – Smuts, Randolph Churchill and Brendan. Question is – should this be done before or after the next Big Three Meeting, of which exact date not yet known.

4. Bernays had been killed in an aeroplane accident over Italy in 1944.

July 17th   Very interesting morning at Zionist Office listening to Moshe's Report, especially about the future of Brigade Group, now on borders of Austria. Their desire was at first to take part in the occupation of Germany, according to the P.M.'s public promise, and Moshe had been very anxious to press this, but some of his colleagues in Jerusalem saw real objections, one being that their position would be very isolated, now that the non-fraterniza-tion order is withdrawn, for they could not fraternize with Germans. Moshe was convinced and begins to turn his mind to bringing them back to Palestine, largely because it appears to be H.M.G.'s policy (*quite* mad) to bring the Transjordan and other armed Arab forces, inside Palestine, and this was made very evident in the King's Birthday Parade, when the Jewish units were tucked away in a most humiliating manner. Whenever I listen to Moshe I am struck afresh with his intelligence and lucidity of thought, if only he could say what he has to say a little more shortly.

July 18th   The destination of the Brigade is out of our hands. Moshe heard this morning that they are going to Germany! Well, that is doubtless part of God's pattern, and I am personally relieved. I do not want them in Palestine in the present state of political tension. It puts an end however to an extraordinary and moving development. The Magen David[5] in the centre of Europe has been proving a magnet for young Jewish refugees of both sexes. They hike and hitch-hike, sometimes thousands of miles, to come to it. Some even from Turkestan. These are Polish Jews, who got themselves sent back to Poland, and thence got across the Russian border. The Soviets are showing themselves very hostile to all Jewish emigration out of Russia. What strength there is in Jewish nationalism! It is idle as well as idiotic to try to damp it down. I wrote to Brendan today and told him that the Confer-ence[6] will precipitate a crisis unless the P.M. gives Chaim something to go upon.

July 23rd A very important Yeshiva this morning . . . on the question of what Chaim should say in his opening speech to the Conference. It was decided that headings should be prepared by a small Committee consisting of Moshe, Berl, Brodetsky and Lewis. Chaim said to me that he had not asked me to attend the first Meeting, but they would probably call me in later. I think his reason was that they might feel freer to decide how far to attack H.M.G. if I were not present, but this is unnecessary scrupulosity, for Chaim would never go further than I would be prepared to assent to. And if this Con-ference results in a clash with H.M.G. in Palestine, Chaim would certainly have to resign, in which case I should no longer be in the Political Committee. I pray it has not come to this, but the sands are running out!

5. The Star of David.
6. The forthcoming Zionist conference.

July 26th—Election Day! ... Returns so far 'not good'. *Evening News* bought in Strand confirmed this, I got to Cousin Maud Selborne's[7] in time for one o'clock news, after which she said, 'By all the signs this is a landslide.' Stayed there till the next batch of results at 2 p.m. which began to indicate an absolute Labour majority. Went back to office, found colleagues rather bewildered. I told Berl Locker I was handing him 'my headache'. He asked, 'How so?' I answered, 'Anxiety lest my Party should not behave decently with regard to Palestine.'

Chaim rang up, I pointed out to him that the whole tone of his speech must be changed. Neither he nor the others seemed at first to appreciate the revolution, but Moshe did presently say this would 'save the Conference' and should remove fear of any Jewish upheaval in Palestine at present ...

Lewis dined alone with me, we went through the old draft of Chaim's speech. He is anxious the new one should contain high tribute to Winston. I do not think this should go beyond what Chaim really feels, he has felt so bitter at the do-nothing policy ... Tonight my own feeling is that the Country (especially the Forces) wanted a change, disliking instinctively a One Man Government. Interesting the practical extinction of Liberal Party (and that is the end of a great epoch in English history!) and was utterly against all freak parties, which is a remarkably healthy sign in such an inexperienced Electorate. Also interesting to observe the small power of the Press in this country. Look at the circulation of Beaverbrook papers in London, which has practically all gone Labour!

Well, Labour has power for the first time. It is just forty years since the landslide of 1906, when A.J.B. said the only interesting thing was their emergence as a political force. I think it takes longer than forty years to create a governing class. Lewis thinks that *as* a Governing Class we are finished. It will be as individuals. But tradition and instinct for rule die very hard.

August 1st—London The Zionist Conference opened at 3 p.m. at Royal College of Surgeons in Queen's Square. Chaim presiding. He called on the Jewish Chaplain of the Forces, who was in uniform, to recite the Prayer for the Dead. All stood. Then he welcomed them and made the speech we had settled on. He read it, and as it struck a very moderate note the whole effect did not seem to me adequate to the occasion. The only other political speech of the day was Brodetsky's, nothing in it. The great emotions were reserved for Rabbi Baeck, the Chief Rabbi of Berlin till 1943 when he was deported to Oswecim, and Dobkin's[8] report on his recent visit to the Camps, where the Jews are still living in scandalously bad conditions. What I chiefly felt

7. Lady Maud Cecil: Mrs Dugdale's cousin; daughter of 3rd Marquess of Salisbury; married 2nd Earl of Selborne.
8. Eliyahu Dobkin: Member of Jewish Agency Executive and Director of its Department of Immigration.

today was the great gulf fixed between the Europeans who have actually suffered and the Americans and British. There is great (and perhaps unreasonable) feeling that the latter have not done enough.

August 3rd Conference again all day, hotting up, a lot of criticism of the Executive's handling of these six years; but not I think very formidable. As Chaim said to me, they all assume that the world has been as concentrated on their problems as they are themselves.

The new Government announced today. Colonial Secretary is that old fool George Hall, which is bad. Creech-Jones is Under-Secretary and has let Berl know that he stipulated that he should be consulted on all Palestine matters. Very good — if it works, but unless the Cabinet takes a very firm new line on Palestine I fear Sir George Gater and the Permanent officials will just make rings round both these little men. It takes a long, long time to make a Governing Class.

August 8th ... Spent all morning at the Conference, a big row in the morning, which led to Rabbi Silver putting himself at the head of the extremists, and the Mizrachi uttering a declaration of discontent with the Executive and its whole policy, and withdrawing their representative from the Executive. I think Chaim handled the Conference badly yesterday, he poured *iced* water on the hopes of a Jewish State at once, whereas all they could really stand was tepid water. But Ben-Gurion was not helpful, the whole thing came from over-strained nerves.

Chaim gave a wonderful supper at the Dorchester to the 'Polar Expedition' i.e. our dear old Yeshiva, with the Palestinian inner circle, and Vera, Mrs Ben-Gurion, Malkah Locker, Mrs Brodetsky and Miss May. It was really a sort of farewell to Lewis, who is returning to his history work, though we do not believe he is really withdrawing entirely from Zionist work. Chaim made a beautiful speech, mostly about him, and several of us spoke also. Brodetsky made a really wonderfully generous tribute, especially as they have not always got on, and Ben-Gurion spoke of Berl Katznelson and what *he* had felt about Lewis. I am sure dear Lewis was pleased. He made a very moving little speech. I spoke about him too, and also about what it means to me to have been made so one with them all. It was one of the most utterly harmonious gatherings of friends it has ever been my lot to take part in.

September 20th—London Lunched at Club, then U.N.A. (L.N.U.) Executive. Very rambling, everybody older and deafer than ever!

At 4.30 went to Chaim. Moshe there. They told me this Government has gone back on all the Labour policy and intends to go on with the White Paper, with certain concessions! This was unofficially communicated by Greenwood to Locker. Bevin has not seen Chaim, but sent a young fool of a

Private Secretary (Hector McNeil[9]) who tried to drive a wedge between Chaim and Moshe, insinuating that the proposals would be acceptable to Chaim. He was told off, but of course there is black despair, they had hoped so much from the change of Government! They will not consent to any negotiation on basis of White Paper, and in the evening I made a draft of a letter to Attlee telling him so, and warning that Chaim's position becomes untenable. A few 'illegal' ships have been reaching Palestine recently. The first attempt to stop them will signal an outbreak. We are on the edge of the precipice at last! But President Truman has butted in, asking for 100,000 certificates for Jews from American Zone in Germany alone. This will doubtless upset the Cabinet, who (we hear) are already sharply divided, Dalton being chief among our friends. But they are all so inexperienced as well as being gutless, one cannot foresee what the reaction will be. Blast them!

September 21st Went to the office in the morning, found everybody very distracted, nothing settled yet. Did not join the Yeshiva, Chaim indicated that David Ben-Gurion had rather felt the responsibility must be theirs only at this supreme crisis. Quite right, I was relieved, for life and death to many may hang on what Chaim does. His resignation may precipitate a crisis which would undo the work of thirty years. He said to me, 'Have I the right to do that?' But what else *can* he do? A statement is in draft, saying that every Jew who tries to enter Palestine will have the support of all the People. But this will *not* be issued this weekend.

October 8th Intensively busy day at the office. First, Chaim's Report of an interview with Bevin, nothing conclusive, but it ended by Bevin saying he must see him again shortly, which Lewis and I considered very important, but Ben-Gurion wanted to throw a spanner into the works and refuse to talk at all to any Minister till the White Paper is abolished. However, the Yeshiva was against this silly proposal, and I suspect B.-G. would not otherwise have made it. I think Walter was right and H.M.G. will try to procrastinate on *any* decision! . . .

October 10th . . . Great perturbation at the office for Bevin asked Chaim to come and see him today, and when Chaim asked to bring Moshe, said he would prefer to see him alone! Ben-Gurion disapproves of any more interviews with H.M.G. while the White Paper stands. Chaim exploded and said he could not go on if there were to be two policies in the Executive. However, he is going to see Bevin.

October 11th Zionist Office. Bevin did not say much to Chaim, but Chaim spoke very plainly to him. We suspect they mean to get Arab consent to

---

9   Hector McNeil: Under-Secretary of State at the Foreign Office, 1945–46; Minister of State, 1946–50; Secretary of State for Scotland, 1950–51.

about 2,000 a month. This means continuing the White Paper, and the Jews will not play on those terms . . .

October 21st—Sunday . . . went to see Chaim, who is far from well, and had had a very unpleasant interview with George Hall the Colonial Secretary, a caddish sort of fool, who tried to browbeat him, and (we think) is perhaps anxious for his resignation, as an excuse for short-circuiting the Jewish Agency. This is a new suspicion and requires much consideration.

October 27th   Lunched at Club. Lewis here in the afternoon and for tea, we discussed Zionist affairs, the Government statement still delayed. Our policy must be to sit tight and whatever happens Chaim should not play into their hands by resigning. Lewis and I dined with him and Vera at the Dorchester, and Lewis was very strong on this.

November 1st . . . At Zionist Office Yeshiva was discussing Chaim's departure for U.S.A. when Bakstansky brought in early edition of evening paper, saying widespread attack of sabotage on railways, ports etc.[10] We were not surprised but consternated. Moshe thinks this bears the mark of Hagana, not terrorist work. Chaim insisted we must issue immediate statement, repudiating . . . had a heavy afternoon drafting with Moshe and Locker, constantly on telephone to Chaim, finally we got an accepted compromise wording, but not till Chaim had threatened to resign unless the word 'abhor' was used as well as 'repudiate'.

November 13th—London . . . To Zionist Office where found everybody on the jump, as Moshe and Ben-Gurion were summoned to Colonial Office for directly after lunch to hear the Statement on Palestine which Bevin read out to the House of Commons this afternoon. They returned at once and read it out to Locker, Brodetsky and myself. First impressions are that it might have been worse. The salient points seem to be that U.S.A. is associated with the new Commission of Enquiry,[11] and that by implication the White Paper has to go. The mention of Indian Moslem opinion (for the first time) is a very serious feature. Ben-Gurion considers it a very 'clever' document, from the point of view of keeping the Labour Party quiet. It was decided that no opinion ought to be expressed about it until further study, and the full Executive meets in Jerusalem. Meantime we drafted a statement re-

10. This was a joint Haganah-Irgun-Stern Gang operation, which was subsequently dubbed 'the night of the bridges'. The Palmach—the élite troops of the Haganah—sank three small naval craft and sabotaged the railway network of Palestine in fifty places; the Irgun attacked the railway station at Lydda; while the Stern Gang raided the oil refineries at Haifa.
11. The Anglo-American Commission of Enquiry. Composed of six Englishmen: Sir John Singleton, chairman, Sir Frederick Leggett, Lord Morrison, Mr. Crick, Major Manningham-Buller, and Mr. Richard Crossman, M.P.; and six Americans: Judge Joseph Hutchinson, Ambassador Phillips, Professor Aydelotte, Mr. Buxton, Mr. MacDonald, and Mr. Bartley Crum. The secretaries were Mr. Vincent and Mr. Beeley.

affirming the Jewish point of view re immigration and a Jewish State. There is to be a Debate in Parliament next week.

November 26th   At the office preparations for departure of whole Yeshiva for Jerusalem, to take part in the crucial Executive Meeting to consider reply to Bevin's Statement. But Chaim stays in U.S.A. and will not be there. It is the great Fade Out. I do not think he can again recover real leadership.

1946 *January 4th*   A little warmer, and a little less bronchitic. At Zionist Office Gershon Girsch just back from Central Europe began a most interesting account of the Jewish conditions and a heart-rending description of the utter poverty and starvation in Hungary, but everywhere the indomitable Zionist spirit prevailing. General Morgan[1] speaks of a 'conspiracy' (though I don't believe he meant this ill-chosen phrase in an anti-Semitic way). But there certainly *is* a highly organised Jewish migration away from Poland all along the routes which will lead them eventually to Palestine. We are only beginning to get glimpses of it here, but it is epic in size and quality. The great question is how to get money, clothes and food to them in time. Hirsch says even the organisers are breaking down for need of these things.

January 17th All day at the office beginning to prepare the evidence etc. for the Committee of Enquiry, which comes to London in about ten days.

January 25th   All morning and part of afternoon at first sitting of the Committee of Enquiry at Royal Empire Society in Northumberland Avenue. Not an impressive body of men, judging by their questions, and Leonard Stein contrasted them to me very unfavourably with the first-class brains of the Royal Commission. I heard Brodetsky and Leonard Montefiore giving evidence, on the whole good, but too verbose and made Mr Justice Singleton (who has very bad manners) impatient. Montefiore behaved very well, considering his opinions, and was determined not to be enticed into letting the Zionists down.

January 27th   Chaim predicts that Committee of Enquiry will recommend partition—H.M.G. will say they need six Divisions to carry that through and will ask the U.S.A. to send some. U.S.A. will refuse and H.M.G. will be delighted for excuse to do nothing, and the Yishuv will then lose patience. He is very gloomy and bitter.

January 28th   Most of the day listening to evidence. Rabbi Koppel Rosen in a class by himself, dignified, moving, highly intelligent and quite unshake-

---

1. General Sir F. E. Morgan: Chief of UWRRA operation in Germany, 1945–46.

able. A new star in the Jewish firmament! Too young still I fear to succeed to the Chief Rabbinate, now vacant.

January 29th   At Committee[2] General Spears and Dr Maude Royden[3] appeared. I must say that when I heard they had called her I thought it did show signs of bias that they had declined to call me! I think Beeley the Secretary is biased against us, and probably the Chairman, Mr Justice Singleton, is also. I had lunch with a Jewish lawyer named Abrahams, who often appears in his Court and says he loses no opportunity of displaying anti-Semitism. But after listening to Mr Crossman cross-examining Louis Spears, I revise my first opinion that he too is anti-Semitic.

General Spears was really disgusting and I think his statements were so bad that they did us more good than harm. But one never knows! I do not believe this Committee are sufficiently heavyweight to cut much ice, whatever they report. They remind me of the Bander-log,[4] chattering in the tree-tops while the great creatures pursue their own ways unnoticed below.

January 30th   Leonard Stein gave evidence, not very good from our point of view, he being against a Jewish State. Lord Samuel ditto, but some of his evidence very valuable. In the afternoon Leo Amery, who of course was first-class, and as Secretary to Lloyd George Cabinet in 1917 of course knew exactly what were the intentions. He revealed that he drafted the Balfour Declaration! He was giving evidence for over two hours. He quite consoled me for not having been called myself.

February 4th   We discussed the problem troubling Chaim, whether the Jews should now turn to Russia. Very tentative hints have been given by Maniulsky, their Ukrainian stooge, that he would like to see Chaim while he is here for U.N.O. The Foreign Office would certainly get to know of it, but would that be a bad thing? My instinct is not to venture on such slippery ground, at any rate till we see the Report of the Committee.

February 14th . . . In the evening spoke on 'The Jewish Case' to a small U.N.A. meeting in Palestine House. Chairman, the local parson, definitely prejudiced against, but I got it across pretty well. It is instructive to address these Gentile Meetings as it shows the amount of resistance to the Zionist idea in this country, which one is so apt to forget.

February 17th—Sunday . . . visited Chaim and Vera at the Dorchester. Chaim in good form. Said that Oliver Stanley is coming to see him before the Palestine Debate. He means to tell him that for the first time since 1917

2. The London sessions of the Anglo-American enquiry.
3. Dr Maude Royden: Lecturer and author; wrote extensively on behalf of the Arab cause.
4. 'Mowgli, thou hast been talking with the Bander-log — the Monkey-People' from R. Kipling's, *The Jungle Books*.

the interests of Great Britain, the Jews and the Arabs all coincide. Only together have they a chance of blocking the advance of Russia in the Middle East, which will be against the interests of them all. If only Britain would see this, stop trying to build on Arab friendship, which is less than nothing, stop alienating the Jews who are the stable element, and try to act as honest broker between them and the Arabs. It is not quite too late, though he expects to find the position in Palestine far worse than it was even a year ago.

February 23rd   Began to be impatient to know my exact date of departure for Palestine.

March 3rd—Sunday. Weizmann House, Rehovoth!   What bliss to be here once more! The orange groves are a mass of fruit and flowers! No great changes visible in this part of the country. Chaim and Harry Sacher in the garden, lovely warm afternoon, not too hot . . . Vera in bed. My own old room with the lily-of-the-valley chintz. This beautiful house more beautiful than ever . . .

There is a dispute between Chaim and the Executive as to whether he should ask for a Declaration that there is to be a Jewish State. He is against it, but rather to my surprise Harry Sacher sides with the others, on the principle of 'those who don't ask, don't want' and that his silence would be interpreted as that. We also discussed 'activism' and I found myself alone in believing that it is the right policy now. I promised Chaim to say nothing to encourage Ben-Gurion in this. Certainly it is a very slippery slope, and might easily become indistinguishable from terrorism, but it is not yet, and *is* bringing results . . .

March 4th—Rehovoth   Sat out in the loggia all the morning . . . Read draft of Chaim's Statement before the Committee,[5] thought it slightly lacking in definiteness about Jewish State, and asked him if I might make a suggested re-draft of a sentence or two, which I did in the afternoon and perhaps he will accept. Moshe came from Jerusalem for lunch, gave us an account of a very friendly interview he had with the Emir Abdullah just before he went to London. Abdullah wants Jewish capital etc. in Transjordan, but dare not say so. He spoke of Ibn Sa'ud as his greatest enemy . . .

March 8th—Rehovoth   Chaim gave evidence today in Jerusalem, opening the Jewish Agency's case. He spoke for one and three-quarter hours in the morning and about one and a quarter hour's cross-examination in the afternoon. A truly magnificent performance. I never knew him rise to a higher level, and I do not think he made one error. His mind was like a giant's among the pigmies (which is all this Committee is). Many Arabs were listening, among them the villainous Jemal Husseini, the Mufti's cousin. But

---

5. The Anglo-American Commission was now gathering information in Palestine.

R

one could not guess at the thoughts behind those dark impassive faces. Several times Chaim repeated that he had not given up hope of an understanding with the Arabs, and was at any moment ready to talk with them.

But he spoke very frankly of them and what they had gained, and how little they had done in the two wars. He coined a phrase for what British policy should be—'the line of least injustice'. He begged for a clear line of British policy. He condemned terrorism and said he would do all he could to put it down. But the Agency was losing influence. He was quite definite about a Jewish State. Not the least sign of bitterness or strong language, but the Jewish case has never been so strongly or so nobly put. The Committee were obviously impressed and every shade of opinion among the Jews were utterly delighted. I only hope that no more political evidence will be given by the Agency, for that would only spoil the effect of Chaim's. We drove home as soon as he had finished, arriving well before the 6 p.m. curfew, in time for a late tea. Chaim very tired, but very cheerful, obviously feeling he had done well . . .

March 9th—Rehovoth   Before tea arrived two members of the Commission, Mr Crum and Mr Crossman, to dine and sleep. Vast amount of most interesting talk. Crum is openly 100% on Jewish side. I am less sure of Crossman, but he is an intelligent man. Both have obviously learnt a great deal in their tour of European D.P.[6] Camps, and feel the urgency of getting the people out of them. Moshe was also here, and they asked many pertinent questions about Agency plans for absorbing refugees, if they get the 100,000. Crum has his eye on U.S.A. public opinion if they do not, and Crossman told us confidentially that the British authorities in Europe say that transport need be no difficulty, 100,000 could be brought over in a month. I fancy their coming will be recommended. But on Palestine policy I fancy there will be a division of opinion between British and Americans. Chaim urged that they should insist on leaving a small working Committee in being to see that their Report is carried out. The Peel Commission dissolved without doing that and had no more power.

March 10th—Sunday, Rehovoth   Drove to Jerusalem early with Moshe, had some breakfast at Eden hotel and then went to St. Andrew's Church. A short Communion after, which they have every Sunday, for visitors. Two A.T.S. and myself—very uplifting in this place. Also we sang the Old Hundreth. A good congregation, a lot of R.A.F. and some soldiers . . . It is a lovely Church.

March 12th   Dollik Horowitz[7] came from Jerusalem to lunch, he talked of the Commission, thinks that the two Chairmen and Manningham Buller

---

6. Displaced Persons.
7. Dollik Horowitz: Director of Economic Department of Jewish Agency; later, Governor of Bank of Israel.

are the least friendly to our side. Crossman coming round, and is the most intelligent of the lot . . . thinks probability will be no final solution recommended, but a big immigration. But partition is not ruled out, and Crossman wants to combine it with a big water-scheme, with Jews and Arabs as well as Government on board. We all pray for some final solution, but doubt whether these men are capable of formulating one.

March 14th The quiet of the day was disturbed in the evening by news that some 2,000 Jews had marched up to Berya, near Safad, where the British Military had lately arrested all the people in a Hagana training camp, and attempted to establish there another, purporting however to be a kibbutz. Chaim most upset by this, considering it a breach of promise of quiet while the Committee are here, a foolishly provocative act, and also he suspects that a movement of that size must have been known to and approved of by the Executive beforehand. He suspects Ben-Gurion, but he does that now about everything! Is there a touch of jealousy of the old leader for his successor? Ben-Gurion *may* be 'playing for power', but it is not at the expense of anyone else, for there is no one else, with the possible exception of Rabbi Silver, who certainly wants it, but Chaim thinks it would not do.

March 21st—Eden Hotel, Jerusalem We came before lunch, and Martin Charteris came by appointment to see me in the morning. He is a Colonel and head of Military Intelligence. Frank talk and very interesting. He is *not* a Zionist, or an anti. Sees all from British angle, and especially security angle. Is therefore against partition, as not likely to bring peace and giving one more frontier to defend. Takes Hagana very seriously and knows a lot about it, understanding that it is a movement of the whole nation, and therefore impossible to put down. He also showed great knowledge of internal Zionist politics, is impressed by Ben-Gurion, whom he calls an 'Israelite without guile' which *I* think is true. He asked whether Ben-Gurion or Rabbi Silver is likely to be the next President—I answered I would bet on Ben-Gurion.

March 23rd—Rehovoth . . . the evidence given in camera by Mr Shaw, the Chief Secretary,[8] is the most important. Shaw says things cannot go on as they are—either there must be a Jewish State, or the Jewish Agency must be liquidated. The latter (to my mind) has become impossible without unleashing civil war. Partition at the moment does not seem to hold the field . . .

March 28th—Rehovoth Very warm day. Martin Charteris arrived about 11.30 and had a long talk with Chaim before lunch, which seemed to have gone well, as he was asked to return here any time when passing. He tried to disabuse Chaim of the idea that the British want to continue the White Paper and dissolve the Agency and nothing else . . .

8. Of the Palestine Administration.

The Committee of Enquiry have taken flight to Lausanne—thank goodness!

March 30th—Shabat, Rehovoth My last day! Packing and pottering. Chaim's sisters at lunch. For tea came Moshe and Zipporah Shertok. Moshe said the latest gossip before the Committee left for Lausanne was that they would propose no solution, but indicate several possibilities; state how their opinion was divided, and leave it to the two Governments to decide. That would seem too feeble to be possible, if it were not that they *are* a feeble and mediocre bunch, who have not pulled themselves into an entity for want of leadership, and may be capable of nothing more. But it will be a disastrous result. More authentic was Moshe's news that the Arab Higher Committee is splitting—Jemal [Huseini] leading faction advocating violence whatever the Committee's Report may be, reasoning that it *must* break the White Paper, and so cannot but be bad for them. So I think I leave Palestine in as great a mess as I found it, but nevertheless as a place to live in it can give points to most countries outside the Americas today!

April 6th—London I left Cairo on Thursday afternoon—reached Airways House at 10 p.m. tonight—thirty hours late . . . But I would not believe it, till we were safely down—in England!

April 7th—Sunday Spent all day in. Tidying up, telephoning to people, writing letters, attending to house . . .

April 8th . . . to Zionist Office where all seemed as pleased to see me as I them. Reported all my news to Linton and Locker. Lunched at Chandos with Lewis, full of his 'Coloured Books' but not too much so as to be uninterested in what I had to say . . .

April 25th—London . . . After breakfast went to the Office where I found Linton agog with news of the Committee's Report. It is *said* to be unanimous, but only concerned with short-term policy, which would be to let 100,000 Jews in at once. If that is so it tears the White Paper right across, and I think should be accepted, however bad other parts may be, and they are said to be very bad. Many of the Yeshiva are now in Paris, they will be here on Monday and we shall know the facts. Ben-Gurion is said to be very angry. I hope he won't wreck the whole thing! One ought to be used by now to all these alarums and excursions, which are seldom quite as predicted.

April 26th Under seal of secrecy Berl Locker produced the text of the operative chapter of the Committee of Enquiry's Report, which he acquired in Paris. Harry Sacher read it aloud to a few of us. Chief points are:—

100,000 certificates for European refugees should be allotted immediately to Jewish Agency for distribution and immigration begin as soon as conditions possible, as many as can in 1946. No definite limit set to further immigration. No Jewish *or* Arab State (this means no partition). Mandate to continue till U.N.O. trusteeship begins and meanwhile is to be carried out (this means the end of the White Paper).

Land purchase restrictions of White Paper to be definitely *rescinded,* but smallholders to be safeguarded.

J.N.F. and Wakf[9] rules about inalienable land to be done away with.

More money to be spent on raising Arab standards of living—hospitals—education etc. out of taxes. This means, Jews pay but Government controls.

No private armies.

No 'illegal' immigration.

At first reading we agreed Jews cannot reject this, but Berl warns that study shows a nigger in every one of these wood-piles, especially as Administration becomes more powerful than ever, and nothing is said about reforming it.

It is a woolly document, especially as regards long term policy, and I do not think it will settle the 'Palestine Problem' but I would say it is about 65% pro-Jewish, and to get rid of the White Paper is a great thing. The obvious tactics are to accept in generous spirit, and proceed to argue specific points. I expect the Arabs will make a shindy at once, which would be a very good thing.

Broadly speaking *No Partition* is the important point of policy, especially as I know this to coincide with British Military Opinion. If the British and American Governments accept this Report, it means I think that it will be the beginning of a common front against Russia in the Middle East, for I cannot suppose H.M.G. would accept it without promise of U.S.A. co-operation in case of trouble, for I am sure the Arabs will make trouble somehow. I have no idea when this Report will be published, but it is leaking heavily, the 100,000 certificates are already spoken of as a fact.

April 29th   A big Yeshiva, with Moshe and Ben-Gurion here from the Continent, and Simon Marks and Harry Sacher also present. The question was policy and tactics when the Report comes out. Of course Ben-Gurion's desire is to say Yes and No at the same time! But I think he realizes he cannot do that. Acceptance cannot however be unconditional, the Jews cannot give up their claim to a State in the future, though they may accept Trusteeship now. And there are other things e.g. the idea that they are to pay for Arab development, while H.M.G. keeps control of all the expenditure. I think there is something in the idea of the Jews making a test of sincerity in the way the immigration and new land legislation is put into operation *at once.* I consider it all important that the world should understand that the Jews do not refuse to play. As for tactics—much depends on whether

9. Moslem religious endowments.

the publication of the Report is accompanied by announcement of its acceptance by the Governments. I think it *must* be so.

April 30th   Terrifically busy day—helping prepare the 'hand-out' for the Press on the Report, and writing (by request) my own comments for *The Manchester Guardian*. Had no lunch but a couple of sandwiches in the office with Ben-Gurion, who all day was his very nicest and most reasonable self, and made one understand, what sometimes seems inexplicable, why he has so much influence as a leader . . .

May 1st—London   The Government have done what I thought impossible —published the Report before it has discovered what the U.S.A. intends to do in sharing responsibility for carrying it out. This complicates the whole situation, and moreover Attlee's statement to the House implied that they will make the 100,000 conditional on arms in Palestine being given up! This will *not* happen as things are, and may cause a serious crisis. I feel very worried.

May 3rd . . . Walter told me something of Winston's conversation at the Other Club last night, where Smuts and Sir John Singleton also were, and there was talk about the Palestine Report—mixed up with India, and World Affairs generally. Winston is obsessed with the idea of the strength and power of U.S.A. in the world. He spoke of it as like a mighty eagle, sitting motionless on a rock until it chooses its moment to spread its wings in flight. This seems to me more rhetorical than sensible, but the upshot may be that Winston's attitude to the Palestine Report may be that if U.S.A. cooperates he will back it with his whole strength. If not — not.

May 26th—Sunday   After tea went to consult Dr Kounine about my health. He gave me a thorough overhaul and thinks I am suffering from bronchial-asthma and high blood pressure, but which is causing which he cannot tell for a week or two . . . What an intelligent man he is! I did well to pick him out! Almost the only doctor I have ever met who did not put one against obeying his advice!

June 12th   Wet and cold as usual. Went to Zionist Office. Found Ben-Gurion there . . . Berl at Bournemouth at Labour Conference, where Bevin has made a very inimical speech on the Committee Report[10] and everything is pretty black . . .

   At 6.30 p.m. I went to see Dr Kounine who said my bronchial trouble was enormously better, but took a serious view of blood pressure and heart,

10. Bevin virtually rejected the admission of 100,000 refugees into Palestine as recommended by the Commission. He argued that it would cost Great Britain another division and two hundred million pounds. This was also the occasion when Bevin lambasted the Americans, accusing them of pressing for the immediate admission of the Jews into Palestine in order to keep them out of New York.

and impressed on me that I must go quietly for a time. I feel this myself, being so drowsy and breathless . . .

June 29th . . . The evening paper had the news of the Palestine arrests.[11] Moshe and Bernard Joseph headed the list! No use trying to put down here one's feelings. I got through to Locker and Linton on the telephone and heard that our London Yeshiva had already put out a statement . . .

Chaim, we heard, had been summoned to see the High Commissioner. I feel he should have refused to go until his colleagues were released.

What imbecility as well as what evil this Government is capable of!

July 2nd Evidence accumulates of wanton destruction. It is true what Chaim said, the work of the Yishuv for fifty years can be destroyed in a week. I think that *is* the Government's policy.

July 4th Work goes on. Office full of Mizrachi, and also a new 'young entry' of Jews who were in the Forces and now doing their best in the Information Department. Linton had four minutes on telephone with Eliahu Epstein[12] in Washington, who said the Jews are *not* taking an active part in the Loan question,[13] but what has happened in Palestine will inevitably count. The stories of looting and destruction by troops multiply, and even the British authorities are taking steps. But nothing except the *immediate* release of the Jewish Agency and the Trade Union leaders could restore the situation in the least degree. Irreparable harm has been done . . .

July 7th—Sunday Went to Church. Lunched at Allies Club and by 3 p.m. was at Beaver Hall near Mansion House, where took part in the Meeting which passed the Resolution there.[14] In due course the main part of the marchers, who had started from Absa Hall in the Commercial Road, came along, we joined them, and all marched to Trafalgar Square, which was already nearly full of people. Our procession was nearly two miles, led by ex-servicemen and the Youth Movements. There were finally at least 20,000 in the Square. A most inspiring sight, especially when the multitude sang Hatikvah at the end. All passed off with perfect dignity and order. I was one of the six chosen to go to Downing Street and present the Resolution.

11. On 29 June the Palestine Administration arrested the leaders of the Jewish Agency; they were detained in a camp at Latrun.
12. E. Epstein [later Elath]: Head of the Middle and Near East division of Jewish Agency. 1934–45; political representative of Jewish Agency in U.S., 1945–48; since then has held high office in Israel in diplomatic service.
13. This apparently refers to the Senate hearings on the Anglo-American loan. The agreement had been signed in December 1945 and had been the subject of much criticism in the U.S.
14. A special emergency conference of the Zionist Federation had been held at Beaver Hall at which resolutions were adopted protesting against 'the aggressive action taken by British Forces on the orders of His Majesty's Government against the Jewish community in Palestine', and demanding 'the immediate release of the Jewish leaders, the cessation of attacks on Jewish settlements, and the immediate opening of Palestine to 100,000 Jews'.

I thought it disgusting that, in spite of notice having been given, there was not even a Secretary at Number Ten to receive it—only the Messenger on duty!

July 19th   Chaim came to office and reported on Palestine.[15] He thinks only his presence has so far restrained 'rivers of blood', for the Army were longing for an excuse to wipe out the Yishuv, and on the Yishuv's side the hatred and anger against Britain will never be wiped out except by partition and a Jewish State. Chaim is very well despite all this.

July 22nd   Went as usual to Zionist Office. My article was in type when the dreadful news came at lunch-time of the blowing up of the King David Hotel, with fearful loss of life.[16] Of course I had to scrap everything written. This confirms Chaim's worst fears of what might happen after he left Palestine, and may change the whole course of affairs.

July 23rd   Zionist Office. The whole Yeshiva, especially of course Bakstansky, insistent that it would be disastrous and impossible for Chaim to cancel his meeting[17] now. But Chaim himself was in a most irrational frenzy of anger, and would not come near the office, nor discuss anything calmly on telephone. He includes Berl in his wild rage against Moshe, Sneh,[18] and especially of course Ben-Gurion. He considers that he had been deceived and defied about Hagana.

July 24th   At the office we were in conclave about briefs for the M.P.'s in next week's debate, when the White Paper about connexion of Jewish Agency with Hagana and Irgun was brought in. At first sight a very disastrous document, but even then we soon saw some very odd mysteries about 'telegrams' cited in evidence.

July 25th—(Nunk's birthday!)   Chaim still in very bad state, physically and mentally. Linton was there and we went on together to the office. Heard from him that only *one* of the telegrams cited in the White Paper was ever received at No. 77. This was the only one which is not anonymous, and the only one not published under the vague address of 'London'. Odd! The Yeshiva decided this morning to make a Statement regarding this, and the evening papers carried a similar denial from Jerusalem . . .

August 2nd   Chaim telephoned for Locker and me to come to the Dor-

15. He had arrived in London the previous day.
16. The hotel was blown up by the Irgun; 91 people were killed and 45 wounded, including British, Arabs and Jews.
17. A public rally at which Elliot had agreed to take the chair.
18. Moshe Sneh: Commander-in-Chief, Haganah, 1940–46; member of Jewish Agency Executive and Director of its Political Department, 1945–47; afterwards prominent in Israel political life. Weizmann was concerned at the activist turn in Haganah policy.

chester to hear report of talk he had this morning with the Colonial Secretary, who invited Jewish Agency for talks on the scheme. Chaim said he must consult his colleagues now in Paris, and gave his idea of certain conditions. (1) Viable frontiers; (2) the 100,000 or some of them; (3) High Commissioner *not* to appoint Ministers. He said something had snapped in British-Jewish relations, which seemed to take Mr Hall aback! Also release of Moshe and the others 'even on bail'. This was a mistake. Moshe would not come out on bail. He has now been five weeks behind barbed wire and no charge preferred! Chaim's impression was that H.M.G. is getting a bit scared that their case is not good enough!

August 5th—Bank Holiday Wrote article for Zionist Revue, packed etc. Michael arrived before tea in his car, to drive me down to Fifehead tomorrow.[19] I dined with Chaim and Vera—David Bergmann there and Linton, just back from the Executive Meeting in Paris. He brought messages from everybody, imploring Chaim to come, if only for twenty-four hours. But he will not, and Vera is determined he shall not. It is a fatal mistake and equivalent to abdication in my view. I am not surprised that they will not let Chaim carry out the projected second interview with the Colonial Secretary this week. They do not want to start negotiations on basis of present plan, especially as Truman has not yet accepted it. Chaim thinks this utterly wrong. I do not feel quite convinced.

August 29th Zionist Office. People back from Paris. Yeshiva met to discuss answer to H.M.G.'s invitation.[20] Still divided in opinion. At 5 p.m. we all met again in a room at the Dorchester to continue talk, but a new turn was given it by arrival of Nahum Goldmann from Paris, having had a forty minute talk there with Mr Bevin this very morning. *He* is sincere in wishing the Palestine Conference to succeed, whatever may be the desire of the Foreign Office and General Barker.[21] His ignorance of facts, geographic and others, appears to be unfathomable. He alluded to Stettin as a port on the Adriatic! But he implored that the Jews should not refuse the invitation, and said he would see what could be done during the weekend to make the basis more aceptable to them (i.e. the 'Peel' not the 'Morrison' plan[22]).

19. To Michael Dugdale's house in Dorset. Mrs Dugdale had been ordered by her doctor to take three weeks' rest.
20. To participate in yet another Palestine conference.
21. Lieutenant-General Sir Evelyn Barker: Commander-in-Chief, Palestine; author of the notorious non-fraternization letter issued immediately after the blowing up of King David Hotel. This letter accused the Yishuv of complicity in terrorist activities. Consequently a non-fraternization order was put into effect to punish 'the Jews in a way the race dislikes more than any, by striking at their pockets and showing our contempt for them'.
22. The Morrison-Grady plan had been drawn up by an Anglo-U.S. 'technical committee'. It was an unusually complicated cantonal system. The Jewish and Arab areas were endowed with a degree of administrative autonomy; while the Jerusalem area and the Negev were to be administered by the Government. The vital question of immigration remained in the hands of the Administration, though it was stipulated that cantonal recommendations, based on economic absorptive capacity, were normally to be accepted. The British Government accepted the plan; the U.S., the Zionists, and the Arabs, all rejected it.

September 25th   Locker rang up from Jerusalem. Decision *not* to go into Conference under present circumstances, but Executive asked to go on trying to alter these. They had much better have said straight out that the Agency won't go in till its Members are released. People would understand that. Chaim is said to be in an awful state of mind, and talks of resigning. I think he had better not, and I don't believe he means to. It is just as well that Rosh Hashana [the Jewish New Year] now intervenes, and prevents any Jewish activities for four days! But what a mess everybody has made of everything![23]

September 30th   Enormous Yeshiva, discussing the terms on which the Jewish Agency should start the informal talks with H.M.G. I am appalled by our lack of preparedness, but the circumstances have been very difficult, with Ben-Gurion stuck in Paris, and others perpetually flying between London and Jerusalem. Although I was one of those against going into Conference while Shertok and Co. are interned, I would not make this a pre-condition for the informal talks.

October 1st—London   First day of the 'informal talks' between the Government and the Jewish Agency. Chaim went to the Foreign Office at 11.30 accompanied by Brodetsky, Rabbi Fischman, Nahum Goldmann, Kaplan, Locker, Meyer Weisgal and Linton. In the afternoon Locker reported to the rest of us, and we had a meeting at teatime at the Dorchester.

I do not think there is much hope of good coming out of these talks. Bevin is obviously full of goodwill, but as far as ever from understanding the elements of the Jewish case. They insist on separating a 'Truce' from the political question, and including the 'releases' under that heading, which is to be discussed separately with the Colonial Office alone. This is a clever move on the Government's part, and it looks to me as if our people had rather allowed themselves to fall into a trap over it. It has however been agreed that *releases* and *immigration* should have priority as Jewish conditions for coming into a Conference . . .

October 9th   Colleagues in conference all day with Colonial Office. They say there is a definite improvement in atmosphere now that Creech-Jones has replaced George Hall as Colonial Secretary,[24] but what it will lead to I know not. At present the discussions are simply on the terms on which the Agency would enter the Conference. They will insist on the release of Moshe and Co. H.M.G. wants a Declaration against terrorism. This would be easy enough, so long as it does not include a Declaration against sabotage, for all that turns on relaxation of the stoppage of immigration, and we think (although they won't admit it) that H.M.G. has probably given the Arabs an assurance that there shall be no change in their policy about that while the Conference

23. Discussions as to whether or not the Zionists should go to Conference had been in progress since the end of August. They had been distinguished only by their indecision.
24. On 4 October.

is in abeyance. Meantime the shadow of the forthcoming Congress begins to affect our political manoeuvrings!

November 5th   At the Yeshiva this morning Berl Locker told us he has heard officially that 'the releases' take place today. Over four months, without charge! The story of the Rabbi and the Goat applies—but after all the Rabbi was right, and the atmosphere *was* changed! . . . then Berl went off to see the Colonial Secretary and hear details. He came back not unhappy, for there are no conditions attached, although we think it a pity that the Government Statement does make it look as if the releases were a *quid pro quo* for the Agency's anti-terrorist statement of last week. But Creech-Jones had also told him in confidence of some small immigration relaxations— some people to be brought in from Cyprus and even Europe in the next few weeks, etc. Altogether our 'atmosphere' in Great Russell Street has been brighter than for many weeks. I think Berl especially has suffered very much psychologically from being here when Moshe and the others were shut up.

December 3rd—Hotel Drei Könige, Basle   Flew here today, for the Zionist Congress . . .

December 5th . . . After tea Agronsky turned up, and from him I got at last some accurate dope as it is today, but this is a very fluid period, for the Parti-gruppen are only now getting together and holding conferences. It seems that Chaim's chances of re-election to the Presidency are almost nil! This was a great shock to me, and I think it will be to him. But it is all bound up with the question of partition, and even Chaim's most faithful adherents do not think him a good negotiator. Of the whole American Delegation he will only get eight votes (led by Rabbi Wise, who is Silver's enemy). General Zionists and Mapai may be split. Revisionists may be split on some questions but united against Chaim.

While we were discussing these things in the lounge, Chaim and Vera arrived from Lugano, with Linton and Meyer Weisgal. They only passed through the hall, and went up to their rooms, both looking very well, and Chaim's eyes obviously much better, he recognized me right across the lounge.

Agronsky strongly advised me to know nothing of what he had been telling me, if asked. He thinks that in two or three days it might be advisable for Chaim to take the initiative, and let his position be known in advance, and make quite plain that if they don't like it they must do without him, but not yet. I am very thankful that Agronsky is here, I think he is a better adviser than any of the others who surround Chaim, with the possible exception of Linton. It seems that many of Chaim's best friends in all parties feel that the British connection means to much to him that H.M.G. might get the better of him.

I dined with him and Vera, we sat some time in the lounge, I think because he was dying of curiosity to hear the gossip. Various people gathered round—Dr Wise, Mrs Epstein (of Hadassah). Later, with Linton and Miss May, we went to the Weizmanns' sitting-room. Chaim said he was sure Ben-Gurion does not want to stand against him, but he is equally sure that 'activism' is not rooted out, and he will not be President unless Ben-Gurion gives certain assurances on that point, which he does not believe Ben-Gurion *could* give. For the rest, Chaim stands for going into the London Conference, and for Partition. Dr Silver has arrived, we all went up in the lift together, everybody as polite as possible to everybody else!

December 6th   The Executive met this morning. Linton says Chaim was in great form, surprising many who expected to see a broken old man. On the whole the tide seems to be setting a bit more our way, but it is early days, and there is certainly a strong feeling against going into the Conference unconditionally. As for Partition—I hope the line may not be to advocate it, but to pass no resolution which would shut it out. About the 'Morrison Plan' I think it very important that Chaim should make very clear in his opening speech that the Jews will not be prepared even to discuss that. Many people think he is so keen not to break with Britain that if he goes to the Conference he might be inveigled into discussion and thence into acceptance of an improved Morrison Plan.

December 7th . . . Talked with Ben-Gurion after breakfast. He was quiet, but very unoptimistic about getting anything out of H.M.G. He thinks their ignorance is too great to be vanquished . . .

Moshe came to the hotel to have tea with me. Spoke of his life in Latrun—intolerable, mainly because he did not know how long it would last; the days passed quickly for he was very busy. The British are quite unfit to run a police State. His mail (uncensored and unknown to the authorities) was delivered to him every morning punctually at eleven. His lonely evenings were spent in writing political directives. In fact Moshe is always Moshe! But he began to feel himself losing touch, like a man who is gradually going blind. Then we talked about the position here. I am sure from what he says that Chaim is deceived about his position; it is not so strong as he thinks, unless he turns it by his opening speech, which he has touched up today in the direction of making it more pro-British. I think this a mistake.

December 9th   The Congress opened at 4 p.m. Hall packed (about 2,000 people I think). I had a seat in Vera's box. I am *not* happy about Chaim's reception. There was no fire in it. He read his speech, a tremendous effort, gallantly carried through, but of course it was not very effective to listen to, and it took an hour and a half. There was hardly any applause but I *hope* that was due to English not being very well understood, for if it were otherwise the reception would be decidedly cold.

When we returned we drank some tea in the lounge, people gathered round us of course. Dr Goldmann told Chaim that if a vote were taken *tonight* on going in to the Conference or not, it would be against. But I don't believe they will dare to be such fools. For if not—then what? The Parties are divided, but broadly speaking the Americans and the Palestinians oppose the Conference. Chaim says that if they do *not* enter the Conference, Zionism is dead as a constructive political movement for a generation.

December 10th Spent most of the day at the Congress. Chaim was elected President of the Congress by a great majority (show of hands) and very satisfactory enthusiasm. But this does not mean much . . . The interest of the afternoon was Dr Silver's speech. He threw down the gauntlet—against partition and in favour of 'resistance'—but not one word to distinguish it from terrorism. Significant and satisfactory that he did not seem to have the applause of about two-thirds of the hall.

December 11th Last night Ben-Gurion made an extraordinary speech, in which he attempted to say two contradictory things: (1) that the Executive holds to the Biltmore Programme;[25] (2) that they would discuss partition if proposed. This has put the cat among the pigeons with a vengeance.

December 12th Went to Congress this morning and had a talk with Mr Lipsky,[26] begging him to get his American colleagues to see how fatal it would be to refuse to enter the Conference, thus alienating British sympathies, and giving Palestine over to a continuance of a police State which in a short time would destroy the constructive work of fifty years. Lipsky said that, apart from about a dozen, the whole American delegation is thirled [Scottish legal word meaning tied or bound to] to Silver's policy of break with Britain, and are not open to argument.

However the day ended more cheerfully. Nahum Goldmann made a very courageous speech, in favour of going into the Conference and of partition, and was listened to without interruption and got a great ovation at the end. Moreover, Simon Marks and Harry Sacher are organizing private meetings of the General Zionists and bringing many of them round.

December 14th . . . Chaim seems really in earnest this time when he says he cannot work with either Silver or Ben-Gurion, but Harry Sacher pooh-poohed this later, saying that Chaim knows perfectly well that he must see the London Conference through. All agree that Ben-Gurion has lost an

25. The Biltmore programme had been adopted by a Zionist conference held in New York in May 1942. It called for the fulfilment of the orginal purpose of the Balfour Declaration and the Mandate: the foundation in Palestine of a Jewish commonwealth.
26. Louis Lipsky: A prominent U.S. Zionist leader; editor of *New Palestine*.

immense amount of his prestige and influence by his speech, giving no lead and bewildering the people. The best speech of the Congress so far has been Nahum Goldmann's.

December 16th At about five we all went to the Congress, for the final act of the General Debate. Dr Silver spoke, followed by his opponent Dr Wise. Then Ben-Gurion, whose Yiddish I can never understand, but I gather he still failed to give a clear lead. Then Chaim—in Yiddish. The greatest speech of his life. Perhaps the greatest I have ever heard. Perhaps the last he will ever make to a Zionist Congress, for we enter now upon the last lap, and either we shall be on the road to a Jewish State, or the conduct of battle must pass into younger hands. But he showed, physically and mentally, all the fire and vigour of fifteen years ago. His voice was strong. He must have shown the Congress that the idea of an Honorary Presidency is a foolish one. Either Chaim Weizmann leads the Zionist Movement, in fact as well as in name, or he retires to be an Elder Statesman.

The most moving moment was when he rebuked Neumann,[27] who shouted from the audience 'demagogue'—Chaim retorted he had a right to say what he had said, as every tree, every stone, every inch of Palestine soil was dear to him. Spontaneously the whole audience rose, friend and foe, except Neumann himself and that fool Silver, who committed the fearful error of remaining seated on the platform.

Chaim's triumph was great. But speeches seldom change opinions. We have still to see!

December 17th Today one hears some of the criticisms of Chaim's speech. Too flippant—much too pro-British, etc. He almost seemed to excuse the arrests of June 29th, etc. (this from B.G.). The Congress is still very undecided, the battle sways, Chaim very calm, determined to have his own policy or pull right out . . .

December 18th When I came down to breakfast Mrs Ben-Gurion waylaid me, begging me to 'use my influence' with Chaim to accept the Honorary Presidency. I answered that I had no influence, and anyway would not wish my worst enemy a greater curse than responsibility without power. Linton told me at breakfast that the Mapai Party[28] would probably offer Chaim that, but did not wish him to conduct the Conference if they go into it. This is Ben-Gurion's doing. Chaim would never dream of accepting the Honorary Presidency. The chances of his defeat are reckoned at about 50/50. I still think that when it comes to the point they will not commit suicide. But I

27. E. Neumann: Member of Jewish Agency, Jerusalem, 1931–39, 1946–47; represented Jewish Agency in negotiations with British Government, 1947; member of Executive of Jewish Agency and World Zionist Organization, 1951.
28. The largest and most influential group within the Palestine labour movement, led by Ben-Gurion and Shertok.

must leave tomorrow before it is decided, and, for the first time, almost glad to go. It is an age of pygmies, and so much squalor, spite, folly and party hatreds seem to be devouring Zionist politics. I think the day is done for Zionists of the old school.

December 24th—Fifehead Neville, Dorset . . . news that the Congress has voted, by a narrow majority, against going into the Conference. So Chaim has not stood again for Presidency, as that is the defeat of his policy. He flies home today. That is all I know.

December 25th—Christmas Day　Before breakfast I spoke to Chaim at the Dorchester. He said the final intriguing had been below belief—Ben-Gurion and Shertok mixed up in it. No Executive is yet chosen. He would not put it past them, now they have succeeded in getting rid of him, to go to the Conference after all. He will be off to Rehovoth as soon as he can.

December 29th　Zionist Executive formed—seems to include everybody, friends and foes alike! And no President, so there can be no policy. Silver and Ben-Gurion are the outstanding figures. But how are they to work together? The whole thing will break up in confusion, *or* they will go into the London Conference without a pilot!

1947 *January 4th—London* Lunched with Chaim and Vera. Isaiah Berlin there. Back in the old Zionist atmosphere! Ben-Gurion had had an interview with Creech-Jones (he came to see Chaim after and complained that C.J. had talked too much, which we thought funny from B.-G.!). Nothing very tangible seems to have emerged, though the usual carrot is being dangled before the donkey's nose—a satisfactory settlement in three months! But if things drift as they are doing for three months more, the Irgun will be in virtual control of Palestine.

Chaim saw Ben-Gurion but refuses to see Moshe—who (he says) *abstained* on the vote about going into the Conference. The only one of our old Yeshiva who, he says, fought valiantly to the end was Locker. And yet Locker, too, has joined the present Executive. Chaim agrees that my present position at Great Russell Street must now be brought to an end. I cannot work for or with any Executive that is pursuing a policy of non-cooperation with Britain. But it may not be the end of my Zionist work. Chaim is thinking of forming a group of his own. But we must wait and see whether the Executive does or does not go into Conference with H.M.G.

Then went to see Lewis, who is in bed in the London Clinic after an appendix operation, stayed some time and told him all these things.

January 7th Joe Linton lunched with me at the Club. Long talk about Zionist affairs. He holds on (Chaim has told him to) but he thinks it will not be for long. He told me more than I realized at the time about the Basle intrigues to get Chaim out. Very horrible!

January 10th . . . Lunched with Berl Locker at the Akropolis. Had long frank talk with him about the political position, and especially about my regret that he and Kaplan had entered this Executive. He did not agree, of course. I have met it before, people who think they will act as brakes upon a policy, and are in fact nothing but flies upon a wheel! He was (naturally) very averse to Chaim forming an Opposition Group. Thinks he should 'bide his time'. He does not realize that when people are leaders by nature, nature bids them react when they are thrown out of leadership.

S

January 16th . . . Looked in at the Office. But I shan't go again. The rift is bound to widen between the present Executive and Chaim and his friends. If only Berl Locker had not stayed on the wrong side of the fence!

January 26th—Sunday . . . Walter and I dined with the Weizmanns. Chaim in a more fighting mood than ever. He does not think that the Executive talks with H.M.G. are likely to lead to much, he hears that the Cabinet are divided—Creech-Jones remains a friend, and (more important) Herbert Morrison is said to be coming over to a decent partition scheme, but Bevin still takes the Foreign Office view, and carries Attlee. If the talks break down, anything may happen in Palestine.

January 27th A judge in Palestine has now been carried off by Irgun while sitting in Court, as another hostage! It is very shocking, but I cannot help admiring the efficient audacity of it.
. . . I stayed in all day unable to face the fearful cold.

January 28th . . . Cold intensified, one remembers nothing like it.

January 29th Cold continues . . .
Went to a Committee at Palestine House and then to see Harry Sacher and show him some notes I made by request for Chaim's speech to E.Z.F.[1] next Sunday. I dined with the Weizmanns and David Bergmann. Linton came in after dinner, to give Chaim an account of the first of the informal 'talks' between the new Executive and H.M.G. Creech-Jones had presided, Bevin was there (displaying incredible ignorance of the facts of the situation) referring to the White Paper as 'the agreement' of 1939, and constantly referring to his officials. He is obviously *against* partition, which tallies with what Chaim heard last week. But H.M.G. seem to have succeeded in passing the baby to the Jewish Agency, telling them that they have no cut and dried plan and want them to put forward their own scheme. This will embarrass Ben-Gurion extremely, for he will hardly have the courage to put forward any partition scheme! Linton says there is reason to think that H.M.G. have in mind a cantonization very much more favourable to the Jews than the Morrison plan, both as regards boundaries and powers. Chaim said that *he* would accept this.

January 30th Walter told me on telephone that Shadow Cabinet decided yesterday to ask for a Debate on State of Security in Palestine. This in spite of being unable to make constructive suggestions, owing to division of opinion in the Party, but Oliver Stanley is confident that he can keep debate on lines criticizing H.M.G. for lack of policy. I rang up Chaim and told him this, but did not pass it on to No. 77. Chaim, I should record, was terribly hurt that none of his friends on the Executive took the trouble

1. English Zionist Federation.

yesterday to ring him up and tell him what had passed with H.M.G. But for Linton he would have known nothing. I am surprised at Locker! Even from the point of view of expediency this is not the way to treat him. This lion is by no means toothless, as they will find.

January 31st The Palestine Debate took place. Walter got me a ticket for the Gallery. It went very well from our point of view. The Government had neither defence nor defenders for its lack of policy, and its handling of terrorism.

February 10th . . . I was at the Carlton Grill, lunching with Moshe at two p.m. when the afternoon cuts began. It is perhaps worth recording that the only light in that place was a small candle on each table!

It was the first time I had seen Moshe since Basle. Our friendship is as warm as ever. He told me first the details of H.M.G.'s proposals, handed to the Jews two days ago. *Quite* unacceptable, being worse in most respects than the Morrison Plan, especially as regards the crucial point of control of immigration. This afternoon the Agency will go to the Colonial Office and announce their rejection and why. But it will probably be a day or two before the public statement is made. It seems obvious to Moshe that Bevin has killed the idea of Partition, and aims at an Arab State with a Jewish minority. It is impossible to say what the effect of the breakdown of the talks will be in Palestine. I saw Barney Janner later in the afternoon, white with consternation. He thinks that the Government's difficulties over the fuel crisis will work against Zionist interest—(a) by distracting the Cabinet's attention (for we have some friends there to set against Bevin) and (b) by making our friends in the Labour Party more unwilling to embarrass the Government.

March 11th Stories of spreading floods all over the country. The blizzard has moved North. Ghastly destruction of livestock, especially sheep, is being revealed. This poor country is undergoing afflictions like the Ten Plagues. Could the reason be the same? Too fantastic an idea to utter! 'Let My People Go'.

March 16th . . . Lewis came with me to Crown Court where Moffett preached a fine sermon. Lewis and I lunched at my club and then, after lunch, he told me that he intends to be baptized and is going to marry Julia de Beausobre! Of course the two steps are connected . . . He spoke with great dignity and simplicity. He is more Zionist than ever, convinced that Judaism and Christianity must in the end be reconciled, and this can only happen in Palestine. I never felt so warm towards him, he is now my oldest *great* surviving friend! He deserves to be very happy.

April 18th Went to the Office and had a talk with Linton, just back from Palestine. Not very cheerful. Terrorism gains strength. On the other hand the country develops, capital is invested, there is faith in the future. Chaim is reported very bitter, but absorbed in his research Institute and very well and vigorous.

July 24th   Soon after breakfast Maurice Rosette[2] came here about the crisis arising over the deportation of the 'illegals' back to France from Palestine. Then ensued a day quite like old times. I went with him to consult Leo Amery, then to the office where a sort of Yeshiva was in progress, but neither Locker nor Linton are in London . . . News came in from Paris of rapid changes in the situation. The French will probably not give in to Foreign Office pressure to land the refugees in France whether they like it or not. Great tension in Palestine. Strong rumours that H.M.G. means to 'liquidate' the Jewish Agency! I cannot believe that even they would be such fools!

July 27th—Sunday   To Church, and in the afternoon to a Protest Meeting about the deportation back to France of the Jews on the *President Warfield*.[3] No one of much note spoke, but a good deal of heat generated. But *à quoi bon?* There will be no press publicity at all. But I think H.M.G. has made *such* a mess over this ship that the Opposition are missing an opportunity in not making more row about it.

August 3rd—Sunday, Fifehead Neville   The weekend news is all bad. As regards Palestine the hanging by the Irgun of the three sergeants[4] blackens the whole picture, and no wonder. As regards everything else, the economic crisis is upon us, and looks like being worse even than was anticipated. Michael says we shall look back on 1947 as our last year of luxury! . . .

The diaries continue intermittently throughout August and come to an end on 10 September 1947.

2. Maurice Rosette: Head of the information department of Jewish Agency, 1942-48; Secretary to the Khesseth from 1948.
3. Later re-named *The Exodus*.
4. In fact two British sergeants, Paice and Martin, were found hanging from a eucalyptus tree just outside Natanya; the ground underneath their bodies had been booby-trapped. The Irgun Zvei Leumi claimed responsibility for this outrage.

INDEX

with Jewish Agency, 27; discusses Palestine, 28; discusses Royal Commission's Report, 47–48, 66–67; views on Report, 52; to continue with declared policy, 69–70; regards Palestine as liability, 73; doesn't consult Weizmann, 78; contemplates bartering part of Galilee, 83; and crisis over Eden, 83–86; and Austrian crisis, 88; authorizes negotiations on self-determination, 98; agrees to give away Sudeten districts, 99; puts pressure on Czechs, 102; short-term policy of, 114; achieves understanding with Arabs, 129; considers postponement of statement, 134; indecisive, 149–50; at war with Germany, 150; cabinet to decide on Palestine, 154; Halifax and policy of, 166; criticized over conduct of war, 168–69; will fight alone, 172; agrees to a Jewish Fighting Force, 177; decides against deportation of refugees, 179; attitude towards Jewish Fighting Force, 187; favours Palestine as part of British Empire, 197; Palestine policy of, 201; no longer guided by White Paper, 203; embarks on new Palestine policy, 206; to continue with mandate, 220; 'mad' policy of, 222

Greenwood, Arthur, 149–50, 162–63, 171, 224
Grigg, Sir J., 185, 197
Grossmann, M., 59–60, 64, 147
Gunston, Derrick, 3, 104, 191
Gunston, Gardenia, 3, 111, 191
Gunther, John, 189

Ha-Cohen, David, 136
Haganah (see also, Jewish Army, Palmach), discipline of, 16; financing of, 116; members arrested, 153; memo against, 161; members released, 182; 'Night of the Bridges', 226; training camp, 233; relations with Jewish Agency, 238
Hahn-Warburg, Lola, 184
Haifa, 13–14, 18, 40, 44–45, 47, 51, 80, 133–34; Great Britain's intentions towards, 52; garrisoned by Jews, 66; loss of interest in, 71–72; refugees in, 135; immigrants brought to, 160, 178
Haining, Gen., 83, 95, 115, 133, 174; to settle new frontiers, 88; authorizes occupation of new land purchases, 134
Haldane, R. B. (Viscount Haldane), 39
Halifax, Viscount, 44, 87, 88–90, 104–05, 110, 112–13, 118, 122, 126–27, 129, 133, 140, 154–55, 166, 168, 170, 178–79, 181, 185; succeeds Eden, 84; sends for Masaryk, 103; meets Weizmann, 113; letter to Weizmann, 156; supports MacDonald, 164; as potential prime minister, 169
Halutzim, 57, 133–34, 160, 167
Hall, G., 214; appointed colonial secretary,

224; interviews Weizmann, 226; invites Jewish Agency for talks, 239; replaced as colonial secretary, 240
Hammersley, S. S., 207
Hanita, heroes of, 133–34
Hankey, Sir Maurice, 18; and Permanent Mandates Commission, 141–42
Hannon, Sir P., 165
Harmsworth, E. (2nd Viscount Rothermere), 32
Harris, Air Chief Marshal, 196
Harris Plan, 96
Hartington, Marquess of (10th Duke of Devonshire), 43, 153–54
Harvey, Sir O., 152
Heathcoat-Amory, D. (1st Viscount), 38
Henderson, Sir Neville, 96
Henlein, Konrad, 90
Herzl, Theodore, 58–59
Hess, Rudolf, 184
Hirsch, Gershon, 229
Histradruth, 13, 57–58
Hitler, Adolf, 8, 10, 89, 93–97, 99, 102, 105, 127, 137, 147–48, 152, 206; breaks Locarno treaties, 6; proposals of, 6n; and Sudetenland, 103–04; plot against, 151; 'converses' with Napoleon, 186–87; success of anti-semitic policies, 189
Hoare, Sir Samuel (Lord Templewood), 2, 7, 9, 22, 29, 74, 114
Hodza, Dr Milan, 98
Hoesch, Leopold von, 7, 9
Holland, war against, 120; invaded by Germany, 169
Holmes, Mrs 175, 176
Hore-Belisha, Leslie, 69, 91, 98, 140, 153, 160; appointed secretary of state for war, 43; vetoes Jewish legions, 151; resignation of, 159–60
Horowitz, David, 232
Hos, Dov, 17–18, 20, 44, 50, 80, 117, 146, 171, 173–74, 178
Hudson, Hannah, 2, 22, 30, 69, 77, 86, 104, 137, 143, 184, 187
Hudson, R. S., 2, 19, 22, 30, 34, 69, 77, 86, 187; and German loan episode, 143–44
Hulah, 44
Hungary, fate of Jewry in, 213–15, 229
Husaini, Jemal, 231, 234
Husaini, Haj Amin al (Mufti of Jerusalem), 48, 54, 63–64, 66, 79–80, 82, 119–22, 128–29, 137, 231; and disturbances, 15; conversations with Nuri, 83; unable to unite Arabs, 131; opposed by Palestine Arabs, 136

Ibn Sa'ud, 48, 66, 80, 95–96, 125, 161, 219, 231
India, 122, 189, 226, 236